DEPARTMENT OF PUBLIC INFORMATION

BASIC FACTS
ABOUT THE UNITED NATIONS

UNITED NATIONS

New York, 1998

P9-EKH-515

LIST OF ACRONYMS

DDA	Department for Disarmament Affairs
DESA	Department of Economic and Social Affairs
DGAACS	Department of General Assembly Affairs and Conference Services
DM	Department of Management
DPA	Department of Political Affairs
DPI	Department of Public Information
DPKO	Department of Peacekeeping Operations
ECA	Economic Commission for Africa
ECE	Economic Commission for Europe
ECLAC	Economic Commission for Latin America and the Caribbean
ECOSOC	Economic and Social Council
ESCAP	Economic and Social Commission for Asia and the Pacific
ESCWA	Economic and Social Commission for Western Asia
FAO	Food and Agriculture Organization of the United Nations
IAEA	International Atomic Energy Agency
IBRD	International Bank for Reconstruction and Development (World Bank)
ICAO	International Civil Aviation Organization
ICJ	International Court of Justice
ICRC	International Committee of the Red Cross
IDA	International Development Association (World Bank)
IFAD	International Fund for Agricultural Development
IFC	International Finance Corporation (World Bank)
ILO	International Labour Organization
IMF	International Monetary Fund
IMO	International Maritime Organization
INSTRAW	International Research and Training Institute for the Advancement of Women

ITC	International Trade Centre UNCTAD/WTO
ITU	International Telecommunication Union
MIGA	Multilateral Investment Guarantee Agency (World Bank)
MINURCA	United Nations Mission in the Central African Republic
MINURSO	United Nations Mission for the Referendum in Western Sahara
MIPONUH	United Nations Civilian Police Mission in Haiti
MONUA	United Nations Observer Mission in Angola
OCHA	Office for the Coordination of Humanitarian Affairs
ODCCP	Office for Drug Control and Crime Prevention
OHCHR	Office of the United Nations High Commissioner for Human Rights
OIOS	Office of Internal Oversight Services
OLA	Office of Legal Affairs
OSG	Office of the Secretary-General
UNCHS	United Nations Centre for Human Settlements (Habitat)
UNCTAD	United Nations Conference on Trade and Development
UNDCP	United Nations International Drug Control Programme
UNDOF	United Nations Disengagement Observer Force
UNDP	United Nations Development Programme
UNEP	United Nations Environment Programme
UNESCO	United Nations Educational, Scientific and Cultural Organization
UNFICYP	United Nations Peacekeeping Force in Cyprus
UNFPA	United Nations Population Fund
UNHCR	Office of the United Nations High Commissioner for Refugees
UNICEF	United Nations Children's Fund
UNICRI	United Nations Interregional Crime and Justice Research Institute
UNIDIR	United Nations Institute for Disarmament Research
UNIDO	United Nations Industrial Development Organization
UNIFEM	United Nations Development Fund for Women
UNIFIL	United Nations Interim Force in Lebanon

UNIKOM	United Nations Iraq-Kuwait Observation Mission
UNIPOM	United Nations India-Pakistan Observation Mission
UNITAR	United Nations Institute for Training and Research
UNMIBH	United Nations Mission in Bosnia and Herzegovina
UNMOGIP	United Nations Military Observer Group in India and Pakistan
UNMOP	United Nations Mission of Observers in Prevlaka
UNMOT	United Nations Mission of Observers in Tajikistan
UN/NGLS	United Nations Non-Governmental Liaison Service
UNOMIG	United Nations Observer Mission in Georgia
UNOMSIL	United Nations Observer Mission in Sierra Leone
UNOPS	United Nations Office for Project Services
UNPREDEP	United Nations Preventive Deployment Force
UNRISD	United Nations Research Institute for Social Development
UNRWA	United Nations Relief and Works Agency for Palestine Refugees in the Near East
UNSO	United Nations Sudano-Sahelian Office
UNTSO	United Nations Truce Supervision Organization
UNU	United Nations University
UNV	United Nations Volunteers
UPU	Universal Postal Union
WFP	World Food Programme
WHO	World Health Organization
WIPO	World Intellectual Property Organization
WMO	World Meteorological Organization
WTO	World Trade Organization

FOREWORD

The United Nations is in the midst of change, critically assessing its performance and seeking to strengthen its central role in meeting the many demands of a world in transition. For a truly global organization which incorporates so many views and concerns, such fundamental change requires the unprecedented creativity, cooperation and political will of all 185 Member States.

Through this determined, multidimensional effort, a modern and efficient Organization is emerging. In recent years, Member States have reaffirmed its founding Charter; discussed comprehensive agendas for furthering peace and development; taken new steps to fight injustice and crime and to protect human rights and the rule of law; and initiated organizational reforms which will better enable the United Nations to meet the diverse responsibilities assigned by the international community.

Since my assuming office in January 1997, Member States have repeatedly shown their support for the reforms and revitalization of the Organization, demonstrated vividly by the General Assembly's adoption of the reform plans carefully elaborated over the course of that year. These are significant breakthroughs, but much remains to be accomplished. We have not yet succeeded in putting the Organization on a sound financial basis. Also pending are decisions regarding the evolution of such organs as the Security Council and the Economic and Social Council to reflect today's economic and political realities. Still, the Organization is increasingly speaking with one voice, a voice which is being heard more clearly by people everywhere. It is an Organization which acts in concert, offering assistance, guidance and hope for a better life to billions of persons. It remains a uniquely universal expression of our collective desire for a just and stable world.

This edition of *Basic Facts about the United Nations* describes the core mission and objectives of the Organization, taking note of the many changes that are occurring, changes that are essential to ensure the Organization's continuing relevance and viability as the centrepiece of the international community. It also reflects the wide range of concerns and the many ways in which the United Nations touches the lives of people everywhere. From helping to reconcile warring parties to ensuring safe water for rural villages and urban homes; from removing landmines to protecting the rights of workers; from feeding millions of refugees and displaced people to ensuring the safety of air travel, the United Nations and its family of agencies are striving to meet the goals of the Organization's founding Charter — to help bring peace, justice and prosperity to all peoples. In describing the work of the United Nations system, *Basic Facts about the United Nations* provides us with a blueprint of our concerns, problems and determined efforts to find solutions.

Today, the international community faces a multitude of challenges that bring both threat and opportunity to our hopes for world peace and prosperity. The spread of democratic principles is bringing wider freedoms than ever before. The era of globalization is equally transforming the world, bringing knowledge, information and economic opportunity into virtually all corners of the world.

But these profound changes are also bringing new threats to social cohesion, to cultural diversity, to the environment, and allowing longstanding problems, such as drug trafficking and organized crime, to spread. The end of the cold war opened new prospects for peace and cooperation, but it also unleashed nationalistic and ethnic tensions that continue to bring war and misery to millions. The era of economic opportunity has still to bring hope to hundreds of millions more — mostly women and children — who spend every day of their lives in desperate poverty.

The need for a single, universal organization capable of building global consensus and acting in the name of all nations to meet these challenges is greater than ever. The United Nations is that body. The comprehensive reforms now being implemented or being discussed will ensure that we have the unity of purpose and the coherence and responsiveness of action to meet the needs of the international community. I trust that this new edition will be a welcome companion in the long journey ahead.

Kofi A. Annan
Secretary-General

PART ONE

Chapter 1

THE UNITED NATIONS: ORGANIZATION

THE UNITED NATIONS: ORGANIZATION

The name "United Nations", coined by United States President Franklin D. Roosevelt, was first used in the "Declaration by United Nations" of 1 January 1942, when representatives of 26 nations pledged their Governments to continue fighting together against the Axis Powers during the Second World War.

The United Nations Charter was drawn up by the representatives of 50 countries at the United Nations Conference on International Organization, which met in San Francisco from 25 April to 26 June 1945. Those delegates deliberated on the basis of proposals worked out by the representatives of China, the Soviet Union, the United Kingdom and the United States at Dumbarton Oaks in August-October 1944. The Charter was signed on 26 June 1945 by the representatives of the 50 countries. Poland, which was not represented at the Conference, signed it later and became one of the original 51 Member States.

The United Nations officially came into existence on 24 October 1945, when the Charter had been ratified by China, France, the Soviet Union, the United Kingdom and the United States and by a majority of other signatories. United Nations Day is celebrated on 24 October each year.

United Nations Charter

The United Nations Charter is the constituting instrument of the Organization, setting out the rights and obligations of Member States, and establishing the United Nations organs and procedures. An international treaty, the Charter codifies the major principles of international relations — from the sovereign equality of States to the prohibition of the use of force in international relations.

The Charter opens with a Preamble, and includes chapters on United Nations Purposes and Principles, Membership, Organs, Pacific Settlement of Disputes, Action with Respect to Threats to the Peace, Breaches of the Peace and Acts of Aggression, International Economic Cooperation, and Non-Self-Governing Territories.

Preamble to the Charter

The Preamble to the Charter expresses the ideals and common aims of all the peoples whose Governments joined together to form the United Nations:

> "WE THE PEOPLES OF THE UNITED NATIONS DETERMINED to save succeeding generations from the scourge of

Amendments to the United Nations Charter

The United Nations Charter may be amended by a vote of two thirds of the Members of the General Assembly and ratification by two thirds of the Members of the United Nations, including the five permanent members of the Security Council. So far, four Charter Articles have been amended, one of them twice:

- in 1965, the membership of the Security Council was increased from 11 to 15 (Article 23) and the number of affirmative votes needed for a decision was increased from seven to nine, including the concurring vote of the five permanent members for all matters of substance rather than procedure (Article 27);
- in 1965, the membership of the Economic and Social Council was increased from 18 to 27, and in 1973, was further increased to 54 (Article 61);
- in 1968, the number of votes required in the Security Council to convene a General Conference to review the Charter was increased from seven to nine (Article 109).

war, which twice in our lifetime has brought untold sorrow to mankind, and to reaffirm faith in fundamental human rights, in the dignity and worth of the human person, in the equal rights of men and women and of nations large and small, and to establish conditions under which justice and respect for the obligations arising from treaties and other sources of international law can be maintained, and to promote social progress and better standards of life in larger freedom,

"AND FOR THESE ENDS to practice tolerance and live together in peace with one another as good neighbours, and to unite our strength to maintain international peace and security, and to ensure, by the acceptance of principles and the institution of methods, that armed force shall not be used, save in the common interest, and to employ international machinery for the promotion of the economic and social advancement of all peoples,

"HAVE RESOLVED TO COMBINE OUR EFFORTS TO ACCOMPLISH THESE AIMS. Accordingly, our respective Governments, through representatives assembled in the city of San Francisco, who have exhibited their full powers found to be in good and due form, have agreed to the present Charter of the United Nations and do hereby establish an international organization to be known as the United Nations."

Purposes and principles

The **purposes** of the United Nations, as set forth in the Charter, are:

- To maintain international peace and security;
- To develop friendly relations among nations based on respect for the principle of equal rights and self-determination of peoples;
- To cooperate in solving international economic, social, cultural and humanitarian problems and in promoting respect for human rights and fundamental freedoms;
- To be a centre for harmonizing the actions of nations in attaining these common ends.

The United Nations acts in accordance with the following **principles**:

- It is based on the sovereign equality of all its Members;
- All Members are to fulfil in good faith their Charter obligations;
- They are to settle their international disputes by peaceful means and without endangering international peace and security, and justice;
- They are to refrain from the threat or use of force against any other State;
- They are to give the United Nations every assistance in any action it takes in accordance with the Charter, and shall not assist States against which the United Nations is taking preventive or enforcement action;
- Nothing in the Charter is to authorize the United Nations to intervene in matters which are essentially within the domestic jurisdiction of any State.

Membership

Membership of the United Nations is open to all peace-loving nations which accept the obligations of the Charter and, in the judgement of the Organization, are willing and able to carry out these obligations (*for a full list of the current 185 Member States, see Part Three, pages 287-292*).

New Member States are admitted by the General Assembly on the recommendation of the Security Council. The Charter provides for the suspension or expulsion of a Member for violation of the principles of the Charter, but no such action has ever been taken.

Official languages

Under the Charter, the official languages of the United Nations are Chinese, English, French, Russian and Spanish. Arabic has been added

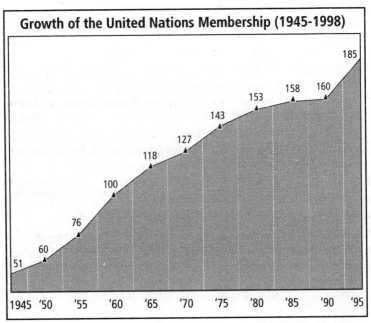

Growth of the United Nations Membership (1945-1998)

For a full list of Members States' accession to the United Nations, see Part Three, page 293-294

as an official language of the General Assembly, the Security Council and the Economic and Social Council.

Structure of the Organization

The Charter established six principal organs of the United Nations, which are the: General Assembly, Security Council, Economic and Social Council, Trusteeship Council, International Court of Justice and Secretariat. The United Nations family, however, is much larger, encompassing 15 agencies and several programmes and bodies (*see page 21, and the chart on pages 22-23*).

General Assembly

The General Assembly is the main deliberative organ. It is composed of representatives of all Member States, each of which has one vote. Decisions on important questions, such as those on peace and security, admission of new Members and budgetary matters, require a two-thirds majority. Decisions on other questions are adopted by a simple majority.

Functions and powers

Under the Charter, the functions and powers of the General Assembly include:

- To consider and make recommendations on the principles of cooperation in the maintenance of international peace and security, including the principles governing disarmament and arms regulation;
- To discuss any question relating to international peace and security and, except where a dispute or situation is being discussed by the Security Council, to make recommendations on it*;
- To discuss and, with the same exception, make recommendations on any question within the scope of the Charter or affecting the powers and functions of any organ of the United Nations;
- To initiate studies and make recommendations to promote international political cooperation, the development and codification of international law, the realization of human rights and fundamental freedoms for all, and international collaboration in economic, social, cultural, educational and health fields;
- To make recommendations for the peaceful settlement of any situation, regardless of origin, which might impair friendly relations among nations;
- To receive and consider reports from the Security Council and other United Nations organs;
- To consider and approve the United Nations budget and to apportion the contributions among Members;
- To elect the non-permanent members of the Security Council, the members of the Economic and Social Council and those members of the Trusteeship Council that are elected; to elect jointly with the Security Council the Judges of the International Court of Justice; and, on the recommendation of the Security Council, to appoint the Secretary-General.

---

* Under the "Uniting for peace" resolution adopted by the General Assembly in November 1950, the Assembly may take action if the Security Council, because of a lack of unanimity of its permanent members, fails to act in a case where there appears to be a threat to international peace, breach of the peace or act of aggression. The Assembly is empowered to consider the matter immediately with a view to making recommendations to Members for collective measures, including, in the case of a breach of the peace or act of aggression, the use of armed force when necessary to maintain or restore international peace and security.

Sessions

The General Assembly's regular session usually begins each year in September. The 1998-1999 session, for example, will be the fifty-third regular session of the General Assembly. At the start of each regular session, the Assembly elects a new President, 21 Vice-Presidents and the Chairpersons of the Assembly's six Main Committees. To ensure equitable geographical representation, the presidency of the Assembly rotates each year among five groups of States: African, Asian, Eastern European, Latin American and the Caribbean, and Western European and other States.

In addition, the Assembly may meet in special sessions at the request of the Security Council, of a majority of Members of the United Nations, or of one Member if the majority of Members concur. Emergency special sessions may be called within 24 hours of a request by the Security Council on the vote of any nine members of the Council, or by a majority of the United Nations Members, or by one Member if the majority of Members concur.

At the beginning of each regular session, the Assembly holds a general debate, often addressed by heads of State and Government, in which Member States express their views on a wide range of international matters. Most questions are then discussed in its six Main Committees:

- **First Committee** (Disarmament and International Security);
- **Second Committee** (Economic and Financial);
- **Third Committee** (Social, Humanitarian and Cultural);
- **Fourth Committee** (Special Political and Decolonization);
- **Fifth Committee** (Administrative and Budgetary);
- **Sixth Committee** (Legal).

Some issues are considered only in plenary meetings, rather than in one of the Main Committees. All issues are voted on through resolutions passed in plenary meetings, usually towards the end of the regular session, after the committees have completed their consideration of them and submitted draft resolutions to the plenary Assembly.

Voting in committees is by a simple majority. In plenary meetings, resolutions may be adopted by acclamation, without objection or without a vote, or the vote may be recorded or taken by roll-call.

While the decisions of the Assembly have no legally binding force for Governments, they carry the weight of world opinion on major international issues, as well as the moral authority of the world community.

The work of the United Nations year-round derives largely from the decisions of the General Assembly — that is to say, the will of the majority of the Members as expressed in resolutions adopted by the Assembly. That work is carried out:

- By committees and other bodies established by the Assembly to study and report on specific issues, such as disarmament, peacekeeping, development and human rights;
- In international conferences called for by the Assembly; and
- By the Secretariat of the United Nations — the Secretary-General and his staff of international civil servants.

Security Council

The Security Council has primary responsibility, under the Charter, for the maintenance of international peace and security.

The Council has 15 members: 5 permanent members — China, France, the Russian Federation,* the United Kingdom and the United States — and 10 elected by the General Assembly for two-year terms.

Each Council member has one vote. Decisions on procedural matters are made by an affirmative vote of at least 9 of the 15 members. Decisions on substantive matters require nine votes, including the concurring votes of all five permanent members. This is the rule of "great Power unanimity", often referred to as the "veto" power. If a permanent member does not agree with a decision, it can cast a negative vote, and this act has power of veto. All five permanent members have exercised the right of veto at one time or another. If a permanent member does not support a decision but does not wish to block it through a veto, it may abstain.

Under the Charter, all Members of the United Nations agree to accept and carry out the decisions of the Security Council. While other organs of the United Nations make recommendations to Governments, the Council alone has the power to take decisions which Member States are obligated under the Charter to carry out.

Functions and powers

Under the Charter, the functions and powers of the Security Council are:

- To maintain international peace and security in accordance with the principles and purposes of the United Nations;

---

* The Union of Soviet Socialist Republics was an original Member of the United Nations from 24 October 1945. In a letter dated 24 December 1991, Boris Yeltsin, the President of the Russian Federation, informed the Secretary-General that the membership of the Soviet Union in the Security Council and all other United Nations organs was being continued by the Russian Federation with the support of the 11 member countries of the Commonwealth of Independent States.

- To investigate any dispute or situation which might lead to international friction;
- To recommend methods of adjusting such disputes or the terms of settlement;
- To formulate plans for establishing a system to regulate armaments;
- To determine the existence of a threat to the peace or act of aggression and to recommend what action should be taken;
- To call on Members to apply economic sanctions and other measures not involving the use of force to prevent or stop aggression;
- To take military action against an aggressor;
- To recommend the admission of new Members;
- To exercise the trusteeship functions of the United Nations in "strategic areas";
- To recommend to the General Assembly the appointment of the Secretary-General and, together with the Assembly, to elect the Judges of the International Court of Justice.

The Security Council is so organized as to be able to function continuously, and a representative of each of its members must be present at all times at United Nations Headquarters. The Council may meet elsewhere than at Headquarters; in 1972, it held a session in Addis Ababa, Ethiopia, and the following year it met in Panama City, Panama.

When a complaint concerning a threat to peace is brought before it, the Council's first action is usually to recommend that the parties try to reach agreement by peaceful means. In some cases, the Council itself undertakes investigation and mediation. It may appoint special representatives or request the Secretary-General to do so or to use his good offices. It may set forth principles for a peaceful settlement.

When a dispute leads to fighting, the Council's first concern is to bring it to an end as soon as possible. On many occasions, the Council has issued ceasefire directives which have been instrumental in preventing wider hostilities.

The Council also sends United Nations peacekeeping forces to help reduce tensions in troubled areas, keep opposing forces apart and create conditions of calm in which peaceful settlements may be sought. Under Chapter VII of the Charter, the Council may decide on enforcement measures, economic sanctions (such as trade embargoes) or collective military action (*see Chapter 2 for further details*).

Economic and Social Council

The Charter established the Economic and Social Council as the principal organ to coordinate the economic and social work of the United Nations and the specialized agencies and institutions — known as the United Nations family of organizations (*see page 21*). The Council has 54 members, who serve for three-year terms. Voting in the Council is by simple majority; each member has one vote.

Functions and powers

The functions and powers of the Economic and Social Council are:

- To serve as the central forum for discussing international economic and social issues, and for formulating policy recommendations addressed to Member States and to the United Nations system;
- To make or initiate studies and reports and make recommendations on international economic, social, cultural, educational, health and related matters;
- To promote respect for, and observance of, human rights and fundamental freedoms;
- To call international conferences and prepare draft conventions for submission to the General Assembly;
- To coordinate the activities of the specialized agencies, through consultations with and recommendations to them, and through recommendations to the General Assembly and the Member States;
- To consult with non-governmental organizations concerned with matters with which the Council deals.

ECOSOC has been strengthening its coordinating functions, particularly coordination of system-wide socio-economic activities, including the follow-up to global conferences, and oversight of operational activities for development.

Sessions

The Economic and Social Council generally holds one five-week-long substantive session each year, alternating between New York and Geneva. The session includes a high-level special meeting, attended by Ministers and other high officials, to discuss major economic and social issues. The year-round work of the Council is carried out in its subsidiary bodies — commissions and committees — which meet at regular intervals and report back to the Council.

Subsidiary and related bodies

The subsidiary machinery of the Council includes:

- Nine functional commissions, which are deliberative bodies whose role is to consider and make recommendations on issues in their areas of responsibility and expertise: Statistical Commission, Commission on Population and Development (*see Chapter 3, page 176*), Commission for Social Development (*see Chapter 3, page 159*), Commission on Human Rights *(see Chapter 4, pages 224-225)*, Commission on the Status of Women *(see Chapter 3, page 178, and Chapter 4, pages 235-236)*, Commission on Narcotic Drugs (*see page 187*), Commission on Crime Prevention and Criminal Justice (*see Chapter 3, page 190*), Commission on Science and Technology for Development (*see Chapter 3, page 155*) and Commission on Sustainable Development (*see Chapter 3, page 197-200*);
- Five Regional Commissions as grouped by the United Nations: Economic Commission for Africa (Addis Ababa, Ethiopia), Economic and Social Commission for Asia and the Pacific (Bangkok, Thailand), Economic Commission for Europe (Geneva, Switzerland), Economic Commission for Latin America and the Caribbean (Santiago, Chile) and Economic and Social Commission for Western Asia (Beirut, Lebanon). The basic mandate of these Regional Commissions is to initiate measures that promote the economic development of each region and strengthen the economic relations of the countries in that region, both among themselves and with other countries of the world (*see also Chapter 3, page 128*).
- Four standing committees: Committee for Programme and Coordination, Commission on Human Settlements, Committee on Non-Governmental Organizations and Committee on Negotiations with Intergovernmental Agencies;
- A number of expert bodies on subjects such as development planning, natural resources, and economic, social and cultural rights;
- The executive committees and boards of various United Nations bodies (United Nations Children's Fund, Office of the United Nations High Commissioner for Refugees, United Nations Development Programme/United Nations Population Fund, World Food Programme, International Research and Training Institute for the Advancement of Women). Also related to the Council is the International Narcotics Control Board (*see Chapter 3, pages 187-188*).

As requested by the General Assembly, ECOSOC is now carrying out a review of its functional commissions and expert groups and bodies, as well as a general review of the Regional Commissions.

Relations with non-governmental organizations

Under the Charter, the Economic and Social Council consults with non-governmental organizations (NGOs) concerned with matters within its competence. Over 1,500 NGOs have consultative status with the Council. The Council recognizes that these organizations should have the opportunity to express their views to the Council, and that they possess special experience or technical knowledge of value to the Council's work.

The Council classifies NGOs into three categories: category I organizations are those concerned with most of the Council's activities; category II organizations have special competence in specific areas; and organizations that can occasionally contribute to the Council are placed on a roster for ad hoc consultations.

NGOs with consultative status may send observers to meetings of the Council and its subsidiary bodies and may submit written statements relevant to the Council's work. They may also consult with the United Nations Secretariat on matters of mutual concern.

Over the years, the relationship between the United Nations and affiliated NGOs has developed significantly. Increasingly, NGOs are seen as partners who are consulted on policy and programme matters and seen as valuable links to civil society. NGOs around the world, in increasing numbers, are working daily with the United Nations community to help achieve the objectives of the United Nations Charter.

Trusteeship Council

The Trusteeship Council, one of the main organs of the United Nations, was established to supervise the administration of Trust Territories placed under the Trusteeship System, which was set up under the Charter to promote the advancement of the inhabitants of the 11 original Trust Territories and their progress towards self-government or independence. The Trusteeship Council is made up of the five permanent members of the Security Council — China, France, the Russian Federation, the United Kingdom and the United States.

The Charter authorizes the Trusteeship Council to examine and discuss reports from the Administering Authority on the political, economic, social and educational advancement of the peoples of Trust Territories; to examine petitions from the Territories; and to undertake special missions to the Territories.

To date, all Trust Territories have attained self-government or independence, either as separate States or by joining neighbouring independent countries. In 1994, the Security Council terminated the United Nations Trusteeship Agreement for the last of the original 11 Territories on its agenda — the Trust Territory of the Pacific Islands (Palau), administered by the United States. The Trusteeship Council, by amending its rules of procedure, will now meet as and where occasion may require (*see also Chapter 7, page 276*).

International Court of Justice

The International Court of Justice, based at The Hague, the Netherlands, is the principal judicial organ of the United Nations. It settles legal disputes between States parties and gives advisory opinions to the United Nations and its specialized agencies. Its Statute is an integral part of the United Nations Charter.

The Court is open to the parties to its Statute, which automatically includes all Members of the United Nations. A State which is not a United Nations Member may become a party to the Statute, as is the case for Switzerland and Nauru. The Court is not open to private individuals.

All countries which are parties to the Statute of the Court can be parties to cases before it. Other States can refer cases to it under conditions laid down by the Security Council.

Both the General Assembly and the Security Council can ask the Court for an advisory opinion on any legal question; other organs of the United Nations and the specialized agencies, when authorized by the Assembly, can ask for advisory opinions on legal questions within the scope of their activities.

Jurisdiction

The jurisdiction of the Court covers all questions which States refer to it, and all matters provided for in the United Nations Charter or in treaties or conventions in force. States may bind themselves in advance to accept the jurisdiction of the Court, either by signing a treaty or convention which provides for referral to the Court or by making a declaration to that effect. Such declarations accepting compulsory jurisdiction may exclude certain classes of cases.

In accordance with its Statute, the Court decides disputes by applying:

- International conventions establishing rules expressly recognized by the contesting States;
- International custom as evidence of a general practice accepted as law;

- The general principles of law recognized by nations; and
- Judicial decisions and the teachings of the most qualified scholars of the various nations.

Membership

The Court consists of 15 Judges elected by the General Assembly and the Security Council, voting independently. They are chosen on the basis of their qualifications, not on the basis of nationality, and care is taken to ensure that the principal legal systems of the world are represented in the Court. No two Judges can be from the same country. The Judges serve for a nine-year term and may be re-elected. They cannot engage in any other occupation during their term of office.

The Court normally sits in plenary session, but it may form smaller units called chambers if the parties so request. Judgments given by chambers are considered as rendered by the full Court. The Court also has a Chamber for Environmental Matters and forms annually a Chamber of Summary Procedure (*see also Chapter 6*).

Secretariat

The Secretariat — an international staff working in offices around the world — carries out the diverse day-to-day work of the Organization. It services the other principal organs of the United Nations and administers the programmes and policies laid down by them. At its head is the Secretary-General, who is appointed by the General Assembly on the recommendation of the Security Council for a five-year, renewable term.

The duties carried out by the Secretariat are as varied as the problems dealt with by the United Nations. These range from administering peacekeeping operations to mediating international disputes, from surveying economic and social trends and problems to preparing studies on human rights and sustainable development. Secretariat staff also sensitize and inform the world's communications media about the work of the United Nations; organize international conferences on issues of worldwide concern; monitor the extent to which the decisions of United Nations bodies are being carried out; and interpret speeches and translate documents into the Organization's official languages.

Now, some 8,600 women and men, under the regular budget, from some 170 countries make up the Secretariat staff. As international civil servants, they and the Secretary-General answer to the United Nations alone for their activities, and take an oath not to seek or receive instructions from any Government or outside authority. Under the Charter, each Member State undertakes to respect the exclusively international character of the responsibilities of the Secretary-General and the staff and to refrain from seeking to influence them improperly.

The United Nations, while headquartered in New York, maintains a significant presence in Geneva, Vienna and Nairobi. The United Nations Office at Geneva (UNOG) is a centre for conference diplomacy and a forum for disarmament and human rights. The United Nations Office at Vienna (UNOV) is the headquarters for United Nations activities in the fields of international drug-abuse control, crime prevention and criminal justice, peaceful uses of outer space and international trade law. The United Nations Office at Nairobi (UNON) is headquarters for United Nations activities in the fields of environment and human settlements.

Secretary-General

The Secretary-General is described by the Charter as the "chief administrative officer" of the United Nations. The Secretary-General is, of course, much more than that. Equal parts diplomat and activist, conciliator and advocate, the Secretary-General stands before the world community as the very emblem of the United Nations and of the values embodied in the Charter. The task demands great vigour, sensitivity and imagination, to which the Secretary-General must add a tenacious sense of optimism — a conviction that the principles expressed in the Charter can be made a reality. The present Secretary-General of the United Nations, and the seventh occupant of the post, is Mr. Kofi Annan of Ghana, who took office on 1 January 1997.

The work of the Secretary-General involves a certain degree of inherent, creative tension that stems from the Charter's definition of the job: both Secretary, as the chief executive of the Secretariat responsible for its administration, and General, as spokesperson and embodiment of the will of the international community. The Secretary-General must speak and act for peace, and yet he would fail if he did not take careful account of the concerns of major Powers and regional groups that comprise the Member States.

The extraordinary influence the Secretary-General can wield over international events through his good offices was demonstrated in February 1998 when Mr. Kofi Annan went to Baghdad amidst a stand-off between the Security Council and Iraq over weapons inspections, and returned with an agreement that averted a conflict that could have led to large-scale death and destruction and which could have had catastrophic political consequences (*see Chapter 2, page 104*). The Secretary-General went to Baghdad, however, only after a careful and full sounding of the views of the members of the Security Council and with their support.

Previous Secretaries-General

Mr. Annan's predecessors as Secretary-General were: Boutros Boutros-Ghali, of Egypt, who held office from January 1992 to December 1996; Javier Pérez de Cuéllar, of Peru, who served from January 1982 to December 1991; Kurt Waldheim, of Austria, who held office from January 1972 to December 1981; U Thant, of Burma (now Myanmar), who served from November 1961, when he was appointed acting Secretary-General (he was formally appointed Secretary-General in November 1962) to December 1971; Dag Hammarskjöld, of Sweden, who served from April 1953 until his death in a plane crash in Africa in September 1961; and Trygve Lie, of Norway, who held office from February 1946 to his resignation in November 1952.

The Charter empowers the Secretary-General to bring to the attention of the Security Council any matter which appears to threaten international peace and security. It also requires him or her to perform "such other functions" as are entrusted by the Security Council, the General Assembly and the other main United Nations organs. While clearly limiting the powers of the Office, these broad guidelines do grant the Secretary-General considerable scope for action, as the Baghdad intervention demonstrated.

The Secretary-General's work entails continuous daily consultations with world leaders and other individuals, attendance at sessions of various United Nations bodies, and worldwide travel as part of the overall effort to apprise himself of all aspects of international concern before the Organization, and of the views of all its 185 Member States, as well as the concerns of representatives of civil society. Each year, the Secretary-General issues a report on the work of the Organization which appraises its activities and outlines future priorities.

One of the most vital roles played by the Secretary-General is the use of his "good offices" — drawing upon the Secretary-General's stature and impartiality — in the interests of "preventive diplomacy". This refers to steps taken by the Secretary-General, publicly and in private, to prevent international disputes from arising, escalating or spreading. Since becoming Secretary-General, Kofi Annan has made dynamic use of his good offices to revive the peace process in a number of long-standing disputes, including Afghanistan, Angola, Cyprus, East Timor, Tajikistan and Western Sahara.

Each Secretary-General also defines his tasks by taking into consideration the contemporary demands being made on the Organization. Secretary-General Kofi Annan has made reform of the Organization a priority of his administration, accelerating the process of streamlining and reorganization designed to make the world body more responsive to the rapidly evolving and dramatically changed political and economic environment of the post-cold-war period and to make it a more relevant force for the world's people.

Reform measures

In his first year, Mr. Annan presented a sweeping reform package that was largely adopted by the General Assembly in 1997. Reflecting Member States' concern both to streamline the Organization and to strengthen its practical impact, the reforms have been both administrative — including an unprecedented zero-growth budget and rigorous efforts to upgrade management practices — and organizational, with the emphasis on enabling the Organization to respond more effectively and quickly to the growing demands being placed on it, particularly at the country and regional levels. The changes have already had an impact on the Organization, particularly the work of the Secretariat, and will enhance programmes, policy-making and coordination throughout the system, particularly in the key areas of peace and security, economic and social development, human rights and humanitarian assistance.

A new post — that of **Deputy Secretary-General** — was created to assist the Secretary-General in the array of responsibilities assigned to his office. The first holder of this new position is Louise Frechette, who was Canada's Deputy Minister of National Defence before her appointment in January 1998. One of her principal current tasks is to oversee implementation of the reform effort. The Deputy Secretary-General also has direct authority over the newly created Office for Development Financing as part of the overall drive to enhance the Organization's profile and leadership in the development sphere.

Measures have also been taken to consolidate programmes relating to development, human rights and humanitarian assistance, as well as the fight against organized crime and drug trafficking (*see Chapter 3, pages 128 and 187, and Chapter 4, page 217*). An important new priority is to strengthen outreach to civil society — NGOs, trade unions, business groups and others — to foster practical partnerships to further the goals and mandates of the Organization. These efforts have met with a strong, positive response, including significant private donations to further enhance the work of the various arms of the United Nations system. One of the most prominent of these was by Time-Warner co-chairman Ted Turner, who in 1997 made a $1 billion contribution to the United Nations.

The General Assembly continues to consider important institutional changes, including the expansion of the Security Council, the reorganization of the Economic and Social Council, changes in the proportion of assessment of dues paid by Member States to the Organization, as well as ways to improve the overall coordination of the United Nations and its family of specialized agencies. These longer-term changes are seen as key to ensuring the solid political and financial basis required for the United Nations to play a central role in the world community in the decades ahead.

Budget of the United Nations

The regular budget of the United Nations (excluding the specialized agencies and UN programmes) is approved by the General Assembly for a two-year period. The budget is initially submitted by the Secretary-General and reviewed by the **Advisory Committee on Administrative and Budgetary Questions** (made up of 16 experts who are nominated by their Governments and elected by the General Assembly but who serve in their personal capacity). The programmatic aspects are reviewed by the **Committee for Programme and Coordination** (made up of 34 experts who are elected by the General Assembly and who represent the views of their Governments).

The budget approved for the two years 1998-1999 is $2,532 million, $10.1 million lower than the 1996-1997 appropriations. The budget covers the costs of the United Nations programmes in areas such as political affairs, international justice and law, international cooperation for development, public information, human rights and humanitarian affairs (*for details, see Part Three, pages 305-306*).

The main source of funds for the regular budget is the contributions of Member States, who are assessed on a scale approved by the Assembly on the recommendation of the **Committee on Contributions** (made up of 18 experts selected by the General Assembly on the recommendation of its Administrative and Budgetary Committee). The fundamental criterion on which the scale of assessments is based is the ability of countries to pay. This is determined by considering their relative shares of total gross national product, adjusted to take into account a number of factors, including their per capita incomes. In 1998, the Assembly fixed a maximum of 25 per cent of the budget for any one contributor and a minimum of 0.001 per cent until the year 2000 (*for the scale of assessments of Member States, see Part Three, pages 287-291*).

The overall financial situation of the United Nations has been precarious for several years because of the continuing failure of many Member States to pay, in full and on time, their assessed contributions to the regular budget or to peacekeeping operations, which are budgeted separately. The United Nations has managed to continue to

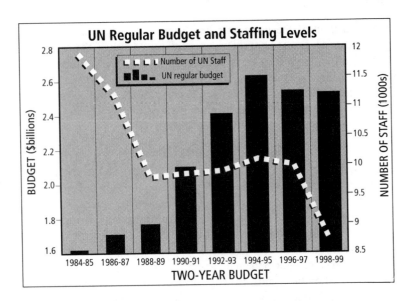

UN Regular Budget and Staffing Levels

Legend: Number of UN Staff; UN regular budget

BUDGET ($billions) — vertical axis: 1.6, 1.8, 2.0, 2.2, 2.4, 2.6, 2.8

NUMBER OF STAFF (1000s) — vertical axis: 8.5, 9, 9.5, 10, 10.5, 11, 11.5, 12

TWO-YEAR BUDGET — horizontal axis: 1984-85, 1986-87, 1988-89, 1990-91, 1992-93, 1994-95, 1996-97, 1998-99

operate, thanks to voluntary contributions from some countries and to its Working Capital Fund (to which Member States advance sums in proportion to their assessed contributions), and by borrowing from peacekeeping operations.

For 1998, as of 15 June, Member States' unpaid contributions to the regular budget totalled $990 million. Out of this amount, Member States owed more than $638 million to the regular budget for 1998 and $352 million for 1997 and previous years. Out of 185 assessed Member States, on 31 December 1997, only 100 had paid their assessments for the regular budget in full. The remaining 85 had failed to meet their statutory financial obligations to the Organization.

In addition to the regular budget, Member States are also assessed, in accordance with a modified version of the basic scale, for the costs of the United Nations peacekeeping operations around the world (*see Part Three, pages 301-303, for list of peacekeeping operations as of June 1998*).

The cost of United Nations peacekeeping peaked at $2.8 billion in 1995, reflecting in particular the expense of operations in the former Yugoslavia. Peacekeeping costs fell in 1996 and 1997, to $1.4 billion and some $1.3 billion respectively; estimated budgetary requirements for 1998 are expected to drop under $1 billion. As of 31 December 1997, outstanding contributions for current and previous peacekeeping operations were a little under $1.6 billion. Shortfalls in the receipt of assessed contributions were met by delaying reimbursements to

States that have contributed troops, equipment and logistical support, thus placing an unfair burden on them.

In 1997, the approved regular budget of the United Nations, including its offices and programmes, and of the specialized agencies (except the World Bank, the International Monetary Fund and the International Fund for Agricultural Development) amounted to $3.165 billion.

The bulk of resources for operational programmes and funds (such as the United Nations Development Programme and the World Food Programme) are financed on a voluntary basis. Contributions are provided by Governments, and also by individuals, as in the case of the United Nations Children's Fund.

The United Nations Family of Organizations

The United Nations family of organizations (the "United Nations system") is made up of the United Nations Secretariat, the United Nations programmes and funds (such as the United Nations Development Programme and the United Nations Children's Fund) and the specialized agencies. These bodies, linked to the United Nations through special agreements, report to the Economic and Social Council and/or the General Assembly. They have their own budgets and governing bodies, set their own standards and guidelines, and provide technical assistance and other forms of practical help in virtually all areas of economic and social endeavour (*see below*).

The **Administrative Committee on Coordination (ACC)**, composed of the Secretary-General and the heads of the specialized agencies and the International Atomic Energy Agency, ensures full coordination between all branches of the UN system.

Secretariat

The United Nations Secretariat is made up of nine departments and other Offices, described below. The Office of the Secretary-General, composed of the Secretary-General and his senior advisers, provides overall administrative guidance to the Organization. The Secretariat has its headquarters in New York and has offices in all regions of the world, including the offices of its Regional Commissions in Addis Ababa, Bangkok, Beirut, Geneva and Santiago. Three main centres of activities are the United Nations Office at Geneva (UNOG), headed by Under-Secretary-General Vladimir Petrovsky (Russian Federation), the United Nations Office at Vienna, headed by Under-Secretary-General Pino Arlacchi (Italy), and the United Nations Office at Nairobi (UNON), headed by Under-Secretary-General Klaus Topfer (Germany).

The UNITED NATIONS system

PRINCIPAL ORGANS OF THE UNITED NATIONS

INTERNATIONAL COURT OF JUSTICE

GENERAL ASSEMBLY

- Main and other sessional committees
- Standing committees and ad hoc bodies
- Other subsidiary organs and related bodies

▷ **UNRWA**
United Nations Relief and Works Agency for Palestine Refugees in the Near East

■ **IAEA**
International Atomic Energy Agency

▲ **INSTRAW**
International Research and Training Institute for the Advancement of Women

▲ **ODCCP**
United Nations Office for Drug Control and Crime Prevention

▲ **OHCHR**
Office of the United Nations High Commissioner for Human Rights

ECONOMIC AND SOCIAL COUNCIL

■ **ILO**
International Labour Organization

■ **FAO**
Food and Agriculture Organization of the United Nations

■ **UNESCO**
United Nations Educational, Scientific and Cultural Organization

■ **WHO**
World Health Organization

SECURITY COUNCIL

- Peacekeeping Operations
- Military Staff Committee
- Standing committees and ad hoc bodies
- International Tribunal for the former Yugoslavia
- International Criminal Tribunal for Rwanda
- **UNSCOM**
United Nations Special Commission (Iraq)

TRUSTEESHIP COUNCIL

SECRETARIAT

OSG
Office of the Secretary-General

OIOS
Office of Internal Oversight Services

OLA
Office of Legal Affairs

DPA
Department of Political Affairs

DDA
Department for Disarmament Affairs

DPKO
Department of Peacekeeping Operations

OCHA
Office for the Coordination of Humanitarian Affairs

DESA
Department of Economic and Social Affairs

DGAACS
Department of General Assembly Affairs and Conference Services

DPI
Department of Public Information

DM
Department of Management

UNCHS
United Nations Centre for Human Settlements (Habitat)

UNCTAD
United Nations Conference on Trade and Development

UNDP
United Nations Development Programme

UNIFEM
United Nations Development Fund for Women

UNV
United Nations Volunteers

UNEP
United Nations Environment Programme

UNFPA
United Nations Population Fund

UNHCR
Office of the United Nations High Commissioner for Refugees

UNICEF
United Nations Children's Fund

UNICRI
United Nations Interregional Crime and Justice Research Institute

UNIDIR
United Nations Institute for Disarmament Research

UNITAR
United Nations Institute for Training and Research

UNOPS
United Nations Office for Project Services

UNU
United Nations University

WFP (UN/FAO)
World Food Programme

ITC
International Trade Centre UNCTAD/WTO

FUNCTIONAL COMMISSIONS
Commission for Social Development
United Nations Research Institute for Social Development (UNRISD)
Commission on Human Rights
Commission on Narcotic Drugs
Commission on Science and Technology for Development
Commission on Sustainable Development
Commission on the Status of Women
Commission on Population and Development
Commission on Crime Prevention and Criminal Justice
Statistical Commission

REGIONAL COMMISSIONS
Economic Commission for Africa (ECA)
Economic Commission for Europe (ECE)
Economic Commission for Latin America and the Caribbean (ECLAC)
Economic and Social Commission for Asia and the Pacific (ESCAP)
Economic and Social Commission for Western Asia (ESCWA)

SESSIONAL AND STANDING COMMITTEES

EXPERT, AD HOC AND RELATED BODIES

WORLD BANK GROUP

IBRD
International Bank for Reconstruction and Development

IDA
International Development Association

IFC
International Finance Corporation

MIGA
Multilateral Investment Guarantee Agency

IMF
International Monetary Fund

ICAO
International Civil Aviation Organization

UPU
Universal Postal Union

ITU
International Telecommunication Union

WMO
World Meteorological Organization

IMO
International Maritime Organization

WIPO
World Intellectual Property Organization

IFAD
International Fund for Agricultural Development

UNIDO
United Nations Industrial Development Organization

WTO*
World Trade Organization

UNSECOORD
Office of the United Nations Security Coordinator

UNOG
UN Office at Geneva

UNOV
UN Office at Vienna

UNON
UN Office at Nairobi

▲ United Nations programmes and organs (representative list only)

■ Specialized agencies and other autonomous organizations within the system

● Other commissions, committees and ad hoc and related bodies

* Not part of the United Nations system although has cooperating arrangements and practices with the Organization

Principal United Nations Offices around the world

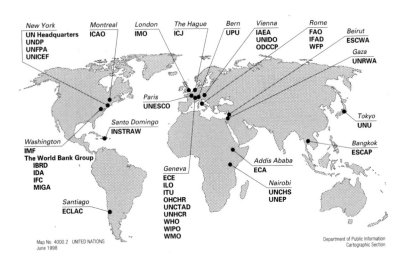

Map No. 4000.2 UNITED NATIONS
June 1998

Department of Public Information
Cartographic Section

Office of Internal Oversight Services (OIOS)

Under-Secretary-General   Mr. Karl Th. Paschke (Germany)

Established in 1994, the Office of Internal Oversight Services (OIOS) assists the Secretary-General in fulfilling his internal oversight responsibilities. In particular, OIOS:

- Evaluates the efficiency and effectiveness of the implementation of programmes and legislative mandates;
- Conducts comprehensive internal audits in accordance with the relevant provisions of the Financial Regulations and Rules of the United Nations;
- Monitors the programme implementation in accordance with the provisions of article V of the Regulations and Rules Governing Programme Planning, the Programme Aspects of the Budget, the Monitoring of Implementation and the Methods of Evaluation;
- Conducts ad hoc inspections of programmes and organizational units;
- Investigates reports of mismanagement and acts of misconduct;
- Advises programme managers on the effective discharge of their responsibilities;

- Monitors the implementation of recommendations emanating from audits, evaluations, inspections and investigations.

The Under-Secretary-General for Internal Oversight Services advises the Secretary-General and senior management on oversight issues and ensures coordination of the Office's work programme with the activities of the Board of Auditors and the Joint Inspection Unit. He is appointed by the Secretary-General, following consultations with Member States, and approved by the General Assembly, for one fixed five-year term without possibility of renewal.

Office of Legal Affairs (OLA)

Under-Secretary-
General
The Legal Counsel   Mr. Hans Corell (Sweden)

The United Nations Office of Legal Affairs (OLA) is the central legal service of the Organization; it provides legal advice to the Secretary-General and acts on his behalf in legal matters. It advises the Secretariat and other United Nations organs on questions of international and national, public, private and administrative law.

Among other things, it deals with questions concerning privileges and immunities and the legal status of the United Nations; prepares drafts of international conventions, agreements, rules of procedure of United Nations organs and conferences and other legal texts; discharges the Secretary-General's responsibilities regarding the registration and publications of treaties as well as the depositary of multilateral conventions; provides secretariat services for the General Assembly's Sixth Committee, the International Law Commission, the Commission on International Trade Law, the United Nations Administrative Tribunal, the Special Committee on the Charter of the United Nations and on the Strengthening of the Role of the Organization and other committees or conferences dealing with legal matters; and as in-house staff of lawyers for the Organization, provides general legal services and public and private law advice in support of the operations and activities of the Organization, including peacekeeping, observer, humanitarian and other missions, as well as the Regional Commissions and the separate funds and programmes such as UNDP, UNICEF and UNFPA.

The head of the Office — the Legal Counsel — deals with legal questions submitted by the Secretary-General and other United Nations organs; certifies legal instruments issued on behalf of the United Nations; represents the United Nations or the Secretary-General at meetings and conferences on legal matters; and advises the Secretary-General on matters of law.

Department of Political Affairs (DPA)

Under-Secretary-
General   Mr. Kieran Prendergast (United Kingdom)

The Department of Political Affairs (DPA) provides advice and support to the Secretary-General in the discharge of his responsibilities related to the prevention, control and resolution of conflicts. It is the focal point within the United Nations for post-conflict peace-building.

The Department also advises and supports the Secretary-General in the political aspects of his relations with Member States and other intergovernmental organizations, especially regional organizations with which the United Nations cooperates. It provides advice on electoral assistance and ensures consideration of and response to Member States' requests for such assistance. It also services the Security Council and its subsidiary bodies as well as the Committee on the Exercise of the Inalienable Rights of the Palestinian People, in addition to providing substantive support to the Special Committee on the Situation with regard to the Implementation of the Declaration on the Granting of Independence to Colonial Countries and People.

The head of the Department — the Under-Secretary-General for Political Affairs — provides political guidance to special envoys of the Secretary-General; directs and manages, on behalf of the Secretary-General, goodwill, fact-finding and other special political missions; undertakes, on behalf of the Secretary-General, consultations and negotiations relating to peaceful settlement of disputes; and acts as the United Nations Focal Point for Electoral Assistance Activities.

Department for Disarmament Affairs (DDA)

Under-Secretary-
General   Mr. Jayantha Dhanapala (Sri Lanka)

The Department for Disarmament Affairs (DDA) promotes the goal of nuclear disarmament, supports and participates in multilateral efforts to strengthen the non-proliferation of weapons of mass destruction, and promotes and supports disarmament efforts in the area of conventional weapons, especially landmines and small arms, which are often used in contemporary conflicts.

The Department provides substantive and administrative support for norm-setting in the area of disarmament through the work of the General Assembly's First Committee, the Disarmament Commission, the Conference on Disarmament and other bodies. It promotes regional disarmament efforts and preventive disarmament measures, such as dialogue and transparency and confidence-building measures; these include the United Nations Register of Conventional Arms (*see Chapter 2, page 100*) and regional forums such as the Standing Advisory Committee on Security Questions in Central Africa. It also provides information on United Nations disarmament efforts.

DDA supports the development of practical measures after a conflict, such as disarming former combatants and helping them to reintegrate into civil society.

Department of Peacekeeping Operations (DPKO)

Under-Secretary-
General   Mr. Bernard Miyet (France)

The Department of Peacekeeping Operations (DPKO) was created in 1992 to provide executive direction, management and logistical support to United Nations peacekeeping operations worldwide. As of mid-1998, approximately 14,500 soldiers and civilian police worldwide were serving in 17 United Nations peacekeeping missions at an annualized estimated cost of slightly over $1 billion. DPKO also offers administrative and logistical support to political and humanitarian missions, and coordinates all United Nations activities related to landmines.

Office for the Coordination of Humanitarian Affairs (OCHA)

Under-Secretary-
General for Humanitarian Affairs
Emergency Relief
Coordinator   Mr. Sergio Vieira de Mello (Brazil)

The mandate of the Office for the Coordination of Humanitarian Affairs (OCHA) is to strengthen coordination among the United Nations bodies that provide assistance in response to emergencies.

The Office works to secure agreement among agencies of the United Nations system on the division of responsibilities such as the establishment of coordination mechanisms, the mounting of need-assessment missions, the preparation of consolidated appeals and resource mobilization.

The core functions of the Emergency Relief Coordinator are:

- Policy development and coordination, ensuring that all humanitarian issues, including those which fall between gaps in existing mandates of agencies — such as protection and assistance for internally displaced persons — are addressed;
- Advocacy of humanitarian issues with political organs, notably the Security Council; and
- Coordination of humanitarian emergency response, by ensuring that an appropriate response mechanism is established on the

ground. This is done through deliberations of the Inter-Agency Standing Committee (IASC), which is chaired by the Emergency Relief Coordinator.

Department of Economic and Social Affairs (DESA)

Under-Secretary-
General   Mr. Nitin Desai (India)

The Department of Economic and Social Affairs (DESA) has three broad, interlinked areas of work.

First, DESA compiles, generates and analyses a broad range of social, economic and environmental data and information on relevant issues and trends. This enables Member States to carry out informed discussions and take stock of policy options and their consequences. Second, it facilitates negotiations in many intergovernmental bodies that meet on economic, social and environmental matters in the United Nations, providing support to Member States as they negotiate common courses of action to address ongoing or emerging global challenges. Finally, at the request of interested Governments, DESA advises them on the ways and means of translating the policy frameworks agreed at the recent series of global conferences in the economic, social and environmental fields into programmes at the country level. Through technical assistance, it also helps them build national capacities in these fields.

DESA's work includes the promotion of sustainable development, gender issues and the advancement of women, Africa and the least developed countries, development policy analysis, population, statistics, public economics and public administration, and social policy and development. DESA collaborates closely with non-governmental organizations and other representatives of civil society, in recognition of their increasingly important roles as contributors to the policy and operational aspects of development.

Department of General Assembly Affairs and Conference Services (DGAACS)

Under-Secretary-
General   Mr. Yongjian Jin (China)

The Department of General Assembly Affairs and Conference Services (DGAACS) provides technical and secretariat support services to the General Assembly, its Main Committees and subsidiary organs, to the Economic and Social Council and most of its subsidiary bodies, and to meetings and conferences dealing with economic and social matters. It also provides meeting and documentation services to all intergovernmental bodies and expert bodies meeting in New York and in other locations, as well as other translation and publishing services.

The head of the Department — the Under-Secretary-General for General Assembly Affairs and Conference Services — represents the Secretary-General in meetings related to the functions of the Department and is responsible for developing conference-servicing policies and practices for the United Nations worldwide.

Department of Public Information (DPI)

Under-Secretary-
General   Mr. Kensaku Hogen (Japan)

The Department of Public Information was established in 1946 to inform a global audience about the activities and purposes of the United Nations. Its broad-ranging programmes, which place public information at the heart of the Organization's strategic efforts to meet pressing international challenges, are an integral part of the United Nations substantive programme. DPI communicates the complex work of the United Nations system as a whole through a multiplicity of outreach efforts, including the UN web site, which it coordinates and maintains, publications, press releases, radio and television programming, documentary videos, special events, public tours and library facilities, with the assistance of its information centres around the world.

The Department comprises three divisions and one service:

The Media Division provides live television and radio news broadcasts to correspondents and news organizations worldwide on all major United Nations activities. It also produces its own radio, television and video programmes, and provides press accreditation.

The Promotion and Public Services Division conducts public awareness campaigns to promote United Nations conferences, themes and programmes through special events, exhibits and other activities.

The Library and Publications Division oversees the work of the Dag Hammarskjöld Library, which maintains a complete collection of United Nations documentation and provides research and reference services. It also manages the United Nations publications and sales programmes (*for a list of regular DPI publications, see Part Three, pages 327-336*).

The Information Centres Service coordinates 69 United Nations information centres and services and eight United Nations Offices with information components around the world.

The Under-Secretary-General for Communications and Public Information is the principal strategist for United Nations communications policy, ensuring a coordinated, open and transparent flow of information regarding the work of the Organization as a whole. Working closely with other departments as well as with United Nations programmes, funds and specialized agencies, the Under-Secretary-General is responsible for developing a cohesive culture of communications throughout the Organization, reflecting the strategic guidance of the General Assembly and the Secretary-General.

The Office of the Spokesman of the Secretary-General (OSSG) is administered by DPI, and the Spokesman, who reports directly to the Secretary-General, works closely with the Under-Secretary-General and his senior staff. The OSSG is a vital link for journalists covering the United Nations. The Spokesman briefs accredited correspondents and, later, the press officers of the Government missions to the United Nations on a daily basis. The Office is responsible for planning the Secretary-General's media-related activities, including press conferences and interviews.

Department of Management (DM)

Under-Secretary-
General   Mr. Joseph E. Connor (United States)

The Department of Management (DM) provides strategic policy guidance and management support to all entities of the Secretariat in three management areas; finance, human resources and support services. These fall under the purview of the Offices of Programme Planning, Budget and Accounts; Human Resources Management; and Central Support Services respectively.

DM has the central responsibility for formulating and implementing improved management policies in the United Nations Secretariat; the management and training of Secretariat staff; programme planning, budgetary, financial and human resources management; and technological innovations. It also provides the technical servicing for the Fifth Committee of the General Assembly (Administrative and Budgetary), as well as the servicing of the Committee for Programme and Coordination.

The head of the Department — the Under-Secretary-General for Management — provides policy guidance, coordination and direction for the preparation of the medium-term plan and the biennial budgets of the Organization. He represents the Secretary-General on matters relating to management, monitors emerging management issues throughout the Secretariat and has the overall supervision of the internal system of the administration of justice in the Secretariat.

Office of the United Nations Security Coordinator (UNSECOORD)

The Office of the United Nations Security Coordinator (UNSE-COORD) acts on behalf of the Secretary-General and the Executive Heads of United Nations agencies, programmes and funds, to ensure a coherent response by the United Nations system to any emergency situation, and is responsible for all policy and procedural matters related to security. In addition, on behalf of the Secretary-General, the Office takes decisions relating to all aspects of evacuation. The Office formulates detailed recommendations aimed at ensuring the safety and security of staff members and eligible family members of the entire United Nations system and is responsible for coordinating, planning and implementing inter-agency security and safety programmes and for acting as the focal point for inter-agency cooperation.

The Office is funded on an inter-agency basis by all the participants in the Administrative Committee on Coordination.

Regional Commissions

The five United Nations Regional Commissions report to the Economic and Social Council and operate under the authority of the Secretary-General. They are part of the regular United Nations budget (*see page 12 above*).

Economic Commission for Africa (ECA)

ECA was set up in 1958 to focus on the promotion of subregional and regional policies and strategies to increase economic cooperation and integration among African countries, particularly in production, trade, monetary, infrastructure and institutional fields. ECA has 52 member countries. It fosters human-centred development through the enhancement of human capacities in both rural and urban areas and among all productive groups, including women, and through poverty alleviation. Special attention is paid to the enhancement of mass participation of civic society in the development process. The Commission's other areas of focus include the strengthening of policy-making and analytical capacity for development management and measures for the development of entrepreneurship and private-sectors initiatives.

Executive Secretary: Mr. K. Y. Amoako (Ghana)
Address: Africa Hall, P.O. Box 3001, Addis Ababa, Ethiopia
Telephone: (251 1) 51 44 16; Fax: (251 1) 51 44 16
E-mail: uneca@un.org
Internet: www.un.org/Depts/eca/

Economic Commission for Europe (ECE)

ECE was created in 1947 to assist in the economic reconstruction of Europe and the strengthening of the economic relations of the European countries both among themselves and with other countries of the world. ECE, which has 54 member countries in Europe and North America, includes Israel as well. ECE's priority areas of work include environment, transport, statistics, trade facilitation, industry, agriculture and forestry, as well as housing, building and planning. The Commission also undertakes activities designed to assist countries of Central and Eastern Europe in transition to market economies, using the concept of sustainable development as the guiding principle for all its activities.

Executive Secretary: Mr. Yves Berthelot (France)
Address: Palais des Nations, 1211 Geneva 10, Switzerland
Telephone: (41 22)917 4444; Fax: (4122) 917 0505
E-mail: info.ece@unece.org
Internet: www.unicc.org/unece

Economic Commission for Latin America and the Caribbean (ECLAC)

ECLAC was set up in 1948 to coordinate policies for the promotion of economic development in the Latin American and Caribbean region. It collaborates with it 41 member states and six associate member states in the research and analysis of regional and national economic problems and provides assistance in the formulation of development plans. It cooperates with national, regional and international organizations on subjects such as food and agriculture, economic and social planning, industrial, scientific and technological development, international trade and development finance, natural resources and energy, environment and human settlements, population, social development, integration of women into development, statistics and economic projections, regional integration and cooperation, and transnational corporations.

The ECLAC system comprises two organizations: the Latin American and Caribbean Institute for Economic and Social Planning, which undertakes research and provides training as well as further cooperation among the planning services of the region; and the Latin American Demographic Centre, which collaborates with Governments in formulating population policies and provides demographic estimates and projections, documentation and training facilities.

Executive Secretary: Mr. José Antonio Ocampo (Colombia)
Address: Edificio Naciones Unidas, Avenida Dag Hammarskjold,
    Casilla 179-D, Santiago, Chile
Telephone: (56 2) 210 2371; Fax: (56 2) 208 0252, (56 2) 208 1946
E-mail: [first initial][surname]@eclac.cl
Internet: www.eclac.cl

Economic and Social Commission for Asia and the Pacific (ESCAP)

ESCAP, established in 1947, has a mandate to address the economic and social issues of the region. It has 48 members and 10 associate members representing almost 60 per cent of the World's population. ESCAP provides a range of technical assistance, focusing on direct advisory services to Governments, training and pooling of regional experience and information through meetings, publications and inter-country networks. It executes programmes and projects to stimulate growth, improve socio-economic conditions and help build the foundations of modern society. Three regional research and training institutions in agricultural development, statistics and technology transfer operate under its auspices. New areas of priority include promotion of inter-regional trade and investment, transfer of technology, privatization and entrepreneurship, environment, urbanization, poverty alleviation, drug abuse control, population, social development and labour migration.

Executive Secretary: Mr. Adrianus Mooy (Indonesia)
Address: United Nations Building, Rajadamnern Avenue, Bangkok, Thailand
Telephone: (662) 288 1234; Fax: (662) 288 1000
E-mail: [surname].unescap@unorg
Internet: www. unescap.org

Economic and Social Commission for Western Asia (ESCWA)

ESCWA was established in 1973 to facilitate concerted action for the economic and social development of the countries of Western Asia by promoting economic cooperation and integration in the region. ESCWA's substantive programmes address areas such as planning, agriculture, industry, sustainabale economic development, natural resources, social development, statistics and transport and communications. The Commission comprises 13 member states.

Executive Secretary: Mr. Hazem Abdel Aziz El Beblawi (Egypt)
Address: P.O. Box 11-8575, Riad el-Solh Square, Beirut, Lebanon
Telephone: (961) 198 1301; Fax : (961) 198 1510
E-mail: unescwa@e˘cwa.org.lb
Internet: www.escwa.org.lb

UN Programmes and other Bodies

Various offices, programmes, funds and specialized agencies, which carry out cooperation activities for development, are also closely related to the United Nations. Also listed below are six institutions specializing in development research.

United Nations Children's Fund (UNICEF)

The United Nations Children's Fund (UNICEF), the only United Nations organization dedicated exclusively to children, works for child protection, survival and development within the framework of the Convention on the Rights of the Child. Created by the General Assembly in 1946 to meet the emergency needs of children in post-war Europe, UNICEF now supports programmes aimed at improving the lives of children everywhere, particularly those in developing countries. It promotes the full implementation of the Convention on the Rights of the Child, adopted unanimously by the General Assembly in 1989 and almost universally ratified, and the year 2000 goals for children established at the 1990 World Summit for Children.

In cooperation with other United Nations agencies, Governments and non-governmental organizations, and through its worldwide field network, UNICEF supports low-cost community-based programmes in primary health care, nutrition, basic education, water and environmental sanitation, and gender and development. It advocates observance of human rights for all children, especially girls. UNICEF also continues to provide relief and rehabilitation assistance in emergencies.

UNICEF was awarded the Nobel Peace Prize in 1965.

UNICEF is governed by a 36-member Executive Board that establishes policies, reviews programmes and approves budgets. It reports to the General Assembly through the Economic and Social Council. UNICEF has over 6,200 staff in 242 locations in 133 countries, 84 per cent of whom are in the field. The remainder are assigned to headquarters locations in New York, Copenhagen and Florence, as well as the Regional Office for Europe, in Geneva.

UNICEF relies entirely on voluntary governmental and non-governmental contributions; more than 30 per cent of its income comes from non-governmental and private sector sources. In 1997, total income was $902 million. The total programme expenditure was $822 million (89 per cent of total expenditure), of which 33 per cent was spent on child health — the largest programme sector.

Major publications include *The State of the World's Children* and *The Progress of Nations*.

Executive Director: Ms. Carol Bellamy (USA)
Headquarters: UNICEF House, United Nations, New York, NY 10017, USA
Tel.: (1-212) 326 7000; Fax: (1-212) 888 7465
E-mail: webmaster@unicef.org
Internet: www.unicef.org

United Nations Conference on Trade and Development (UNCTAD)

The United Nations Conference on Trade and Development (UNCTAD) was established in 1964 to accelerate trade and economic development, particularly that of developing countries. Since then, eight Conferences have taken place: 1968 (New Delhi), 1972 (Santiago), 1976 (Nairobi), 1979 (Manila), 1983 (Belgrade), 1987 (Geneva), 1992 (Cartagena) and 1996 (Midrand, South Africa).

UNCTAD is the focal point within the United Nations system for the integrated treatment of development and interrelated issues in the areas of trade, finance, technology, investment and sustainable development.

The Trade and Development Board is the executive body of UNCTAD. It is responsible for ensuring the overall consistency of UNCTAD's activities with agreed priorities.

Three Commissions of the Board were established by UNCTAD IX in 1996 to develop policies in their areas of competence: the Commission on Trade in Goods and Services, and Commodities; the Commission on Investment, Technology and Related Financial Issues; and the Commission on Enterprise, Business Facilitation and Development.

Since 1993, UNCTAD has been providing substantive and technical support to the ECOSOC Commission on Science and Technology for Development.

UNCTAD is composed of 188 member States. The secretariat has a staff of approximately 394. Its annual operational budget is approximately $50 million, drawn from the United Nations regular budget. Technical cooperation activities, financed from extrabudgetary resources, amount to about $24 million.

Secretary-General: Mr. Rubens Ricupero (Brazil)
Headquarters: Palais des Nations, CH-1211 Geneva 10,
  Switzerland
Tel.: (41 22) 907 1234; Fax: (41 22) 907 0057
Telex: 412962
E-mail: ers@unctad.org
Internet: www.unctad.org

United Nations Development Programme (UNDP)

Established in 1965, the United Nations Development Programme (UNDP) is the world's largest multilateral source of grants for sustainable human development. It coordinates most of the technical assistance provided by the United Nations system.

UNDP has three overriding goals:

- To help the United Nations become a powerful and cohesive force for sustainable human development;
- To focus its own resources on a series of objectives central to sustainable human development: poverty elimination, environmental regeneration, job creation and advancement of women;
- To strengthen international cooperation for sustainable human development and serve as a major substantive resource on how to achieve this cooperation.

Through a worldwide network of 132 offices, UNDP works with Governments, organizations and people in 174 developing countries and territories. Ninety per cent of UNDP's core resources go to 66 countries that are home to 90 per cent of the world's extremely poor. Eighty-five per cent of UNDP's staff is based in the developing countries where people need help.

The financial resources of UNDP are derived primarily from voluntary contributions. In 1997, these contributions totalled $760 million in core resources. In addition, it received $1.4 billion in other financing for various UNDP-administered funds and special development objectives.

UNDP manages several associated funds. Among them are:

- United Nations Volunteer Programme (UNV)
- United Nations Development Fund for Women (UNIFEM)
- Office to Combat Desertification and Drought (UNSO)
- United Nations Capital Development Fund (UNCDF)
- United Nations Fund for Science and Technology for Development (UNFSDT)
- United Nations Revolving Fund for Natural Resources (UNRFNRE)

UNDP is governed by a 36-member Executive Board, representing both developing and developed countries. Among its major publications is the *Human Development Report*, published annually.

Administrator: Mr. James Gustave Speth (USA)
Headquarters: 1 UN Plaza, New York, NY 10017, USA
Tel.: (1-212) 906-5000; Fax: (1-212) 906-5364
Telex: 125980, 422862
Internet: www.undp.org

United Nations Volunteers (UNV)

United Nations Volunteers (UNV) was created as a subsidiary organ of the United Nations by the General Assembly in 1970 to be an operational programme in development cooperation. As a volunteer-based programme, UNV is both unique within the United Nations family and in its scale as a multilateral undertaking. It assigns mid-career women and men to sectoral and community-based development projects, humanitarian aid and the promotion of human rights and democracy. It seeks also to foster volunteer contributions in general. UNV reports to the Executive Board of UNDP/UNFPA and works through UNDP's country offices around the world.

In any given year, some 4,000 UNV specialists, field workers and national UNVs, short-term business/industry consultants and returning expatriate advisers, comprising more than 140 nationalities, are at work in a similar number of countries. Two thirds are themselves citizens of developing countries and countries in economic transition, and one third come from industrialized countries. More than 16,000 persons have served as UNVs since 1971.

Graduate qualifications and several years' working experience are preconditions for recruitment. Contracts are normally for two years, with shorter assignments for humanitarian, electoral and other missions. UNVs receive a modest monthly living allowance. Funding comes from UNDP, partner UN agencies resources and donor contributions to the UNV Special Voluntary Fund.

UNV is designated by the UN General Assembly as the focal point for the International Year of Volunteers, 2001 (E-mail: iyv2001@unv.org) (Internet: www.unv.org/projects/iyv2001/index.html)

Executive Coordinator: Dr. Sharon Capeling-Alakija (Canada)
Headquarters: Postfach 260111, D-53153 Bonn, Germany
Tel.: (49-228) 815-2000; Fax: (49-228) 815-2001
E-mail: enquiry@unv.org
Internet: www.unv.org

United Nations Office for Project Services (UNOPS)

The United Nations Office for Project Services (UNOPS) manages project resources to help developing nations and countries with economies in transition in their quest for peace, social stability, economic growth and sustainable development.

UNOPS offers the international community a broad range of services, from overall project management to the provision of single inputs. In responding flexibly to its clients' demands, UNOPS tailors management services to their particular needs, applies methods for attaining cost-effective results, and mobilizes diverse implementing partners.

The Office works in partnership with UNDP and other United Nations bodies. It is entirely funded by fees earned for services rendered.

Executive Director: Mr. Reinhart Helmke (Germany)
Headquarters: 220 East 42nd Street, 14th floor, New York, NY 10017, USA
Tel.: (1-212) 906-6500; Fax: (1-212) 906-6501
E-mail: unops.newyork@unops.org
Internet: www.unops.org

United Nations Environment Programme (UNEP)

The United Nations Environment Programme (UNEP) was founded in 1972. Its mission is to provide leadership and encourage partnerships in caring for the environment by enabling nations and peoples to improve their quality of life without compromising that of future generations.

As the principal body in the field of the environment, UNEP sets the global environmental agenda, promotes coherent implementation of the environmental dimension of sustainable development in the United Nations system, and serves as an authoritative advocate of the global environment. UNEP's main functions are: analysing the state of the global environment, assessing environmental trends, providing policy advice and early-warning information on environmental threats, catalyzing and promoting international cooperation and action; furthering development of international environmental law, including interlinkages among conventions; advancing implementation of agreed international norms and policies, and stimulating cooperative action to respond to emerging environmental challenges; coordinating environmental activities in the United Nations system; serving as an implementation agency of the Global Environment Facility; promoting environmental awareness and cooperation involving all sectors of society; serving as an effective link between the scientific community and policy makers; and providing policy and advisory services in key areas of institution-building to Governments and institutions.

Its work programme for 1996-1997 focused on: sustainable management and use of natural resources; sustainable production and consumption; a better environment for human health and well-being; and globalization of the economy and the environment.

Among its publications, every two years UNEP produces *Global Environment Outlook*, which provides a comprehensive overview of regional environmental concerns, policy responses to them and a possible future using modelling techniques.

UNEP's programmes are financed by the Environment Fund, made up of voluntary contributions from Governments and supplemented by trust funds and a small allocation from the United Nations regular budget. The budget for the biennium 1996-1997 was $90 million-$105 million.

UNEP's governing body — the Governing Council — made up of 58 countries, meets annually.

Executive Director: Mr. Klaus Topfer (Germany)
Headquarters: United Nations Avenue, Gigiri, Nairobi, Kenya
Tel.: (254-2) 621234, 520600; Fax: (254-2) 226886 or 226890
Telex: 22068,22173
E-mail: unepinfo@unep.org
Internet: www.unep.org

United Nations Population Fund (UNFPA)

Established in 1969 at the initiative of the General Assembly, the United Nations Population Fund (UNFPA) is the largest multilateral source of population assistance to developing countries.

The three UNFPA core programme areas are:

- Reproductive health of women, including family planning and sexual health, which helps people achieve their desired family size and enjoy greater freedom in planning their lives and contributes to slower and more balanced population growth;
- Population and development strategies which guide developing States in drawing up policies with population issues built in and help them design strategies to improve the quality of life of their people by helping them with fact-gathering and supporting policies for sustainable development;
- Advocacy to promote women's equality, an international consensus on population and sustainable development, as well as on the early stabilization of world population.

UNFPA has the same Executive Board as UNDP. The field offices of UNDP and UNFPA Representatives carry out the Fund's work. Pledges to UNFPA's general resources in 1997 totalled $285.5 million. At year's end, cumulative pledges through 1997 totalled about $4 billion from a cumulative total of 171 donors. The number of donors in 1997 totalled 83. About 63 per cent of UNFPA assistance is used for reproductive health, including family planning and sexual health, to refine approaches to adolescent reproductive health, reduce maternal mortality, provide emergency assistance in refugee situations and address HIV/AIDS. Almost 31 per cent is for population and development strategies to ensure a balance between socio-economic develop-ment and population dynamics by providing information, influencing policy and building national capacity in population programming. The remaining 6 per cent is used for advocacy to mobilize resources and political commitment for population activities.

Executive Director: Dr. Nafis Sadik (Pakistan)
Headquarters: 220 East 42nd Street, New York, NY 10017, USA
Tel.: (1-212) 297-5020; Fax: (1-212) 557-6416
Telex: 422031 or 422038
E-mail: ryaxuv@unfpa.org
Internet: www.unfpa.org

United Nations Relief and Works Agency for Palestine Refugees in the Near East (UNRWA)

The United Nations Relief and Works Agency for Palestine Refugees in the Near East (UNRWA) was established by the General Assembly in 1949 to carry out relief work for Palestine refugees in cooperation with Governments in the region. Its mandate has been periodically renewed, most recently until 30 June 1999.

UNRWA initially provided emergency relief to some 750,000 Pal-estine refugees who had lost their homes and livelihoods as a result of the 1948 Arab-Israeli conflict. By 1997, UNRWA was providing essential health, education, relief and social services to more that 3.4 million registered Palestine refugees. Of this number, some 1.1 million lived in 59 refugee camps served by the Agency in Jordan, Lebanon, the Syrian Arab Republic, the Gaza Strip and the West Bank.

In addition to its approximately 120 international staff, UNRWA employs over 22,000 area staff, mainly Palestine refugees. UNRWA depends almost entirely on voluntary contributions for its regular and emergency operations. The Agency's regular budget for the biennium 1996-1997 included $589.2 million in cash and $77.4 million in kind, for a total of $666.6 million. Over 74 per cent of this budget was devoted to programmes of education, health and relief and social services.

Commissioner-General: Mr. Peter Hansen (Denmark)
Headquarters (Amman, Jordan)
Bayader Wadi Seer, P.O. Box 140157, Amman 11814, Jordan
Tel.: (962 6) 826 171/6; Fax: (962 6) 864 149

Headquarters (Gaza)
Gamal Abdul Nasser Street
P.O. Box 371, Gaza City
or P.O. Box 338 c/o Ashqelon 78100 Israel
Tel.: (972 7) 677 7700; Fax: (972 7) 677 7555

United Nations University (UNU)

The United Nations University (UNU) engages in research, postgraduate training and the dissemination of knowledge on pressing global problems of human survival, development and welfare that are the concern of the United Nations and its agencies. The Charter of the University was adopted in 1973; it commenced operations in 1975.

The University has five research and training centres:

- UNU World Institute for Development Economics Research (UNU/WIDER), Helsinki, Finland;
- UNU Institute for New Technologies (UNU/INTECH), Maastricht, the Netherlands;
- UNU International Institute for Software Technology (UNU/IIST), Macau;
- UNU Institute for Natural Resources in Africa (UNU/INRA), Legon (Accra), Ghana.
- UNU Institute of Advanced Studies (UNU/IAS), Japan.

It also has three specialized programmes: the UNU Programme for Biotechnology for Latin America and the Caribbean (UNU/BIO-LAC), Caracas, Venezuela; the International Network on Water, Environment and Health (UNU/INWEH), Hamilton, Ontario, Canada; and the International Leadership Academy (UNU/ILA), Amman, Jordan.

UNU is financed entirely by voluntary contributions from Governments, agencies, foundations and individual donors. It receives no funds from the United Nations regular budget. The University's basic annual income for operating expenses comes from investment income derived from its Endowment Fund. UNU's expenditure for programmes in 1996-1997 was $80 million.

UNU is governed by a 26-member Council which meets annually.

Rector: Prof. Hans van Ginkel (The Netherlands)
Headquarters: 53-70 Jingumae 5-Chome, Shibuka-Ku,
  Tokyo 150, Japan
Tel.: (81-3) 3499-2811; Fax: (81-3) 3499-2828
Telex: J25442 UNAT UNIV
E-mail: mbox@hq.unu.edu
Internet: www.unu.edu

World Food Programme (WFP)

As the food-aid arm of the United Nations system, the World Food Programme (WFP) is the largest multilateral food-aid organization in the world, responsible for handling around 3 million metric tons of food aid. Established in 1963, WFP's mandate is to help poor people in developing countries by combating world hunger and poverty. It uses food aid to promote economic and social development. In emergencies, WFP provides fast, life-sustaining relief to victims of natural and man-made disasters, and wars. Seventy per cent of WFP resources are used for emergency relief. An estimated 50 million people worldwide benefit from WFP food aid.

WFP has a staff of about 4,115, of which 1,525 are in the field, 581 are at headquarters, and about 2,180 are temporary staff working mainly in emergency operations. In 1997, 2.7 million tons of food was delivered to 53 million people worldwide in 84 countries.

While a large portion of WFP's food supplies are pledged in kind by donor countries, over $300 million is bought by WFP using multilateral and bilateral cash resources. It is the largest purchaser of food and services in developing countries within the United Nations system. In 1997, WFP's total purchases amounted to $323 million.

WFP is governed by the 42-member Committee on Food Aid Policies and Programmes, half of whom are appointed by ECOSOC and half by FAO. The Committee meets twice a year.

Executive Director: Ms. Catherine Bertini (USA)
Headquarters: 426 Via Cristoforo Colombo, 00145 Rome, Italy
Tel.: (39-6) 552-2821; Fax: (39-6) 5960-2111; 5960-2348
Telex: 626675 WFP
E-mail: [surname]@wfp.org
Internet: www.wfp.org

Office of the UN High Commissioner for Human Rights (OHCHR)

The General Assembly in 1993 established the post of United Nations High Commissioner for Human Rights as the United Nations official with principal responsibility for United Nations human rights activities. The High Commissioner is charged with promoting and protecting the enjoyment by all of civil, cultural, economic, political and social rights. The mandate is carried out through the Office of the High Commissioner for Human Rights (OHCHR), formerly known as the United Nations Centre for Human Rights.

OHCHR acts as the focal point for all human rights activities of the United Nations. It prepares reports and undertakes research at the request of the General Assembly and other policy-making bodies. It cooperates with Governments and international, regional and non-governmental organizations for the promotion and protection of human rights. It acts as the secretariat for the many meetings held by United Nations human rights bodies.

The Office of the High Commissioner, which includes a Deputy High Commissioner and which has a staff of some 200, is organized into three branches:

1. The Research and Right to Development Branch does research and analysis on human rights issues, develops and oversees the implementation of a strategy for the realization of the right to development;

2. The Support Services Branch ensures support for United Nations human rights bodies, like the Commission on Human Rights and the treaty bodies;

3. The Activities and Programme Branch carries out an extensive programme of technical assistance to countries in the area of human rights, provides support to fact-finding bodies (Special Rapporteurs, Working Groups, etc.) that are looking into alleged violations, and plays a support and training role for human rights field activities.

High Commissioner: Ms. Mary Robinson (Ireland)
Headquarters: Palais des Nations, 8-14 Avenue de la Paix,
    1211 Geneva 10, Switzerland
Tel.: (41 22) 917 31 34; Fax: (41 22) 917 02 45
E-mail: Secrt.hchr@unog.ch
Internet: www.unhchr.ch

United Nations Centre for Human Settlements (Habitat)

The United Nations Centre for Human Settlements (Habitat) promotes sustainable human settlements development through policy formulation, capacity-building, knowledge creation and the strengthening of partnerships between Governments and civil society.

In 1996, the General Assembly designated Habitat as the focal point for the implementation of the Habitat Agenda — the global plan of action adopted at the second United Nations Conference on Human Settlements. The Centre, established in 1978, is the lead agency for coordinating human settlements development activities within the United Nations family, focusing on the following priority areas:

- Shelter and social services;
- Urban management;
- Environment and infrastructure; and
- Assessment, monitoring and information.

Habitat supports — and works in partnership with — Governments, local authorities, non-governmental organizations and the private sector. In 1998, the Centre had over 200 programmes and projects under way in over 80 countries, focusing on urban management, housing, basic services and infrastructure development.

Most of these programmes are implemented in partnership with other bilateral support agencies.

In the biennium 1996-1997, Habitat's expenditures reached a total of approximately $100 million.

Habitat is governed by the 58-member Commission on Human Settlements, which meets every two years.

Acting Executive Director: Mr. Klaus Topfer (Germany)
Headquarters: United Nations Avenue, Gigiri, Nairobi, Kenya
Tel.: (254-2) 621-234; Fax: (254-2) 624-266;1-267
E-mail: habitat@unchs.org
Internet: www.unhabitat.org

Office of the UN High Commissioner for Refugees (UNHCR)

The Office of the United Nations High Commissioner for Refugees (UNHCR) was created by the UN General Assembly in 1951 and its mandate is to help the world's more than 20 million people who come under its concern. They include refugees, as well as certain groups of people displaced within the borders of their own country. UNHCR has helped more than 30 million refugees to start a new life.

The work of UNHCR is humanitarian. Its principal functions are to provide international protection to refugees, seek durable solutions to their plight and furnish them with material assistance. This is done by either voluntary repatriation to their original homes, integration in the countries where asylum was first sought, or resettlement to a third country.

Today, there are 5,475 UNHCR workers in 246 offices in 122 countries working to solve the refugee problem. Over 453 non-governmental organizations work as UNHCR's operational partners.

The High Commissioner follows policy directives given to her by the General Assembly and ECOSOC, and is advised by a 53-member Executive Committee, which meets annually to approve the budget. UNHCR depends entirely on voluntary contributions for its programmes of protection and assistance, but some of its basic administrative costs are covered by the regular United Nations budget. Its budget for 1997 was $1.22 billion.

Every two years, UNHCR produces *The State of the World's Refugees*, a comprehensive analysis of problems and policies related to refugees and other displaced people.

UNHCR was awarded the Nobel Peace Prize in 1954 and in 1981.

High Commissioner: Mrs. Sadako Ogata (Japan)

Headquarters: 94 Rue Montbrillant, Geneva, Switzerland
Tel.: (41-22) 739-85-02; Fax: (41-22) 731-73-15
Telex: 415740 UNHCR CH
E-mail: webmaster@unhcr.ch
Internet: www.unhcr.ch

Office for Drug Control and Crime Prevention (ODCCP)

The Office for Drug Control and Crime Prevention (ODCCP) was established on 1 November 1997 to enable the United Nations to focus on and enhance its capacity to address the interrelated issues of drug control, crime prevention and international terrorism. It consists of:

* The United Nations International Drug Control Programme (UNDCP); and
* The Centre for International Crime Prevention (CICP).

UNDCP is the central drug control entity responsible for coordinating and leading all United Nations drug control activities. It serves as the repository of technical expertise in this field, and provides technical advice to Member States on drug control matters. It carries out its mandate at the national, regional and global levels through a network of field offices.

CICP is the central entity responsible for activities in the field of crime prevention and criminal justice. The Centre pays special attention to combating transnational organized crime, illicit trafficking in human beings, financial crimes and terrorism.

The total ODCCP budget for 1998-1999 was $16.88 million, out of which $16.1 million was for UNDCP and $7.7 million was for CICP. Ninety per cent of UNDCP's and 29 per cent of CICP's resources come from voluntary contributions. The remainder was derived from the United Nations regular budget.

Executive Director: Mr. Pino Arlacchi (Italy)
Headquarters: Vienna International Centre, Wagramerstrasse 5,
   P.O. Box 500, A-1400 Vienna, Austria
Tel.: (43-1) 21345-0; Fax: (43-1) 21345-5866
Telex: 135612
E-mail: undcp_hq@undcp.un.or.at
Internet: www.odccp.org

United Nations Development Fund for Women (UNIFEM)

The United Nations Development Fund for Women (UNIFEM) promotes the economic and political empowerment of women in developing countries. UNIFEM works to ensure the participation of women in all levels of development planning and practice. It also acts as a catalyst within the UN system for efforts to link the needs and concerns of women to all critical issues on the national, regional and global agendas.

UNIFEM works in autonomous association with UNDP. It reports to a Consultative Committee consisting of representatives from all regions and to the Executive Board of UNDP. UNIFEM is represented at the regional and country levels by its 12 Regional Programme Advisors.

UNIFEM works in three key programme areas of strategic importance to women:

1. Strengthening women's economic capacity as entrepreneurs and producers;
2. Engendering governance and leadership that increase women's participation in decision-making processes that shape their lives;
3. Promoting women's human rights to eliminate all forms of violence against women and transform development into a more equitable process.

Since the 1995 Fourth World Conference on Women in Beijing, UNIFEM has been working to support implementation of the Beijing Platform for Action, which is aimed at enhancing women's empowerment on all issues concerning their lives.

UNIFEM's annual budget is approximately $20 million.

Director: Ms. Noeleen Heyzer (Singapore)
Headquarters: 304 East 45th Street, 6th floor, New York, NY 10017, USA
Tel.: (1-212) 906-6400; Fax: (1-212) 906-6705
E-mail: unifem@undp.org
Internet: www.unifem.undp.org

International Research and Training Institute for the Advancement of Women (INSTRAW)

The International Research and Training Institute for the Advancement of Women (INSTRAW) was established in 1976 to serve as a vehicle to undertake policy research and training programmes at the international level to contribute to the advancement of women; to enhance their active and equal participation in the process of development; to raise awareness of gender issues; and to create networks worldwide for the attainment of gender equality. Thus, the Institute aims to improve conceptual and methodological tools, collect and disseminate gender-focused information, offer training programmes in line with its research results to trainers and policy makers, and advocate policy measures for the ultimate goal of the advancement of women as equal partners in the private as well as public spheres of life. In this regard, the Institute networks and collaborates with as well as assists the initiatives of international governmental and non-governmental organizations and disseminates research findings, training experience and information to widen the scope of the Institute's advocacy role for gender-sensitive policy and practice.

The Institute, an autonomous body within the framework of the United Nations, is governed by an 11-member Board of Trustees and is funded solely from voluntary contributions made by Member States, intergovernmental bodies, NGOs, foundations, philanthropic institutions and individuals.

INSTRAW's expenditure for the 1996-1997 biennium was $4.158 million.

Director: Dr. Yakin Erturk (Turkey)
Headquarters: César Nicolás Pensón 102-A, Santo Domingo, Dominican Republic
Tel.: (1-809) 685-2111; Fax: (1-809) 685-2117
E-mail: instraw.hq.sd@codetel.net.do
Internet: www.un.org/instraw

United Nations Institute for Training and Research (UNITAR)

The United Nations Institute for Training and Research (UNITAR) was established in 1965 as an autonomous institution within the United Nations with the purpose of enhancing the effectiveness of the United Nations through appropriate training and research. Each year, UNITAR designs and organizes some 70 training programmes for about 3,000 participants around the world. Training is provided at various levels to persons, particularly from developing countries, for assignments with the United Nations or its specialized agencies and for assignments in their national civil services connected with the work of the United Nations system and institutions operating in related fields.

UNITAR is governed by a Board of Trustees and is headed by an Executive Director. The Institute is sponsored by voluntary contributions from Governments, intergovernmental organizations, foundations, and other non-governmental sources.

UNITAR's budget for 1996-1997 was approximately $10 million.

The activities of the Institute are conducted out of its Headquarters in Geneva, as well as through its New York Office.

Executive Director: Mr. Marcel Boisard (Switzerland)
Headquarters: Palais des Nations, 8-14 Avenue de la Paix. CH-1211 Geneva 10, Switzerland
Tel.: (41-22) 798-84-00; Fax: (41-22) 733-13-83
E-mail: info@unitar.org
Internet: www.unitar.org

United Nations Institute for Disarmament Research (UNIDIR)

The United Nations Institute for Disarmament Research was established in 1980 for the purpose of undertaking independent research on disarmament and related international security issues.

UNIDIR has a small core staff. It relies heavily on project-related, short-term contracts to implement its research programme.

Main areas of research are:

- A non-proliferation and disarmament programme which covers projects such as nuclear policies in south Asia and the debate surrounding a fissile material cut-off, as wel las other disarmament efforts;
- Work on the evolution of collective security within the context of the development of an African peacekeeping capacity;
- A regional security issues programme, covering projects such as confidence-building in the Middle East, West Africa and Latin America;
- Work on the ways and means (both regional and global) of stemming the destructive impact of the excessive accumulàtion and transfers of small arms and light weapons.

The Institute is financed by voluntary contributions from States and public or private foundations. The budget for 1997 was $1.2 million.

Director: Dr. Patricia Lewis (United Kingdom)
Headquarters: Palais des Nations, CH-1211 Geneva 10, Switzerland
Tel.: (41 22) 917 3186 or (41 22) 917 4293; Fax: (41 22) 917 0176
Telex: 412962
E-mail: plewis@unog.ch or ccarle@unog.ch
Internet: www.unon.ch/unidir

United Nations Research Institute for Social Development (UNRISD)

Founded in 1963, the United Nations Research Institute for Social Development (UNRISD) engages in research on the social dimensions of problems affecting development. The Institute provides Governments, development agencies, grass-roots organizations and scholars with a better understanding of how development policies and processes of economic, social and environmental change affect different social groups.

Current research themes include business responsibility for sustainable development; community perspectives on urban governance; integrating gender into development; globalization and citizenship; grass-roots initiatives for land reform in developing countries; information technologies and social development; mass tourism in developing countries; public sector reform and crisis-ridden States; and rebuilding war-torn societies.

UNRISD relies wholly on voluntary contributions for financing its activities. Contributions received in 1997 amounted to approximately $1.5 million and came from Denmark, Finland, Mexico, the Netherlands, Norway, Sweden and Switzerland. Additional funding for specific projects was also received from a variety of other bodies, bilateral donors and United Nations agencies. An 11-member Board approves UNRISD's budget and research programme.

Director: Mr. Thandika Mkandawire (Sweden)
Headquarters: Palais des Nations, CH-1211 Geneva 10, Switzerland
Tel.: (41 22) 798 8400; Fax: (41 22) 740 0791
Telex: 412.962 UNO CH
E-mail: info@unrisd.org
Internet: www.unrisd.org

United Nations Interregional Crime and Justice Research Institute (UNICRI)

The United Nations Interregional Crime and Justice Research Institute (UNICRI), established in 1968, carries out research, training and information activities:

- It promotes and supports research in collaboration with the countries concerned to:
  1. Establish a reliable base of knowledge and information on organized crime;
  2. Identify strategies for the prevention and control of crime so as to contribute to socio-economic development and the protection of human rights;
  3. Design practical systems aimed at providing support for policy formulation, implementation and evaluation;
- It designs and carries out training activities at the interregional and national levels;
- It promotes the exchange of information through its international documentation centre on criminology.

The Institute is funded by voluntary contributions to the United Nations Crime Prevention and Criminal Justice Fund from Member States, governmental and non-governmental organizations, as well as academic institutions.

Officer-in-charge: Mr. Alberto Bradanini (Italy)
Headquarters: Via Giulia 52, 00186 Rome, Italy
Tel.: (39 6) 687 7437; Fax: (39 6) 689 2638
E-mail: unicri@unicri.it
Internet: www.unicri.it

International Trade Centre UNCTAD/WTO (ITC)

The International Trade Centre UNCTAD/WTO (ITC) is the technical cooperation arm of the World Trade Organization (WTO) and the United Nations Conference on Trade and Development (UNCTAD) for operational and enterprise-oriented aspects of international trade development. As the United Nations focal point for technical cooperation in trade promotion, ITC works with developing countries and economies in transition to set up effective trade promotion programmes to expand their exports and improve their import operations.

ITC is a joint subsidiary organ of WTO and the United Nations, the latter acting through UNCTAD. Headquarters operations are financed by the United Nations and WTO. Technical cooperation programmes are funded by UNDP and voluntary contributions from individuals, Governments and organizations. ITC's 1998-1999 budget was $40.1 million.

Executive Director: Mr. J. Denis Bélisle (Canada)
Headquarters: Palais des Nations, CH-1211 Geneva 10, Switzerland
Tel.: (41 22) 73 01 11; Fax: (42 22) 733 44 39
Telex: 414 119 ITC CH
E-mail: itcreg@intracen.org
Internet: www.intracen.org

United Nations Non-Governmental Liaison Service (UN/NGLS)

The United Nations Non-Governmental Liaison Service (NGLS) was established in 1975 to increase cooperation between the United Nations and non-governmental organizations (NGOs) in the field of development education, information and policy advocacy on global sustainable development issues. It has offices in Geneva and New York and supports an active programme of publications, consultations and ongoing liaison.

NGLS collaborates with all UN organizations working for development, particularly the agencies and programmes which carry out development activities.

NGLS reports annually to the United Nations Programme and Coordination Committee and to the Joint United Nations Information Committee (JUNIC). UNCTAD is NGLS' administering agency and UNDP is its lead agency.

Coordinator: Mr. Tony Hill (United Kingdom)
Headquarters: Palais des Nations, CH-1211, Geneva 10, Switzerland
Tel.: (41 22) 907-2076; Fax: (4122) 907-0057
E-mail: ngls@igc.apc.org
Internet: http://ngls.tad.ch

Specialized Agencies and other Organizations

International Labour Organization

The International Labour Organization (ILO) was established in 1919, its Constitution forming a part of the Treaty of Versailles. In 1946, ILO became the first specialized agency associated with the United Nations.

ILO works to promote social justice for working people everywhere. It formulates international policies and programmes to help improve working and living conditions; creates international labour standards to serve as guidelines for national authorities in putting these policies into action; carries out an extensive programme of technical cooperation to help Governments in making these policies effective in practice; and engages in training, education and research to help advance these efforts.

ILO is unique among world organizations in that workers' and employers' representatives have an equal voice with those of Governments in formulating its policies. It is composed of three bodies:

- The International Labour Conference brings together governmental, employer and worker delegates from member countries every year. It adopts the budget and sets international labour standards;
- The Governing Body meets twice a year and directs ILO operations, prepares the programme and budget and examines cases of non-observance of ILO standards;
- The International Labour Office is the permanent secretariat of the Organization.

Opportunities for study and training are offered at the International Training Centre in Turin, Italy. ILO's International Institute for Labour Studies' means of action include research networks; social policy forums; courses and seminars; visiting scholar and internship programmes; and publications. On its fiftieth anniversary in 1969, ILO was awarded the Nobel Peace Prize.

ILO's budget for 1998-1999 was approximately $481 million.

Director-General: Mr. Michel Hansenne (Belgium)
            (from March 1999: Mr. Juan Somavía (Chile))
Headquarters: 4, route des Morillons, CH-1211 Geneva 22,
    Switzerland
Tel.: (41) (22) 799 61 11; Fax: (41) (22) 798 86 85
Telex: 41 56 47
E-mail: webinfo@hql.ilo.ch
Internet: www.ilo.org

Food and Agriculture Organization of the United Nations (FAO)

The Food and Agriculture Organization of the United Nations (FAO) acts as the lead agency for rural development in the United Nations system. It works to alleviate poverty and hunger by promoting agricultural development, improved nutrition and the pursuit of food security — the access of all people at all times to the food they need for an active and healthy life.

FAO was founded at a conference in Quebec City on 16 October 1945. Since 1981, that date has been observed annually as World Food Day.

Special FAO programmes help countries prepare for emergency food crisis and provide relief when necessary. On average, FAO has some 1,800 field projects operating at any one time. FAO-assisted projects attract more than $2 billion per year from donor agencies and Governments for investment in agriculture and rural development. FAO's budget for 1998-1999 was $650 million.

FAO is governed by the Conference of member nations, which meets biennially. The Conference elects a 49-member Council which serves as the governing body between sessions of the Conference.

Director-General: Dr. Jacques Diouf (Senegal)
Headquarters: Viale delle Terme di caracalla, 00100 Rome, Italy
Tel.: (39) (6) 57051; Fax: (39) (6) 5705 3152
Telex: 625852 FAO 1
E-mail: gii-registry@fao.org
Internet: www.fao.org

United Nations Educational, Scientific and Cultural Organization (UNESCO)

UNESCO was created in 1946 to build lasting world peace founded upon the intellectual and moral solidarity of humankind. Its areas of work are education, natural sciences, social and human sciences, culture and communication.

UNESCO's programmes aim at promoting a culture of peace and human and sustainable development. They focus on: achieving education for all; promoting environmental research, through international scientific programmes; supporting the expression of cultural identities; protecting and enhancing the world's natural heritage; and promoting the free flow of information and press freedom, as well as strengthening of the communication capacities of developing countries.

UNESCO is supported by National Commissions, UNESCO Associations, Centres and Clubs. It cooperates with more than 395 nongovernmental organizations and foundations, as well as international and regional networks.

The regular budget for 1998-1999 amounted to $554 million.

UNESCO's governing body — the General Conference — is made up of all member States and meets every two years. The Executive Board, consisting of 58 members elected by the Conference, is responsible for supervising the programme adopted by the Conference.

Director-General: Mr. Federico Mayor Zaragoza (Spain)
Headquarters: 7 Place de Fontenoy, 75352 Paris 07-SP, France
Tel.: (33-1) 4568-1000; Fax: (33-1) 4567-1690
Telex: 204461
E-mail: info@unesco.org
Internet: www.unesco.org

International Civil Aviation Organization (ICAO)

The International Civil Aviation Organization (ICAO) makes it safer and easier to fly from one country to another. Created in 1944, it sets international standards and regulations necessary for the safety, security, efficiency and regularity of air transport, and serves as the medium for cooperation in all fields of civil aviation among its 185 Contracting States.

ICAO has an Assembly, its sovereign body, comprising delegates from all 185 Contracting States, and a Council of representatives of 33 nations elected by the Assembly. The Assembly meets at least once every three years, decides ICAO policy and examines any matters not specifically referred to the Council. The Council is the executive body of ICAO and carries out Assembly directives.

The 1998 budget of ICAO was $54.5 million.

President of the Council: Dr. Assad Kotaite (Lebanon)
Secretary General: Mr. R.C. Costa Pereira (Brazil)
Headquarters: 999 University Street, Montreal, Quebec,
    Canada H3C 5H7
Tel.: (1) (514) 954 8219; Fax: (1) (514) 954 6077
Telex: 05 24513
E-mail: icaohq@icao.org
Internet: www.icao.org

World Health Organization (WHO)

The World Health Organization (WHO), established in 1948, is the premier United Nations institution working in the field of health. Its objective is the attainment by all peoples of the highest possible level of health.

Its main functions are:

• To give worldwide guidance in the field of health;

- To cooperate with Governments to strengthen the planning, management and evaluation of national health programmes; and
- To develop and transfer appropriate health technology, information and standards.

The governing body of WHO is the World Health Assembly; composed of all member States, it meets every year. In 1977, the Assembly set "Health for All" as WHO's overriding priority.

WHO's budget for 1996-1997 was $842 million.

WHO has Regional Offices in Brazzaville, Congo; Washington, D.C., USA; Alexandria, Egypt; Copenhagen, Denmark; New Delhi, India; and Manila, Philippines.

Director-General: Dr. Gro Harlem Brundtland (Norway)
Headquarters: 20 Avenue Appia, CH-1211 Geneva 27, Switzerland
Tel.: (41-22) 791-3223/2584; Fax: (41-22) 791-4858
E-mail: inf@who.ch
Internet: www.who.org

World Bank Group

The World Bank is a group of four institutions: the International Bank for Reconstruction and Development (IBRD), established in 1945; the International Finance Corporation (IFC), established in 1956; the International Development Association (IDA), established in 1960; and the Multilateral Investment Guarantee Agency (MIGA), established in 1988.

The common goal of all four institutions is to reduce poverty around the world by strengthening the economies of poor nations. Their aim is to improve people's living standards by promoting economic growth and development.

The Bank's governing body is the Board of Governors, in which all member States are represented. General operations are delegated to a smaller group, the Board of Executive Directors, with the President of the Bank serving as Chairman of the Board.

Among the major publications produced by the World Bank is the *World Development Report*, which is published annually.

President: Mr. James D. Wolfensohn (USA)
Headquarters: 1818 H Street NW, Washington, D.C. 20433, USA
Tel.: (1-202) 477-1234; Fax: (1-202) 477-6391
E-mail: [surname]@worldbank.org
Internet: www.worldbank.org

International Bank for Reconstruction and Development (IBRD)

The Articles of IBRD were drawn up in 1944 at the Bretton Woods Conference, and the Bank began operations in 1946 with a mandate to promote the international flow of capital for productive purposes and to assist in the reconstruction of nations devastated by the Second World War.

Ninety per cent of the Bank's lending is funded by international capital markets. Over its 51-year history, only $11 billion of capital has been paid in to the Bank by its shareholders, but that amount has leveraged into more than $280 billion in loans.

In fiscal 1997, the Bank's commitments amounted to $14.5 billion. A total of 141 IBRD loans to 42 countries were approved. Adjustment lending loans that are tied to long-term economic reforms amounted to $5,085.7 million or 26.5 per cent of Bank commitments. Assistance to the poorest countries — those with a per capita gross national product of $785 or less — totalled $7.4 billion. The Bank's loans were invested in sectors such as power, oil and gas, industry and mining, transport, urban development , water and sanitation and the financial sector.

International Development Association (IDA)

IDA provides financing on highly concessional terms for the world's poorest countries, those that are not able to service loans from the IBRD. IBRD is responsible for its administration.

IDA loans, known as "credits", are extended mainly to countries with annual per capita incomes of less than $925. IDA "credits" are for a period of 35 to 40 years, without interest, except for a small charge to cover administrative costs. Repayment of principal does not begin until after a 10-year grace period.

The bulk of IDA's resources come from donor Government contributions. These contributions come mainly from richer IDA members, but donor countries also include some countries which are current recipients of IBRD loans. Donors are asked every three years to "replenish" IDA funds. There have been 11 replenishments since IDA was created 30 years ago.

In fiscal 1997, IDA disbursements were a record $5.979 billion. A total of 100 projects were approved for 50 countries in areas such as farming, health, clean water and primary education. IDA has invested heavily in environmental projects and projects concerning women's issues.

International Finance Corporation (IFC)

IFC is the largest multilateral source of equity and loan financing for private-sector projects in developing countries. IFC follows three main principles in its investments:

- It seeks to act as a catalyst to bring private investors together in projects, taking a minority role to mobilize additional funding;
- It functions as a business in partnership with the private sector, taking the same commercial risks in order to create profitable enterprises;
- It participates only in investments where it can make a special contribution (such as attracting foreign investment into a country for the first time).

IFC finances itself primarily by borrowing in the financial markets based on its financial strength and reputation.

IFC is a separate entity within the World Bank Group and its funds are distinct from those of IBRD. In fiscal 1997, IFC's Board of Directors approved 276 projects amounting to $6.7 billion.

Multilateral Investment Guarantee Agency (MIGA)

MIGA was established to encourage the flow of foreign private capital to developing countries by mitigating the major political risks involved in investing in these countries. It does this by providing insurance (guarantees) to foreign private investors against the noncommercial (i.e. political) risks of currency transfer, expropriation, and war and civil disturbance in developing countries.

MIGA's subscribed capital exceeds $1 billion from its 145 member countries. An additional 19 developing countries and economies in transition are in the process of fulfilling membership requirements.

MIGA has successfully promoted the flow of capital to developing countries. To date, it has facilitated more than $15 billion in foreign direct investments in 40 developing countries.

International Monetary Fund (IMF)

Established at the Bretton Woods Conference in 1944, the International Monetary Fund (IMF):

- Facilitates international monetary cooperation;
- Promotes exchange rate stability and orderly exchange arrangements;
- Assists in the establishment of a multilateral system of payments and the elimination of foreign exchange restrictions;
- Assists members by temporarily providing financial resources to correct maladjustments in their balance of payments.

The financial resources of the IMF consist primarily of the subscription ("quotas") of its 182 member countries, which currently total SDR 145,321 billion or approximately $195 billion. Quotas are determined by a formula based upon the relative economic size of the members. IMF has authority to create and allocate to its members international financial reserves in the form of "Special Drawing Rights (SDRs)".

IMF's main financial role consists of providing temporary credits to members experiencing balance-of-payments difficulties. The amounts that IMF members may borrow are limited in proportion to their quotas. Countries receiving IMF financial support for their economic adjustment programmes over several years may borrow as much as four or five times their quotas.

IMF also offers concessional assistance to low-income member countries through its Enhanced Structural Adjustment Facility (ESAF). IMF members qualifying for ESAF funding may borrow a maximum of 190 per cent of their quotas under a three-year ESAF arrangement. This limit may be increased, under exceptional circumstances, to a maximum of 255 per cent of quota.

. IMF's governing body, the Board of Governors, in which all member countries are represented, meets annually. Day-to-day work is conducted by the 24-member Executive Board, advised by the Interim Committee.

IMF has a staff of about 2,600 from 110 countries, headed by a Managing Director who is selected by the Executive Board, a 24-member body responsible for the conduct of the day-to-day business of IMF.

IMF publishes the *World Economic Outlook* twice a year.

Managing Director: Mr. Michel Camdessus (France)
Headquarters: 700 19th Street NW, Washington, D.C. 20431, USA
Tel.: (1-202) 623-7000; Fax: (1-202) 623 4661
E-mail: publicaffairs@imf.org
Internet: www.imf.org

Universal Postal Union (UPU)

The Universal Postal Union (UPU) was established by the Berne Treaty of 1874 and became a specialized agency of the United Nations in 1948.

UPU plays an important leadership role in promoting the continued revitalization of postal services. With 189 member countries, it is the primary vehicle for cooperation between postal services. It advises, mediates and renders technical assistance where necessary. Among its principal objectives are the promotion of universal postal service, growth in mail volumes through the provision of up-to-date postal products and services, and improvement in the quality of postal service for customers. In so doing, UPU fulfils its basic mission of promoting and developing communication between all the people of the world.

UPU sets the indicative rates, the maximum and minimum weight and size limits and the conditions of acceptance of letter-post items, which include priority and non-priority items, letters and aerogrammes, postcards, printed matter and small packets.

The Universal Postal Congress is the supreme authority of UPU. It meets every five years and lays down the general programme of UPU activities, and sets the budget. The twenty-first Congress took place in Seoul in 1994 and the twenty-second Congress is scheduled to take place in Beijing in 1999.

UPU's budget for 1997 was $25.2 million. Its headquarters staff number 151.

Director-General: Mr. Thomas E. Leavey (USA)
Headquarters: Weltpoststrasse 4, Case Postale 3000, Berne 15, Switzerland
Tel.: (41-31) 350-31-11; Fax: (41-31) 350-31-10
E-mail: ib.info@ib.upu.org
Internet: ibis.ib.upu.org/

International Telecommunication Union (ITU)

Founded in Paris in 1865 as the International Telegraph Union, the International Telecommunication Union (ITU) took its present name in 1934 and became a specialized agency of the United Nations in 1947.

The Union's mandate covers the following areas:

- A technical area: to promote the development and efficient operation of telecommunication facilities, in order to improve the efficiency of telecommunication services and their general availability to the public;
- A development area: to promote and offer technical assistance to developing countries in the field of telecommunications, to promote the mobilization of the human and financial resources needed to develop telecommunications, and to promote the extension of the benefits of new telecommunications technologies to people everywhere;
- A policy area: to promote, at the international level, the adoption of a broader approach to the issues of telecommunications in the global information economy and society.

ITU is composed of 188 member States and 482 members (scientific and industrial companies, public and private operators, broadcasters, regional/international organizations). Its supreme governing body is the Plenipotentiary Conference, which meets every four years and which elects the 46-member ITU Council which meets annually. ITU's budget for the 1998-1999 biennium was $22.7 million.

Secretary-General: Dr. Pekka Tarjanne (Finland)
Headquarters: Place des Nations, CH-1211 Geneva 20, Switzerland
Tel.: (41) (22) 730 5111; Fax: (41) (22) 733 7256
E-mail: itumail@itu.int
Internet: www.itu.int

World Meteorological Organization (WMO)

The World Meteorological Organization (WMO), which became a specialized agency of the United Nations in 1951, provides authoritative scientific information on atmospheric environment, the Earth's freshwater resources and climate issues. It develops weather-forecasting services, including seasonal forecasting, and through international collaboration contributes to tracking of global weather conditions, makes possible the rapid exchange of weather information and promotes activities in operational hydrology.

WMO operates a number of major programmes, including the World Weather Watch, World Climate, Atmospheric Research and Environment, Application of Meteorology, Hydrology and Water Resources, Education and Training and Technical Cooperation Programmes.

These programmes provide the basis for better preparation and forewarning of severe weather events such as tropical cyclones, El Niño, floods, droughts and other natural disasters, saving both lives and property, and contribute significantly to our better understanding of the environment and the climate.

The Organization has drawn attention to issues of major concern, such as ozone layer depletion, global warming and diminishing water resources.

WMO has 185 members, comprising 179 States and 6 territories, all of which maintain their own meteorological and hydrological services. WMO's governing body, the World Meteorological Congress, meets every four years. The 36-member Executive Council meets annually. The budget for the financial period 1996-1999 is $177 million.

Secretary-General: Mr. G.O.P. Obasi (Nigeria)
Headquarters: 41, Avenue Giuseppe-Motta, CH-1211 Geneva 20, Switzerland
Tel.: (41) (22) 730 8111; Fax: (41) (22) 734 2326
Telex: 414199 OMM CH
E-mail: gorre.dale_e@gateway.wmo.ch
Internet: www.wmo.ch

International Maritime Organization (IMO)

The International Maritime Organization (IMO), which began functioning in 1959, is the only United Nations agency to be exclusively concerned with safer shipping and cleaner oceans.

The Organization's main objective is to facilitate cooperation among Governments on technical matters affecting international shipping, in order to achieve the highest standards of maritime safety and efficiency in navigation. It helps to protect the marine environment through prevention of pollution of the seas caused by ships and other crafts.

IMO has drafted international conventions and recommendations which Governments have adopted, such as conventions for the safety of life at sea, the prevention of marine pollution by ships, the training and certification of seafarers, the prevention of collisions at sea, and many others.

The IMO International Maritime Law Institute, Valletta, Malta, was established in 1989 to train lawyers in international maritime law.

The IMO International Maritime Academy, Trieste, Italy, established in 1989, offers specialized short courses in a variety of maritime disciplines.

In 1983, IMO established the World Maritime University in Malmö, Sweden, which provides advanced training for administrators, educators and others involved in shipping at the senior level.

IMO's governing body, the Assembly, consists of all member States and meets every two years. It elects the 32-member Council, which is IMO's executive organ.

IMO's budget for 1997-1998 was $58 million. It has a staff of 300.

Secretary-General: Mr. William A. O'Neil (Canada)
Headquarters: 4 Albert Embankment, London SE1 7SR, England
Tel.: (44-171) 735-76-11; Fax: (44-171) 587-32-10
Telex: 235-88 (CALL BACK: IMOLDN G)
E-mail: info@imo.org
Internet: www.imo.org

World Intellectual Property Organization (WIPO)

The World Intellectual Property Organization (WIPO) was established in 1970. Its objectives are to promote the protection of intellectual property throughout the world through cooperation among its 169 member States and to ensure administrative cooperation among the Unions established to afford protection in the field of intellectual property.

The principal Unions so established are those of Paris and Berne.

- The Paris Union, officially the International Union for the Protection of Industrial Property;
- The Berne Union, officially the International Union for the Protection of Literary and Artistic Works.

Intellectual property comprises two main branches: industrial property, chiefly inventions, trademarks, industrial designs and appellations of origin; and copyright, chiefly of literary, musical, artistic, photographic and audiovisual works.

WIPO's three governing bodies are: the General Assembly, made up of WIPO member States which are members of the Paris and/or Berne Union, and which meets every two years; the Conference, made up of all member States, which also meets every two years; and the 68-member Coordination Committee, which meets every year.

WIPO's programme and budget are established biennially by its governing bodies. WIPO's 1998-1999 budget is approximately $280 million.

Director-General: Dr. Kamil Idris (Sudan)
Headquarters: 34 Chemin des Colombettes, 1211 Geneva 20, Switzerland
Tel.: (41-22) 338 91-11; Fax: (41-22) 733-54-28
Telex: 412912
E-mail: publicinf@wipo.int
Internet: www.wipo.int

International Fund for Agricultural Development (IFAD)

To combat hunger and rural poverty in the low-income, food-deficit regions of the world is the mandate of the International Fund for Agricultural Development (IFAD), a multilateral financial institution established in 1977, following a decision by the 1974 World Food Conference.

IFAD's main purpose is to mobilize resources for improved food production and better nutrition among the poor in developing countries. At least 20 per cent of the people in Africa, Asia and Latin America suffer from chronic hunger and malnutrition, and the Fund focuses its attention on the needs of the poorest rural communities. The Fund lends money on highly concessional terms. It works with many other institutions, including the World Bank, regional development banks, other regional financial agencies and United Nations agencies. Many of these institutions co-finance IFAD projects.

For every dollar contributed by IFAD in support of its projects, it has mobilized over three dollars from other external donors. IFAD's average annual investment in loans and grants for projects and research programmes amounts to $323 million. During 1997, IFAD's field investment (loans and grants) was $430.5 million.

IFAD's governing body, the Governing Council, is made up of all member States and meets annually. The Executive Board, consisting of 18 members and 18 alternate members, oversees the Fund's operations.

President: Mr. Fawzi Al-Sultan (Kuwait)
Headquarters: Via del Serafico 107, 00142 Rome, Italy
Tel.: (39-6) 54591; Fax: (39-6) 504-3463
Telex: 620330 IFAD
E-mail: ifad@ifad.org
Internet: www.ifad.org

United Nations Industrial Development Organization (UNIDO)

The United Nations Industrial Development Organization (UNIDO) was established by the General Assembly in 1966. It became a specialized agency of the United Nations in 1985, with a mandate to promote industrial development and cooperation. Its current membership numbers 168 countries. They meet once every two years at the General Conference, which approves the budget and work programme of UNIDO and appoints the Director-General.

UNIDO's activities are grouped into two main areas:

(1) Strengthening of industrial capacities; and
(2) Cleaner and sustainable industrial development.

To support its services, UNIDO has engineers, economists and technology and environmental specialists in Vienna, as well as professional staff in its network of Investment Promotion Service offices and field offices. These field offices are headed by Country Directors. UNIDO's approved budget for 1998-1999 is $129.5 million. A major source of funds for UNIDO projects has been the United Nations Development Programme.

Director-General: Mr. Carlos Magariños (Argentina)
Headquarters: Vienna International Centre, A-1400 Vienna,
  Austria
Tel.: (43) (1) 211 31; Fax: (43) (1) 21131 232 156
Telex: 135612 UNO A
Cable: UNIDO VIENNA
E-mail: unido-pinfo@unido.org
Internet: www.unido.org

International Atomic Energy Agency (IAEA)

Set up in 1957 as an autonomous agency under the aegis of the United Nations, the International Atomic Energy Agency (IAEA) serves as the world's central intergovernmental forum for scientific and technical cooperation in the peaceful uses of nuclear energy.

The Agency provides technical assistance to its 127 member States in the development of self-sufficient nuclear science programmes. Almost half of the Agency's work focuses on programmes that can be applied in areas such as food and agriculture, health, industry and hydrology and environmental pollution, especially marine.

IAEA helps States to verify their compliance with international treaties meant to ensure that nuclear materials are not diverted for military purposes. Some 200 inspectors are deployed worldwide to more than 900 installations and other locations covered under the IAEA Safeguards Programme.

The responsibility of IAEA in the area of nuclear safety has increased as nuclear-power programmes have grown and public attention has focused on safety aspects. IAEA formulates basic safety standards for radiation protection and issues regulations and codes of practice on specific types of operations, including the safe transport of radioactive materials. It also facilitates emergency assistance to member States in the event of a radiation accident.

IAEA's governing bodies are the General Conference, in which all member States are represented and which meets annually; and the Board of Governors, made up of 35 members — 13 designated by the Board and 22 elected by the Conference.

A $221 million regular budget has been appropriated for the Agency's programmes for 1998, with extrabudgetary contributions amounting to about $71 million.

Director-General: Mr. Mohamed ElBaradei (Egypt)
Headquarters: Vienna International Centre, Wagramerstrasse 5,
   P.O. Box 100, A-1400 Vienna, Austria
Tel.: (43-1) 2060-0; Fax: (43-1) 20607
Telex: 1-12645
E-mail: official.mail@iaea.org
Internet: www.iaea.org

World Trade Organization (WTO)

The World Trade Organization (WTO) was established on 1 January 1995, replacing the General Agreement on Tariffs and Trade (GATT) as the only international body overseeing international trade. Although not a specialized agency, it has cooperating arrangements and practices with the United Nations.

At its heart are the 28 WTO agreements, the legal ground rules for international commerce and for trade policy. The agreements have three main objectives:

- To help trade flow as freely as possible;
- To achieve further liberalization gradually through negotiation;
- To set up an impartial means of settling disputes.

These agreements on international trading relations are contained in the Final Act of the Uruguay Round of trade negotiations. The fundamental principles on which these agreements are based include: non-discrimination (the "most-favoured nation" clause), freer trade, encouraging competition, and extra provisions for less developed countries. One of WTO's objectives is to reduce protectionism.

WTO's governing body is the Ministerial Conference, which meets every two years. The General Council carries out day-to-day work. WTO's budget for 1998 is $80 million.

Director-General: Mr. Renato Ruggiero (Italy)
Headquarters: Centre William Rappard, 154 Rue de Lausanne,
   CH-1211 Geneva 21, Switzerland
Tel.: (41 22) 739 51 11; Fax: (41 22) 731 42 06
Telex: 412324 OMC/WTO CH
Internet: www.wto.org

Chapter 2

INTERNATIONAL PEACE AND SECURITY

One of the primary purposes for establishing the United Nations — and a central part of its mandate — is the maintenance of international peace and security. Since its creation, the United Nations has been called upon many times to prevent the threat of conflict escalating into war, to persuade opposing parties to use the conference table rather than force of arms, or to help restore peace when conflict does break out.

Over the decades, the United Nations has successfully helped to end numerous conflicts, often through actions of the Security Council — the primary organ for dealing with international peace and security issues. The end of the cold war brought a time of hope and change and rising expectations for the United Nations, and Member States looked for ways to strengthen the Organization's capacity for preventive diplomacy, for peacemaking and for peacekeeping.

To address a surge in intra-State conflicts, the Security Council authorized innovative and complex peacekeeping operations. In El Salvador and Guatemala, in Cambodia and in Mozambique, the United Nations played a major role in ending civil war and bringing peace. But recent conflicts, many of which have been characterized by ethnic violence, such as in Somalia, Rwanda and the former Yugoslavia, brought new challenges to the United Nations peacemaking role.

The United Nations system as a whole is focusing as never before on peace-building — action to support structures that will strengthen and consolidate peace. Experience has shown that keeping peace, in the sense of avoiding military conflict, is not sufficient for establishing a secure and lasting peace. Such security can only be achieved by helping countries to foster economic development, social justice, protection of human rights, good governance and the democratic process. No other institution has the multilateral experience, competence, coordinating ability and impartiality that the United Nations brings to providing assistance in these tasks.

The **Security Council**, the **General Assembly** and the **Secretary-General** all play major, complementary roles in fostering peace and security, described below. United Nations activities cover the principal areas of *peacemaking* (*see page 69*), *peacekeeping* (*see page 71*), *enforcement* (*see page 76*) and *peace-building* (*see page 77*).

The Security Council

The Charter — an international treaty — obligates Member States to settle their disputes by peaceful means, in such a manner that international peace and security, and justice, are not endangered. They are to refrain from the threat or use of force against any State, and may bring any dispute before the Security Council.

The Security Council is the United Nations organ primarily responsible for maintaining peace and security (*see also Part One, pages 9-10*). Under the Charter, Member States are obliged to accept and carry out the Council's decisions. Recommendations of other United Nations bodies do not have the mandatory force the decisions of the Security Council have, but can influence situations as they express the opinion of the international community.

When a dispute is brought to its attention, the Council's first action is usually to recommend to the parties to reach agreement by peaceful means. In some cases, the Council itself undertakes investigation and mediation. It may set forth principles for a peaceful settlement. It may appoint special representatives or ask the Secretary-General to use his good offices.

When a dispute leads to fighting, the Council's first concern is to bring it to an end as quickly as possible. The Council may issue ceasefire directives that can be instrumental in preventing wider hostilities. In support of a peace process, the Council may deploy military observers or a peacekeeping force to an area of conflict.

Under *Chapter VII* of the Charter, the Council is empowered to take measures to enforce its decisions. It can impose embargoes and economic sanctions, or it can authorize the use of force to ensure that mandates are fulfilled.

In some cases, the Council has authorized, under Chapter VII, the use of military force by a coalition of Member States or by a regional organization or arrangement. But the Council takes such action only as a last resort, when peaceful means of settling a dispute have been exhausted, and after determining that a threat to the peace, a breach of the peace or act of aggression exists.

Also under Chapter VII, the Council has established international criminal tribunals to prosecute persons accused of serious violations of international humanitarian law, including genocide.

The General Assembly

The United Nations Charter (article 11) empowers the General Assembly to "consider the general principles of cooperation in the maintenance of international peace and security" and "make recommendations ... to the Members or to the Security Council or to both". The Assembly offers a means for finding consensus on difficult issues, providing a forum for the airing of grievances and diplomatic exchanges. To foster the maintenance of peace, it has held special or emergency special sessions on issues such as disarmament, the question of Palestine or the situation in Afghanistan.

The General Assembly considers peace and security issues in its First (Disarmament and International Security) Committee and in its Fourth (Special Political and Decolonization) Committee. Over the years, the Assembly has helped promote peaceful relations among nations by adopting declarations on peace, the peaceful settlement of disputes and international cooperation.

The Assembly in 1980 approved the establishment in San José, Costa Rica, of the **University for Peace**, a specialized international institute for studies, research and dissemination of knowledge on peace-related issues.

The Assembly has designated the opening day of its regular annual session in September as International Day of Peace.

Peacemaking

Peacemaking refers to the use of diplomatic means to persuade parties in conflict to cease hostilities and to negotiate a peaceful settlement of their dispute. The United Nations provides various means through which conflicts may be contained and resolved, and their root causes addressed. The Security Council may recommend ways to resolve a dispute or request the Secretary-General's mediation. The Secretary-General may take diplomatic initiatives to encourage and maintain the momentum of negotiations.

The **Secretary-General** plays a central role in peacemaking, both personally and by dispatching special envoys or missions for specific tasks, such as negotiation or fact-finding. Under the Charter, the Secretary-General may bring to the attention of the Security Council any matter which appears to threaten international peace and security.

To help resolve disputes, the Secretary-General may use "good offices" for mediating, or to exercise "preventive diplomacy". The impartiality of the Secretary-General is one of the United Nations' great assets. In many instances, the Secretary-General has been instrumental in averting a threat to peace or in securing a peace agreement.

This was dramatically illustrated in February 1998 when, following consultation with Security Council members, Secretary-General Kofi Annan visited Baghdad and succeeded in resolving a dispute with Iraq

Working Group on an Agenda for Peace

Since 1992, a General Assembly Working Group has been analysing and developing ways to strengthen United Nations action for peace.

With the cold war ended, Member States looked for ways to strengthen the work of the United Nations in maintaining international peace and security. At an extraordinary meeting of the Security Council in 1992 — the first at the level of heads of State or Government — world leaders asked the Secretary-General to prepare recommendations for strengthening the United Nations capacity for preventive diplomacy, peacemaking and peacekeeping. The Secretary-General submitted a series of proposals in a report later that year entitled *An Agenda for Peace: Preventive Diplomacy, Peacemaking and Peacekeeping*.

The proposals included: establishing an early-warning system for assessing possible threats to peace; deploying United Nations forces to an area where conflict appears imminent rather than waiting until war breaks out; creating peace-enforcement units to be deployed when the task of maintaining a ceasefire might exceed the mission of peacekeeping; and increasing the involvement of regional organizations in preventive diplomacy, peacemaking and peacekeeping. These proposals were elaborated in 1995 in the *Supplement* to *An Agenda for Peace*.

A General Assembly Informal Open-ended Working Group has continued to discuss four key themes addressed in the report: preventive diplomacy and peacemaking; post-conflict peace-building; coordination; and the use of sanctions. As a result of the Working Group's deliberations, the Assembly gave the Secretary-General a clear mandate to pursue preventive diplomacy and to strengthen the United Nations capacity to identify potential conflict situations.

over weapons inspections which threatened a renewal of hostilities with that country (*see page 104, below*). A decade earlier, in 1988, action by the Secretary-General led to the end of the war between Iran and Iraq that had raged since 1980. In Afghanistan, mediation by the Secretary-General and his personal envoy led to the 1988 agreements that resulted in the withdrawal of Soviet troops from the country. Cases such as the Middle East, Namibia, Cambodia, Mozambique, Angola, Central America and Cyprus reflect the many different ways the Secretary-General becomes involved as a peacemaker (*see United Nations action for peace, pages 79-108, below*).

Preventive diplomacy refers to action to prevent disputes from arising, to resolve them before they escalate into conflicts or to limit the spread of conflicts when they occur. The United Nations monitors carefully political developments around the world to detect threats to international peace and security, thereby enabling the Security Council to carry out or to foster preventive action. Envoys and special representatives of the Secretary-General are engaged in preventive diplomacy and mediation throughout the world to help reconcile parites in conflict. In many cases this work is undertaken in close cooperation with regional organizations (*see page 73, below*).

Peacekeeping

Peacekeeping operations, which are authorized by the Security Council, are a crucial instrument at the disposal of the international community to advance international peace and security. The role of peacekeeping was recognized by the world in 1988, when the United Nations peacekeeping forces received the Nobel Peace Prize.

While not specifically envisaged in the Charter, peacekeeping was pioneered by the United Nations in 1948 with the establishment of the United Nations Truce Supervision Organization in the Middle East (*see page 96*). Peacekeeping operations are authorized to be deployed by the Security Council with the consent of the host Government, and usually of other parties involved. They may include military and police personnel, together with civilian staff. Operations may involve military observer missions, peacekeeping forces, or a combination of both. Military observer missions are made up of unarmed officers, typically to monitor an agreement or a ceasefire. The soldiers of the peacekeeping forces have weapons, but in most situations can use them only in self-defence.

The military personnel in United Nations peacekeeping operations are voluntarily provided by Member States and are financed by the

---

Preventive deployment

United Nations action in the former Yugoslav Republic of Macedonia is an example of successful "preventive deployment" — the fielding of peacekeepers to forestall probable conflict.

Concerned about being drawn into the Yugoslav conflict *(see page 105)*, the country in 1992 requested the deployment of United Nations observers. The Council agreed, and in 1992 dispatched a peacekeeping contingent to the country's borders with Yugoslavia and Albania. Since then, the 1,100-strong **United Nations Preventive Deployment Force** has been monitoring developments in the border areas that could threaten the country's territory or undermine its stability.

The former Yugoslav Republic of Macedonia has repeatedly requested the extension of the mission, which stands as a model for possible future preventive operations.

---

international community. Participating States are compensated at a standard rate from a special peacekeeping budget (*see Part One, page 20*).

United Nations peacekeeping operations cost some $1.4 billion in 1996 and $1.02 billion in 1997 — less than 0.2 per cent of world military spending.

Since 1948, over 750,000 military, police and civilian personnel from some 110 countries have served in these operations; more than 1,500 peacekeepers have lost their lives.

In recent years, certain prerequisites for the success of peacekeeping operations have become increasingly clear. These include a genuine desire on the part of combatants to resolve their differences peacefully; a clear mandate; strong political support by the international community; and the provision of the resources necessary to achieve the operation's objectives (*see also page 74, below*).

At the same time, the unacceptability of inaction has also become obvious. From Yugoslavia to Rwanda, the international community has seen the horrifying destructive effects of contemporary conflicts. In addition, conflicts have major implications beyond the borders of a particular country, and can generate instability through entire regions if they are unchecked. Even conflicts that are remote from the focus of major Powers can foster problems which have global implications — such as illegal arms flows, terrorism, drug trafficking, refugee flows and environmental degradation.

United Nations operations, because of their universality, offer unique advantages as a means to address conflicts. Their universality adds to their legitimacy and limits the implications for the host country's sovereignty. Peacekeepers from outside a conflict can foster discussion among warring parties while focusing global attention upon local concerns, opening doors that would otherwise remain closed for collective efforts in peacemaking and in building a lasting peace.

Operations are financed through a United Nations budget and include troops from many countries: this "burden-sharing" can offer extraordinary efficiency in human, financial and political terms.

Operations can take many forms, and are constantly evolving in the light of changing circumstances. Among the tasks discharged by peacekeeping operations over the years are:

- Maintenance of ceasefires and separation of forces. By providing "breathing space," an operation based on a limited agreement between parties can foster an atmosphere conducive to negotiations;

- Preventive deployment. Deployed before conflict breaks out, an operation can provide a reassuring presence and a degree of transparency which favour political progress;
- Implementation of a comprehensive settlement. Complex, multi-dimensional operations, deployed on the basis of comprehensive peace agreements, can assist in such diverse tasks as monitoring human rights, providing electoral assistance, observing elections, furnishing humanitarian assistance and coordinating support for economic reconstruction;
- Protection of humanitarian operations during conflict. In many conflicts, civilian populations have been deliberately targeted as a means to gain political ends. In such situations, peacekeepers have been asked to provide protection and support for the delivery of humanitarian aid. However, such tasks can place peacekeepers in difficult political positions, and can lead to threats to their own security.

No catalogue of such roles can be exhaustive. Future conflicts are likely to continue to present complex challenges to the international community. An effective response will require courageous and imaginative use of the tools for peace.

Cooperating with regional organizations

In the search for peace, the United Nations is increasingly cooperating with regional organizations and other external actors and mechanisms provided for in Chapter VIII of the Charter. It has worked closely with the Organization of American States in Haiti, the Economic Community of West African States in Liberia, the Organization of African Unity (OAU) in Somalia and Western Sahara, and the European Community in the former Yugoslavia (*see United Nations action for peace, pages 79-108, below*).

In 1997, the United Nations and the OAU appointed for the first time a joint special representative to address the crises in the Great Lakes region — which includes Burundi, Rwanda and the Democratic Republic of the Congo (*see page 83, below*).

In Liberia, Georgia and Tajikistan, United Nations military observers have been cooperating with peacekeeping forces of regional organizations (*see pages 90 and 104-105, below*). The observers in Tajikistan also cooperate with a civilian mission of the Organization for Security and Cooperation in Europe (OSCE).

In the former Yugoslavia, the United Nations has cooperated with OSCE and the Council of Europe in the areas of human rights, electoral assistance, peacemaking and economic development.

Who commands peacekeeping operations?

Peacekeeping operations are established by the Security Council and directed by the Secretary-General, often through a special representative; depending on the mission, the Force Commander or the Chief Military Observer is responsible for the military aspects.

The United Nations has no military force of its own, and Member States provide, on a voluntary basis, the personnel, equipment and logistics required for an operation. Peacekeepers wear their country's uniform: they are identified as peacekeepers only by a United Nations blue helmet or beret and a badge. Military and civilian police personnel serve under the operational control of the United Nations, but remain members of their own national forces. They are expected to conduct themselves in accordance with the exclusively international character of their mission.

Strengthening future peacekeeping

The international community has drawn lessons from recent peacekeeping experience, and is working to strengthen the United Nations capacity in a number of areas. These include:

- *Enhancing capacity for rapid deployment.* After an operation has been created, its credibility and effectiveness are affected by the promptness with which it is deployed. Rapid deployment can prevent enormous suffering and can spare a country from a legacy of bitterness that can make political reconciliation impossible for years. Several initiatives have been taken to address this need:

  The United Nations **Standby Arrangements System** provides a framework to facilitate the timely planning and deployment of an operation. As of mid-1998, some 70 Member States had identified troops and equipment that were potentially available for service in operations, subject to approval by national authorities on a case-by-case basis.

  Within this system, certain groups of Member States are pursuing initiatives to enhance readiness by pooling their efforts to prepare peacekeepers. One particularly advanced example is the Standby Forces High-Readiness Brigade, whose core staff would be based in Denmark. Troops would remain based in their parent countries and assemble for deployment as necessary. Their capacity for deployment would be enhanced by common procedures and standards for equipment.

In addition, the United Nations is working to create a rapidly deployable mission headquarters, which would constitute a core to be dispatched quickly to the field, around which a peacekeeping operation could be organized.

- *Enhancing ability to function in adversity.* Once deployed, many operations face a difficult or hostile environment. In some situations, an impressive show of force is the best way to avoid having to actually use it. This lesson was successfully applied by the United Nations Transitional Administration in Eastern Slavonia (*see page 108, below*).

To enhance the influence of the peacekeepers with warring parties, it may be necessary to strengthen not only an operation's capacity to dissuade, but its capacity to persuade. This can be achieved through civic action programmes in which peacekeepers perform helpful tasks to gain people's goodwill and cooperation, or by reinforcing an operation's ability to provide benefits to those who cooperate and make political advances possible.

- *Acting comprehensively.* In assisting States in the aftermath of conflict, peacekeepers often confront problems of economic collapse, traditions of abusive use of the instruments of State to advance political power, and adherence to a system where the winner takes all. If restoring peace is to have any durability or meaning, it must pave the way to a comprehensive response to such problems. The institution-building role of peacekeeping operations has thus increased in importance, with mandates including such tasks as ensuring human rights observance, promoting the means to end impunity of human rights violators, and creating the institutions through which legitimate political differences can be expressed.

One response that offers considerable potential is the deployment of operations that are built around a core of civilian police, rather than military peacekeepers. These operations can help reshape the dynamics of society after a conflict while strengthening the foundations for lasting peace. The United Nations has also responded by enhancing coordination within operations.

- *Mustering political will.* Ultimately, the success of peacekeeping operations depends on the political will of the warring parties to resolve their differences. It also depends on the political will of Member States to support such operations and ensure that they are provided with the human, material and financial resources necessary for carrying out their mandates. On this basis, peacekeeping can be an effective instrument for managing and resolving conflicts.

Enforcement

Under Chapter VII of the United Nations Charter, the Security Council can take enforcement measures to maintain or restore international peace and security. Such measures range from economic sanctions to international military action.

Embargoes and sanctions

The Council has resorted to economic sanctions and embargoes as an enforcement tool when peace was threatened and diplomatic efforts had failed. Sanctions were imposed, for instance, against South Africa's apartheid regime in 1977, and subsequently lifted with the end of apartheid in 1994 (*see Chapter 4, pages 233-234*). Recently, sanctions have been imposed against Iraq, the former Yugoslavia, Libya, Haiti, Liberia, Rwanda, Somalia, UNITA forces in Angola, Sudan and Sierra Leone (*see pages 79-108, below*). Economic sanctions have taken many forms, ranging from specific trade bans to full embargoes.

The use of mandatory sanctions brings pressure on a target State or entity to comply with the objectives set by the Security Council without resorting to force. The universal character of the United Nations makes it an especially appropriate body to consider and monitor such measures.

At the same time, Member States have considered the problem of possible unintended consequences of sanctions at various United Nations fora — including the sub-group on sanctions of the General Assembly's Working Group on An Agenda for Peace, where countries have expressed humanitarian concerns on the possible adverse impact of sanctions on the most vulnerable segments of the population, and economic concerns on collateral effects of sanctions.

Authorizing military action

When peacemaking efforts fail, stronger action by Member States may be authorized under Chapter VII of the Charter. The Council has authorized coalitions of Member States to use "all necessary means", including military action, to deal with a conflict — as it did to restore the sovereignty of Kuwait after its invasion by Iraq (1991); to permit humanitarian relief operations in the midst of civil war in Somalia (1992) and Rwanda (1994); to restore the democratically elected Government in Haiti (1994); and to protect humanitarian operations in Albania (1997) (*see pages 79-108, below*).

These actions, though sanctioned by the Security Council, were entirely under the control of the participating States. They were not

United Nations peacekeeping operations, which are established by the Security Council and directed by the Secretary-General.

Peace-building

Today, peace and security are measured not only in terms of the absence of conflict. Lasting peace requires economic development, social justice, environmental protection, democratization, disarmament and respect for human rights. Peace can be durable only if economic and social development are guaranteed.

In the aftermath of a conflict, the United Nations system is thus often called upon to carry out peace-building — action to support structures that will strengthen and consolidate peace. Areas of activity include military security, civil law and order, human rights, elections, local administration, health, education and reconstruction.

Election monitoring

The United Nations broke new ground in 1989, when it supervised the entire election process which led to the independence of Namibia (*see Chapter 7, pages 280-281*). Since then, the United Nations has monitored, at Government request, elections in Nicaragua (1990), Haiti (1990), Angola (1992), Cambodia (1993), El Salvador (1994), South Africa (1994), Mozambique (1994), Eastern Slavonia (Croatia, 1997) and Liberia (1997), as well as the referendum on independence in Eritrea (1993) (*see pages 79-108, below*).

The degree of United Nations involvement depends upon factors such as the requests received from Governments, peace agreements between previously warring parties, or mandates from the Security Council. The United Nations has played a variety of roles ranging from technical assistance to the actual conduct of the electoral process.

United Nations observers typically follow the electoral campaign, the registration of voters and the organization of the polls. On election day, they are deployed to polling stations throughout the country, observe voting and vote counting, and issue a final statement on the validity of the elections.

Since 1992, the United Nations **Electoral Assistance Division** in the **Department of Political Affairs**, working closely with the United Nations Development Programme (UNDP), which coordinates United Nations electoral assistance in the field, and other offices and programmes, has provided technical assistance in the preparation and holding of elections to over 70 countries. Assistance may involve

The fight against landmines

Since the 1980s, the United Nations has been addressing the problems posed by the tens of millions of deadly landmines scattered in over 70 countries around the world. Each year around 30,000 people — most of them children, women and the elderly — are maimed or killed by these "silent killers". In addition to the existing mines and other unexploded ordinance, new landmines continue to be deployed in military actions in various parts of the world.

Since 1993, the General Assembly has called for a moratorium on the export of landmines, to which over 25 States have adhered. In 1996, the States parties to the United Nations–sponsored Inhumane Weapons Convention of 1980, adopted further restrictions to its Protocol dealing with landmines, agreeing that all mines must be detectable, and extending the Protocol to internal conflicts. An international convention banning the production, use and export of landmines, sponsored by Canada, Norway and other countries, was concluded in Ottawa in 1997 (*see page 111*).

Governments are increasingly asking the United Nations to operate mine clearance programmes, often as part of peacekeeping missions. The United Nations not only performs mine clearance, but also trains deminers, carries out public mine-awareness programmes, conducts mine surveys and provides funding for national programmes. Today, some 6,000 deminers are employed in United Nations–supported programmes.

Such programmes have been carried out in several of the countries most affected by the problem — Afghanistan, Angola, Bosnia and Herzegovina, Cambodia, Croatia, Lao People's Democratic Republic, Mozambique, Rwanda and Yemen. The first UN programme started in 1988 in Afghanistan, a country infested with some 10 million mines.

As these programmes have shown, effective, cheap and vital action against landmines is possible. With the right mixture of skills, resources and commitment, the problem can be resolved in a matter of years, not decades.

---

coordination and support, advisory services, logistics, training, computer applications and short-term observation.

United Nations assistance has often been instrumental in building and consolidating democracy. In Mozambique, El Salvador and Guatemala, the United Nations has helped armed opposition movements to transform themselves into political parties.

Building peace through development

A central tool of United Nations action to consolidate peace is development assistance. Many United Nations organizations — including

UNDP, the United Nations Children's Fund (UNICEF), the World Food Programme and the Office of the United Nations High Commissioner for Refugees (UNHCR) — play roles in the recovery stage, which is crucial for providing opportunities for displaced persons and restoring confidence in national and local institutions (*see also Chapter 5, pages 250-251*).

The United Nations can help repatriate refugees, clear landmines, repair infrastructure and stimulate economic recovery; it can help strengthen institutions, monitor elections and promote human rights. This "peace-building" is the best prevention against the recurrence of war.

United Nations action for peace

The following section, structured by regions, offers a wide range of examples of United Nations action for peace.

Africa

In 1997, the Security Council held a special meeting at the ministerial level on Africa at which it expressed "grave concern" over the number and intensity of armed conflicts on the continent and called for an international effort to promote peace and security. Africa has faced a profound economic crisis for many years, and is a priority concern of the United Nations (*see Chapter 3, page 131*).

Africa was the scene of one of the earliest and largest peacekeeping operations, from 1960 to 1964, in what is now the Democratic Republic of the Congo. With a strength of nearly 20,000 military personnel, the **United Nations Operation in the Congo** helped the Government restore the country's independence and territorial integrity (threatened by the attempted secession of the Katanga province), helped maintain law and order, and put into effect a wide programme of technical assistance.

From its earliest days, the United Nations was involved in the international struggle to bring the apartheid system in South Africa to an end, as well as in the efforts to achieve independence for Namibia (*see Chapter 4, pages 233-234 and Chapter 7, pages 280-281*).

More recently, the United Nations has been involved in peacekeeping operations to help resolve conflicts in many parts of the continent that have demonstrated clearly the link between war and dire poverty. Many of these operations have involved close cooperation with regional organizations, such as the Organization of African Unity (OAU). At its 1997 meeting, the Security Council called for a further

Ongoing peacekeeping operations*

- United Nations Truce Supervision Organization (UNTSO, established 1948), in the Middle East;
- United Nations Military Observer Group in India and Pakistan (UNMOGIP, 1949);
- United Nations Peacekeeping Force in Cyprus (UNFICYP, 1964);
- United Nations Disengagement Observer Force (UNDOF, 1974), in the Syrian Golan Heights;
- United Nations Interim Force in Lebanon (UNIFIL, 1978);
- United Nations Iraq-Kuwait Observation Mission (UNIKOM, 1991);
- United Nations Mission for the Referendum in Western Sahara (MINURSO, 1991);
- United Nations Observer Mission in Georgia (UNOMIG, 1993);
- United Nations Mission of Observers in Tajikistan (UNMOT, 1994);
- United Nations Preventive Deployment Force (UNPREDEP, 1995), in the Former Yugoslav Republic of Macedonia;
- United Nations Mission in Bosnia and Herzegovina (UNMIBH, 1995);
- United Nations Mission of Observers in Prevlaka (UNMOP, 1996), in Croatia;
- United Nations Observer Mission in Angola (MONUA, 1997);
- United Nations Civilian Police Mission in Haiti (MIPONUH, 1997);
- United Nations Civilian Police Support Group (1998), in Croatia;
- United Nations Mission in the Central African Republic (MINURCA, 1998);
- United Nations Observer Mission in Sierra Leone (UNOMSIL, July 1998 to present).

---

*As of mid-1998; for a full list of United Nations peacekeeping operations, see Part Three, pages 301-304.

---

strengthening of such collaboration to enhance conflict prevention and resolution on the continent.

Southern Africa

At the end of the 1980s, with the cold war waning, the United Nations was able to reap the fruits of many years of efforts aimed at ending wars that had plagued southern Africa. The decline of the apartheid regime in **South Africa**, whose influence extended to the bordering "frontline" States, and which had supported opposition forces in **Angola** and **Mozambique** (*see below*), was a major factor in these efforts.

Peace efforts by the Secretary-General and his envoys, as well as the involvement of Canada, France, the Federal Republic of Germany,

United Nations Peacekeeping Operations, 1998

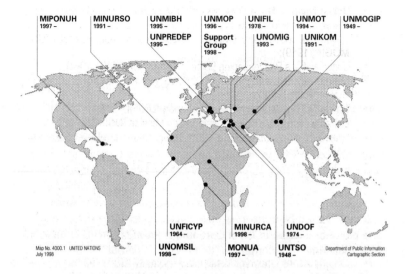

MIPONUH	MINURSO	UNMIBH	UNMOP	UNIFIL	UNMOT	UNMOGIP
1997 –	1991 –	1995 –	1996 –	1978 –	1994 –	1949 –
		UNPREDEP	Support	UNOMIG	UNIKOM	
		1995 –	Group	1993 –	1991 –	
			1998 –			

UNFICYP	MINURCA	UNDOF
1964 –	1998 –	1974 –
UNOMSIL	MONUA	UNTSO
1998 –	1997 –	1948 –

Map No. 4000.1 UNITED NATIONS
July 1998

Department of Public Information
Cartographic Section

the United Kingdom and the United States, led to the historic agreements signed at United Nations Headquarters in 1988 under which Angola, Cuba and South Africa committed themselves to a series of measures to achieve peace in southern Africa. South Africa agreed to cooperate with the Secretary-General to ensure the independence of **Namibia**; and Angola and Cuba signed an agreement on the withdrawal — under United Nations supervision — of Cuban forces from Angola. The agreements opened the way to a solution to the conflicts in the region.

Angola. Since 1988, the United Nations has been involved in efforts to bring peace and reconciliation between Angola's Government and the opposition force, the National Union for the Total Independence of Angola (UNITA), engaged in an intermittent yet devastating civil war since the country's independence in 1975.

United Nations efforts have included mediation by the Secretary-General and his envoys, the organization of peace talks, the imposition of a Security Council arms and oil embargo against UNITA forces, and the monitoring of national elections. Since 1988, the Security Council has established four successive peacekeeping missions (*see Part Three, page 301-304*). The first was in 1989, to monitor the withdrawal of pro-Government Cuban troops from Angola. The second, from 1991, sought to monitor a ceasefire, verify demobilization of combatants and observe elections in 1992 — elections rejected by UNITA when the results were announced, which in turn led to another outbreak of fighting.

Mediation by the Secretary-General's special representative, Mr. Alioune Blondin Beye, brokered the 1994 Lusaka peace accord, which led to a fragile peace. The accord provided for a ceasefire and for UNITA's integration into the Government and into the armed forces. To back the accord and to help the parties to achieve peace and national reconciliation, a third mission was set up in 1995. In a peace-building effort, the Secretary-General himself visited Angola in early 1997 to promote reconciliation and the installation of a Government of national unity, which was inaugurated in April 1997. A fourth United Nations mission was established in 1997 to consolidate peace and assist in the transition. Providing humanitarian assistance, carrying out demining, helping to repatriate some 300,000 refugees and supporting the economic reconstruction of the country have also been continuous features of the United Nations involvement in Angola.

Mozambique. A few years after Mozambique gained independence from Portugal in 1975, the impoverished country was plunged into a long and debilitating civil war between the Government and the Mozambican National Resistance (RENAMO), supported by South Africa's apartheid regime. In 1992, after two years of negotiations in Rome, the two parties signed a General Peace Agreement. As part of the Agreement, the Security Council established the **United Nations Operation in Mozambique (ONUMOZ)** to monitor and support a ceasefire, the demobilization of forces and the holding of national elections.

In early 1993, some 6,500 troops and military observers, led by the Secretary-General's special representative, Mr. Nello Ajello, were deployed. To guarantee the implementation of the Agreement and settle disputes, a Supervisory and Monitoring Commission was established: it was chaired by the United Nations, and composed of the Government, RENAMO, Italy (mediator State), France, Germany, Portugal, the United Kingdom and the United States (observer States at the Rome talks), and the OAU.

In addition to overseeing the electoral process, ONUMOZ launched a humanitarian assistance programme to help the 3.7 million people displaced by war to resettle in their communities. For its part,

UNHCR started in 1993 the repatriation of 1.3 million refugees. The three-year operation was the biggest ever undertaken by UNHCR in Africa. By mid-1994, some 75 per cent of the people internally displaced had been resettled and most refugees had returned to Mozambique.

Demobilization, started in 1994, eventually involved more than 76,000 soldiers from both sides, 10,000 of which ONUMOZ helped integrate into the new national army. ONUMOZ also recovered about 155,000 weapons.

Meanwhile, some 6.3 million voters were registered — 81 per cent of the estimated eligible voters. ONUMOZ helped RENAMO and other opposition groups to transform themselves into political parties and contest the elections effectively. The country's first multi-party elections were held in October 1994, monitored by some 2,300 international observers. The Government's party, FRELIMO, won the parliamentary and presidential elections. The new Parliament and President were inaugurated in December. Its task successfully fulfilled, ONUMOZ left Mozambique in January 1995.

Central Africa

The Great Lakes region of Central Africa has been the focus of particular concern for the United Nations in recent years. Decades of ethnic tension, which culminated in the genocide in **Rwanda** in 1994 (*see page 85*), created a climate of instability affecting all States in the region. In a special initiative to help try and resolve the many areas of dispute, the United Nations and the OAU appointed for the first time in 1997 a joint special representative for the Great Lakes region, Mr. Mohamed Sahnoun, who has been deeply involved in international efforts to help resolve the crises. During 1997, the United Nations planned and prepared for possible missions in Zaire and the Republic of the Congo, in case the Security Council decided to deploy peacekeeping missions.

On the humanitarian front, United Nations agencies have sought to address the emergencies resulting from the mass movements of refugees and displaced people throughout the region. A $324 million appeal was launched in 1997 to provide humanitarian assistance to more than 1.4 million refugees, internally displaced and other war-affected people. A regional humanitarian coordinator, appointed in 1997, has worked to coordinate overall relief efforts.

Burundi. The United Nations Office in Burundi participated in international efforts to help resolve the crisis in that country, where a long-standing internal conflict led in 1993 to a coup attempt in which the first democratically elected President, a Hutu, and six ministers were killed. This ignited factional fighting in which at least 150,000 people died in the following three years. In 1996, the Government and President, who had been put in place in 1994 through an agreement between the Hutu majority and the Tutsi minority, were deposed by a Tutsi-led military coup. Neighbouring countries reacted by imposing sanctions against Burundi; the Security Council condemned the overthrow of the Government and urged the military leaders to restore constitutional order. Fighting between the largely Tutsi army and Hutu rebels followed, resulting in massive internal displacements of people. During 1996 and 1997, some 500,000 people were forcibly transferred to "regroupment camps" as a security measure, and an additional 300,000 people fled to Tanzania to escape the continuing violence.

Democratic Republic of the Congo. Following the massacres in Rwanda in 1994 and the establishment of a new government there, some 1.2 million Rwandese Hutu refugees fled to eastern Zaire, an area inhabited, among others, by ethnic Tutsi. There, a rebellion started in 1996, pitting the Alliance of Democratic Forces for the Liberation of Zaire/Congo (ADFL), led by Laurent Désiré Kabila, against the government of President Mobutu Sese Seko. The ADFL, moving westwards, took the capital in May 1997, establishing the Democratic Republic of the Congo. The civil war resulted in more than 450,000 refugees and internally displaced people. A team of United Nations investigators was dispatched to the country to examine allegations of large-scale human rights abuses and massacres.

Republic of the Congo. In 1997, factional tension, heightened by an attempt by Government forces to disarm the militia of former President Denis Sassou-Nguesso ahead of the July presidential elections, escalated into full-scale fighting between Sassou-Nguesso's supporters and government forces and militia loyal to the incumbent President, Pascal Lissouba. The Security Council called for an immediate end to the violence and a negotiated solution to the crisis. During mediation efforts by President Omar Bongo of Gabon, assisted by the joint OAU/United Nations special representative, a request was made for establishing a peacekeeping operation in the country. The Secretary-General sent a mission to the country and to the region to assess the modalities of such an operation. After four months of fighting, Mr. Sassou-Nguesso seized power. Meanwhile, with 650,000 people displaced by the civil war, the United Nations launched a $17.7 million appeal to meet their needs.

Central African Republic. Following three mutinies in 1996 in the armed forces, several African countries formed an International Mediation Committee which brokered peace agreements between the mutineers and the Government. In 1997, after the signature of the agreements, African States sent to the country an inter-African force to facilitate implementation of the agreements and assure security. A National Reconciliation Conference in February 1998 was attended by several African leaders and by a representative of the Secretary-General. The Security Council in August 1997 placed the inter-African force under Chapter VII of the Charter, and in March 1998 established the United Nations Mission in the Central African Republic (MINURCA), which has replaced the inter-African force and has assisted in maintaining security and stability.

Rwanda. The United Nations involvement in Rwanda started in 1993, when Rwanda and Uganda requested the deployment of military observers along their common border to prevent the military use of the area by the Rwandese Patriotic Front (RPF). The Security Council in June 1993 established the **United Nations Observer Mission Uganda-Rwanda (UNOMUR)** on the Uganda side of the border to verify that no military assistance reached Rwanda.

Fighting had broken out in northern Rwanda in 1990 between the mainly Hutu Government and the Tutsi-led RPF operating from Uganda and areas in northern Rwanda. Peace talks, brokered by Tanzania and the OAU, led to a peace agreement in 1993, which provided for a transitional Government and for elections. At the request of Rwanda and the RPF, the Security Council in October 1993 established another international force, the **United Nations Assistance Mission for Rwanda (UNAMIR)**, to help the parties implement the agreement, monitor its implementation and support the transitional Government.

The United Nations solicited troop contributions, but initially only Belgium with half a battalion of 400 troops, and Bangladesh with a logistical element of 400 troops, offered personnel. It took five months to reach the authorized strength of 2,548. But because of many unresolved issues between the parties, implementation of the agreement was delayed. Consequently, the inauguration of the transitional Government never took place.

In April 1994, the Presidents of Rwanda and of Burundi were killed while returning from peace talks in Tanzania, when the Rwandese plane crashed, in circumstances that are still to be determined, as it was landing in Kigali, Rwanda's capital. This set off a tidal wave of political and ethnic killings: the Prime Minister, cabinet ministers and UNAMIR peacekeepers were among the first victims.

The killings, targeting Tutsi and moderate Hutus, were mainly carried out by the armed forces, the presidential guard and the ruling party's youth militia, as subsequently confirmed by the Special Rapporteur on Rwanda of the United Nations Human Rights Commission. The RPF resumed its advance from the north and the east of Rwanda, and government authority disintegrated.

An interim Government was formed, but failed to stop the massacres. With the RPF's southward push, the number of displaced persons and refugees increased tremendously. On 28 April alone, 280,000 people fled to Tanzania to escape the violence. Another wave of refugees went into Zaire. United Nations and other agencies provided emergency assistance on an unprecedented scale.

UNAMIR sought to arrange a ceasefire, without success, and its personnel came increasingly under attack. After some countries unilaterally withdrew their contingents, the Security Council in April reduced UNAMIR's strength from 2,548 to 270. Despite its reduced presence, UNAMIR troops managed to protect thousands of Rwandese who took shelter at sites under UNAMIR control.

The Security Council in May imposed an arms embargo against Rwanda, called for urgent international action and increased UNAMIR's strength to up to 5,500 troops. But it took nearly six months for Member States to provide the troops.

To contribute to the security of civilians, the Council in June authorized, under Chapter VII of the United Nations Charter, a multinational humanitarian operation. French-led multinational forces carried out "Operation Turquoise", which established a humanitarian protection zone in south-western Rwanda. The operation ended in August and UNAMIR took over in the zone.

In July, RPF forces took control of Rwanda, ending the civil war, and established a broad-based Government. The new Government declared its commitment to the 1993 peace agreement and assured UNAMIR that it would cooperate on the return of refugees.

For their part, when the conflict broke out in April, UNOMUR observers had expanded their monitoring activities in Uganda to the entire border area. But the Security Council gradually scaled down the operation, and UNOMUR left Uganda in September.

By October 1994, estimates suggested that out of a population of 7.9 million, at least half a million people had been killed. Some 2 million had fled to other countries and as many as 2 million people were internally displaced. A United Nations humanitarian appeal launched in July raised $762 million, making it possible to respond to the enormous humanitarian challenge.

A Commission of Experts established by the Security Council reported in September that "overwhelming evidence" proved that Hutu elements had perpetrated acts of genocide against the Tutsi group in a "concerted, planned, systematic and methodical way".

In November 1994, the Security Council established the International Tribunal for Rwanda to prosecute those responsible for genocide and war crimes (*see Chapter 6, page 269*). Located in Arusha, Tanzania, the Tribunal issued the first indictments in 1995 and held the first trials in 1997.

UNAMIR continued its efforts to ensure security and stability, support humanitarian assistance, clear landmines and help refugees to resettle. But Rwanda supported ending the mission, stating that UNAMIR did not respond to its priority needs. The Security Council heeded that request, and UNAMIR left in March 1996.

At a meeting organized by Rwanda and the United Nations Development Programme in 1996, international donors pledged over $617 million towards the reconstruction of the country. United Nations agencies have continued to provide humanitarian aid and to assist in the return of refugees.

Eritrea

Upon the collapse of the military Government in Ethiopia in 1991, the secessionist movement in Eritrea, led by the Eritrean People's Liberation Front, announced the formation of a provisional Government and the holding of a referendum to determine the wishes of the Eritrean people regarding their status in relation to Ethiopia.

The head of Eritrea's Referendum Commission in 1992 invited the United Nations to verify that the referendum process was free, fair and impartial. Endorsing a proposal by the Secretary-General, the General Assembly in December established the **United Nations Observer Mission to Verify the Referendum in Eritrea (UNOVER)**.

UNOVER observed all referendum activities, from voter registration to the announcement of the results. The observers maintained contact with community leaders and social organizations, visited municipalities throughout the country, made random visits to voter registration centres, observed rallies and verified compliance by all parties with the referendum's code of conduct. At the end of the process, about 1.1 million voters had been registered.

Voting took place in April 1993, with the overwhelming majority of voters in favour of independence. The head of UNOVER, Mr. Samir Sanbar, declared the referendum process free and fair. Eritrea was declared independent on 24 May 1993, and joined the United Nations on 28 May.

Somalia

Following the downfall of President Siad Barre in 1991, a civil war broke out in Somalia between the faction supporting Interim President Ali Mahdi Mohamed and that supporting General Mohamed Farah Aidid. The United Nations, in cooperation with the OAU and other organizations, sought to resolve the conflict. The Secretary-General in 1991 dispatched an envoy to whom all faction leaders expressed support for a United Nations peace role.

The United Nations also became engaged in providing humanitarian aid, in cooperation with relief organizations. The war had resulted in nearly 1 million refugees and almost 5 million people threatened by hunger and disease.

The Security Council in January 1992 imposed an arms embargo against Somalia. The Secretary-General organized talks between the parties, who agreed on a ceasefire, to be monitored by United Nations observers, and on the protection of humanitarian convoys by United Nations security personnel. In April, the Council established the **United Nations Operation in Somalia (UNOSOM)**.

The relief effort was hampered by continued fighting and insecurity. The Security Council in August deployed some 3,000 additional troops to protect humanitarian aid. But the situation continued to worsen, with aid workers under attack as famine threatened 1.5 million people.

The United States in November 1992 offered to organize and lead an operation to ensure the delivery of humanitarian assistance. The Security Council accepted the offer and authorized the use of "all necessary means" to establish a secure environment for the relief effort.

The Unified Task Force (UNITAF), made up of contingents from 24 countries led by the United States, quickly secured all major relief centres, and by year's end humanitarian aid was again flowing. UNOSOM remained responsible for protecting the delivery of assistance and for political efforts to end the war.

At a meeting convened by the Secretary-General in early 1993, 14 Somali political movements agreed on a ceasefire and pledged to hand over all weapons to UNITAF and UNOSOM. In March, the United Nations organized an aid conference at which donors pledged over $130 million. At a reconciliation conference organized by the Secretary-General and his special representative, the leaders of 15 political movements endorsed an accord on disarmament, reconstruction and the formation of a transitional Government.

The Security Council in March decided on a transition from UNITAF to **UNOSOM II**, authorizing it to use force if necessary to ensure its mandate — securing a stable environment for the delivery of humanitarian assistance. UNOSOM was also mandated to assist in the reconstruction of economic, social and political life. But while UNITAF had patrolled less than half of the country with 37,000 well-equipped troops, the 22,000 United Nations peacekeepers were given the mandate to cover all of Somalia.

The factions, however, did not observe the ceasefires. In June, 24 UNOSOM II soldiers from Pakistan were killed in an attack in Mogadishu. Subsequently, clashes between UNOSOM and Somali militiamen in Mogadishu resulted in casualties among civilians and UNOSOM.

In October, 18 United States soldiers of the Quick Reaction Force — deployed in support but not part of UNOSOM — lost their lives in an operation in Mogadishu. The United States immediately reinforced its military presence, but later announced that it would withdraw by early 1994. Belgium, France and Sweden also decided to withdraw.

The Secretary-General in October held talks in Somalia, while UNOSOM and United Nations agencies continued their reconciliation and relief efforts. Somali elders held reconciliation meetings in various parts of the country, while over 100,000 refugees returned to relatively peaceful parts of Somalia.

The Security Council in early 1994 revised UNOSOM's mandate, stressing assistance for reconciliation and reconstruction, and setting a March 1995 deadline for the mission.

At talks brokered by a Secretary-General's envoy, the 15 major political movements in March 1994 signed a declaration on reconciliation: it provided for a ceasefire, the disarmament of militias and a conference to appoint a new Government. But preparations for the conference were repeatedly postponed.

The Secretary-General told the Security Council in September that UNOSOM's ability to provide security had been reduced by troop withdrawals, budget restrictions and military actions by the Somali factions. Wider problems included the lack of commitment to peace by the factions and insufficient political will by Member States. The Council approved reductions in the force.

With faction leaders still not complying with the 1993 and 1994 agreements, the Security Council extended UNOSOM for a final period. It urged factions to enact a ceasefire and form a Government of national unity. As no further progress was made, UNOSOM withdrew in March 1995.

During the three-year effort, 154 United Nations peacekeeping personnel had died. But the United Nations had brought relief to millions facing starvation, helped to stop the large-scale killings, assisted in the return of refugees and provided massive humanitarian aid. Under difficult conditions, United Nations agencies have continued their humanitarian work.

Liberia

In Liberia, the United Nations supported the Economic Community of West African States (ECOWAS), a 16-country subregional organization, in its efforts to end a civil war that had broken out in late 1989. These efforts included establishing, in 1990, an observer force, the Military Observer Group (ECOMOG). The Security Council in 1992 imposed an arms embargo on Liberia, and the Secretary-General appointed a special representative to assist in talks between ECOWAS and the warring parties.

After ECOWAS brokered a peace agreement in Cotonou, Benin, in 1993, the Security Council established the **United Nations Observer Mission in Liberia (UNOMIL)**. Its task was to support ECOMOG in implementing the Cotonou peace agreement — especially compliance with and impartial implementation of the agreement by all parties. UNOMIL was the first United Nations peacekeeping mission undertaken in cooperation with a peacekeeping operation already established by another organization. With the ceasefire in force, the United Nations successfully observed the conduct of the 1997 elections. These led to the establishment of a democratically elected Government and the effective end of a war in which over 150,000 people — mostly civilians — were killed and more than 850,000 became refugees.

In November 1997, following the completion of UNOMIL's mandate, the United Nations established a post-conflict, peace-building support office. Headed by a Representative of the Secretary-General, the Office was intended to strengthen and harmonize United Nations peace-building efforts, to help promote reconciliation and respect for human rights, and to help mobilize international support for reconstruction and recovery.

Latin America and the Caribbean

In one of its most complex and successful interventions, the United Nations became directly involved in peacekeeping and peacemaking efforts in Central America in 1989, when Costa Rica, El Salvador, Guatemala, Honduras and Nicaragua requested its assistance in their collective agreement (Esquipulas II agreement) to end the conflicts that were disrupting the entire region, promote democratic elections and pursue democratization and dialogue.

The Security Council established the **United Nations Observer Group in Central America (ONUCA)**, which was deployed in all five countries to verify that they cease assistance to irregular and insurrectionist forces, and not allow their territory to be used for attacks into other countries.

Nicaragua. The five countries also agreed to draw up a plan for demobilizing the Nicaraguan resistance, also known as "contras". Nicaragua announced it would hold elections under international and United Nations monitoring. At Nicaragua's request, the **United Nations Observation Mission for the Verification of Elections in Nicaragua (ONUVEN)** was established in 1989. It observed the entire preparation and holding of the 1990 elections — the first United Nations–observed elections in an independent country.

The success of ONUVEN helped create conditions for the voluntary demobilization of the "contras". ONUCA oversaw that demobilization, as decided by the Security Council, at specific sites in Honduras and Nicaragua. By July 1990, some 22,000 resistance members had turned in their weapons to the United Nations observers. ONUCA remained in Central America, contributing to the peace efforts, until 1992.

El Salvador. Meanwhile, as requested by El Salvador and the Farabundo Martí National Liberation Front (FMLN), the Secretary-General began assisting in talks aimed at ending the civil war in that country. The first major accord was achieved in 1990, when the parties agreed to ensure respect for human rights. To verify this and future agreements, the Security Council established in 1991 the **United Nations Observer Mission in El Salvador (ONUSAL).**

Intense negotiations brokered by the Secretary-General and his personal representative culminated in the Chapultepec Peace Accords of January 1992, which put an end to a conflict that had claimed some 75,000 lives. The Security Council assigned to ONUSAL the mandate to monitor the Accords.

In one of the most comprehensive operations in United Nations history, ONUSAL monitored the accords and verified the demobilization of combatants, their reintegration into society and the respect by both parties of their human rights commitments.

The formal end of the 12-year conflict was proclaimed in December 1992, as FMLN troops completed their demobilization. This was followed by a 50 per cent reduction in the Salvadoran army and the departure of officers allegedly responsible for human rights violations.

ONUSAL also assisted in bringing about reforms needed to tackle the root causes of the civil war — such as judicial reforms, the phasing out of the national police, the training of the new civilian police, and the transfer of land to former combatants and landholders. At the request of the Government, ONUSAL observed the 1994 elections, won by the ruling party, the Republican National Alliance (ARENA), with FMLN emerging as the main opposition party.

ONUSAL's mandate ended in 1995, and a small United Nations office remained in the country to provide good offices and verify implementation of the areas of the peace accord still outstanding.

Guatemala. At the request of Guatemala and the Guatemalan National Revolutionary Unity (URNG), the United Nations from 1991 observed talks between the parties aimed at ending the civil war, which had lasted over three decades and resulted in over 140,000 people killed or missing.

In 1994, the parties concluded accords providing for the United Nations to verify all agreements reached, as well as to establish a human rights mission. The General Assembly in 1994 established the **United Nations Human Rights Verification Mission in Guatemala (MINUGUA).**

The United Nations–moderated talks led to other agreements: on resettling war-displaced people and refugees (1994); on a commission to investigate past human rights violations (1994); on the rights of indigenous people (1995); on socio-economic aspects and the agrarian situation (1996); and on strengthening civilian power and the role of the army (1996).

The URNG announced the suspension of its military operations in early 1996; the Government responded by ordering the army to cease counter-insurgency operations. In December, agreements were concluded on a ceasefire, on constitutional and electoral reforms, and on the legal integration of URNG. Finally, on 29 December 1996, the parties signed in Guatemala City the Agreement on a Firm and Lasting Peace, which ended the war and brought all previously signed agreements into effect.

The last and longest of Central America's conflicts had ended, and the region was at peace for the first time in 36 years. In 1997, a military observer group attached to MINUGUA oversaw the disarmament and demobilization of URNG forces. An expanded MINUGUA has remained in the country to verify compliance with the accords. United Nations agencies have continued to address the social and economic roots of conflict throughout the region.

Haiti

After the departure of "Life President" Jean-Claude Duvalier in 1986, Haiti had a series of short-lived governments. In 1990, the country's provisional Government requested the United Nations to observe the December 1990 elections.

The **United Nations Observer Group for the Verification of the Elections in Haiti (ONUVEH)** observed the preparation and holding of the elections, which were termed as "highly successful" by the head of ONUVEH. Jean-Bertrand Aristide, of the National Front for Change and Democracy, was elected President.

But in 1991, a coup headed by Lieutenant-General Raoul Cédras ended democratic rule. The President went into exile. The Organization of American States (OAS) and the United Nations condemned the coup and began diplomatic efforts for the return to democratic rule. The Secretary-General, at the request of the General Assembly, appointed a special envoy for Haiti, Mr. Dante Caputo, who was also appointed separately as special envoy by the OAS.

In response to the worsening situation, and on the request of Mr. Aristide, a joint United Nations/OAS mission — the **International Civilian Mission in Haiti (MICIVIH)** — was deployed in the country in 1993. Its task was to monitor the human rights situation and to investigate violations.

The special envoy sought to reach an agreement on the appointment of a Prime Minister at the head of a Government of national unity, an amnesty for the coup leaders and the return of the President. But his proposals were not accepted.

In an effort to restore constitutional rule, the Security Council imposed an oil and arms embargo on Haiti in June 1993. General Cédras then agreed to hold talks. Such talks, conducted in New York by the special envoy, led in July to an agreement: Mr. Aristide would return to Haiti in October and appoint a new head of the armed forces.

As provided for by the agreement, the Security Council suspended the embargo following the approval by Parliament of a new cabinet, and established the **United Nations Mission in Haiti (UNMIH)** to assist in modernizing the armed forces and in creating a new police force. But its mandate was undermined by the non-compliance of the military authorities with the agreement.

After a series of incidents, UNMIH, MICIVIH and other international agencies left Haiti in October, and the Security Council resumed the embargo.

After further negotiations, MICIVIH returned to Haiti in 1994. The mission denounced the human rights violations taking place, and was met with harassment and obstruction. The Security Council added to the sanctions a trade embargo, with the exception of medical products and foodstuffs.

The de facto Government declared MICIVIH's international staff undesirable and gave them 48 hours to leave. The Secretary-General, concerned about their security, decided, in agreement with the OAS Secretary-General, to evacuate them.

The Security Council in July authorized Member States to form a multinational force and use "all necessary means" to facilitate the departure of the military leaders and the return to democratic rule. It also decided that a strengthened UNMIH would take over from the multinational force once a secure and stable environment was established.

The Secretary-General dispatched an envoy to seek arrangements for the President's return. But the military leaders declined to meet the envoy. Preparations for an operation to enforce the Council's decision began.

The United States and Haiti's military leaders reached in September an agreement aimed at avoiding further violence. The agreement, mediated by a delegation headed by former United States President Jimmy Carter, provided for the early retirement of various military leaders, the end of the embargo and free parliamentary elections.

The 20,000-strong multinational force, led by the United States, began deploying in Haiti, followed shortly thereafter by an UNMIH advance team.

General Cédras resigned and left Haiti, along with the Chief of Staff. On 15 October, President Aristide returned to Haiti, and the following day the embargo was lifted. MICIVIH also returned, resuming its monitoring and promotion of human rights, and providing assistance to institution-building.

As decided by the Security Council, UNMIH took over in 1995 from the multinational force to assist the Government to maintain the secure and stable environment established by the force. UNMIH helped to create, for the first time in the country's history, a national civil police. The United Nations and OAS oversaw the 1995 parliamentary and local elections, won by a coalition associated with President Aristide.

Its mission concluded, UNMIH was replaced in its functions by the **United Nations Support Mission in Haiti**, which was followed by other operations — the **Transition Mission in Haiti** and the **Civilian Police Mission in Haiti**. The current mission has continued to provide international support to the Government in upgrading the country's national police force. MICIVIH has continued to monitor and promote human rights, and to provide technical assistance in institution-building.

Asia

Korean peninsula

The question of Korea came before the General Assembly in 1947. United Nations efforts to re-establish a unified State through elections were unsuccessful, and two separate governments came into being in 1948. That year the General Assembly called for the withdrawal of occupying forces and created a United Nations Commission on Korea: its task was to lend its good offices to bring about unification, and to facilitate the removal of barriers to economic, social and other friendly relations caused by the division of the country.

In June 1950, the United States and the Commission on Korea informed the United Nations that the Republic of Korea had been attacked by forces from North Korea. The Security Council recommended that Member States furnish the necessary assistance to the Republic of Korea to repel the attack and restore peace and security in the area. In July, the Council recommended that Member States providing military forces make them available to a unified command under the United States; 16 nations made troops available. This force, known as the United Nations Command and authorized by the Council to fly the United Nations flag, was not a United Nations peacekeeping operation placed under the command of the Secretary-General, but an international force acting under the unified command.

The Soviet Union, which had been absent from the Security Council in protest against the Chinese Nationalist government representing China at the United Nations, deemed the Council's decisions illegal as they were adopted in the absence of two permanent members (the Soviet Union and China). Fighting continued until July 1953, when an armistice agreement was signed.

The Middle East

The United Nations has been concerned with the question of the Middle East from its earliest days. It has outlined principles for a peaceful settlement and dispatched various peacekeeping missions, and continues to support initiatives towards a just solution to the underlying political problems.

The Middle East question has its origin in the issue of the status of Palestine. In 1947, Palestine was a Territory administered by the United Kingdom under a Mandate from the League of Nations: it had a population of some 2 million, two thirds Arabs and one third Jews. The General Assembly in 1947 endorsed a plan, prepared by the United Nations Special Committee on Palestine, for the partition of the Territory: it provided for the creation of an Arab and a Jewish State, with Jerusalem under international status. The plan was not accepted by the Palestinian Arabs or by the Arab States.

On 14 May 1948, the United Kingdom relinquished its Mandate over Palestine and the Jewish Agency proclaimed the State of Israel. The following day, the Palestinian Arabs, assisted by Arab States, opened hostilities against the new State. The hostilities were halted through a truce called for by the Security Council and supervised by a Mediator appointed by the General Assembly, assisted by a group of military observers which came to be known as the **United Nations Truce Supervision Organization** — the first United Nations observer mission.

As a result of the conflict, some 750,000 Palestine Arabs lost their homes and livelihoods and became refugees. To assist them, the General Assembly in 1949 established the United Nations Relief and Works Agency for Palestine Refugees in the Near East (UNRWA), which has since been a major provider of assistance and a force for stability in the region (*see Chapter 5, pages 255-256*).

Unresolved, Arab-Israeli hostilities led again to warfare in 1956, 1967 and 1973, each conflict leading Member States to call for United Nations mediation and peacekeeping forces. The 1956 conflict saw the deployment of the first full-fledged peacekeeping force — the **United Nations Emergency Force** — which oversaw troop withdrawals and contributed to peace and stability.

The June 1967 war involved fighting between Israel and Egypt, Jordan and Syria, during which Israel occupied the Sinai peninsula, the Gaza Strip, the West Bank of the Jordan River, including East Jerusalem, and part of Syria's Golan Heights. The Security Council called for a ceasefire and, as a result of subsequent negotiations, authorized the stationing of observers on the Golan Heights and Suez Canal sectors to supervise the ceasefire.

The Security Council, by *resolution 242* of 22 November 1967, defined principles for a just and lasting peace in the Middle East.

These are:

- "withdrawal of Israel armed forces from territories occupied in the recent conflict"; and
- "termination of all claims or states of belligerency and respect for and acknowledgement of the sovereignty, territorial integrity and political independence of every State in the area and their right to live in peace within secure and recognized boundaries, free from threats or acts of force". The resolution also affirmed the need to settle the refugee problem.

After the 1973 war between Israel, and Egypt and Syria, the Security Council adopted *resolution 338* of 22 October 1973, which reaffirms the principles of resolution 242 and calls for negotiations aimed at "a just and durable peace". These benchmark resolutions remain the basis for an overall settlement in the Middle East.

To monitor the 1973 ceasefire, the Security Council established two peacekeeping forces. The second **United Nations Emergency Force** was deployed in the Suez Canal sector in 1973; it remained until its mandate lapsed in 1979. The **United Nations Disengagement Observer Force**, established in accordance with the Disengagement Agreement between Israel and Syria, is still in place on the Golan Heights.

In the following years, the General Assembly repeatedly called for an international peace conference on the Middle East, under United Nations auspices, based on resolutions 242 and 338. The Assembly in 1974 invited the Palestine Liberation Organization (PLO) to participate in the work of the Assembly and in United Nations international conferences as an observer.

Direct negotiations between Egypt and Israel led to the Camp David accords of 1978, which in turn led to the Egypt-Israel peace treaty of 1979. Under that treaty, Israel withdrew from the Sinai, which was returned to Egypt. In 1994, a peace treaty between Israel and Jordan was also concluded.

Lebanon. Since 1972, southern Lebanon had been the theatre of hostilities between Palestinian groups on the one hand, and Israeli forces and its local Lebanese auxiliary on the other. After Israeli forces invaded southern Lebanon in 1978 following a Palestinian commando raid in Israel, the Security Council, by **resolution 425**, called for respect for the integrity, sovereignty and independence of Lebanon, called upon Israel to withdraw, and established the **United Nations Interim Force in Lebanon (UNIFIL)**. This Force was to confirm the withdrawal of Israeli forces, restore international peace and security, and assist Lebanon in re-establishing its authority in the area.

In 1982, after intense exchanges of fire in southern Lebanon and across the Israel-Lebanon border, Israeli forces moved into Lebanon, reaching and surrounding Beirut. Israel withdrew from most of the country in 1985, but retained control of a strip of land in southern Lebanon, where Israeli forces and its local Lebanese auxiliary remained, and which partly overlaps UNIFIL's area of deployment. Hostilities have continued between Israeli and auxiliary forces on the one hand, and Lebanese groups who proclaim their resistance against the Israeli occupation on the other.

The Security Council has maintained its commitment to Lebanon's territorial integrity, sovereignty and independence, while the Secretary-General has continued his efforts to persuade Israel to leave the security zone. Israel has maintained that the zone is a temporary arrangement governed by its security concerns. Lebanon has requested that Israel withdraw, viewing the occupation as illegal and contrary to United Nations resolutions. For its part, UNIFIL has sought to contain the conflict and protect the population.

During the period of widest conflict in Lebanon, a number of foreigners were taken hostage. "Quiet diplomacy" by the Secretary-General and his envoy led in 1991 to the release of several hostages and prisoners. Overall, nine Western hostages held in Lebanon and 91 Lebanese prisoners held by Israel were released.

***Intifada* and self-government.** In 1987, the Palestinian uprising (*intifada*) began in the occupied territories of the West Bank and the Gaza Strip, in a call for Palestinian independence and statehood. The Palestine National Council — the legislative body of the PLO — proclaimed in November 1988 the establishment of the State of Palestine. The General Assembly in December acknowledged that proclamation and decided to designate the PLO as "Palestine".

The Security Council in 1990 reaffirmed its support for negotiations involving all parties, based on resolutions 242 and 338, which would take into account Israel's right to security as well as the rights of the Palestinian people.

In 1991, a Peace Conference on the Middle East opened in Madrid, co-sponsored by the Soviet Union and the United States. The United Nations was invited to participate in 1992, and the Secretary-General appointed a special representative. The General Assembly in 1991 reaffirmed the principles for a lasting peace, and revoked its 1975 determination that Zionism was a form of racism and racial discrimination.

Following Norwegian-mediated negotiations, Israel and the PLO established mutual recognition on 10 September 1993. The PLO recognized Israel's right to exist, and Israel recognized the PLO as the representative of the Palestinian people.

Three days later, Israel and the PLO signed in Washington, D.C., the Declaration of Principles on Interim Self-Government Arrangements. The landmark agreement opened the way to Palestinian self-rule, providing for Israeli withdrawal from the occupied territories and for an interim Palestinian self-government, first in the Gaza Strip and the West Bank town of Jericho, and later in the rest of the West Bank.

Welcoming the agreement, the Secretary-General pledged the assistance of United Nations agencies and programmes. As requested by Israel and the PLO, the United Nations created a task force on the social and economic development of Gaza and Jericho, and appointed a special coordinator for United Nations assistance, who has been overseeing the development work of United Nations programmes and agencies.

The transfer of powers from Israel to the Palestinian Authority in the Gaza Strip and Jericho began in 1994. In 1995, Israel and the PLO signed an agreement on Palestinian self-rule in the West Bank, providing for the withdrawal of Israeli troops and the handover of civil authority in the West Bank to an elected Palestinian Council.

Elections for the Council's 88-member Palestinian Executive Authority were held in the Gaza Strip, the West Bank and East Jerusalem in 1996. PLO Chairman Yasser Arafat was elected President of the Authority.

A number of issues, however, have continued to threaten the peace process. In 1997, the Secretary-General expressed his "shock and horror" at the suicide bombing attacks that killed scores of civilians in Israel. Also in 1997, the resumption of Israeli settlements in the occupied territories was condemned by the General Assembly at an emergency special session. The Assembly demanded that Israel stop building a new settlement near East Jerusalem as well as all other settlements in the occupied territories.

South Asia subcontinent: India-Pakistan

The United Nations has continued to be concerned with the decades-old dispute between India and Pakistan over Kashmir. The issue dates back to the 1940s, when the State of Jammu and Kashmir was one of the princely states which became free, under the partition plan and the India Independence Act of 1947, to accede to India and Pakistan. The Security Council first discussed the issue in 1948, following India's complaint that tribesmen and others, with Pakistan's support and participation, were invading Kashmir and that fighting was taking place. Pakistan denied the charges and declared Kashmir's accession to India illegal. The Security Council recommended measures to stop the fighting, including the use of observers, and to create conditions for a plebiscite. It established a United Nations Commission for India and Pakistan, which made proposals on a ceasefire and troop withdrawals, and proposed that the issue be decided by plebiscite. Both sides accepted the proposal, but could not reach agreement on the modalities for holding the plebiscite. Since 1949, the **United Nations Military Observer Group in India and Pakistan (UNMOGIP)** has been observing the ceasefire line in Kashmir.

Following the 1972 India-Pakistan agreement defining a Line of Control in Kashmir, the two countries undertook to settle their difference peacefully and achieve a final settlement. After the agreement, India took the position that the mandate of UNMOGIP had lapsed — a position not accepted by Pakistan. The Secretary-General, meanwhile, has maintained that only the Security Council can terminate the mission, and has consistently expressed his readiness to facilitate the search for a lasting solution to the overall dispute. Both sides resumed their bilateral dialogue in 1997, after a three-year impasse. They agreed on a comprehensive eight-point agenda for further talks which includes the issue of Jammu and Kashmir. The Secretary-General, welcoming the resumption of dialogue, encouraged the two sides to make progress towards a lasting solution.

Cambodia

In one of its most complex operations, the United Nations in Cambodia oversaw a transition that led to the restoration of civil rule after years of civil war and foreign intervention.

In 1992, as specified in the 1991 Paris Agreements painstakingly negotiated with the help of the Secretary-General, the **United Nations Transition Authority in Cambodia (UNTAC)** assumed control of key sectors of the country's administrative structures — foreign affairs, defence, security, finance and communications — in order to build a stable environment conducive to national elections. At the same time, UNHCR oversaw the successful repatriation and resettlement of some 360,000 refugees and displaced persons. At its peak, UNTAC numbered over 21,000 military and civilian personnel from more than 100 countries.

A major step towards normalization occurred with the elections of May 1993. Twenty parties took part in the elections. UNTAC oversaw the electoral campaign and the registration of voters, as well as the elections. Over 4.2 million people — nearly 90 per cent of the registered voters — cast their ballots to elect a Constituent Assembly. The head of UNTAC declared the elections free and fair. In September, the Constitution was proclaimed and a new government, led by two prime ministers, was inaugurated.

Several United Nations agencies have remained in the country to support reconstruction and development. In 1993, in conformity with the Paris Agreements, the Secretary-General appointed a Special Representative for Human Rights to assist the Government in promoting and protecting human rights. Working closely with the Special Representative, a Cambodia Office of the United Nations High Commissioner on Human Rights seeks to strengthen civil society and build institutions and legal structures for human rights and democracy. In 1994, the Secretary-General appointed a Representative for Cambodia to serve as a liaison with the Government, monitor the political situation and report on developments relating to peace and security.

Friction between the two prime ministers led in 1997 to fighting and the flight of one of the prime ministers, members of his political party and of other opposition groups. To help restore a democratic government, the United Nations sent monitors, with the consent of the authorities, in an initiative intended to assure politicians wanting to return that they would be allowed to resume political activities without harm or intimidation, in view of new elections to be held in 1998.

Cyprus

The **United Nations Peacekeeping Force in Cyprus** has been supervising a ceasefire and maintaining a buffer zone between the Greek Cypriot National Guard and Turkish Forces since 1974 when a *coup d'état* by Greek Cypriot and Greek elements favouring union of the country with Greece was followed by military intervention by Turkey and the de facto division of the island. Since the events of 1974, the Secretary-General and his envoy have been seeking to resolve the decades-old dispute between the island's Turkish-Cypriot and Greek-Cypriot communities. The Secretary-General has used his good offices to bring the two sides together in search of a comprehensive settlement, sanctioned by legal instruments. In 1997, the Secretary-General and his new special adviser on Cyprus initiated a process of fresh rounds of direct talks between the leaders of the two communities, with the strong support of the Security Council.

Iraq

The United Nations response to Iraq's invasion of Kuwait in August 1990 illustrates the range of options it has at its disposal in the pursuit of restoring international peace and security. The Security Council immediately condemned the invasion, demanded the withdrawal of Iraqi forces and imposed comprehensive sanctions against Iraq. The Council subsequently banned air transport to and from Iraq and Kuwait, and endorsed a naval blockade to enforce the sanctions. At the 1990 session of the General Assembly, all Member States condemned Iraq's action.

At the same time, the United Nations undertook many initiatives to avert war. The Secretary-General met with Iraq's Foreign Minister in August 1990, and with the President of Iraq in Baghdad in January 1991. He was also in constant contact with the political leaders involved in the crisis.

The Security Council set 15 January 1991 as the deadline for Iraq's compliance with the Council's resolutions. The Council authorized Member States cooperating with Kuwait to use "all necessary means" to uphold and implement these resolutions and to restore international peace and security in the area. Faced with Iraq's non-compliance, on 16 January coalition forces allied to restore Kuwait's sovereignty began attacks against Iraq. The coalition forces acted in accordance with the Council's authorization, but not under the direction or control of the United Nations. Hostilities were suspended on 27 February after the Iraqi forces had left Kuwait.

By *resolution 687* of 3 April 1991, the Security Council set terms for a ceasefire, demanded that Iraq and Kuwait respect the inviolability of the border, called for plans for deploying United Nations observers, took action on compensation for war damages and decided that Iraq's weapons of mass destruction should be eliminated. The resolution also called for Iraq to cooperate with the International Committee of the Red Cross to facilitate the repatriation of Kuwaiti and third country nationals, and asked the Secretary-General to facilitate the return to Kuwait of all property seized by Iraq.

Observers deployed. The Security Council established a demilitarized zone along the Iraq-Kuwait border and set up an observer mission to monitor the zone. The **United Nations Iraq-Kuwait Observation Mission (UNIKOM)** monitored the withdrawal of the remaining armed forces. Following a series of incidents, the Council in 1993 expanded UNIKOM's mandate to include an armed force capable of preventing or redressing small-scale violations.

Border demarcation. As called for in resolution 687, the **Iraq-Kuwait Boundary Demarcation Commission** was established in 1991. It included one representative from Iraq, one from Kuwait and three independent experts appointed by the Secretary-General. Iraq stopped participating in the work of the Commission in 1992. The

Commission demarcated the boundary as agreed by Iraq and Kuwait in 1932 and again in 1963.

The Security Council demanded that Iraq and Kuwait respect the inviolability of the boundary. Iraq informed the Secretary-General in November 1994 that it recognized Kuwait's sovereignty, territorial integrity and international boundaries.

Elimination of banned weapons. Resolution 687 also dealt with the elimination of Iraq's weapons of mass destruction and missiles with a range greater than 150 kilometres, together with related items and facilities. To verify implementation of these provisions, the Security Council established the **United Nations Special Commission (UN-SCOM)**, with powers of no-notice inspection. The International Atomic Energy Agency (IAEA) was asked to undertake similar tasks in the nuclear area, with UNSCOM assistance.

UNSCOM and IAEA have uncovered and eliminated much of Iraq's banned weapons programmes and capabilities — including a nuclear weapons programme, major chemical weapons and biological warfare programmes, and scores of ballistic missiles. But despite the considerable progress made, UNSCOM and IAEA have been unable to determine that Iraq has fulfilled all the obligations it accepted. A monitoring and verification system has been put in place to detect and deter rearmament efforts.

Compensation for damages. Under resolution 687, the Security Council established a fund to compensate foreign Governments, nationals or corporations for any loss, damage or injury resulting from Iraq's invasion. Iraq was required to pay to the fund an amount not exceeding 30 per cent of the annual value of its oil exports. A **Compensation Commission**, made up of nine jurists and experts, has examined claims and recommended compensation.

In the aftermath of the Persian Gulf war, the Secretary-General launched in 1991 the **United Nations Humanitarian Programme for Iraq**, which has promoted the return of those displaced and provided humanitarian assistance to the population. He also appointed a coordinator of the humanitarian work of the United Nations system and other relief agencies. The humanitarian situation has remained critical. Economic sanctions, which have remained in place, have taken a severe toll on the most vulnerable people, especially children. In 1997, a UNICEF study estimated that chronic malnutrition affected nearly 1 million children.

Oil-for-food programme. In August 1991, the Security Council offered Iraq the opportunity to export limited amounts of oil, under specified conditions, to provide funds for purchasing humanitarian goods. Under *resolution 986* (1995), the Security Council authorized States to permit the import of up to $1 billion worth of Iraqi oil every 90 days, to generate resources for the humanitarian needs of the Iraqi people. While sanctions have remained in place, in 1996 an "oil-for-food" agreement between the United Nations and Iraq was concluded. A committee of the Security Council has been overseeing this matter and authorized the supply of food, medicine and other humanitarian items.

In February 1998, the Security Council expanded the "oil-for-food" agreement by authorizing Iraq to sell $5.2 billion worth of oil over a six-month period. Also in February, a visit by the Secretary-General in Baghdad led to an agreement to resolve a peace-threatening stand-off on UNSCOM inspections.

Tajikistan

Following the breakup of the Soviet Union, Tajikistan became an independent republic in 1991. The country soon faced an acute social and economic crisis, and its stability was upset by regional and political tensions, further compounded by differences between secularists and pro-Islamic traditionalists. A civil war erupted in 1992, and the Tajik opposition — a coalition of Islamic and other groups — seized power. After suffering defeat in 1992, most of the opposition forces crossed the border into Afghanistan; from there, they carried out armed attacks into Tajikistan. The war resulted in an estimated 50,000 deaths, some 400,000 refugees and 600,000 internally displaced persons.

Since 1993, a special representative of the Secretary-General has been mediating between the Government and the opposition. Talks under his auspices led to a ceasefire agreement signed in Tehran in 1994. The Security Council in 1994 established the **United Nations Mission of Observers in Tajikistan (UNMOT)** to assist the Joint Commission — composed of representatives of the Government and of the opposition — to monitor the ceasefire agreement.

After three years of United Nations–sponsored peace negotiations, a peace agreement was signed in Moscow in 1997: it provided for a transitional period during which all the provisions of the agreement were to be implemented, thus creating the political, legislative and security environment under which new parliamentary elections could be held.

The Security Council in 1997 strengthened the mandate of UN-MOT to allow it to help promote peace and reconciliation and assist in implementing the peace agreement. UNMOT has cooperated closely with a peacekeeping force of the Commonwealth of Independent States (CIS) and a mission of the Organization for Security and Cooperation in Europe (OSCE).

An international donor conference organized by the United Nations in 1997 resulted in many pledges for activities related to the implementation of the peace agreement. In 1998, the United Nations launched a $34.5 million appeal to meet urgent humanitarian needs in the country.

Europe

Georgia

Georgia, one of the republics of the Soviet Union, became independent in 1991. Within Georgia, Abkhazia had been an autonomous republic since 1931. Attempts by Abkhazia's local authorities to separate from Georgia escalated into a series of armed confrontations in 1992. Hundreds of people died and some 30,000 fled to the Russian Federation. An envoy of the Secretary-General, appointed in 1993, began mediation among the parties. A ceasefire agreement was reached in 1993, and to verify compliance with it, the Security Council established the **United Nations Observer Mission in Georgia (UNOMIG)**.

But fighting resumed, turning into civil war in September 1993 and leading to the displacement of some 250,000 people. Another ceasefire was finally reached in Moscow in 1994. The parties agreed to the deployment of a peacekeeping force of the Commonwealth of Independent States (CIS) to monitor compliance with the agreement, with UNOMIG monitoring implementation of the agreement and observing the operation of the CIS force. The Secretary-General's special representative has continued negotiations towards a lasting settlement, focusing on the question of the political status of Abkhazia and the return of refugees and displaced persons. A United Nations office for the protection and promotion of human rights in Abkhazia was established in 1996. At a meeting held under United Nations auspices in November 1997, both sides agreed to establish a Coordinating Council and, within its framework, three working groups to address the military, political and economic aspects of the peace process.

The former Yugoslavia

A founding Member of the United Nations, the Federal Socialist Republic of Yugoslavia comprised six republics — Bosnia and Herzegovina, Croatia, Macedonia, Montenegro, Serbia, and Slovenia. At the end of the 1980s, in the midst of economic and political crisis, Slovenia and Croatia moved towards separation, both declaring independence in June 1991. Serbs living in Croatia, supported by the Yugoslav National Army, opposed the move, and war between Croatia and Serbia broke out. The European Community sought to resolve the crisis, without success.

The United Nations became involved in September 1991, when the Security Council imposed an arms embargo on Yugoslavia. The Secretary-General appointed a personal envoy, Mr. Cyrus Vance (later replaced by Mr. Thorvald Stoltenberg), to support the peace efforts of the European Community.

The Security Council in early 1992 established the **United Nations Protection Force (UNPROFOR)**, to create the conditions for negotiating a settlement. UNPROFOR was deployed in Croatia in four "protected areas" in which Serbs were the majority or a large minority, to ensure the demilitarization of such areas and to protect the population from attacks. But by October, Member States had provided less than 10 per cent of the 14,000 authorized troops.

Bosnia and Herzegovina declared independence in March 1992 — an act supported by Bosnian Croats and Muslims but opposed by Bosnian Serbs. The war had extended to that republic, with the Yugoslav and Croatian armies intervening. The Security Council in May imposed economic sanctions on rump Yugoslavia (consisting by then of Serbia and Montenegro). Also in May, Bosnia and Herzegovina, Croatia and Slovenia became Members of the United Nations.

By mid-1992, there were widespread reports of "ethnic cleansing" — forcible removal or elimination by the ethnic group controlling an area of members of other ethnic groups — mostly conducted by Bosnian Serb forces. The United Nations sought to assist the 2.2 million refugees and displaced persons — the largest refugee crisis in Europe since the Second World War.

In the light of continued fighting in Bosnia, the Security Council in June 1992 authorized UNPROFOR to protect the delivery of humanitarian aid. The General Assembly suspended participation of the Federal Republic of Yugoslavia (Serbia and Montenegro) in the Assembly's work, and condemned the country for violating Bosnia's sovereignty.

The former Yugoslav Republic of Macedonia, concerned about being drawn into the war, requested the deployment of United Nations observers. The Security Council, in December 1992, dispatched an UNPROFOR contingent to the country's borders with Yugoslavia and Albania (*see page 71, above*). The former Yugoslav Republic of Macedonia became a Member of the United Nations in 1993.

The United Nations created, for the first time, an international court to prosecute war crimes: the International Criminal Tribunal for the former Yugoslavia, established by the Security Council in early 1993 to prosecute those responsible for grave violations of international humanitarian law (*see also Chapter 6, page 268*).

The European Community mediator, Mr. David Owen, and the envoy of the Secretary-General continued intense peace efforts. But their settlement plan was rejected in April by the Bosnian Serbs.

The Security Council in May 1993 declared the Bosnian capital, Sarajevo, and other Bosnian towns as "safe areas" that should be free from attacks; in June it authorized UNPROFOR to use force in reply to attacks against the safe areas. The Secretary-General informed the Council that peacekeeping commanders needed 35,000 troops to deter attacks. Notwithstanding this recommendation, the Security Council authorized 7,600 troops. Member States made these personnel available only after considerable delay.

To deter continuing attacks against Sarajevo, the North Atlantic Treaty Organization (NATO) decided in early 1994 to authorize air strikes at the request of the Secretary-General.

France, Germany, the Russian Federation, the United Kingdom and the United States formed in April a "Contact Group" in a further attempt to settle the Bosnian conflict. But the Bosnian Serbs refused to agree to the Contact Group's territorial proposals, and as a result the Security Council in September strengthened sanctions against them. Continuing his peace efforts, the Secretary-General in late 1994 went to Sarajevo.

United Nations agencies continued to provide relief aid: overall, they provided humanitarian assistance to some 4 million people in the former Yugoslavia. UNHCR alone delivered over 1.1 million tons of aid to over 3.5 million people.

The Security Council in early 1995 replaced UNPROFOR with three distinct operations in Bosnia and Herzegovina, in Croatia and in the former Yugoslav Republic of Macedonia — as the three countries had requested.

In response to NATO air strikes, Bosnian Serb forces in May 1995 detained about 400 UNPROFOR observers, using some as "human shields" — chained to military targets to deter further strikes. The Secretary-General stressed before the Security Council the contradictions of the Force's mandate: its original peacekeeping task had gradually been enlarged to include enforcement elements, thus causing UNPROFOR to be seen as a party to the war.

Fighting now intensified. Croatia launched in May and August major offensives against its Serb-populated areas, which forced some 200,000 Croatian Serbs to flee the country. The Bosnian Serbs in July took over the Srebrenica and Zepa "safe areas" in Bosnia, during which thousands of refugees disappeared. The Bosnian Serbs' constant shelling of Sarajevo left 33 civilians killed on 28 August alone. NATO responded with massive air strikes against military targets around Sarajevo.

Talks sponsored by the Contact Group led in September to an agreement between Croatia, the Federal Republic of Yugoslavia and Bosnia and Herzegovina to end the Bosnian war. Under the agreement, Bosnia would continue to exist and consist of two entities — a Bosnian-Croat federation and a Serb republic.

A peace initiative led by the United States resulted in various agreements. The three countries concluded an agreement for elections in Bosnia; the Bosnian Serbs signed an agreement to end fighting in Sarajevo by November 1995; Croatia and the Croatian Serbs concluded an agreement on Eastern Slavonia, Baranja and Western Sirmium — areas of Croatia with a mainly Serb population.

Peace talks in Dayton, Ohio, United States, culminated in the December 1995 peace agreement between Bosnia and Herzegovina, Croatia and the Federal Republic of Yugoslavia: all pledged to respect each other's sovereignty and independence, refrain from using force, and settle disputes peacefully. The 42-month war had come to an end.

To help ensure compliance with the agreement, the Security Council authorized the deployment of a multinational Implementation Force (IFOR), mainly formed by NATO troops. In December, IFOR took over from UNPROFOR, whose mandate was terminated. Over 230 United Nations peacekeepers and other United Nations personnel had died in the war.

Whereas the Security Council had sent 30,000 lightly-equipped United Nations peacekeepers to deal with all-out war in Bosnia, the NATO-led operation deployed 60,000 heavily armed and fully supported troops after the peace agreement was concluded.

The Security Council established in Bosnia and Herzegovina a **United Nations International Police Task Force**, which in 1996 became part of a larger **United Nations Mission in Bosnia and Herzegovina (UNMIBH)**.

As requested by the parties to the 1995 agreement between Croatia and Croatian Serbs, the Security Council in early 1996 established the **United Nations Transitional Administration for Eastern Slavonia, Baranja and Western Sirmium (UNTAES)**. The mission supervised the demilitarization of the region, assisted in the return of refugees and displaced persons, and organized and supervised elections, successfully held in 1997. The mission ended in January 1998.

Disarmament

Since its foundation, the United Nations has made the goals of multilateral disarmament and arms limitation central issues in the maintenance of international peace and security. Highest priority has been given to the reduction and eventual elimination of the weapons of mass destruction, which have posed the greatest threat to humankind. While the objective of reducing the threat of nuclear, chemical and biological weapons remained constant through the years, the scope of the deliberations and negotiations on disarmament has changed, reflecting the evolving political realities and international conditions. In the post-cold-war period, the international community has begun to consider more closely the threats related to the excessive and destabilizing accumulation of conventional armaments, the proliferation of small arms and light weapons, and the humanitarian crisis caused by the massive deployment of landmines in conflict areas.

United Nations role

The United Nations machinery for disarmament was established by the Charter and subsequent decisions of the General Assembly. The Charter has given the General Assembly the chief responsibility of considering "the general principles of cooperation in the maintenance of international peace and security, including the principles governing disarmament and the regulation of armaments" (article 11).

The Assembly has two subsidiary bodies dealing with disarmament issues, open to all Member States: the **Disarmament and International Security Committee** (the First Committee), which meets during the regular session and deals with all disarmament issues on the agenda of the Assembly; and the **United Nations Disarmament Commission**, a specialized deliberative body that focuses on specific issues, such as the creation of nuclear-weapon-free zones and guidelines for international arms transfers. The General Assembly held special sessions on disarmament in 1978, 1982 and 1988.

The Conference on Disarmament is the international community's single multilateral negotiating forum for disarmament agreements. This body, working strictly on the basis of consensus in matters that touch the national security interests of States, has a limited membership, expanded in 1996 from 38 to 61, and a unique relationship with the General Assembly. It defines its own rules and develops its own agenda, but takes into account the recommendations of the Assembly and reports to it annually. Most recently, the Conference successfully negotiated both the *Chemical Weapons*

Convention (1993) and the *Comprehensive Nuclear-Test-Ban Treaty* (1996) (*see below*).

In the United Nations Secretariat, the **Department for Disarmament Affairs** implements the decisions of the Assembly in matters of disarmament. Its responsibilities include maintaining and operating the Register of Conventional Arms, exchanging information called for in various arms agreements, facilitating the discussion of disarmament issues in the General Assembly and the Conference on Disarmament, and supplying impartial information for educational purposes in pursuit of the goals of the Organization in this field (*see Part One, pages 26-27*).

The **United Nations Institute on Disarmament Research (UNIDIR),** based in Geneva, undertakes research on disarmament and related problems, particularly international security (*see Part One, page 48*).

Recent highlights

The sweeping political changes of recent years have led to important achievements in multilateral disarmament, some of which had been sought for decades, such as the culmination of the 40-year effort to agree on the *Comprehensive Nuclear-Test-Ban Treaty*. The achievements highlight the prominent contribution that the United Nations, through persistent and long-term effort, can make to global stability and a safer and more secure world.

The most prominent recent achievements have been:

- The signature in 1993 and entry into force in 1997 of the *Chemical Weapons Convention (CWC)*, which outlawed an entire class of weapons of mass destruction (such as those equipped with the chemical agents: mustard gas, soman, sarin and VX), thus completing a process that started in 1925, when the Geneva Protocol prohibited the use of poison gas weapons (*see also page 114, below*).
- In 1995, the States Parties to the 1968 *Treaty on the Non-Proliferation of Nuclear Weapons (NPT)* decided to extend indefinitely its provisions. Under the Treaty, States parties undertake to pursue negotiations in good faith on measures to end the nuclear arms race and on nuclear disarmament, as well as on general and complete disarmament. The indefinite extension of the Treaty underscored the broad and growing consensus within the international community on the need for more systematic and progressive efforts toward nuclear disarmament, with the ultimate goal of the total elimination of nuclear weapons (*see also pages 112-113, below*).

- In 1996, an overwhelming majority of Members of the General Assembly adopted the *Comprehensive Nuclear-Test-Ban Treaty (CTBT)*, which banned underground nuclear-test explosions — an objective originally proposed in 1954 and sought for nearly four decades. The Treaty thus extended the 1963 partial prohibition on nuclear test explosions to all physical environments. With nearly 150 signatory States participating in the Preparatory Commission for the CTBT Organization, located in Vienna, preparations are under way in the Provisional Technical Secretariat, established in 1997, to ensure that an international monitoring system is operational by the time the Treaty enters into force.
- The signature by over 120 States of the *Convention on the Prohibition of the Use, Stockpiling, Production and Transfer of Antipersonnel Mines and on Their Destruction (Ottawa Convention)* in 1997 is a major step towards addressing the humanitarian crisis sparked by the indiscriminate use of anti-personnel landmines. The Convention marks the first time that a multilateral disarmament agreement bans completely a weapon that is in widespread, active use in the military arsenals of many States. The Convention has spurred the campaign to reduce needless human suffering by increasing resources for mine clearance, mine awareness and mine assistance (*see also page 115, below*).

Containing nuclear weapons

During the cold-war period, a variety of nuclear-disarmament initiatives were put forward, both in and outside the framework of the United Nations, at the unilateral, bilateral, regional and international levels.

In January 1946, less than a year after the dawn of the nuclear age, the General Assembly adopted its very first resolution dealing with the issue of nuclear weapons. The **International Atomic Energy Agency (IAEA)** was established in 1957, to promote the peaceful uses of atomic energy under a system of IAEA safeguards (*see below*). Later, the Agency was given the task of verifying that nuclear material not be diverted for military purposes, as stipulated by the NPT.

Bilateral agreements on nuclear weapons

While international efforts to contain nuclear weapons continued in different forums, it was generally understood that the nuclear-weapon powers held special responsibility for maintaining a stable and secure international security environment. During and after the cold war, the two major powers arrived at agreements that have significantly reduced the threat of nuclear war. In the 1970s, the *Strategic Arms*

Bilateral agreements

- The 1972 *Treaty on the Limitation of Anti-Ballistic Missile Systems (ABM Treaty)* limits the number of anti-ballistic missile systems of the United States and the former Soviet Union to one each. A 1997 "demarcation" agreement between the United States and the Russian Federation distinguishes between "strategic", or long-range ABMs, which are still prohibited, and "non-strategic" or shorter-range ABMs, which are not.
- The 1987 United States-Soviet Union *Intermediate- and Shorter-Range Nuclear Forces Treaty (INF Treaty)* eliminated an entire class of nuclear weapons, which includes all land-based ballistic and cruise missiles with a range of 500 to 5,500 km. By the end of 1996, all the weapons slated for destruction under the provisions of the Treaty had been eliminated.
- The 1991 United States–Soviet Union *Strategic Arms Limitation and Reduction Treaty (START I)* places a ceiling of 6,000 warheads on 1,600 deployed long-range nuclear missiles for each side by the year 2001, thereby reducing the 1991 stockpile levels by about 30 per cent.
- The 1992 *Lisbon Protocol to START I* committed the Russian Federation, Belarus, Kazakhstan and Ukraine, as successor States to the Soviet Union, to abide by the START I Treaty; Belarus, Kazakhstan and Ukraine were to adhere to the NPT as non-nuclear-weapon States. By 1996, these three States had removed all nuclear weapons from their territories.
- The 1993 *Strategic Arms Limitation and Reduction Treaty II (START II)* commits both parties to reduce the number of warheads on long-range nuclear missiles to 3,500 on each side by the year 2003, and eliminated MIRVed (multiple independently targetable re-entry vehicle) ICBMs (intercontinental ballistic missiles). A 1997 agreement extends the deadline for destruction of the launching systems — missile silos, bombers and submarines — to the end of 2007.
- In 1997 in Helsinki, agreement was reached to begin START III negotiations on further reductions in nuclear weapons stocks, once START II has entered into force.

Limitation Talks (SALT I and *II)* not only performed the vital confidence-building function of keeping the lines of communication open between the two powers, but also resulted in limiting and containing the nuclear arms race. Several bilateral treaties have proved to be important steps towards nuclear disarmament (*see box above*).

Multilateral agreements

Commonly recognized as the cornerstone of international efforts to contain the proliferation of nuclear weapons, the *Treaty on the Non-*

Proliferation of Nuclear Weapons has near universal membership, including the five States which acknowledged possession of nuclear weapons (China, France, the Russian Federation, the United Kingdom and the United States.) The indefinite extension of the NPT in 1995 made permanent the commitment of the non-nuclear-weapon States parties not to acquire nuclear weapons. It also legally extended the commitment of the nuclear-weapon States parties, under article VI of the Treaty, to pursue nuclear disarmament.

Agreements have been reached to limit the spread of nuclear weapons by prohibiting them from certain environments or geographic regions. For example, treaties have been concluded to prohibit the deployment and testing of nuclear weapons on Antarctica (1959), in outer space (1967) and on the ocean floor (1971).

Nuclear-weapon-free zones

In a development that was to herald a new movement in regional arms control, the signing of the 1967 *Treaty for the Prohibition of Nuclear Weapons in Latin America and the Caribbean (Treaty of Tlatelolco)* established for the first time a nuclear-weapon-free zone (NWFZ) in a populated area of the world.

Since that landmark agreement, three other NWFZs have been established: in the South Pacific (*Treaty of Rarotonga*, 1985), Southeast Asia (*Treaty of Bangkok*, 1995) and Africa (*Treaty of Pelindaba*, 1996). By virtue of such treaties, the whole of the populated southern hemisphere has nuclear-weapon-free status, greatly reducing the chance of nuclear proliferation. Proposals have been made for establishing nuclear-weapon-free zones in Central Asia, Central Europe, the Middle East and South Asia.

Preventing nuclear proliferation

The **International Atomic Energy Agency (IAEA)** plays a prominent role in international efforts aimed at preventing the proliferation of nuclear weapons. IAEA serves as the world's international inspectorate for the application of nuclear safeguards and verification measures covering civilian nuclear programmes.

By the end of 1997, there were some 221 safeguards agreements in force in 137 member States (and in Taiwan, China). To verify their implementation, 200 IAEA experts conduct daily on-site inspections in every part of the world, for a total of some 2,500 safeguards inspections a year. Their aim is to ensure that the nuclear material held in 1,000 nuclear installations in some 70 countries is not diverted away from legitimate peaceful uses to military purposes. IAEA thus contributes to international security, and reinforces efforts to halt the spread of arms and move towards a world free of nuclear weapons.

Various types of safeguards agreements can be concluded with IAEA. Those in connection with the NPT, the Model Protocol Additional to Existing Safeguards Agreements, the Treaty of Tlatelolco, the Treaty of Pelindaba and the Treaty of Rarotonga (*see page 113, above*) require non-nuclear-weapon States to submit their entire nuclear-fuel-cycle activities to IAEA safeguards. Other types of agreement cover safeguards at single facilities. IAEA safeguards under the NPT are an integral part of the international regime for non-proliferation, and play an indispensable role in ensuring implementation of the Treaty.

Current priorities

Nuclear disarmament and non-proliferation

Though the cold war is over, nuclear disarmament and non-proliferation of nuclear weapons remain the priority concerns in the area of multilateral disarmament. Many Governments, their militaries and the public are weighing the security benefits versus the security risks of the remaining weapons of mass destruction that have not been prohibited by international agreement. There is a growing body of opinion, in nuclear-weapon and non-nuclear-weapon States alike, that much more rapid progress towards total nuclear disarmament is needed in the years to come.

In response to a request by the General Assembly for an advisory opinion on the question of the legality of the use or threat of use of nuclear weapons, the International Court of Justice in 1996 stated unanimously that States are under an obligation "to pursue in good faith and bring to a conclusion negotiations leading to nuclear disarmament in all its aspects". The adoption of the CTBT in 1996 also added impetus to the momentum in that direction.

Many States feel that efforts should focus on the adoption of a time-bound phased programme of nuclear disarmament, while others stress that the States possessing nuclear weapons have made unprecedented progress through negotiations and can continue to do so. At the multilateral level, efforts will be pursued within the framework of the General Assembly, the Conference on Disarmament and the annual preparatory meetings leading to the next review of the NPT in the year 2000.

Chemical and biological weapons

With the *Chemical Weapons Convention*, a stringent international verification regime to oversee the implementation of a treaty banning weapons was created for the first time. The Convention established for that purpose the **Organisation for the Prohibition of Chemical Weapons (OPCW)**, located in The Hague, the Netherlands. The OPCW has initiated the international verification regime involving, among other things, the collection of information on chemical facilities on a worldwide basis and a routine global inspection system to verify that States parties are complying with the Treaty's terms.

The *Biological Weapons Convention (BWC)*, which prohibits the development, production and stockpiling of such weapons, was concluded in 1972 and entered into force in 1975. To build confidence in the effectiveness of the prohibition, States parties exchange detailed information each year on such items as their high-risk biological research facilities. Since 1995, they have been striving, through the convening of expert groups, to find ways to strengthen the verification of compliance procedures of the Convention.

Conventional weapons, confidence-building and transparency

The geopolitical rivalries of the cold war greatly influenced the entire range of disarmament initiatives. There was a tendency to highlight weapons of mass destruction to the exclusion of conventional weapons used in conflicts throughout the world, which are no less destructive to human life.

The growing proliferation of landmines around the world has been a particular focus of attention. In 1995, a review of the *Convention on Certain Conventional Weapons* (so-called *Inhumane Weapons Convention* or *CCW*) produced an *Amended Protocol II* strengthening restrictions on certain uses, types (self-destroying and detectable) and transfers of anti-personnel landmines.

Not satisfied with what they considered an inadequate response to a serious humanitarian crisis, a group of like-minded States negotiated an agreement on a total ban on all anti-personnel landmines — the *Convention on the Prohibition of the Use, Stockpiling, Production and Transfer of Anti-personnel Landmines* — which opened for signature on 3 December 1997 in Ottawa. Further efforts are being undertaken to make universal adherence to the Convention. It has been proposed that the Conference on Disarmament conduct multilateral negotiations to seek an approach to the total ban acceptable to those States that have not adhered to the Ottawa Convention.

The CCW review also achieved a prohibition on the use and development of blinding laser weapons, thus precluding their ever being deployed as weapons of war.

An abbreviated chronology of important international disarmament and arms regulation measures concluded through negotiations in multilateral and regional fora includes:

- 1959 *Antarctic Treaty:* demilitarizes the continent and bans the testing of any kind of weapon;
- 1963 *Treaty Banning Nuclear Weapon Tests in the Atmosphere, in Outer Space and under Water (Partial Test-Ban Treaty):* restricts nuclear testing to underground sites only;
- 1966 *Treaty on Principles Governing the Activities of States in the Exploration and Use of Outer Space, including the Moon and Other Celestial Bodies (Outer Space Treaty):* mandates that outer space be used for peaceful purposes only and that nuclear weapons not be placed or tested in outer space *(see also page 118)*;
- 1967 *Treaty for the Prohibition of Nuclear Weapons in Latin America and the Caribbean (Treaty of Tlatelolco):* prohibits testing, use, manufacture, storage, or acquisition of nuclear weapons by the countries of the region. All five nuclear-weapon States are parties to it;
- 1968 *Treaty on the Non-Proliferation of Nuclear Weapons (NPT):* the non-nuclear-weapon States agree never to acquire nuclear weapons and, in exchange, are promised access to civilian nuclear power technologies; nuclear-weapon States pledge to seek to carry out negotiations relating to cessation of the nuclear arms race and to nuclear disarmament;
- 1971 *Treaty on the Prohibition of the Emplacement of Nuclear Weapons on the Sea-Bed and the Ocean Floor and in the Subsoil Thereof (Sea-bed Treaty):* bans the emplacement of nuclear weapons, or any weapon of mass destruction, on the seabed or ocean floor;
- 1972 *Convention on Bacteriological (Biological) Weapons (BWC):* places a ban on the development, production, and stockpiling of biological and toxin agents, as well as providing for the destruction of such weapons and their means of delivery. A verification protocol, which could not be elaborated when the Convention was negotiated, is now being considered by the States parties;

Register of Conventional Arms

To provide greater transparency and confidence in the area of the transfer of advanced-conventional-weapon systems, the General Assembly agreed in 1992 to establish the Register of Conventional Arms. The arrangement allows for Governments to provide information on a voluntary basis on their transfers to other States of major weapons systems, such as aircraft, tanks, battleships and artillery. Such data are compiled and published annually by the United Nations as official United Nations documents, available to the general public.

arms regulation agreements

- 1980 *Convention on Certain Conventional Weapons (CCW)*: prohibits certain conventional weapons deemed excessively injurious or having indiscriminate effects. The Convention is considered an umbrella agreement, to which additional agreements can be added. As of 1997, it contains four Protocols.
  Protocol I bans weapons which explode fragments that are by X-ray undetectable within the human body; *Amended Protocol II* (agreed in 1995) limits the use of certain types of mines, booby-traps, and other devices; *Protocol III* bans incendiary weapons designed to set fire to targets; and *Protocol IV* bans the use of blinding laser weapons;
- 1985 *South Pacific Nuclear Free Zone Treaty (Treaty of Rarotonga)*: bans the stationing, acquisition or testing of nuclear explosive devices and the dumping of nuclear waste within the prescribed zone. It has been signed by, among others, all five nuclear-weapon States;
- 1990 *Treaty on Conventional Armed Forces in Europe (CFE Treaty)*: limits the numbers of various conventional armaments in a zone stretching from the Atlantic ocean to the Ural mountains;
- 1993 *Chemical Weapons Convention (CWC)*: prohibits the development, production, stockpiling and use of chemical weapons worldwide and requires their destruction;
- 1995 *Southeast Asia Nuclear-Weapon-Free Zone Treaty (Treaty of Bangkok)*: bans the development or stationing of nuclear weapons on the territories of the States party to the treaty;
- 1996 *African Nuclear-Weapon-Free Zone Treaty (Treaty of Pelindaba)*: bans the development or stationing of nuclear weapons on the African continent;
- 1996 *Comprehensive Nuclear-Test-Ban Treaty (CTBT)*: places a worldwide ban on nuclear test explosions of any kind and in any environment;
- 1997 *Landmines Convention (Ottawa Convention)*: prohibits the use, stockpiling, production and transfer of anti-personnel mines and provides for their destruction.

Small arms and light weapons

Efforts are also being made to promote at the global and regional levels the control and reduction of small arms and light weapons — the primary weapons used in contemporary conflicts. The General Assembly has called upon all States to implement the recommendations made by a 1997 United Nations study on small arms: these include aiding the improvement of internal security forces, strengthening international cooperation among police, intelligence, customs and border control services, and boosting both security and overall development.

Peaceful uses of outer space

The United Nations works to ensure that outer space be used for peaceful purposes and that the benefits from space activities be shared by all nations. This concern in the peaceful uses of outer space began soon after the launch of the Sputnik — the first man-made satellite — by the Soviet Union in 1957, and has kept in step with the subsequent advances in space technology.

The United Nations intergovernmental body active as the focal point in this area is the **Committee on the Peaceful Uses of Outer Space**, set up by the General Assembly in 1959 and made up of 61 Member States. It reviews the scope of international cooperation in peaceful uses of outer space, devises programmes and directs United Nations technical cooperation in this field, encourages research and dissemination of information, and contributes to the development of international space law.

The Committee has two Subcommittees:

- The **Scientific and Technical Subcommittee** currently discusses matters such as remote sensing of the earth by satellite, the use of nuclear power sources in outer space, space debris, space transportation systems, space activities related to the earth's environment, astronomy and planetary exploration.
- The **Legal Subcommittee** currently addresses such items as the definition and delimitation of space, ways to ensure the rational and equitable use of the geostationary orbit, and review of the status of the five international legal instruments governing outer space (*see below*).

The Committee and its two Subcommittees meet annually to consider questions put before them by the General Assembly, reports submitted to them and issues raised by Member States. Working on the basis of consensus, the Committee makes recommendations to the General Assembly.

Legal instruments

The work of the Committee and its Legal Subcommittee has resulted in the adoption by the General Assembly of five legal instruments, all of which are in force:

- The 1966 *Treaty on Principles Governing the Activities of States in the Exploration and Use of Outer Space, including the Moon and Other Celestial Bodies* (commonly known as the *"Outer Space Treaty"*) provides that space exploration shall be carried out for the benefit of all countries, irrespective of their degree of development. It seeks to maintain outer space as the province of all humankind, free for exploration and use by all States, solely for peaceful purposes, and not subject to national appropriation;

- The 1967 *Agreement on the Rescue of Astronauts, the Return of Astronauts and the Return of Objects Launched into Outer Space* (the *"Rescue Agreement"*) provides for aiding the crews of spacecraft in case of accident or emergency landing, and establishes procedures for returning to the launching authority a space object or its components found beyond the territory of that authority;
- The 1971 *Convention on International Liability for Damage Caused by Space Objects* (the *"Liability Convention"*) provides that the launching State is liable for damage caused by its space objects on the Earth's surface, to aircraft in flight and to space objects of another State or persons or property on board such objects;
- The 1974 *Convention on Registration of Objects Launched into Outer Space* (the *"Registration Convention"*) provides that launching States shall maintain registries of space objects and provide information on objects launched to the United Nations. Under the 1974 Convention, the **Office for Outer Space Affairs** maintains a United Nations Registry on objects launched into outer space. Information has been provided by all launching States and by the European Space Agency (ESA);
- The 1979 *Agreement Governing Activities of States on the Moon and Other Celestial Bodies* (the *"Moon Agreement"*) elaborates the principles relating to the Moon and other celestial bodies set out in the 1966 Treaty, and sets up the basis to regulate the future exploration and exploitation of natural resources on those bodies.

On the basis of the work of the Committee and its Legal Subcommittee, the General Assembly has also adopted the following set of principles on the conduct of space activities:

- The *Principles governing the use by States of artificial Earth satellites for international direct television broadcasting* (1982) recognize that such use has international political, economic, social and cultural implications. Such activities should respect the sovereign rights of States, including the principle of non-intervention, should promote the dissemination and exchange of information and knowledge, and should foster development.
- The *Principles relating to remote sensing of the Earth from outer space* (1986) state that such activities are to be conducted for the

benefit of all countries, respecting the sovereignty of all States and peoples over their natural resources, and for the rights and interests of other States. Remote sensing is to be used to preserve the environment and to reduce the impact of natural disasters.

- The *Principles on the use of nuclear power sources in outer space* (1992) recognize that such sources are essential for some missions, but that their use should be based on a thorough safety assessment. The Principles also provide guidelines for the safe use of nuclear power sources and for notification of a malfunction of a space object where there is a risk of re-entry of radioactive material to the Earth.

- The *Declaration on international cooperation in the exploration and use of outer space for the benefit and in the interest of all States, particularly developing countries* (1996) provides that States are free to determine all aspects of their participation in international cooperation in space activities on an equitable and mutually acceptable basis, and that such cooperation should be conducted in ways that are considered most effective and appropriate by the countries concerned.

Office for Outer Space Affairs

The Vienna-based **United Nations Office for Outer Space Affairs** serves as the secretariat for the Committee on the Peaceful Uses of Outer Space, and assists developing countries in using space technology for sustainable development.

The Office disseminates space-related information to Member States through its International Space Information System. Through its **United Nations Programme on Space Applications**, the Office provides technical advisory services to Member States in conducting pilot projects, and undertakes training and fellowship programmes in such areas as remote sensing, satellite communication, satellite meteorology and basic space science.

The Office provides technical assistance to Regional Centres for Space Science and Technology Education affiliated with the United Nations. The Centres help to develop skills and knowledge of scientists and researchers in the aspects of space science and technology that can help to develop human resources for space technology applications and sustainable development. The Centre in Asia and the Pacific became operational in India in 1995; the Centres in Africa and in Latin America and the Caribbean are expected to be operational in 1998.

The Office works in close cooperation with organizations such as ESA, the International Astronautical Federation (IAF) and the Committee on Space Research (COSPAR).

In addition to the Office, other United Nations organizations are active in areas such as space communication, satellite meteorology, space science and remote sensing. To coordinate the space activities of the United Nations system, an **Inter-Agency Meeting on Outer Space Activities** convenes once a year.

UNISPACE conferences

The United Nations has organized two major world conferences on outer space — the **First and Second United Nations Conferences on the Exploration and Peaceful Uses of Outer Space**, held in Vienna in 1968 and 1982. The first conference examined the practical benefits deriving from space research and exploration, and the extent to which non-space countries, especially developing countries, might enjoy them.

The second conference (UNISPACE 82) reflected the growing involvement of all nations in outer space activities; assessed the state of space science and technology; considered the applications of space technology for development; and discussed international space cooperative programmes.

The third conference (UNISPACE III) will be convened as a special session of the Committee on Outer Space in Vienna in July 1999. Intergovernmental and non-governmental organizations with space activities as well as space-related industries will also participate in UNISPACE III, which will seek to promote the use of space technology to solve regional and global problems, and to strengthen the capability of Member States, particularly developing countries, to use space-research application in the service of development.

PART TWO

Chapter **3**

ECONOMIC AND SOCIAL DEVELOPMENT

ECONOMIC AND SOCIAL DEVELOPMENT

Although most people associate the United Nations with the issues of peace and security, the vast majority of the Organization's resources are in fact devoted to advancing the Charter's pledge to "promote higher standards of living, full employment and conditions of economic and social progress and development". United Nations development efforts have profoundly affected the lives and well-being of millions of people throughout the world. Guiding the United Nations endeavours is the conviction that lasting international peace and security are possible only if the economic and social well-being of people everywhere is assured.

Many of the economic and social transformations that have taken place globally in the last 50 years have been significantly affected in their direction and shape by the work of the United Nations. As the global centre for consensus-building, the United Nations has set priorities and goals for international cooperation to assist countries in their development efforts and to foster a conducive and supportive global economic environment.

This consensus has been expressed through a series of *International Development Decades*, the first beginning in 1961 (*see box, page 127*). These broad statements of policy and goals, while emphasizing certain issues of particular concern in each decade, have consistently stressed the need for progress on all aspects of development, social as well as economic, and the importance of narrowing the disparities between industrialized and developing countries.

As a forum for innovative thinking, the United Nations has been responsible for formulating and promoting key new developmental objectives on the international agenda, such as sustainable development. It has articulated the need for incorporating issues such as the advancement of women, human rights, environmental protection and good governance into the development paradigm.

International debate on economic and social issues in recent years has increasingly reflected the commonality of interests between rich and poor countries alike in solving the many problems that transcend national boundaries. Issues such as refugee populations, organized crime, AIDS and drug trafficking are seen as global problems requiring coordinated action. The impact of persistent poverty and unemployment in one region can be quickly felt in others, not least through migration, social disruption and conflict. Similarly, in the age of a global economy, financial instability in one country will be felt almost instantaneously in the markets of others.

In 1997, the General Assembly, reflecting this growing interdependence, agreed on the *Agenda for Development* which, along with the action plans from the series of world conferences held during the first half of the 1990s (*see box, page 157*), provides an all-encompassing framework for international cooperation on development — a coherent blueprint for tackling the common threats to global development.

The *Agenda* represents one of the most far-reaching agreements on this central issue ever attained by Member States at the General Assembly, not only bringing together the familiar components of development, such as economic growth, poverty eradication, trade, finance, employment and human resources development, but also emphasizing the role of democracy, human rights, popular participation, governance and the empowerment of women. Its insistence that international development can be based only on partnerships, not on competing interests, and its clear recognition of the need for strengthened institutional cooperation are important features of the *Agenda*. In particular, the *Agenda* not only affirms the United Nations role in the field of development, but also identifies ways of reinforcing the capacities and effectiveness of its various offices and agencies.

Coordinating development activities

Despite advances on many fronts, gross disparities in wealth and well-being continue to characterize the world. Reducing poverty and redressing inequalities, both within and between nations, remain fundamental goals of the United Nations. The United Nations system works in a variety of ways to promote its economic and social goals — by formulating policies, advising Governments on their development plans and programmes, setting international norms and standards, and by mobilizing funds totalling over $25 billion annually, including from financial institutions, to carry out programmes for development (*see page 129*). It is through the work of its various Offices and Programmes and its family of specialized agencies, in areas as diverse as education, air safety, environmental protection and labour conditions, that the work of the Organization touches the lives of people everywhere.

Under the Charter, the **Economic and Social Council (ECOSOC)** is the principal body coordinating the economic and social work of the United Nations and its operational arms. The Council is also the central forum for discussing international economic and social issues and for formulating policy recommendations (*see Part One, pages 11-13*).

UN Development Decades

1961   First United Nations Development Decade (1961-1970) outlines broad policies designed to achieve economic growth in developing countries of at least 5 per cent a year;

1969   Declaration on Social Progress and Development stresses the interdependence of social and economic development;

1970   The International Development Strategy for the Second United Nations Development Decade (1971-1980) calls for promoting international economic cooperation on a just and equitable basis;

1974   A special session of the General Assembly calls for the establishment of a New International Economic Order. The Assembly subsequently adopts the Charter of Economic Rights and Duties of States, which stipulates the right of States to exercise full sovereignty over their wealth and natural resources;

1980   The International Development Strategy for the Third United Nations Development Decade (1981-1990) again calls for changes to the world economy through global negotiations;

1990   At a special session, the General Assembly adopts the Declaration on International Economic Cooperation, in particular the revitalization of Economic Growth and Development of the Developing Countries. It subsequently adopts the International Development Strategy for the Fourth United Nations Development Decade (1991-2000) which singles out four priority areas — poverty and hunger, human resources and institutional development, population, and the environment.

United Nations development activities are carried out through several bodies. Guided by the policy framework laid out by the recent United Nations global conferences in the economic, social and environmental spheres, the United Nations **Department of Economic and Social Affairs (DESA)** gathers and analyses economic and social data; carries out policy analysis and coordination; and provides substantive and technical support to Member States in the areas of sustainable and social development, statistics and population, gender issues and the advancement of women, public economics and public administration, development policy analysis and development of Africa (*see also Part One, page 28*). Its substantive support to intergovernmental processes in those areas facilitates the task of Member States to set norms and standards and agree on common courses of action in relation to ongoing or emerging global challenges. DESA thus constitutes a crucial interface between global policies and national action and between research, policy and operational activities at the national and international levels.

The United Nations competitive advantage

The only global institution for furthering development, the United Nations system has bettered the lives of countless people in the poorest parts of the world through practical programmes for development.

The United Nations has unique strengths in promoting development:

- Its *universality*: all countries have a voice when major policy decisions are made;
- Its *impartiality*: it does not represent any particular national or commercial interest, and can thus develop special relations of trust with countries and their people to provide aid with no strings attached;
- Its *global presence*: it has the world's largest network of country offices for delivering assistance for development;
- Its *comprehensive mandate*, spanning social, economic and emergency needs: it supports development, delivers relief aid, encourages democratization and promotes reconstruction;
- Its *commitment* to "the peoples of the United Nations".

The five **Regional Commissions** facilitate similar exchanges of economic and social information and policy analysis in the regions of Asia and the Pacific, Western Asia, Africa, Latin America and the Caribbean and Europe (*see Part One, pages 12 and 32-33*). In addition, the various funds and programmes of the United Nations deal with operational activities for development in programme countries. The specialized agencies of the United Nations are also engaged in providing support and assistance to development efforts of developing countries and economies in transition. At a time of increasingly limited resources, both human and financial, enhanced coordination and cooperation between the various arms of the system are vital if development goals are to be realized.

Recognizing this, the Secretary-General in 1997 established two bodies to assist in the management and coordination of economic and social affairs and development work within the Organization — the **Executive Committee on Economic and Social Affairs** and the Executive Committee on development cooperation, known as the **United Nations Development Group**. Both executive bodies, which are comprised of the relevant Secretariat departments and offices as well as the Regional Commissions and relevant Funds and Programmes, work to enhance the coordination and cooperation between policy entities and the distinct operational programmes.

Economic development

The world has witnessed enormous economic development in recent decades, but the generation of wealth and prosperity has been very uneven, so uneven that economic imbalances are seen to exacerbate serious social problems and political instability in virtually every region of the world. The end of the cold war and the accelerated emergence of a global economy have not solved persistent problems of extreme poverty, indebtedness, underdevelopment and trade imbalances, especially in developing regions.

One of the founding principles of the United Nations is the conviction that economic development for all peoples of the world is the surest way to achieve political, economic and social security. It is a central preoccupation of the Organization that over 60 per cent of the world's population, most of them in Asia, Africa and Latin America and the Caribbean, subsist on $2 or less per day. About 1.3 billion people live in extreme poverty. Nearly 1 billion people are illiterate, and over 1 billion lack access to safe water. Every day, some 840 million go hungry or face food insecurity.

The United Nations continues to be the single institution dedicated to finding ways to ensure that economic expansion and globalization are guided by policies aimed at ensuring human welfare, sustainable development, the eradication of poverty, fair trade policies and the reduction of crippling indebtedness.

The United Nations urges the adoption of macroeconomic policies that address these imbalances, particularly the growing gap between the North and South, the persistent problems of the least developed countries, and the unprecedented requirements of the economies in transition from centralized to market economies. The Organization has worked at the global and national levels for the creation of an enabling environment for development. It is engaged everywhere in helping the efforts of people to escape from the trap of poverty and hunger, and in promoting child survival, environmental protection, women's progress, human rights and democracy. For millions in poor countries, these programmes of assistance *are* the United Nations.

Official development assistance

Through their policies and financial flows, the Organization's lending institutions have, collectively, an enormous influence on the economies of developing countries. This is especially true for the least developed countries (LDCs), which include 48 nations whose extreme poverty and indebtedness have marginalized them from global growth

Declining assistance to development

In 1980, industrialized countries pledged at the General Assembly to devote 0.7 per cent of their gross national product (GNP) to official development assistance (ODA) to developing countries. But that target has been reached by only a few countries — currently Denmark, Finland, Norway, Sweden. In fact, Nordic countries by themselves provide over 20 per cent of total ODA each year. On average, ODA has remained at less than half of the targeted level, or about 0.3 per cent of industrialized countries' GNP. With the end of the cold war, ODA has fallen by 14 per cent in real terms between 1992 and 1995. By 1996, ODA, at $58 billion, represented a mere 0.25 per cent of the GNP of the 21 main donor countries — its lowest level in 30 years. The largest donor continued to be Japan, followed by the United States, Germany and France.

In the past, official development finance from northern Governments represented the bulk of the financial resources going into developing countries. But in the last few years, private investment in developing countries has increased dramatically, and private investments and loans now far outweigh official flows. Of total resource flows from donor countries in 1996 of $304 billion, $238 billion was private flows, and only $66 billion was official flows, including non-ODA funds.

Both the World Bank and the United Nations Conference on Trade and Development carefully monitor these financial flows and point to serious problems that still must be addressed. Eighty per cent of the private capital flow to developing countries, for example, goes to just 12 countries; the poorest countries attract less than 1 per cent of total foreign investment flows; and nearly 50 developing countries are not receiving any foreign capital at all.

Reflecting concern over these issues, the General Assembly decided in 1997 to convene an international conference or a special session of the Assembly by the year 2001 which would be devoted exclusively to the issue of financing for development. The high-level meeting would address, among other things, the continuing high level of indebtedness, the mobilization of innovative domestic and private resources for development, and governance of the international monetary, financial and trade systems.

and development. The LDCs are the focus of several United Nations assistance programmes, including the *Programme of Action for the Least Developed Countries for the 1990s*, whereby LDCs, the majority of which are in Africa, are targeted as priorities for international development cooperation. Donor countries have agreed to commit 0.15 per cent of their gross national product (GNP) to this group of nations. Small island developing States (*see also page 205*), landlocked developing countries and countries with economies in transition to market economies also suffer from critical problems requiring

Africa — a United Nations priority

The United Nations, reflecting the concern of the international community, has made the critical socio-economic conditions in Africa a priority concern. In affirming its commitment to support the region's development, it has devised special programmes to find durable solutions to external debt and debt-service problems, to increase foreign direct investment, to enhance national capacity-building, to deal with the shortage of domestic resources for development and to facilitate the integration of the African countries into subregional, regional and world trade.

At its 1986 special session on Africa, the General Assembly adopted the **Programme of Action for African Economic Recovery and Development 1986-1990 (UNPAERD)**, which sought to mobilize political and financial support for economic reforms. Reviewing the Programme of Action in 1991, the Assembly called for a **New Agenda for Development of Africa in the 1990s** to ensure continued support for the region by achieving an average real growth rate in gross domestic product of at least 6 per cent a year through out the 1990s. The New Agenda accords special attention to human development and increased employment, and to programmes which promote rapid progress in life expectancy, the integration of women in development, child and maternal health, and the provision of adequate nutrition, water and sanitation, education and shelter.

To ensure coordination of United Nations policy-making and of its extensive programmes in the region, the General Assembly launched in 1996 the **United Nations System-wide Special Initiative on Africa (UNSIA)** to help accelerate Africa's development in the decade to 2005. UNSIA is designed to rationalize and maximize the impact of United Nations assistance, including that of UNDP, UNESCO, UNICEF and the Bretton Woods institutions, through more effective coordination at headquarters and at the country level. The Initiative's mechanisms work to forge coherent partnerships to focus on priorities already identified by African countries.

---

special attention from the international community and are similarly priorities in the assistance programmes of the United Nations system.

Official development assistance (ODA) to all developing countries has averaged around $60 billion a year in the 1990s (*see box on opposite page*). United Nations ODA is derived from two sources: grant assistance from United Nations specialized and technical agencies and United Nations funds and programmes, which has averaged around $4.5 billion; and loans from lending institutions of the United Nations system, such as the International Fund for Agricultural Development (IFAD) and the World Bank.

ODA from the United Nations system is widely distributed among 130 countries. Africa receives nearly 40 per cent of all United Nations system grant resources, Asia and the Pacific and Latin America each receive 22 per cent, Europe 6.6 per cent and Western Asia 6 per cent.

In 1996, the latest year for which a detailed breakdown is available, the sector comprising humanitarian assistance and disaster management was the largest single recipient of grant-financed development activities of the United Nations system, accounting for over a quarter of total outlays, followed by the health sector. This does not include expenditures by the Office of the United Nations High Commissioner for Refugees which in recent years have averaged around $1 billion annually (*see Chapter 5, page 253*). In addition, IFAD invests over $250 million a year in loans and grants aimed at relieving hunger and rural poverty (*see pages 145 and 163*). Finally, the World Bank provides loans totalling over $20 billion a year, while the other so-called Bretton Woods institution, the International Monetary Fund, also offers various forms of support to countries in financial difficulties (*see pages 135 and 136 respectively*).

But the activities of the United Nations system have been affected by the marked decline of the share of ODA in total resource flows (*see box on page 130*). Moreover, the share of United Nations system development grants in declining total ODA has dropped from around 8 per cent ($4.9 billion) in 1993 to less than 7.5 per cent ($4.3 billion) in 1996.

As general (core) resources provided to United Nations agencies and bodies have declined, there has been a relatively rapid increase in non-core resources provided for specific programmes, projects or funds. While all countries contribute to development cooperation, nearly 90 per cent of core resources is provided by only 15 industrial countries. The traditional donor base has been static, despite significant changes in the global economy.

Promoting development worldwide

The **United Nations Development Programme (UNDP)** is the United Nations system's largest source of grant funding for development, and is the main body for coordinating United Nations development assistance (*see also Part One, pages 35-37*).

Through a network of 132 country offices, UNDP's mission is to help countries to develop their own national capacity to build sustainable human development — development that both is people-centred and respects the environment — giving top priority to poverty eradication, environmental regeneration, job creation and the advancement of women. In support of these goals, UNDP is often asked to assist in promoting sound governance and market development, and to support rebuilding societies in the aftermath of war and humanitarian emergencies (*see also Chapter 2, page 77 and Chapter 5, page 251*).

Ninety per cent of UNDP's core programme funds go to 66 countries that are home to 90 per cent of the world's extremely poor (*see page 160, below*). In 1996, UNDP and its funds provided $1.5 billion in development assistance. Countries that receive UNDP-administered assistance cover more than half of total project costs through personnel, facilities, equipment and supplies.

UNDP plays a leading role in efforts at the country level to enhance a more integrated approach to the provision of United Nations development assistance. In several developing countries it has established a **United Nations Development Assistance Framework (UNDAF)** made up of United Nations teams under the leadership of the local United Nations Resident Coordinator, who is usually the Resident Representative of UNDP. UNDAFs articulate a coordinated response to the main development challenges, goals, strategies and priorities identified for the United Nations by Governments.

In addition to redeploying some 20 per cent of staff at headquarters in New York to the field in recent years, UNDP is central to efforts to create **United Nations Houses** in many countries to provide common premises and pool facilities for United Nations agencies and programmes in the field. UNDP Resident Representatives devote about 40 per cent of their time to issues relating to their roles as Resident Coordinators and another 20 per cent on behalf of United Nations organizations without country representation. Resident Coordinators regularly serve as coordinators of humanitarian assistance in cases of human disasters, natural disasters and complex emergency situations (*see also Chapter 5, pages 249-251*).

Together with the World Bank and the United Nations Environment Programme, UNDP is one of the managing partners of the **Global Environment Facility** (*see page 200, below*), and UNDP is one of the six sponsors of the **Joint United Nations Programme on HIV/AIDS (UNAIDS)** (*see page 166, below*).

UNDP supports a range of economic development projects. For instance:

- In *China*, it is central to a seven-year programme to raise the quality of life of the 80 million people still living below the poverty line. The programme features a participatory, self-help approach to improving income, health and education. Its United Nations partners in this programme include the World Food Programme, UNICEF and IFAD.

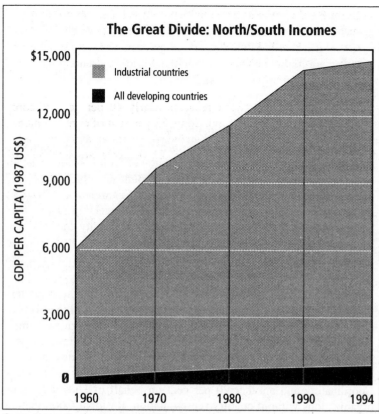

The Great Divide: North/South Incomes

GDP PER CAPITA (1987 US$)

Industrial countries

All developing countries

Source: Human Development Report 1997

- After *Madagascar* adopted a free-market economy, the UNDP-supported First International Industrial Forum attracted 307 potential investors from 16 countries; agreements were signed for 55 investment opportunities, expected to bring in $50.3 million and create 4,000 new jobs.
- In *Viet Nam*, many policy makers have learned how other countries manage macroeconomic reforms through UNDP-financed study tours, fellowships and in-country training. Additional assistance is helping to improve the banking system, enhance public revenues through tax reform, streamline and decentralize public administration, and promote legal reforms in support of a market-based economy.

- *Costa Rica*'s national development plan is based on a policy of sustainable development and was formulated with UNDP support. It has resulted in promotion of clean industry, legislation on policies to reduce energy demand, and improved energy conservation.

UNDP's anti-poverty work receives nearly 40 per cent of core resources (*see page 160, below*). Some 32 per cent of core resources are related to democratization, including electoral assistance and strengthening of the judiciary. About 21 per cent are directed to programmes focusing on the environment.

Lending for development

The **World Bank** works to strengthen economies and expand markets and to help integrate marginalized populations into the local economies with the aim of reducing poverty. Unlike aid programmes and agencies, the Bank does not make grants: it lends money to developing countries — and the loans are repaid (*see also Part One, pages 54-56*).

Developing countries borrow from the Bank because they need capital, technical assistance and policy advice. There are two types of Bank lending. The first type is for developing countries that are able to pay near-market interest rates. The money for these loans comes largely from investors around the world, who buy bonds issued by the Bank.

The second type of loan goes to the poorest countries, which are usually not creditworthy in the international financial markets and are unable to pay near-market interest rates on the money they borrow. Lending to the poorest countries is done by a World Bank affiliate, the **International Development Association (IDA)**. IDA credits are free of interest, carry a low 0.75 per cent annual administrative charge, and are very long-term — 35 or 40 years, including 10 years grace. Countries with per capita incomes of less than $925 (in 1996 dollars) are eligible for IDA credits, but most IDA credits go to countries that are much poorer. But again, the credits are repaid. Funded largely by contributions from the richer member countries, IDA lends an average of about $6 billion a year to the world's poorest countries (*see also page 161, below*).

Under its Articles of Agreement, the Bank can lend only to member Governments, but it works closely with local communities, non-governmental organizations (NGOs) and private enterprise. Its projects are designed to assist the poorest sectors of the population. Successful development requires that Governments and communities "own" their development projects. The Bank encourages Governments to work closely with NGOs and civil society to strengthen participation by people affected by Bank-financed projects. NGOs based in borrowing countries collaborate in about half of Bank-supported projects.

The Bank encourages the private sector by advocating stable economic policies, sound government finances, and open, honest and accountable governance. It works in close collaboration with other members of the United Nations system and actively seeks to establish additional partnerships in areas where private-sector development is making rapid inroads — industry, finance, power, telecommunications, information technology, oil and gas. While the Bank's Articles of Agreement prohibit the Bank from lending directly to the private sector, a Bank affiliate — the **International Finance Corporation (IFC)** — was established in 1956 expressly to invest in private sector enterprises (*see page 138, below*). Another affiliate to the Bank, the **Multilateral Investment Guarantee Agency (MIGA)**, facilitates private-sector investment to developing countries (*see page 138, below*).

The Bank does much more than lend money: it also routinely includes technical assistance in projects. This may cover advice on issues such as the overall size of a country's budget and where the money should be allocated, or how to set up village health clinics, or what sort of equipment is needed to build a road. The Bank funds a few projects each year devoted exclusively to providing expert advice and training. It also trains people from borrowing countries on how to create and carry out development programmes.

In the area of sustainable development, the Bank supports projects for reforestation, pollution control and land management; invests in water, sanitation and agriculture to combat the environmental problems that afflict the poor; promotes economic policies and national environmental action plans which help to conserve natural resources; and is the main funder of the Global Environment Facility (*see page 200, below*).

Lending for stability

Many countries turn to the **International Monetary Fund (IMF)**, a specialized agency of the United Nations system, when internal or external factors seriously undermine their balance-of-payments stability, fiscal stability or capacity to meet debt service commitments. The IMF makes policy recommendations to overcome these problems and often makes financial resources available to members in support of economic reform programmes under a range of policies and facilities (*see also Part One, page 56*).

Members with balance-of-payments problems generally avail themselves of the IMF's financial resources by purchasing other members' currencies with an equivalent amount of their own currencies. The IMF levies charges on this operation, and requires that members repurchase their own currencies from the IMF over a specified time.

The main IMF facilities are:

- *Stand-by arrangements*, designed to provide short-term balance-of-payments assistance for deficits of a temporary or cyclical nature; drawings are phased and their release is conditional on meeting performance criteria;
- *Extended Fund Facility*, designed to support medium-term programmes aimed at overcoming balance-of-payment difficulties stemming from macroeconomic and structural problems; performance criteria are applied;
- *Enhanced Structural Adjustment Facility* (*ESAF*), a concessional facility designed for the low-income member countries with protracted balance-of-payment problems: it makes available low-interest loans — not purchases of other members currencies; they are made in support of three-year programmes and carry an interest rate of 0.5 per cent, with a 5-year grace period and a 10-year maturity;
- *Compensatory and Contingency Financing Facility*, a special facility designed to provide financial assistance to members experiencing temporary export shortfalls, and compensatory financing for excesses in cereal import costs, as well as for external contingencies in IMF arrangements.

In lending to its members, the IMF is guided by two principles. First, the pool of currencies at the IMF's disposal exists for the entire membership, and therefore a member borrowing currency is expected to return it as soon as its payment problems are solved, so as not to limit other members' access. Second, before the IMF releases any money from the pool, the member must demonstrate how it intends to solve its payments problems, so that it can repay the IMF within the repayment period — normally three to five years, and up to 10 years under ESAF.

The IMF's technical assistance consists of expertise provided to its members in several broad areas: the design and implementation of fiscal and monetary policy; institution-building, such as the development of central banks or treasuries; the collection and refinement of statistical data; and the training of member countries' officials at the IMF institutes in Washington, D.C., Singapore and Vienna.

Investment and development

As foreign direct investment has continued to expand dramatically, developing countries have increasingly opened up their economies to such investment. Various parts of the United Nations system monitor and assess developments, and, such as FAO (*see page 143, below*), UNDP (*see page 134, above*) and UNIDO (*see page 145, below*), assist developing-country Governments in attracting investment.

Two affiliates of the World Bank—the International Finance Corporation and the Multilateral Investment Guarantee Agency—help promote investment in developing countries. The **International Finance Corporation (IFC)** encourages private-sector activity in developing countries. It does this mainly through three types of activities: financing private-sector projects, helping companies in the developing world to mobilize financing in the international financial markets, and providing advice and technical assistance to businesses and Governments. IFC thus promotes development by encouraging the growth of productive enterprise and efficient capital markets in member countries. The largest multilateral source of loan and equity financing for private-sector projects in the developing world, IFC invested more than $8 billion in fiscal 1997.

Partly in response to the debt crises of the 1980s, member countries established a new investment insurance affiliate to the Bank—the **Multilateral Investment Guarantee Agency (MIGA)**. Its goal is to facilitate the flow of private investment for productive purposes to developing member countries, by offering to investors long-term political risk insurance—that is, coverage against the risks of expropriation, currency transfer, war and civil disturbance—and by providing advisory services. MIGA carries out promotional programmes, disseminates information on investment opportunities, and provides technical assistance that enhances national investment promotion capabilities.

The **United Nations Conference on Trade and Development (UNCTAD)** assists Governments, government agencies as well as NGOs to improve the general understanding of: global trends in foreign direct investment flows and related policies, the interrelationship between foreign direct investment, trade, technology and development and the development implications of a possible multilateral framework on investment (*see also Part One, page 35*). The results of

Foreign direct investment and development

Foreign direct investment continues to be a driving force in the global economy. The current boom of investment flows underscores the central role played by transnational corporations in both industrialized and developing countries. According to UNCTAD's *World Investment Report 1997*:

- The number of transnational corporations worldwide has continued to expand — up to 44,000 by the mid-1990s;
- Of these, 7,900 were based in developing countries, up from 3,800 at the end of the 1980s;
- In 1995, the some 280,000 foreign affiliates of the world's transnationals produced goods and services worth an estimated $7 trillion;
- Between 1982 and 1994, the output of foreign affiliates almost tripled and their share of world output rose from 5 to 6 per cent;
- The worldwide assets of foreign affiliates was valued at $8.4 trillion in 1994;
- The largest 100 transnationals controlled one fifth of the total global foreign assets of transnationals in 1995;
- In 1995, for the first time, two corporations from developing countries entered the list of the world's 100 biggest corporations: Daewoo Corporation (Republic of Korea) and Petroleos de Venezuela.

---

its work are reported in the annual *World Investment Report* and other studies, which are the basis for policy discussions in UNCTAD's **Commission on Investment, Technology and Related Financial Issues**.

In addition, UNCTAD's **Division on Investment Technology and Enterprise Development** disseminates information on its work in these areas; organizes discussions; and holds seminars to sensitize policy-makers in developing countries and representatives from transnational companies on the development issues originating from foreign direct investment. It also provides guidance on appropriate policy choices and on improving policy-formulation capacity in developing countries.

The Division's Advisory Services on Investment and Technology integrates most of the technical cooperation activities concerning the creation of an enabling investment environment and the improvement of investment promotion and technology diffusion in developing countries. In this connection, the World Association of Investment Promotion Agencies is receiving UNCTAD's support in maintaining its network of investment promotion agencies from more than 95 countries.

Trade and development

International trade has been growing strongly at an annual rate of 10 per cent since the mid-1980s, enabling many developing countries to enjoy remarkable gains in prosperity and growth. But major disparities persist, with many of the poorest countries still participating only marginally in international trade.

Ensuring the integration of all countries in global trade is the task of the **United Nations Conference on Trade and Development (UNCTAD)** — the focal point within the United Nations for dealing with development-related issues in the areas of trade, finance, technology, investment and sustainable development. UNCTAD works to maximize the trade, investment and development opportunities of developing countries, and to help them face challenges arising from globalization and to integrate into the world economy on an equitable basis.

UNCTAD pursues these goals through research and policy analysis, intergovernmental deliberations, technical cooperation, and interaction with civil society and the business sector.

In particular, UNCTAD:

- Examines trends in the global economy and evaluates their impact upon development;
- Helps developing countries, particularly the least developed, to maximize the positive impact of globalization and liberalization by helping them integrate into the international trading system;
- Examines global trends in foreign direct investment flows, and their impact on trade, technology and development;
- Helps developing countries to attract investment;
- Helps developing countries to develop enterprises and entrepreneurship;
- Helps developing countries and countries in transition improve the efficiency of their trade-supporting services, and supports the formulation of national policies and regulations;
- Promotes global electronic commerce by facilitating access to information technologies, particularly through its *Global Trade Point Programme* (*see page 142, below*).

Enterprise Development. UNCTAD promotes enterprise development, particularly for small and medium-sized enterprises (SMEs), through regular intergovernmental discussions and through its technical cooperation (*see also Industrial development, pages 145-146, below*). The **Commission on Enterprise and Business Facilitation and Development** and its expert meetings have examined ways to formulate and implement effective enterprise development strategies.

Promoting fair trade

Intergovernmental negotiations under UNCTAD's auspices have resulted in:

- Agreement on a *Generalized Systems of Preferences* (1971), which facilitates the preferential treatment of $70 billion of developing-country exports to industrialized countries annually;
- Agreement on a *Global System of Trade Preferences* among developing countries (1989);
- Agreement on a set of principles and rules to control restrictive business practices (1980);
- International commodity agreements, including those for cocoa, sugar, natural rubber, jute and jute products, tropical timber, tin, olive oil and wheat;
- The *Common Fund for Commodities*, which provides financial backing for the operation of international stocks and for research and development projects in the area of commodities (1989);
- Debt relief: more than 50 developing countries have benefited from debt relief of over $6.5 billion since a resolution on the retroactive adjustment of terms of the ODA debt of low-income developing countries was approved in 1978;
- Guidelines for international action on debt rescheduling (1980);
- Agreement on a Special New Programme of Action for the Least Developed Countries (1981) and on a Special New Programme of Action for the Least Developed Countries for the 1990s (1990); and
- *United Nations Conventions* in the area of maritime transport: *on a Code of Conduct for Liner Conferences* (1974), *on the Carriage of Goods by Sea* (1978), *on International Multimodal Transport of Goods* (1980), *on Conditions for Registration of Ships* (1986) and *on Maritime Liens and Mortgages* (1993).

Discussions have focused on promoting public-private sector dialogue and policy coherence for SME development as well as identifying best practices in providing appropriate support measures to SMEs.

UNCTAD also assists developing countries to attract investors through the provision of reliable, transparent and comparable financial information at the corporate level (*see pages 138-139, above*). Its **Intergovernmental Working Group of Experts on International Standards of Accounting and Reporting** reviews trends in international accounting and monitors emerging issues such as environmental accounting and accounting for SMEs. Examples of its technical cooperation include entrepreneurship training (*see page 142, below*), and projects to strengthen women entrepreneurs, promote networking among Asian and African entrepreneurs, restructure the Gambian business development agency, rebuild the business sector in Somalia, and retrain 500 auditors in Azerbaijan.

UNCTAD's technical cooperation activities involve over 300 projects in more than 100 countries, for which it provides about $24 million annually. Some interregional projects include:

- The *Automated System for Customs Data*, using state-of-the-art technology, helps Governments modernize customs procedures and management. Used by more than 50 countries, the system is fast becoming the internationally accepted standard for customs automation;
- The *Advance Cargo Information System* helps African countries to develop their transport sector, using computer technology to track cargo along land and sea routes;
- The *EMPRETEC Programme* promotes small and medium-sized enterprise training and development. An information network provides entrepreneurs with access to business databases;
- The *Global Trade Point Programme*, which connects traders throughout the world: small business owners in developing countries, otherwise unable to find trading partners abroad, use the Trade Points as gateways to the global market. The Trade Point matches their needs with those of other traders and facilitates their transactions. Trade Points are interconnected in a worldwide electronic network which facilitates communications across borders, provides easy access to international databases, and opens doors to electronic trade — which is expected soon to be a $100 billion business. Under this programme, some 114 countries have set up trade facilitation centres to reduce trade transaction costs and provide small and medium-size enterprises with better access to trade-related information, services and global networks.

(For UNCTAD's work in the area of science and technology, see page 155, below.)

The **International Trade Centre UNCTAD/WTO (ITC)** is the focal point in the United Nations system for technical cooperation with developing countries in trade promotion (*see also Part One, page 50*). It works with developing countries and countries in transition to set up trade promotion programmes to expand their exports and improve their import operations.

ITC's field of specialization covers six areas:

- Product and market development;
- Development of trade support services;

- Trade information;
- Human resource development;
- International purchasing and supply management;
- Needs assessment and programme design for trade promotion.

Technical cooperation projects in trade promotion are carried out by ITC specialists working in close liaison with local trade officials. National projects often take the form of a broad-based package of services to expand country exports and improve import operations.

Agricultural development

The majority of people on the planet continue to live in rural areas. In recent decades, the quality of rural life has deteriorated and, in the rush to industrialization, insufficient investment has been made in the agricultural sector. The United Nations has sought to address this imbalance in a variety of ways.

The **Food and Agriculture Organization of the United Nations (FAO)** is the lead agency for agriculture, forestry, fisheries and rural development (*see also Part One, page 52, and page 162 below*). It gives practical help to developing countries through a wide range of technical assistance projects. A specific priority is encouraging sustainable agriculture and rural development, a long-term strategy for increasing food production and food security while conserving and managing natural resources.

In promoting sustainable agricultural development, FAO gives practical help to developing countries through a wide range of technical assistance projects. FAO encourages an integrated approach, with environmental, social and economic considerations included in the formulation of development projects. In some areas, for example, particular combinations of crops can improve agricultural productivity, provide a source of fuelwood for local villagers, improve soil fertility and reduce the impact of erosion.

On average, FAO has some 1,800 field projects operating at any one time. They range from integrated land-management projects to policy and planning advice to Governments in areas as diverse as forestry programmes and marketing strategies. FAO usually takes one of three roles: implementing its own programme; executing a programme on behalf of other agencies and donors; or providing advice and management assistance to national projects. FAO's **Investment Centre** assists developing countries in formulating investment projects in agricultural and rural development. Each year, it assists investment projects worth over $2 billion.

Protecting consumers

FAO looks after consumers: for instance, together with the World Health Organization, it establishes helpful standards for foodstuffs. The FAO/WHO **Codex Alimentarius** *(Food Code)* **Commission** was the first to recommend at the international level that an expiry date be indicated on food products. It also sets norms with regard to additives and limits for residues of pesticides; for some pesticides, the Commission does not accept any trace at all. FAO also defines the criteria to determine what is a "low-fat" product, which is a product with less than 3 per cent fat content.

To fight against the spread of the so-called "mad cow" disease, FAO is drafting a code of conduct to regulate the contents of cattle feed.

FAO is active in land and water development, plant and animal production, forestry, fisheries, economic and social policy, investment, nutrition, food standards, and commodities and trade. For instance:

- When 2 million Rwandan refugees returned to their farms in 1996, FAO helped assess the inputs — such as seeds, hoes, pesticides and fertilizers — needed to restore agricultural activity. It provided expertise and helped mobilize the donor community, raising pledges of around $6.8 million;
- Using integrated pest management techniques promoted by FAO, Asian rice farmers have increased yields and reduced the use of pesticides, helping protect the environment and food quality while saving Governments more than $150 million per year in pesticide subsidies;
- FAO promotes aquaculture because of its great potential as a source of food and income. Aquaculture's contribution to world fishery production tripled between 1984 and 1995, from less than 7 million tonnes to 21.3 million tonnes;
- FAO promotes sustainable water management techniques such as water harvesting and the use of simple pumps. Results from the Sahel region of Africa show that rain harvested from one hectare to irrigate another can triple or even quadruple production.

FAO applies an extensive network of monitoring systems and satellite surveillance to supporting food security. The most important is the **Global Information and Early Warning System**, which monitors current and prospective food supply and demand situations, especially in vulnerable developing countries. It also provides timely predictions on such areas as production, consumption, stocks, imports and exports, emergency food requirements, donor commitments, and shipments (*see also Chapter 5, page 252*).

The **International Fund for Agricultural Development (IFAD)** finances agricultural development projects that alleviate rural poverty and improve nutrition in the developing world (*see also Part One, page 61, and page 163 below*). Unlike the World Bank and the IMF, which have a broad range of objectives, IFAD has a single mandate: to combat hunger and rural poverty in developing countries. In fulfilling its mandate, IFAD provides direct funding and mobilizes resources for programmes specifically designed to promote the economic advancement of the rural poor, mainly by improving the productivity of farm activities.

IFAD's beneficiaries are the poorest of the world's people: small farmers, the rural landless, nomadic pastoralists, artisanal fisherfolk, indigenous people and — across all groups — poor rural women.

The bulk of IFAD's resources are made available to poor countries on highly concessional terms, repayable over 40 years, including a grace period of 10 years, and a 0.75 per cent service charge per annum.

Since its establishment in 1977, IFAD has financed 489 projects in 111 countries, to which it has committed $5.67 billion in grants and loans. Recipient countries have contributed $6.41 billion, and donors have provided $5.44 billion in cofinancing. These projects have helped 30 million poor rural households, equivalent to some 200 million people.

Industrial development

The United Nations system's lead organization for industrial development, the **United Nations Industrial Development Organization (UNIDO)** promotes industrial development in developing countries and fosters industrial cooperation (*see also Part One, page 62*). The ultimate aim is to create a better life for people by laying the industrial foundations for long-term prosperity and economic strength.

Acting as a global forum for industrial development, UNIDO brings together representatives of government, industry, and the public and private sectors from developed and developing countries, as well as from countries with economies in transition. UNIDO is also a service organization, putting into practice through its technical cooperation programmes the principles developed at the global level.

UNIDO has two main areas of activity:

- *Strengthening of industrial capacities*, through the promotion of industrial investment and technology, and through the provision of advice on industrial policy, institutional capacity-building, quality standardization and metrology, industrial statistics, and industrial information through networking, including information on the transfer of technology;

- *Cleaner and sustainable industrial development*, through support programmes on environmentally sustainable industrial development strategies and technologies, including transfer of environmental technologies; and through development of norms and standards relating to environmentally sustainable industrial development strategies and technologies, and the application of international environmental treaties.

While maintaining its universal character and vocation, UNIDO concentrates its activities on:

- Services to the least developed countries, particularly in Africa;
- Services in support of agro-based industries and their integration into national industry; and
- Services in support of small- and medium-scale enterprises and their integration into national industry.

UNIDO's **Investment Promotion Service** operates through a network of offices in Austria, Bahrain, Belgium, China, France, Greece, India, Italy, Japan, Poland, the Republic of Korea, the Russian Federation and the United Kingdom. These offices establish contacts between prospective business partners in their host countries and other countries.

Labour

Concerned with both the economic and social aspects of development, the **International Labour Organization (ILO)** is one of the specialized agencies that predates the United Nations, established in 1919 by the Treaty of Versailles (*see also Part One, page 51*). Its long and diverse work in the setting and monitoring of labour standards in the workplace has provided the framework of international labour standards and guidelines that have been adopted in national legislation in virtually all countries. ILO is guided by the principle that social stability and integration can be sustained only if they are based on social justice, particularly the right to employment with fair compensation in a healthy workplace. Over the decades, ILO has helped to create such hallmarks as the eight-hour day, maternity protection, child-labour laws, and a whole range of policies that promote safety in the workplace and peaceful industrial relations (*see also Chapter 4, pages 231-232*).

Specifically, ILO engages in:

- The formulation of international policies and programmes to promote basic human rights, improve working and living conditions and enhance employment opportunities;
- The creation of international labour standards — backed by a unique system to supervise their application — to serve as guidelines for national authorities in putting sound labour policies into practice;
- An extensive programme of technical cooperation, formulated and carried out in partnership with beneficiaries, to help countries make these policies effective;
- Training, education, research and information activities to help advance all these efforts.

Employment promotion. ILO has long provided assistance to job creation programmes and such efforts have been made more urgent during the last decade by the steady rise in poverty linked to unemployment and underemployment. ILO provides research, analysis and advice to assist policy makers and tripartite constituents to make the right choices and formulate optimal strategies in the effort to create more and better jobs. It lays main emphasis on:

- Exploring the employment effects of economic policies, with particular attention to new approaches that would enhance productivity and boost living standards;
- Developing labour market policies that enhance the supply of labour across various sectors, while achieving productive efficiency and social equity;
- Attending to the employment, income and social requirements of unprotected and unorganized workers who form the vast majority of the world's workforce;
- Advising in the transition from centrally planned to market economies, particularly on employment, labour markets, human resources, industrial relations and social protection;
- Responding to a host of labour market problems, including migratory pressures, racial and sexual discrimination, and health and safety questions.

Technical cooperation. ILO's technical cooperation focuses on support for democratization, poverty alleviation through employment creation and the protection of workers. In particular, ILO helps countries to develop their legislation and take practical steps towards implementing ILO standards — for instance by developing occupational health and safety departments, social security systems and worker-education programmes. Projects are implemented through close cooperation between recipient countries, donors and ILO, which maintains a network of area and regional offices worldwide. ILO has technical cooperation programmes in some 140 countries and territories; in the last decade, it spent an average of some $130 million annually on technical cooperation projects.

ILO's **International Training Centre**, located in Turin, Italy, carries out training for senior and mid-level managers in private and public enterprises, leaders of workers' and employers' organizations, government officials and policy makers. Over 55,000 people from 172 countries have been trained since the Centre opened in 1965. The Centre doubles as the **United Nations Staff College**, providing training to United Nations managers working in peacekeeping, humanitarian emergencies, human rights and social and economic development.

ILO's **International Institute for Labour Studies**, located in Geneva, promotes the study and public discussion of policy issues of concern to ILO. It works to identify, for future ILO action, the new social and labour issues being generated by global competition, changes in the international organization of production and social exclusion.

Transport and communications

The United Nations is involved in the standard setting, training and technical exchanges that help to make international transport, communications and travel safer, more reliable and more efficient. There are two United Nations specialized agencies that deal with aviation and shipping.

International aviation

International air traffic in 1997 grew by 9 per cent, and international passenger traffic rose by 8 per cent. The number of international passengers carried annually has grown to over 300 million — more than the population of the United States. International passenger traffic is expected to expand by 7 per cent annually over the period 1995-2005, with freight traffic expanding by 7.5 per cent.

The safe and orderly growth of international flight is overseen by the **International Civil Aviation Organization (ICAO)**. ICAO also works to encourage the design and operation of civil aircraft; support the development of airways, airports and air navigation facilities; and meet the need of the public for safe, regular, efficient and economic international air transport (*see also Part One, page 53*).

To meet those objectives, ICAO:

- Has adopted international standards and recommended practices which specify the design and performance of aircraft and much of their equipment;
- Such standards also govern the performance of airline pilots, flight crews, air traffic controllers, and ground and maintenance crews; the carriage of dangerous goods by commercial aircraft; security requirements and procedures at international airports; and the interdiction of illicit drug transportation by air;
- Formulates visual and instrument flight rules, as well as the aeronautical charts used for international navigation; aircraft telecommunications systems, radio frequencies and security procedures are also its responsibility;
- Facilitates the movement of aircraft, passengers, crews, baggage, cargo and mail across borders, by reducing customs, immigration, public health and other formalities.

ICAO meets requests from developing countries for help in establishing or improving air transport systems and training for aviation personnel. It has established regional training centres in several developing countries: these take students of many nationalities, for which host Governments pay a large share of the costs. ICAO technical cooperation experts have gone on missions to nearly 100 countries. Over 100,000 students have attended training schools registered with ICAO.

ICAO is now developing a satellite-based system to meet the future communications, navigation, surveillance/air traffic management (CNS/ATM) needs of civil aviation. The system applies high technology in satellites and computers, data links and deck avionics to cope with expanding operational needs. This integrated global system will produce economies, efficiencies and greater safety and will have an impact on the way air traffic services are currently organized and operated. The system, which has been endorsed by ICAO member States, is now in its implementation phase: this task includes the development of standards, practices and guidance which will be applied well into the twenty-first century.

ICAO cooperates with the International Air Transport Association, the Airports Council International, the International Federation of Airline Pilot Associations and the International Council of Aircraft Owner and Pilot Associations.

International shipping

In 1958, collisions between ships caused the loss of 56,000 tons of merchant shipping, while grounding or striking wrecks resulted in the loss of 115,000 tons. Nearly half of these casualties were caused by navigational error or deficiency. The same year, the **International Maritime Organization (IMO)** was established, issuing the first safety measures in 1959. Four decades later, losses have dropped dramatically, with over 96 per cent of the world's merchant fleets adhering to three key safety conventions developed by IMO.

Thanks to this United Nations specialized agency, measures to improve the safety of international shipping and to prevent marine pollution from ships are in force worldwide. IMO is also involved in legal matters, including liability and compensation issues and the facilitation of international maritime traffic *(for IMO action against marine pollution, see page 207, below; see also Part One, page 60)*.

The adoption of maritime legislation is IMO's best known responsibility. IMO has adopted around 40 conventions and protocols, most of them amended in line with changes taking place in world shipping.

When IMO began operations, its chief concern was to develop international treaties and other legislation concerning safety and marine pollution prevention. This was largely completed by the late 1970s, and the Organization has subsequently concentrated on keeping legislation up to date and ensuring that it is ratified by as many countries as possible. This has been so successful that some conventions now apply to more than 98 per cent of world merchant shipping tonnage.

The main IMO treaties on maritime safety include:

- *International Convention for the Safety of Life at Sea* (1960 and 1974);
- *International Regulations for Preventing Collisions at Sea* (1972);
- *International Convention for Safe Containers* (1972);
- *International Convention for the Safety of Fishing Vessels* (1977);
- *International Convention on Maritime Search and Rescue* (1979).

Other measures introduced by IMO have concerned the safety of containers, bulk cargoes, liquefied gas tankers and other ship types. Special attention has been paid to crew standards, including the adoption in 1978 of a convention on standards of training, certification and watchkeeping.

Safety standards around the world have improved considerably since the late 1970s, when such treaties began to enter into force and the number of ratifications rose to record levels.

IMO works to establish communications systems guaranteeing greater safety at sea. The enormous strides made in communications technology have made it possible for IMO to introduce major improvements in the marine distress system. In the 1970s, a global search and rescue system was initiated. The International Maritime Satellite Organization (Inmarsat), established in the 1970s, has greatly improved the provision of radio and other messages to ships. In 1992, a further advance was made when the Global Maritime Distress and Safety System became operative. When this system is fully in force in 1999, a ship in distress anywhere in the world will be virtually guaranteed assistance, even if its crew does not have time to radio for help, as the message will be transmitted automatically.

A number of IMO conventions address the question of liability and compensation issues — among them the 1971 *Convention relating to Civil Liability in the Field of Marine Carriage of Nuclear Materials*, and the 1976 *Convention on Limitation of Liability for Maritime Claims*.

IMO's technical cooperation programme assists Governments which lack the technical knowledge and resources needed to operate a shipping industry successfully. The emphasis is on training, and perhaps the best example is IMO's **World Maritime University** in Malmö, Sweden. Established in 1983, it provides advanced training for the men and women involved in maritime administration, education and management.

Telecommunications

Telecommunications have become a key to the global delivery of services: banking, tourism, transportation and the information industry all depend on quick and reliable global telecommunications. The sector is being revolutionized by powerful trends, such as globalization, deregulation, restructuring, value-added network services, intelligent networks and regional arrangements. Such developments have transformed telecommunications from its earlier status of public utility to one having greater links with commerce and trade. The global telecommunications market is expected to grow over the coming decade to some $1,000 billion.

Against this background works the **International Telecommunication Union (ITU)**, the world's oldest intergovernmental organization, dating back to 1865. Within ITU, the public and private sectors cooperate for the development of telecommunications and the

Facilitating global telecommunications

ITU is in the forefront of telecommunications development. For instance:

- ITU has helped to develop a new system called "international freephone numbers", through which businesses will be able to use a single number which customers anywhere in the world can dial at no cost to place an order, get product information or obtain after-sale assistance. Having a "freephone number" is the equivalent of opening an office in every country one wants to do business in — at a fraction of the cost.
- ITU has played a major role in the introduction of the third-generation mobile phone system, called IMT-2000. ITU allocated the radio frequency spectrum needed to start operation, and provided the forum to reach a global agreement on the transborder use of the global satellite component of IMT-2000. It is now preparing the necessary standards for IMT-2000, including the details of the integration of the satellite components. IMT-2000 will make it possible to connect, on a global scale, mobile fax, messaging, data and even two-way voice and broadband multimedia, via small, hand-held phone sets, computer-mounted terminals or laptops. The aim is to integrate and seamlessly interconnect the various satellite, terrestrial, fixed and mobile systems currently being deployed for global communications.
- As more and more information is processed and distributed electronically, the work of ITU in developing global standards which facilitate the interconnection of different systems has become increasingly important. ITU adopted in early 1998 a landmark decision on technical specifications of a new type of modem, expected to be widely used for applications such as the Internet and on-line service access. Increased modem transmission speed cuts down the time needed by computers to transfer information, resulting in lower telephone bills. The new modem is expected to foster continued dramatic growth of the Internet.
- Also in the area of the Internet, ITU took an active part in the restructuring of the domain-of-names registration system. The aim is to introduce a self-governing structure that will lead to competition in the lucrative market for registration of generic Internet top-level domain names, with adequate and diverse public review and input. The new system also aims at improving the stability, flexibility and transparency of the future growth of the network.

---

harmonization of national telecommunications policies (*see also Part One, page 58*).

Specifically, ITU:

- Develops standards which foster the interconnection of national communications infrastructures into global networks, allowing the seamless exchange of information — be it data, faxes or phone calls — across the world;

- Works to integrate new technologies into the global telecommunications network, allowing for the development of new applications, such as the Internet, electronic mail and multimedia;
- Adopts international regulations and treaties governing the sharing of the radio frequency spectrum and satellite orbital positions — finite natural resources which are used by a wide range of equipment including television and radio broadcasting, mobile telephones, satellite-based communications systems, aircraft and maritime navigation and safety systems, and wireless computer systems;
- Strives to expand and improve telecommunications in the developing world by providing policy advice, technical assistance, project management and training programmes, and by fostering partnerships between telecommunications administrations, funding agencies and private organizations.

In addition to its 188 member States, ITU is made up of more than 480 sector members, representing scientific and industrial companies, public and private operators and broadcasters, and regional and international organizations.

International postal service

Some 6.2 million postal employees working in over 700,000 post offices all over the world handle across national borders an annual total of more than 400 billion letters, printed matter items and parcels. The United Nations specialized agency regulating this service is the **Universal Postal Union (UPU)**: the postal services of its 189 member countries form the largest physical distribution network in the world (*see also Part One, pages 57-58*).

UPU forms a single postal territory of countries for the reciprocal exchange of letter-post items. The primary vehicle of cooperation between national postal services, UPU works to secure the organization and improvement of international postal services, to provide postal customers in every country with harmonized and simplified procedures for their international mail, and to make available a universal network of up-to-date products and services. Every member State agrees to transmit the mail of all other members by the best means used for its own mail.

UPU sets the indicative rates, the maximum and minimum weight and size limits, and the conditions of acceptance of letter-post items — which include priority and non-priority items, letters, aerogrammes, postcards, printed matter and small packets. It also prescribes the methods for calculating and collecting transit charges (for letter-post items passing through one or more countries) and terminal dues (for imbalance of mails). It establishes regulations for registered and air mail, and for items requiring special precautions, such as infectious and radioactive substances.

Thanks to UPU, new products and services are integrated into the international postal network. In this way, such services as registered letters, postal money orders, international reply coupons, small packets, postal parcels and expedited mail services have been made available to the great majority of the world's citizens.

UPU provides technical assistance through multi-year integrated projects aimed at optimizing national postal services. It also conducts short projects which may include study cycles, training fellowships, and the service of development consultants who carry out on-the-spot studies concerning training, management or postal operations. UPU has also made international financial institutions increasingly aware of the need for investment in the postal sector.

Around the world, postal services are making a determined effort to revitalize the postal business. As part of a communications market that is experiencing explosive growth, they have to adapt to a rapidly changing environment. UPU is playing a leadership role in promoting this revitalization.

Intellectual property

Intellectual property has become a central issue in international trade relations. Over 3.7 million patents, 11 million registrations of trademarks and 1.3 million registrations of industrial design are in force around the world. Each year, around 1 million books and 5,000 feature films are produced, and 3 billion copies of disks and tapes are sold.

A United Nations specialized agency, the **World Intellectual Property Organization (WIPO)**, is responsible for promoting the protection of intellectual property all over the world through cooperation among States, and for administering various international treaties dealing with the legal and administrative aspects of intellectual property (*see also Part One, pages 60-61*).

Intellectual property comprises two main branches: industrial property, which chiefly means inventions, trademarks, industrial designs, and appellations of origin; and copyright, which chiefly means literary, musical, artistic, photographic and audiovisual works.

To promote the protection of intellectual property throughout the world, WIPO encourages the conclusion of new international treaties and the modernization of national legislation, promotes administrative cooperation among countries, gives technical assistance to developing countries, and maintains services for making it easier to obtain international protection of inventions, marks and industrial designs.

WIPO administers 19 "Unions" or treaties, covering crucial aspects of intellectual property, dating back to the 1880s. Two key treaties are the *Paris Convention for the Protection of Industrial Property* (1883) and the *Berne Convention for the Protection of Literary and Artistic Works* (1886).

A substantial part of WIPO's activities and resources is devoted to development cooperation. WIPO offers to developing countries its sophisticated services with respect to international patent applications, trademark registration and deposits of industrial designs. It encourages developing countries to make full use of intellectual property for fostering domestic creative activity, for facilitating the acquisition of foreign technology and the use of literary and artistic works of foreign origin, and for organizing easier access to the scientific and technological information contained in millions of patent documents.

WIPO's cooperation consists mainly of advice, training and the furnishing of documents and equipment. The advice is given by WIPO staff and consultants, or through international meetings organized by WIPO. Training involves courses, seminars and workshops as well as individual scholarships and fellowships.

Science and technology for development

Since the 1960s, the United Nations has been promoting the application of science and technology for the development of its Member States. The **Commission on Science and Technology for Development (CSTD)**, a functional commission of ECOSOC, is mandated to promote the science and technological development of developing countries and at the same time to coordinate the activities of the United Nations system in this area. Made up of 53 States and meeting every two years, the CSTD selects different themes for its inter-sessional work and its deliberations. Since 1993, the themes covered have included: technology for small-scale activities; gender implications of science and technology; science technology and integrated land management (in cooperation with the Commission on Sustainable Development); the contribution of new and emerging technologies to industrialization; and information and communication technologies. In the next two years, the CSTD will cover issues such as science and technology partnerships, in particular the energy and biotechnology sectors; biotechnology and food production; and the development of a common vision for the future contribution of science and technology to development.

In addition to providing substantive and secretariat support to the Commission, UNCTAD promotes policies favouring national technological capacity-building, innovation and investment and technology flows to developing countries through its work on: country reviews on science, technology, innovation and investment policies; research and analysis on national innovation systems, on the developmental impact of new technologies such as biotechnology, information and communication technologies and on environmentally sound technologies; and the provision of technical assistance, including in the area of information technologies. It also promotes technological-capacity building at the enterprise level through cooperative arrangements among firms such as partnerships and networking.

UNCTAD encourages a coherent approach to trade, investment, science, technology and innovation policies through the exchange of experiences among countries in intergovernmental discussions, seminars, technical cooperation or training courses. FAO, IAEA, ILO, UNDP, UNIDO and WMO also address scientific and technological issues within their specific mandates. Science for development is also an important element in UNESCO's work (*see page 191, below*).

Social development

Inextricably linked to economic development, social development has been a cornerstone of the work of the United Nations from its inception. Over the decades, the United Nations has emphasized the social aspects of development to ensure that the aim of better lives for all people remains the central target of overall development efforts.

In its early years, the United Nations organized ground-breaking research and data gathering in the areas of demographics, health and education, which witnessed the compilation, often for the first time, of reliable data on social indicators on a global scale. It also catalogued and undertook efforts to protect the cultural heritage, from architectural monuments to languages, reflecting concern for those societies particularly vulnerable to the rapid processes of change.

The Organization has been in the forefront of supporting government efforts to extend social services relating to health, education, family planning and housing and sanitation to all people. In addition to developing models for social programmes, it has helped to integrate economic and social aspects of development. The United Nations sees poverty — particularly extreme poverty — as the factor underlying most of our social problems, including malnutrition, illiteracy, inadequate housing or ethnic strife. Its evolving policies and programmes have always underscored the understanding that the multifaceted

Recent major world conferences

World Conference on Education for All, 5-9 March 1990, Jomtien (Thailand)

Second UN Conference on the Least Developed Countries, 3-14 September 1990, Paris

World Summit for Children, 29-30 September 1990, New York

Eighth UN Conference on Trade and Development, 8-25 February 1992, Cartagena (Colombia)

UN Conference on Environment and Development (UNCED), 3-14 June 1992, Rio de Janeiro

World Conference on Human Rights, 14-25 June 1993, Vienna

Global Conference on the Sustainable Development of Small Island Developing States, 25 April-6 May 1994, Bridgetown (Barbados)

World Conference on Natural Disaster Reduction, 23-27 May 1994, Yokohama (Japan)

International Conference on Population and Development, 5-13 September 1994, Cairo

World Summit for Social Development, 6-12 March 1995, Copenhagen

Ninth UN Congress on the Prevention of Crime and the Treatment of Offenders, 29 April-8 May 1995, Cairo

Fourth World Conference on Women: Action for Equality, Development and Peace, 4-15 September 1995, Beijing

Ninth UN Conference on Trade and Development, 27 April-11 May 1996, Midrand (South Africa)

Second UN Conference on Human Settlements (Habitat II), 3-14 June 1996, Istanbul (Turkey)

World Food Summit, 13-17 November 1996, Rome

Progress for each of the major conferences on development issues is reviewed at five-year intervals. Special sessions of the General Assembly will assess implementation of the action plans of the Conferences on Population and Development (1999), Small Island Developing States (1999), Women (2000) and Human Settlements (2001), as well as of the World Summits for Social Development (2000) and for Children (2001).

---

elements of development — social, economic, environmental and cultural — are interconnected, and cannot be pursued in isolation.

The Organization's work in the social area has become ever more closely associated with a "people-centred" approach that places individuals, families and communities at the centre of development strategies. In recent years, the Organization has placed new emphasis on social development, in part out of concern that economic and political problems have dominated the international agenda: sometimes at the expense of social issues, among them health, education and population; or of social groups such as women, children, minorities, youth and the elderly.

World Summit for Social Development

Concerned by the serious social problems experienced by virtually all countries in the world, the General Assembly convened a Summit for Social Development (Copenhagen, Denmark, 1995) at which heads of State and political leaders from 117 countries pledged themselves to confront the "profound social problems" facing the world's disadvantaged. The "Social Summit" addressed core issues common to all countries:

- Promoting social integration, particularly of the disadvantaged and marginalized groups;
- Alleviating and reducing poverty; and
- Expanding employment.

The Summit's Declaration and Programme of Action recommended measures to eliminate inequalities — within and among countries — and to foster social development policies and programmes. Specifically, world leaders committed themselves to:

- Support full employment as a basic policy goal;
- Promote social integration based on the protection of human rights;
- Achieve equality and equity between women and men;
- Accelerate the development of Africa and the least developed countries;
- Ensure that "structural adjustment" programmes (economic and fiscal reforms designed to stabilize and streamline national economies) include social development goals;
- Increase the resources allocated to social development;
- Create an environment enabling people to achieve social development;
- Attain universal access to education and primary health care;
- Strengthen cooperation for social development through the United Nations and other multilateral institutions.

Governments committed themselves to the goal of eradicating poverty. They agreed to take measures ensuring that poor people have access to productive resources such as credit, land, education and training. They also pledged to strengthen policies geared to combating poverty, meeting the basic needs of all people and reducing inequality.

Coordination and support in implementing the outcome of the Summit rests with the United Nations Department of Economic and Social Affairs. The Department also carries out technical cooperation activities strengthening the capacity of countries to follow up on the decisions taken at the Summit.

A special session of the General Assembly in 2000 will review and appraise implementation of the Summit, and consider further actions and initiatives to extend the practical implications of the agreements reached in Copenhagen.

Reflecting this concern, most of the global conferences convened by the United Nations over the past decade have focused on the problems of social development in order to compensate for this shortcoming (*see box on page 157, above*). In a related effort to encourage allocation of increasingly scarce national resources to the social sector, the 1995 World Summit for Social Development urged interested countries to adopt *the 20/20 formula* — an initiative which calls on Governments of developing countries to set aside at least 20 per cent of their budgets for basic social services, and, correspondingly, that donor countries earmark 20 per cent of their official development assistance for such services.

The diverse issues of social development, the United Nations argues, are challenges for developing and developed countries alike. To differing degrees, all societies are confronted by the problems of unemployment, social fragmentation and persistent poverty. And a growing number of social problems — from forced migration to drug abuse, organized crime and the spread of diseases — can be successfully addressed only through concerted international action.

The United Nations addresses the issues of social development through the **General Assembly** and the **Economic and Social Council (ECOSOC)**, where system-wide policy and priorities are set and programmes endorsed. One of the General Assembly's six main committees, the **Social, Humanitarian and Cultural Committee**, takes up those agenda items designated to the social sector.

Under ECOSOC, the main intergovernmental body dealing with social concerns is the **Commission for Social Development.** Made up of 46 Member States, the Commission advises ECOSOC and Governments on social policies and on the social aspects of development. Meeting annually, it focuses on policies designed to promote social progress, setting goals, programme priorities and research in areas affecting social and economic development. The Commission was assigned primary responsibility within the United Nations for monitoring the follow-up to the World Summit for Social Development.

Within the Secretariat, the **Department of Economic and Social Affairs**, newly consolidated through the organizational reforms adopted during 1997, services these bodies, providing research, analysis and expert guidance as requested. System-wide there are many specialized agencies, funds, offices and programmes which address different aspects of social development, many of which are referred to below.

Reducing poverty

Governments, often in collaboration with the United Nations system, have made significant progress in reducing poverty worldwide. In the past 30 years, developing countries as a whole have halved child death

Trends in Poverty in Developing Countries

(poverty line at $1 a day per person, 1985 PPP$)

Region or country group	People below the poverty line (%)		Share of all the poor people (%)		Number of poor people (millions)
	1987	1993	1987	1993	1993
Arab States	5	4	1	1	11
East Asia and South-East Asia and the Pacific	30	26	38	34	446
East Asia and South-East Asia and the Pacific (exc. China)	23	14	10	7	94
Latin America and the Caribbean[a]	22	24	7	9	110
South Asia	45	43	39	39	515
Sub-Saharan Africa	38	39	15	17	219
Developing countries	34	32	100	100	1,301

a. Poverty line at $2 a day.
Source: Human Development Report 1997

rates, reduced malnutrition by one third and raised school enrolment by one fourth.

Despite these gains, about 1.3 billion people continue to live on less than $1 a day — one clear indicator of extreme poverty; and more than 800 million people are chronically hungry. More than 100 million people live in poverty in the richer countries of North America, Asia and Europe, where 37 million are jobless. And most of the world's poor are women and children. In at least 30 countries, the United Nations calculates that overall levels of human development have declined since 1970, and in some regions poverty is increasing. In the republics of the former Soviet Union, for example, the number of people living below the poverty line has surged in less than 10 years from 4 million to 120 million.

To highlight these unacceptable trends, the General Assembly proclaimed 1997-2006 as the **International Decade for the Eradication of Poverty**. The objective is to eradicate absolute poverty, and reduce overall global poverty through decisive national action and international cooperation in implementing the outcome of the United

Nations global conferences. The United Nations system continues to make poverty reduction a priority.

A key player is the **United Nations Development Programme (UNDP)**, which assists people in 174 countries and territories to implement policies and programmes that focus on poverty eradication, environmental regeneration, job creation and the advancement of women. UNDP's mission is to help countries build their own capacity to achieve "sustainable human development", giving priority to eliminating poverty and building equity (*see also pages 131-134, above*). UNDP allocates 90 per cent of its core resources to the 66 low-income countries that are home to 90 per cent of the world's extremely poor.

The heart of UNDP's anti-poverty work, which receives nearly 40 per cent of core resources, lies in empowering the poor. UNDP supports their access to productive assets such as credit, skills, job opportunities, and links to national and international markets.

The international financial institutions of the United Nations system play a central role in funding numerous programmes that focus on the social aspects of poverty eradication. In 1996, 32 per cent of **World Bank** lending was directly targeted to the poor. The World Bank seeks to increase poor people's employment and earning opportunities by investing in human resource development — health, education and family planning. The world's largest lender for human-resources development, its loans for education, population, health and nutrition have totalled more than $34 billion. It also helps borrowing countries in designing social safety nets for the poorest, most vulnerable groups.

As a development institution focused on poverty reduction, the Bank advocates strategies that make use of the most abundant asset of the poor — labour. It also favours investing in people by providing basic social services to the poor, from building roads to educating girls. Its **Social Protection Sector** has been developing ways to better identify vulnerable individuals and groups for whom a disruptive "shock" — such as natural disasters, changes in social policy, or international problems — would aggravate poverty. To address such vulnerability, the Bank supports the development of drought-resistant crops, for example, and measures that make social-security systems more resilient.

The Bank's **International Development Association (IDA)** is the largest source of donor funds for basic social services in the poorest countries. Funds from IDA, for example, have ensured that African pupils have received over 6 million textbooks, girls' enrolment in rural schools in Bangladesh has risen by one third, and 230,000 poor people in Bolivia have received vocational training. IDA lends on average about $5 to $6 billion a year for development projects. Since 1960, IDA has provided over $97 billion in credit to some 90 countries, making basic investments in farming, health, clean water and education.

Fighting hunger

Food production has increased at an unprecedented rate over the past 50 years, outpacing the doubling of world population over the same period. Since the early 1960s, the proportion of hungry people in the developing world has been reduced from more than 50 per cent to 20 per cent. But that 20 per cent represents more than 800 million people — more than the whole population of Europe. The United Nations estimates that world food production will have to increase by more than 75 per cent over the next 30 years to ensure adequate food supplies for a world population expected to reach 8.3 billion by the year 2025. The United Nations has made it clear that hunger, and famine in particular, result not so much from the scarcity of food as from the poverty of the affected populations.

While economic development is seen to be the most effective way to reduce hunger, most of the United Nations bodies fighting hunger have important social programmes to advance food security for the poorer sectors of the population, particularly those in rural areas. Since its establishment, the **Food and Agriculture Organization of the United Nations (FAO)** has been working to alleviate poverty and hunger by promoting agricultural development, improved nutrition

Promoting food security

In 1996, FAO hosted the **World Food Summit** in Rome, which was attended by 186 countries. The Summit approved a Declaration and Plan of Action on World Food Security, which outline ways to achieve universal food security and aim to halve hunger by 2015. The Plan of Action contains seven commitments on the part of Governments which are expected to lead to significant reductions in chronic hunger:

- Assuring the general conditions for economic and social progress conducive to food security;
- Eradicating poverty and ensuring access to adequate food;
- Ensuring sustainable increases in food production;
- Taking steps to ensure that trade contributes to food security;
- Being prepared to prevent and to respond to food emergencies;
- Ensuring optimal investment in human resources, sustainable production capacity and rural development;
- Cooperating in the implementation and monitoring of the Plan of Action.

and the pursuit of food security — the access of all people at all times to the food they need for an active and healthy life. FAO's **Committee on World Food Security** is responsible for monitoring, evaluating and consulting on the international food security situation. It analyses food needs, assesses availability and monitors and disseminates information on stock levels. FAO, through its **Global Information and Early Warning System**, also oversees an extensive network of monitoring systems and satellite surveillance that keep track of current and prospective food supply/demand needs.

FAO's *Special Programme for Food Security* targets the 86 countries that are home to the vast majority of the world's chronically hungry people. The Programme seeks to increase food production and to make conditions better for farming families. During a pilot phase, farmers choose and demonstrate selected technologies to increase food production. Successful strategies are then made widely available during an expansion phase. This is complemented by an emergency prevention system for animal and plant pests and diseases which offers farmers preventive protection for their farm products.

The **International Fund for Agricultural Development (IFAD)** provides development funding to combat rural poverty and hunger in the poorest regions of the world. To ensure that development aid actually reaches those who need it most, IFAD involves the rural poor, both men and women, in their own development. This means identifying their needs, building on their own knowledge and skills, and promoting successful traditional livelihoods and resource management.

The social dimensions of IFAD's work include the organization and mobilization of farming and fishing associations in poor communities. Using loans to finance basic inputs such as seeds, fertilizers, tools and nets to buy food-processing equipment or to start up microenterprises, millions of rural women and men have been able to organize beyond the traditional levels of subsistence production and lift their families and communities out of poverty. Over the past two decades, 489 IFAD projects have created an estimated 3.6 million jobs in 111 countries. IFAD has assisted more than 200 million rural poor, once marginalized, to participate in their national economies. Once organized, the rural poor are excellent repayers, with a loan-repayment rate of 97 per cent, a fact that has greatly encouraged the establishment of small-loan programmes around the world.

The **World Food Programme (WFP)** is the largest food-aid organization in the world, providing food aid to more than 53 million people worldwide in 1997. WFP buys more goods and services from developing countries, in an effort to reinforce their economies, than any other United Nations agency. WFP has regularly delivered two thirds of the world's emergency food assistance, saving millions of lives. Over the past three decades, WFP has invested about $14 billion in development and relief assistance to more than 90 countries (*see also Chapter 5, pages 251-252 amd Part One, pages 41-42*).

Where people are chronically hungry, WFP provides "food-for-work" assistance, helping them to become self-reliant. It uses innovative social development projects to help overcome the obstacles of hunger and poverty. It provides food in ways that prepare people to help themselves and to reduce reliance on international food assistance. WFP's "food-for-work" projects pay workers with food to build roads and ports in Ghana, repair dykes in Viet Nam, terrace hillsides in China and replant forests in Ethiopia.

"Food-for-growth" projects in countries like Haiti, Angola and Mozambique provide an incentive to children to attend schools. Nutritional lunches also enhance the children's ability to participate in their schooling. For instance, in Pakistan WFP promotes female literacy by distributing rations of vegetable oil to parents who send their daughters to school.

United Nations programmes have proved over and over again that hunger and poverty can be overcome with socially relevant and carefully planned programmes that address the longer-term needs of the affected populations. Many countries that once received food aid are now among the largest markets for food exports — countries like South Korea, Mexico and China. Even Ethiopia, the scene in the 1970s and 1980s of some of the worst famines the world has ever seen, has reported food surpluses in recent years.

Health

In most parts of the world, people are living longer, infant mortality is decreasing and illnesses are kept in check as more people have access to basic health services, immunization, clean water and sanitation. The United Nations has been deeply involved in many of these advances, particularly in developing countries, including supporting health services, fighting infectious diseases, delivering essential drugs, making cities healthier and providing health assistance in emergencies.

Infectious diseases, however, remain the main cause of death in the world, and new diseases, such as Ebola and HIV/AIDS, continue to emerge with alarming virulence. Globalization of trade and travel has increased the chances for the spread of infections. Diseases that seemed under control, such as diphtheria and tuberculosis, are making a deadly comeback among extremely poor populations. These persist-

Victory over river blindness

When the United Nations first organized the **Onchocerciasis Control Programme** (OCP) in 1974, millions of the inhabitants of 11 West African countries had little protection from the dreaded blackfly, whose bite transmits the parasitic worms that cause a disease also known as river blindness. Even today, some 18 million people who live outside the OCP control area continue to be infected, demonstrating symptoms including skin rashes and lesions, serious visual impairment and blindness.

Over the course of two decades, OCP focused on attacking the reproductive system of the blackfly by destroying its larvae through aerial spraying of breeding sites in fast-flowing rivers. By the early 1990s, the OCP campaign, sponsored by the World Bank, UNDP, FAO and WHO, and supported by a coalition of 22 donor countries and agencies, entered its final stage of spraying and monitoring to ensure the lasting elimination of the parasites, which can live for 14 years in an infected person. In recent years, the introduction of the drug *ivermectin*, which kills the microscopic parasites in the body, has lead to the virtual elimination of the disease in West Africa and progress towards its eradication throughout the entire continent.

Millions of people born since 1974 are now free from risk of contracting the disease. Millions more who had once been infected have recovered with no traces of the parasite left. And over 25 million hectares of fertile land near rivers have been made safe for resettlement and cultivation. By the time OCP is scheduled to be phased out in the year 2002, the estimated total cost for the programme will be $550 million, or less than $1 per year for each protected person. Based on the success of this initial programme, it is being extended to 19 additional endemic countries in Africa.

ent problems can be addressed effectively only through a coordinated, global response.

For decades, the United Nations system has been in the forefront of the fight against disease through the creation of policies and systems that address the social dimensions of health problems. UNICEF focuses on child and maternal health and the United Nations Population Fund focuses on reproductive health and family planning. The specialized agency coordinating global action against disease is the **World Health Organization (WHO)** (*see also Part One, pages 53-54*). WHO has set ambitious goals for achieving health for all, achieving reproductive health, building partnerships for health and promoting healthy lifestyles and environments.

WHO and its member countries aim at the attainment of the highest possible level of health — a goal WHO views as "one of the fundamental rights of every human being". The World Health Assembly,

The UN combats HIV/AIDS

HIV/AIDS has become a health disaster of global proportions. Some 23 million people are living with HIV/AIDS, while the number of worldwide AIDS-related deaths has reached 1.5 million a year. The epidemic is still expanding at the rate of about 8,500 new infections per day.

To tackle this global threat, six United Nations agencies have pooled their resources in the **Joint United Nations Programme on HIV/AIDS (UNAIDS)** — an effort aimed at preventing transmission, providing care and support, reducing vulnerability of individuals and communities, and alleviating the impact of the disease. In a large number of countries, the United Nations provides support to address issues of HIV/AIDS prevention, care and rights, with the focus on school-based communication, children at risk and youth health intervention. Specific UNICEF-supported programmes in sub-Saharan Africa, Asia and Latin America assist children who have lost one or both parents to AIDS. In addition to its extensive work in the field, UNFPA prepares an annual publication called *AIDS Update*, which provides a country-by-country summary of the Fund's HIV-prevention activities as well as an overall analysis of its country-level support for HIV prevention. The fund provides over $20 million for HIV/AIDS-prevention activities in over 125 countries each year.

Among other things, the Programme seeks to increase commitment against AIDS among political leaders, to promote world research on AIDS, and to foster an environment supportive of people affected by HIV/AIDS. The participating agencies are UNICEF, UNDP, UNFPA, UNESCO, WHO and the World Bank.

WHO's governing body comprised of all member States, has promoted this goal through the campaign "Health for All", committing Governments and WHO to the attainment of levels of well-being that ensures that all people will have the opportunity to lead socially and economically productive lives.

WHO was the driving force behind two historic achievements. The first was the global eradication of smallpox in 1980, achieved after a 10-year campaign. The second was the elimination of poliomyelitis from the Americas in 1994 — the first step towards the goal of eradicating the disease worldwide by the end of 2000.

Between 1980 and 1990 a joint UNICEF-WHO effort raised global immunization coverage against six killer diseases — polio, tetanus, measles, whooping cough, diphtheria and tuberculosis — from 5 to 80 per cent, saving the lives of 3 million children a year.

WHO possesses the capacity to combat new and re-emerging diseases, and can mobilize and dispatch teams on site within 24 hours of notification of an outbreak to initiate epidemic control measures. This was the case with the outbreak of the deadly Ebola fever in Central Africa in 1995: WHO was instrumental in setting up the international Scientific and Technical Committee that successfully controlled the epidemic. WHO uses field technology and public health training programmes to support country surveillance and disease control, and is developing a network of public health laboratories to strengthen international collaboration in detecting and controlling outbreaks. A WHO information system supports global surveillance of drug-resistant diseases (see also Chapter 5, pages 252-253).

WHO is active in all major areas of health. For instance, a UNDP/World Bank/WHO programme on tropical diseases combats six groups of widespread tropical diseases, such as malaria and leprosy. The programme aims to devise new control products and methods and to improve existing ones. As a result, more than 30 disease control products were in use in 1997, and about 30 others were in the development or trial stage.

Standard setting. WHO also establishes international standards on biological, pharmaceutical and similar substances. It has developed the concept of "essential drugs and vaccines" as a basic component of primary health care, and works with countries to ensure the equitable supply of safe and effective drugs at the lowest possible cost and with the most effective use. To this end, it has developed a "Model List" of some 306 drugs and vaccines considered essential to help prevent or treat over 80 per cent of all health problems. More than 140 countries have adapted the list to their own requirements. WHO also helps to design national drug policies; over 80 countries have formulated comprehensive drug policies covering drug supply, financing, control and use.

Through the international access afforded the United Nations, WHO oversees the global collection of information on communicable diseases, and compiles comparable health and disease statistics, sets international standards for safe food, as well as for biological and pharmaceutical products. It also provides unmatched evaluation of the cancer-producing risks of pollutants, and has put into place the universally accepted guidance for global control of HIV/AIDS.

Child health

In the area of child health, the **United Nations Children's Fund (UNICEF)** works to prevent and treat the main causes of childhood illness and death, such as respiratory infections, diarrhoea, malaria, measles and malnutrition (see also Part One, page 34). Together with WHO, it has promoted an integrated approach to prevent and manage such illnesses.

- Dehydration due to diarrhoeal diseases kills 2.2 million children a year in developing countries. UNICEF works to expand the use of oral rehydration therapy (ORT), a simple, inexpensive antidote to diarrhoeal dehydration that saves the lives of over 1.5 million children every year — 4,500 every day. UNICEF estimates that some form of ORT is used by about three quarters of households in the developing world.

- Exclusive breastfeeding for at least the first six months of a baby's life provides the best nutrition and the best protection against common childhood diseases. In just six years, over 13,000 hospitals in 117 countries have been designated "baby-friendly" because they follow the WHO/UNICEF guidelines on breastfeeding.

- Some 1.1 billion people lack access to safe drinking water, and water-related diseases contribute to nearly 4 million child deaths each year. From 1990 to 1995, programmes assisted by UNICEF and other partners helped almost 800 million people gain access to safe drinking water.

- Guinea worm disease, a debilitating water-borne parasitic disease also known as dracunculiasis, afflicted some 3 million people in Africa and Asia in 1990. In 1995, UNICEF, WHO and other partners announced its virtual eradication: surveillance programmes and low-cost water filters helped reduce the number of cases by over 97 per cent.

- An estimated 585,000 women die every year as a result of pregnancy and childbirth, largely because of inadequate maternal health care. Another 50 million women live with a permanent injury or chronic disabilities due to complications from pregnancy or delivery. UNICEF and its partners support educating communities about safe motherhood and the rights of women, training of midwives, expanding access to obstetric care, family planning and improved health and nutrition.

- Each year 2 million girls in at least 28 countries undergo female genital mutilation. UNICEF advocates legislation banning the practice, which it sees as a violation of the human rights of girls and women and the cause of life-long health hazards. It also advocates social mobilization and community-based interventions aimed to train teachers, volunteers and midwives about the hazards of the practice. Several African countries have taken steps to eliminate the practice; Burkina Faso, Egypt and Ghana have made it a legal offence.

Human settlements

Ours is an urbanizing world. By 2025, the United Nations calculates, over 60 per cent of the world's population will live in cities — up from an estimated 47 per cent in 2000 and 38 per cent in 1975. Yet our housing and urban problems are daunting, with millions of people throughout the world living in housing conditions that are below the minimum standards necessary for healthy families and communities.

Addressing these problems is the **United Nations Centre for Human Settlements (Habitat)**: it serves as the lead agency for the human settlements development activities of the United Nations family, as well as the focal point for the global exchange of information about human settlements conditions and trends (*see also Part One, pages 43-44*). Habitat's programme of policy advice, operational research and technical cooperation focuses on the following priority areas:

Shelter and social services. Most poor people in all regions of the world lack access to adequate shelter and social services. In the developing world, at least 600 million urban dwellers — half of them children — live in housing that is of such poor quality and with such inadequate provision for water, sanitation, drainage and garbage collection that their lives and health are continually at risk. Every year, several million urban dwellers are forcibly evicted from their homes, adding to the growing numbers of homeless, currently estimated at 100 million people.

Habitat promotes policies, strategies and delivery systems for housing and social services that respond to the needs of the poor and other vulnerable groups. It fosters the realization of the human right to housing through the development of equitable shelter policies, through community participation, and by encouraging Governments to remove institutional and regulatory constraints which hinder people's access to land and housing. Specifically:

- The *Community Development Programme* empowers poor communities to improve their living and working conditions and strengthens the capacities of community-based organizations, local authorities and Governments to sustain local development;
- The *Women and Habitat Programme* supports the empowerment of women by fostering gender-awareness and by promoting equal participation of women — especially at decision-making levels — in all aspects of human settlements development.

Urban management. Rapid urbanization, the concentration of populations in large cities, the sprawl of cities into wider geographical

Adequate shelter for all

At the **United Nations Conference on Human Settlements (Habitat II)**, held in Istanbul, Turkey in 1996, world leaders made commitments to better standards of living for their people and to support the right to adequate housing and sustainable human development. They addressed issues and problems relating to human settlements, both rural and urban, into the next century.

The Conference's main themes were "adequate shelter for all" and "sustainable human settlements in an urbanizing world". The event saw a strong participation by civil society: in addition to representatives of 171 Member States, it was attended by over 500 mayors of cities and towns, hundreds of community groups, over 2,100 NGOs, the private sector and academic institutions.

Habitat II developed a Declaration and Global Plan of Action (the "Habitat Agenda") to achieve sustainable human settlements and shelter for all. Governments agreed to address:

- Unsustainable consumption and production patterns, particularly in industrialized countries;
- Unsustainable population changes;
- Homelessness;
- Unemployment;
- Lack of basic infrastructure and services;
- Growing social insecurity and violence;
- Increased vulnerability to disasters.

The General Assembly has designated the Centre for Human Settlements (Habitat) as the focal point within the United Nations for monitoring the implementation of the Agenda, including analysing global trends in urbanization and the impact of urban policies. The "City Summit" took place 20 years after the first United Nations Conference on Human Settlements, held in 1976 in Vancouver, Canada.

---

areas, and the rapid growth of "megacities" — cities with more than 10 million inhabitants — are among the most significant transformations of our era. The development of almost every country will largely depend on how well cities are managed.

Habitat works closely with local authorities and other urban management institutions to put into practice the Habitat Agenda (*see box, above*) at the city level. It seeks to improve urban governance and local leadership mainly through:

- The joint Habitat-UNDP *Urban Management Programme*, which strengthens the capacities of urban management institutions and promotes the development of consultative mechanisms for preparing and carrying out city plans of action aimed at poverty reduction, environmental improvement and participatory govern-ance;

- The *Local Leadership and Management Training Programme*, which helps national institutions to train local government offi-cials and urban managers. Activities include preparing training manuals and management tools, developing assessment needs methodologies and holding seminars on capacity-building.

Environment and infrastructure. Urban development is impor-tant for sustainable development because cities have the ability to support efficiently large numbers of people within a limited space. But without sound planning and management, cities can become sources of serious health, environmental and economic problems brought on by air pollution, water contamination, poor sanitation and disasters. Habitat seeks to improve the environment by assisting Gov-ernments, local authorities and communities to establish local envi-ronmental policies and to plan, operate and maintain infrastructure and services — particularly in the areas of water supply, waste dis-posal, sanitation, transportation and energy. Habitat focuses on promoting environmental management, transfer of environmentally sound infrastructure technologies, disseminating best practices in im-proving the environment, and strengthening capacities of local insti-tutions through:

- The joint Habitat-UNEP *Sustainable Cities Programme*, which supports urban environmental planning and management at city and national levels through capacity-building and networking;

- The *Localizing Agenda 21 Programme*, which translates the hu-man settlements components of *Agenda 21*, the action plan for the environment agreed at the 1992 Earth Summit (*see page 195*), into local action by stimulating joint ventures between local authorities, the private sector and community groups;

- The *Settlements Infrastructure and Environment Programme*, which assists Governments and communities to develop policy options, planning and implementation aids and local capacity in critical areas of infrastructure delivery and management;

- The *Disaster Management Programme*, which assists national and local Governments, as well as communities, to carry out post-disaster reconstruction and rehabilitation, particularly in the areas of housing, infrastructure and resettlement.

Assessment, monitoring and information. Habitat has been assigned the task of assessing and monitoring implementation of the Habitat Agenda *(see box, page 170)*.

Habitat promotes policy change regarding social, economic and environmental problems by raising awareness through targeted information materials, via the Internet and through its two main periodicals: the *Global Report on Human Settlements* (last published in 1996) and the quarterly *Habitat Debate*.

Education

Great strides have been made in education in the past decades: enrolment in primary and secondary schools in developing countries has risen since 1960 from an estimated 270 million children to around 760 million in 1995. But millions of children — more girls than boys — never go to school, and many who start attending are forced to leave because of poverty or other family or social pressures. Despite enormous literacy efforts, the absolute number of illiterate adults increased from 877 million in 1980 to 885 million in 1995 — all but 13 million of whom live in developing countries.

The research carried out by several UN bodies, particularly UNICEF, UNDP, UNFPA and the World Bank has demonstrated repeatedly the close relationship between access to education and improved social indicators. This has a special multiplier effect for women. A woman who is educated, for example, will typically be healthier, have fewer children and have more opportunities to increase household income. Her children, in turn, will experience lower mortality rates, better nutritional intake and better overall health. For this reason, girls and women are the focus of many education programmes systemwide.

Many parts of the United Nations system are involved in the funding and development of a variety of education and training programmes. These range from traditional basic schooling and promotion of lifelong learning to technical training for human resource development in areas such as public administration, agriculture and health services to public awareness campaigns to educate people about HIV/AIDS, drug abuse, human rights, family planning, and many other issues. Both UNHCR and UNRWA, for example, have extensive programmes for the education of refugee children, youths and adults.

The lead organizations in the areas of literacy and schooling are **UNICEF** and the **United Nations Educational, Scientific and Cultural Organization (UNESCO)**: they jointly work with Governments to train teachers and make primary education free and

Education for all

The Universal Declaration of Human Rights asserts that "everyone has a right to education". In 1990, UNDP, UNESCO, UNICEF and the World Bank jointly convened the **World Conference on Education for All** in Jomtien, Thailand, at which delegates from 155 countries, including policy makers and specialists in education, as well as representatives from scores of development agencies and non-governmental organizations (NGOs), adopted the Jomtien Declaration on Education for All and the Framework for Action to Meet Basic Learning Needs. These agreements represent a worldwide consensus on an expanded vision of basic education and a renewed commitment to ensure that the basic learning needs of all children, youth and adults are met effectively in all countries. They highlight the fact that one third of the world's adults still do not have access to the printed knowledge, new skills and technologies that can improve the quality of their lives and help them to shape and adapt to the social, economic and cultural changes that are taking place at an ever-accelerating pace.

The Framework outlines the guidelines for implementing this enormous task, describing concerted action within individual countries, cooperation among groups of countries sharing certain characteristics and concerns, and multilateral and bilateral cooperation in the world community. It calls for universal access to, and completion of, primary education, as well as reduction of the adult illiteracy rate to one half its 1990 level by the year 2000. The United Nations, led by UNESCO, is seen as an essential partner and resource in working with Governments and NGOs to realize these goals.

---

compulsory for every child. As part of its wider mandate for the protection and development of children, UNICEF has pledged to more than double its funding for basic education over the rest of the decade, with special attention to girls' schooling. In 1997, UNICEF devoted 14 per cent of its programme expenditure, or over $100 million, to education and early childhood care and development.

Education is one of UNESCO's four central activities (*see also Part One, page 52, and pages 191-193, below*). Under its programme of promoting lifelong education for all, UNESCO supports and fosters national projects to renovate education systems and develop alternative strategies to make lifelong education accessible to all. The programme also seeks to widen access to basic education and improve its quality, reform higher education systems throughout the world and promote adult and continuing education.

UNESCO's innovative interdisciplinary project, "Educating for a sustainable future", helps member States to improve and reorient their national education and training activities dealing with environment, population and development, including health education and the prevention of drug abuse and AIDS.

Some 4,250 schools in 137 countries are involved in UNESCO's Associated Schools Project, an international network elaborating ways and means for enhancing the role of education in learning to live together in a world community. More than 5,000 UNESCO Clubs in 116 countries, mainly comprising teachers and students, carry out a wide range of educational and cultural activities.

Research and training

Academic work in the form of research and training is carried out by a number of specialized United Nations organizations. This work is aimed at enhancing understanding of the global problems we face, as well as fostering the human resources required for more technical aspects of economic and social development.

The **United Nations University (UNU)** is an international community of scholars engaged in research, postgraduate training and the dissemination of knowledge to further the purposes and principles of the United Nations Charter (*see also Part One, page 41*). The UNU has two basic goals: to strengthen the capacities of institutions of higher learning in developing countries to carry out high-quality research and education; and to make scholarly and policy-relevant contributions to the work of the United Nations.

The UNU comprises networks of its own research and training centres and programmes, which work with associated and cooperating institutions and individual scholars in many parts of the world.

The UNU's academic work addresses specific problems and issues of concern to the United Nations. Currently, its activities are grouped within four programme areas: development, environment, peace and governance, and science and technology. Academic activities are carried out by the Academic Division at the UNU Centre in Tokyo, and through eight research and training centres and programmes located in various parts of the world. These include:

- **UNU World Institute for Development Economics Research (UNU/WIDER)**, Helsinki, Finland (established 1985) concentrates on policy-oriented socio-economic research to solve global problems;
- **UNU Institute for New Technologies (UNU/TECH)**, Maastricht, the Netherlands (1990), examines the social and economic impact of new technologies, particularly in developing countries;
- **UNU International Institute for Software Technology (UNU/IIST)**, Macau (1992), concentrates on advanced joint re-

search and development projects, postgraduate curriculum development, dissemination of public domain software and publications;

- **UNU Institute for Natural Resources in Africa (UNU/INRA)**, Legon, Ghana, with a Mineral Resources Unit in Lusaka, Zambia (1990), develops scientific technological capacities in Africa for managing the continent's resources;
- **UNU Institute of Advanced Studies (UNU/IAS)**, Tokyo, Japan (1995), works on eco-restructuring for sustainable development, megacities and urbanization, and multilateralism and governance;
- **UNU Programme for Biotechnology for Latin America and the Caribbean (UNU/BIOLAC)**, Caracas, Venezuela (1988), develops and promotes biotechnology in the region;
- **UNU International Network on Water, Environment and Health (UNU/INWEH)**, Hamilton, Ontario, Canada (1996), integrates international expertise into a programme of education, training, research and technology transfer on major issues relating to water, environment and health; and
- **UNU International Leadership Academy (UNU/ILA)**, Amman, Jordan (1995), serves as a focal point for the exchange of information and experiences among young potential and future leaders.

The United Nations Research Institute for Social Development (UNRISD) engages in research on the social dimensions of contemporary problems affecting development (*see also Part One, page 48*). Working through an extensive network of national research centres, the Institute collaborates with Governments, development agencies, grass-roots organizations and scholars on the formulation of effective development policies. Its current research themes include business responsibility for sustainable development; community perspectives on urban governance; integrating gender into development; grass-roots initiatives for land reform in developing countries; information technologies and social development; and mass tourism in developing countries, among others.

The **United Nations Institute for Training and Research (UNITAR)** works to enhance the effectiveness of the United Nations in its work in peace and security and development through training and research (*see also Part One, page 47*). Each year, UNITAR designs and organizes some 70 training programmes for about 3,000 participants around the world, particularly from developing countries, for assignments with the United Nations or its specialized agencies and for assignments in their national civil services connected with the work of the United Nations system and institutions operating in related fields.

UNITAR's programmes comprise courses on multilateral diplomacy and international cooperation, offered primarily to diplomats accredited to the Organization. A wide range of training programmes cover the area of social and economic development, with training in environmental management as the fastest-growing sector. Various other programmes are offered, including on international environmental law, peacemaking and preventive diplomacy, and new information and communication technologies.

The **International Research and Training Institute for the Advancement of Women (INSTRAW)** carries out policy research and training activities worldwide to enhance women's role as key agents of development (*see page 180 below*).

Population and development

The rapid growth of the world's population became an urgent concern of the United Nations in the 1960s. World population more than doubled between 1950 and 1990, increasing from 2.5 billion to 5.3 billion; it is currently estimated at 5.8 billion. While the rate of growth is on the decline, absolute increments currently exceed 80 million persons per year; most of these people are born in developing regions. The United Nations estimates there will be between 7.7 billion and 11.1 billion people in 2050, with 9.4 billion the most likely projection, depending in part on the effectiveness of family planning programmes.

Overall population growth has weighed heavily on the earth's resources and environment, often outstripping efforts towards development. The United Nations has addressed the relationship between population and development in many ways, placing special emphasis in recent years on the importance of the advancement of the status of women, which is increasingly seen as key to progress in social and economic development.

Over the decades, the best known work of the United Nations in regard to population issues has been its quantitative and methodological work, particularly its authoritative estimates and projections of population size and change and the preparation of research manuals. But population concerns are reflected in many programmes throughout the system.

The 44-member **Commission on Population and Development** (originally known as the Population Commission) provides guidance to the United Nations population programme. Its tasks include advising ECOSOC; preparing studies on population issues and trends; integrating population and development strategies, policies and programmes; and providing population assistance. It has primary responsibility for reviewing the implementation of the Programme of Action of the International Conference on Population and Development (*see box on next page*).

The United Nations **Population Division** within the Department of Economic and Social Affairs (DESA) serves as the secretariat of the Commission. It also provides timely data, information and analyses of population trends and policies and provides assistance to Member States in these areas. The Division maintains major databases, including World Population 1950-2050 and the *Global Review and Inventory of Population Policies (GRIPP)*. DESA also coordinates the *Population Information Network (POPIN)*, which promotes the use of the Internet to facilitate global sharing of population information.

The **United Nations Population Fund (UNFPA)**, which leads the operational population activities of the United Nations system, helps developing countries find solutions to their population problems (*see also Part One, page 39*). It assists countries to improve reproductive-health and family-planning services on the basis of individual choice, and to formulate population policies in support of efforts towards sustainable development. It also promotes awareness of population problems and ways to deal with them and assists Governments in dealing with population issues in ways best suited to each country's needs.

The largest internationally funded source of population assistance to developing countries, UNFPA manages one fourth of global population assistance. It is primarily a funding organization: many of the projects and programmes which it supports are carried out by Governments, United Nations agencies and NGOs. UNFPA provides support to some 160 countries annually.

About half of UNFPA's assistance is used for reproductive health programmes, including maternal and child health care, family planning and sexual health. About 20 per cent is allocated to population information, education and communication. UNFPA does not provide any support for abortion or abortion-related activities. Rather, it seeks to prevent abortion by increasing access to family planning.

The Fund also provides support for population data collection and analysis, research on demographic and socio-economic relationships, and policy formulation. Other priority areas include improving the situation of women, HIV/AIDS control and prevention, and population and the environment.

Recognizing continued population growth in most developing countries and increasing demand for good-quality, low-cost contraceptives and other reproductive health commodities, UNFPA created

The Population Conference, 1994

Attended by 179 countries, the **International Conference on Population and Development** (Cairo, Egypt, 1994) focused on the theme of population, sustained economic growth and sustainable development. Governments adopted a 20-year Programme of Action that aims to make reproductive health care, including family planning, universally available by the year 2015 or sooner. The Programme recognizes that the formulation and implementation of population policies are the responsibility of each country and should take into account the economic, social, environmental and cultural diversity of conditions in each country, including religious beliefs and ethical values.

The Programme emphasizes the link between population and development, and focuses on meeting the needs of individual women and men rather than demographic targets. Key to this approach is empowering women and providing them with more choices through increasing their access to education, health services and employment opportunities.

For the first time, it calls on Governments to address unsafe abortion as a leading cause of maternal mortality and a "major public health concern". The Programme also addresses issues relating to international migration and to population, the environment and consumption patterns.

Previous world population conferences were held in 1974 (Bucharest, Romania) and 1984 (Mexico City). UNFPA is the lead United Nations organization for the follow-up and implementation of the Programme of Action of the ICPD, for which it is undertaking a mid-decade review in 1998.

---

in 1989 the *Global Initiative on Contraceptive Requirements and Logistics Management Needs in Developing Countries*. Through indepth field studies, the initiative has undertaken a series of 10-year estimates of contraceptive requirements and examined logistics management systems, local production options and financing issues in a variety of selected countries.

UNFPA also addresses the reproductive health needs of adolescents as a priority activity. In Angola, for example, reducing the high level of unprotected sexual relations among adolescents is part of the main strategy to reduce maternal mortality and abortion. In Eritrea, adolescent-friendly services are being provided in all hospitals and health centres in the programme's two target provinces. Uganda is taking steps to expand youth-friendly reproductive health counselling and services in quintupling the number of multi-purpose youth centres by the year 2000.

Women's issues and gender mainstreaming

Gender equality and the advancement of women, like human rights, are cross-cutting issues relevant to all aspects of the work of the Organization, whether policy issues, research, programme activities, or its own staffing policies. The many obstacles to overcoming poverty have underscored the crucial role that women play in social and economic development. In the developing world, for example, women manage 50 to 80 per cent of food production, processing and marketing, and run 70 per cent of small enterprises. The United Nations, in its efforts to eradicate poverty, supports women's empowerment and enjoyment of their human rights through its development assistance activities.

The **Commission on the Status of Women,** under ECOSOC, examines progress towards women's equality throughout the world and makes recommendations for promoting women's rights in the political, economic and social fields. The Commission has prepared four global conferences on women's issues, including the **Fourth World Conference on Women,** held in Beijing in 1995, and monitors implementation of the resulting *Platform for Action.* Conventions adopted by the General Assembly regarding the elimination of gender discrimination and violence against women are the result of the work of the Commission and other United Nations bodies to advance the status of women (*see also Chapter 4, pages 235-238*). General Assembly directives on achieving the target of 50 per cent gender balance at the professional and highest levels in the United Nations Secretariat also stem from the Commission's advocacy and monitoring. The **Committee on the Elimination of Discrimination against Women,** supported by the **Division for the Advancement of Women** in the Department of Economic and Social Affairs, monitors adherence to the *United Nations Convention on the Elimination of All Forms of Discrimination against Women.* The Committee's concluding comments and general recommendations have contributed to a better understanding of women's economic and social rights, their political and civil rights and the means to ensure women's enjoyment of these rights.

In addition to the work done by the **Division for the Advancement of Women** to advance the global agenda and serve as a catalyst for gender mainstreaming in the UN system as a whole, all the members of the United Nations family of organizations address women and gender issues in their policies and many of their programmes. Women are central to UNICEF's work for children. Much of UNFPA's mandate revolves around women's health and reproductive rights. UNDP,

UNESCO, WFP, ILO and others have active gender programmes and targets.

In 1997, the Secretary-General designated a **Special Adviser on Gender Issues and Advancement of Women**. The Special Adviser, with the Division for the Advancement of Women, plays a key coordinating role in promoting widespread attention to women's issues and the application of a gender perspective in the work of the Organization. In addition, two other entities have an exclusive focus on women's issues.

The **United Nations Development Fund for Women (UNIFEM)** is a voluntary fund that works to promote the political and economic empowerment of women in developing countries (*see also Part One, pages 45-46*). UNIFEM works primarily in three areas: strengthening women's economic capacity as entrepreneurs and producers; engendering governance and leadership that increase women's participation in decision-making; and promoting women's human rights.

UNIFEM has helped tens of thousands of women in more than 100 countries to improve the quality of life for themselves and their families. It supports innovative programmes and projects benefiting women; provides direct technical and financial support to women's initiatives; and disseminates information to women's groups regarding best practices and lessons learned from the successes and failures of its diverse programmes.

In Central America, for example, UNIFEM works directly with justice administration officials, police officers and judges to raise awareness of women's legal rights in six different countries. In Cameroon, it has helped to import labour-saving cassava processing technologies, which have translated into increased productivity, enhanced family income and greater access to marketing opportunities for women.

The **International Research and Training Institute for the Advancement of Women (INSTRAW),** established in 1976 on the recommendation of the first World Conference on women, undertakes policy research and training programmes at the international level to contribute to the advancement of women; to enhance their active and equal participation in development; to raise awareness of gender issues; and to create networks worldwide for the attainment of gender equality (*see also Part One, page 46*). INSTRAW's work is primarily concerned with the economic and political empowerment of women through specific research programmes, which in 1998-1999 focuses on engendering the political agenda, violence against women and temporary labour migration of women.

INSTRAW works to improve conceptual and methodological tools, collect and disseminate gender-focused information, and offer training programmes in line with its research results to trainers and policy makers. Its training material covers topics such as women, environmental management and sustainable development; gender statistics and indicators for policy use; measurement and valuation of unpaid work; women, water supply and sanitation and waste management; and women and new and renewable sources of energy.

(Further information is available on the Internet at www.un.org/ womenwatch.)

Assistance to children

As the United Nations sees the family as the primary unit of society, it has always placed special emphasis on children and women. Despite great progress in improving conditions for families, nearly 12 million children in the developing world continue to die each year from largely preventable causes. The healthy development of many millions more is stifled by poverty, lack of formal education, discrimination and the trauma of armed conflicts, exploitation and abuse.

Since 1946, the **United Nations Children's Fund (UNICEF)** has been the Organization's lead agency for children, working with Governments, local communities and other partners in over 160 countries to provide children with health care, nutrition, education, and safe water and sanitation (*see also Part One, page 34*). Emphasis is placed on low-cost, community-based programmes in which people take an active part and train in such skills as health care, midwifery and teaching.

As the only United Nations organization exclusively dedicated to children, UNICEF speaks on their behalf and promotes the full implementation of the *Convention on the Rights of the Child* (*see Chapter 4, pages 238*).

As a result of efforts by UNICEF, the **World Summit for Children** was held at United Nations Headquarters in 1990, attended by leaders from more than 150 countries. The Summit recognized the rights of the young to "first call" on their nation's resources.

Governments worldwide have written the Summit's objectives into their policies and plans, ensuring that they will continue to make determined efforts to improve their children's welfare. Considerable progress has been made: under-five mortality rates, child nutrition, primary school attendance and adult literacy have continued to improve globally. Polio and dracunculiasis (guinea worm disease) are almost eradicated. Use of oral rehydration therapy and measles immunization coverage have increased dramatically. Improvements in

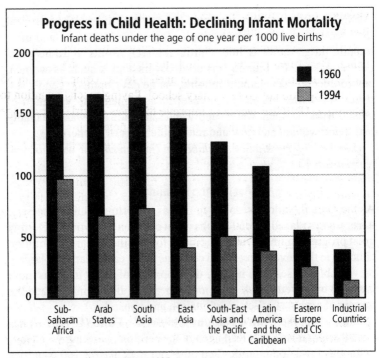

Progress in Child Health: Declining Infant Mortality
Infant deaths under the age of one year per 1000 live births

- ■ 1960
- ▨ 1994

Source: *Human Development Report 1997*

breastfeeding, access to safe water and early childhood development, as well as reductions in iodine deficiency disorders, vitamin A deficiency and gender gaps have been achieved in numerous countries.

In cooperation with WHO, UNICEF supports immunization programmes that every year prevent more than 3 million child deaths and untold suffering from six diseases — diphtheria, measles, pertussis (whooping cough), poliomyelitis, tetanus and tuberculosis (*see also page 166 above*).

Millions of children are at special risk because of acute poverty, wars, natural calamities or disabilities. Children in such situations often become separated from their relatives and are vulnerable to terrible forms of exploitation and abuse. UNICEF works to reunite them with their parents or families (*see also Chapter 5, pages 250-251*).

As many as 250 million children in the world work for their own and their families' survival. They labour in oppressive and often dangerous factory jobs, in domestic service, on city streets or in degrading conditions of sexual exploitation. UNICEF supports special projects for these children, helping provide education, counselling and care. It vigorously opposes exploitation of children as a violation of their rights, and promotes an immediate end to exploitative and hazardous child labour.

Girls face discrimination that often threatens their lives and well-being. They often receive less food and medical care than boys, and far less education: 75 million girls aged 6 to 11, compared with 55 million boys, do not go to primary school. Paying special attention to schooling, UNICEF works to improve the lives of girls and change the beliefs and practices that undermine their potential.

Close to 3 million children under 15 years of age are believed to be infected with the virus that causes AIDS, and many more have lost their parents to the disease. Education, life skills training and access to reproductive health services are essential if the disease is to be contained. UNICEF is working with Governments and NGOs in addressing issues of HIV/AIDS prevention, care and rights, and supports programmes for AIDS orphans.

Social integration

There are several social groups that the United Nations has come to recognize as requiring special attention over the years, including **youth, the elderly, people with disabilities, minorities,** and **indigenous populations.** All of these subjects are overseen by the General Assembly, ECOSOC and the Commission for Social Development. Specific programmes for these groups are carried out within the Department of Social and Economic Affairs.

The United Nations has been instrumental in the defining and defending the human rights of vulnerable groups (*see Chapter 4, page 239-242*). The Organization makes additional concerted efforts to highlight these special populations through the organization of research and data-gathering, as well as the special years and decades based on the specific theme, intended to encourage international action and events. The cycle of United Nations conferences, together with numerous other symposia organized throughout the United Nations system, have contributed to the formulation of international norms, standards and recommendations for action regarding these social groups. This normative work is intended to be adopted and incorporated into social policies by Governments, NGOs and other intergovernmental organizations.

Families in the development process

Recognizing the need for increased international cooperation on family issues as part of the global efforts to address the objectives of social development, the General Assembly proclaimed 1994 as the **International Year of the Family**. With its theme, "Family: Resources and

Responsibilities in a Changing World", the International Year served to highlight the role of families as basic social units and the need to pay adequate attention to the family dimension of development efforts. As part of the International Year, four regional preparatory meetings were convened to identify the priorities and concerns of each region. During these meetings, in Beijing, Cartagena, Tunis, and Valletta, Declarations on actions of benefit to families were adopted. Also, the General Assembly, during its 1994 session, convened in New York an **International Conference on Families**. As a result of the Year, Governments formulated national action plans on the family, established ministries devoted to the family and passed family-oriented legislation.

Follow-up action by Governments, NGOs and other members of civil society has focused on the welfare of the family. Activities relating to families have been integrated into the work programme of the United Nations **Division for Social Policy and Development**. The aims of the work of the United Nations in this area are to stimulate and encourage actions at all levels which respond to problems affecting, and affected by, the situation of families, and help increase awareness of family issues among Governments and civil society.

The **International Day of Families** was proclaimed by the General Assembly in 1993. The United Nations promotes the annual worldwide observance of the International Day on 15 May. The International Day provides an opportunity to increase awareness of issues relating to families as basic units of society, as well as to promote appropriate action.

The General Assembly established the **United Nations Trust Fund on Family Activities** (formerly the Voluntary Fund for the International Year of the Family) to provide assistance for activities specific to the family and projects of direct benefit to it. Grants from the Fund support practical actions by Governments and NGOs at the national, regional and global levels, with special focus on least developed and developing countries, and countries with economies in transition.

Youth

The General Assembly has adopted several resolutions and campaigns specific to youth, and the Secretariat has overseen the actual programmes and information campaigns on the issue.

- In 1965, the General Assembly adopted the *Declaration on the Promotion among Youth of the Ideals of Peace, Mutual Respect and Understanding between Peoples,* stressing the importance of the role of youth in today's world.

- Two decades later, the General Assembly proclaimed 1985 **International Youth Year: Participation, Development, Peace,** to emphasize the contribution of young people to development. The Assembly adopted guidelines for further planning and suitable follow-up in the field of youth — a global long-term strategy for youth work. The United Nations has subsequently promoted the implementation of the guidelines, assisting Governments in developing youth policies and programmes, and strengthening communication between the United Nations and youth organizations.

- In 1995 — the tenth anniversary of the Year — the United Nations strengthened its commitment to young people by adopting the **World Programme of Action for Youth to the Year 2000 and Beyond,** an international strategy to address the problems of young people and to increase opportunities for their participation in society. The Programme provides a policy framework and practical guidelines for national action and international support to improve the situation of youth, and proposes action to promote the well-being and livelihood of young people. It also called for a World Conference of Ministers Responsible for Youth to meet regularly under the aegis of the United Nations to provide a global focus on youth. The first session of that Conference was convened in Lisbon by Portugal in cooperation with the United Nations to be held in August 1998, and to focus on the implementation of the World Programme of Action for Youth by adopting a *Lisbon Declaration on Youth* and specific recommendations for action at the national, regional and world levels.

- The **United Nations Youth Fund** has continued to support projects involving young people. The **Youth Unit** of the United Nations Division for Social Policy and Development promotes operational activities through that Fund and has co-sponsored three sessions of the **World Youth Forum** of the United Nations system. The third was to be convened in partnership with the Portuguese National Youth Committee in Braja, Portugal, in August 1998. Some 500 delegates from youth and student movements and organizations from around the world were scheduled to meet with representatives of the United Nations system and other intergovernmental organizations. The theme of the third forum was "Youth Participation for Human Development".

Older persons

During the past 50 years, the average life expectancy worldwide has increased by 20 years. At the same time, fertility is declining. The combined effect results in an expansion in the absolute numbers of older persons, and increases their proportion of overall population. The populations of different countries are ageing at varying rates. Developing country populations are ageing later than developed countries, and very much faster.

The ageing of populations is posing new and unprecedented challenges and opportunities for the organization of individual lives and the organization of the socio-economic and cultural environment.

For the later years to flourish, the earlier years need to be adjusted for continuing education, skills upgrading, healthy lifestyles and saving.

For ageing societies to flourish, systems and facilities need to be adjusted for age-appropriate use and access, as well as enhanced availability of adult education, gradual retirement and part-time work arrangements, and intergenerational contracts for sustainable income security and health care in old age.

In response to global ageing, the United Nations has taken several initiatives:

- The **World Assembly on Ageing** (Vienna, 1982) adopted the *International Plan of Action on Ageing*, endorsed by the General Assembly later that year. The Plan recommends action in such sectors as employment and income security, health and nutrition, housing, education and social welfare. It sees older persons as a diverse and active population group with wide-ranging capabilities and, at times, particular health-care needs.
- The *United Nations Principles for Older Persons*, adopted by the General Assembly in 1991, establish universal standards pertaining to the status of older persons in five areas: independence, participation, care, self-fulfilment and dignity of senior citizens.
- In 1992 — the tenth anniversary of the adoption of the Plan of Action — the Assembly devoted four plenary meetings to an **International Conference on Ageing**. The Conference adopted the *Proclamation on Ageing*, laying out the main direction for implementing the Plan of Action in its second decade, and proclaimed **1999** the **International Year of Older Persons**. The Assembly also adopted the global targets on ageing for the year 2001 as a practical strategy on ageing.
- The conceptual framework for the observance of the International Year, presented by the Secretary-General to the General Assem-

bly in 1995, introduced four dimensions for exploration during the Year: the situation of older persons; lifelong individual development; relationships between generations; and the relationship between development and the ageing of populations. Overall priority is given to promoting the Principles for Older Persons. The Year's unifying theme is "Towards a society for all ages".

- The operational framework for observance of the Year, presented by the Secretary-General in 1997, was also structured along four dimensions: raising awareness (reiterating the four conceptual dimensions); looking ahead beyond 1999; reaching out to non-traditional actors including the development community, the media, the private sector and youth; and, finally, networking with the aid of new technologies so as to facilitate collaboration across nations and sectors, and to better link research with policy formulation. The operational framework provided a *Menu of ideas* for activities at the national level.

(On the rights of minorities, indigenous peoples, and of disabled persons, see Chapter 4, pages 239-243.)

Uncivil society: crime, illicit drugs and terrorism

Organized international crime, illicit drug trafficking and terrorism have become social, political and economic forces capable of altering the destinies of countries and entire regions. Recent trends include large-scale bribery of public officials, the growth of "crime multinationals" and international money-laundering operations, trafficking in illegal migrants, illegal shipments of toxic wastes, illicit drugs and many other "commodities". The use of terrorism to intimidate communities large and small and to sabotage economic development is also regarded as a threat which requires international cooperation to combat effectively. Facing these threats to good governance and social equity and justice for all citizens, the United Nations has become increasingly involved in orchestrating efforts to combat these problems, which respect no national borders.

Because drugs and organized crime considerably overlap, the Organization's work in these two areas was consolidated in 1997. The Vienna-based **Office for Drug Control and Crime Prevention**, under a single Executive Director, is spearheading the global efforts to combat drug-trafficking, organized crime and international terrorism — what the Secretary-General has called the "uncivil" elements of society.

The Office is comprised of the **United Nations International Drug Control Programme (UNDCP)** and the **Centre for International Crime Prevention** (*see also Part One, page 45*).

Drug control

The United Nations is deeply involved in international drug control. With an estimated total revenue of $400 billion per year, illicit drugs represent 8 per cent of total international trade — more than global trade in iron or motor vehicles. Worldwide, more than 200 million people use drugs, and in industrialized countries alone the fight against drugs costs over $120 billion a year in terms of drug enforcement, prosecutions, prisons, and drug prevention and rehabilitation programmes.

The **Commission on Narcotic Drugs**, a functional commission of ECOSOC, is the main intergovernmental policy-making body on international drug control. Made up of 53 Member States and meeting annually, it analyses the world drug abuse situation and develops proposals to strengthen international drug control. It also directs the activities of UNDCP.

The **International Narcotics Control Board** strives to restrict the availability of drugs to medical and scientific purposes and to prevent their diversion into illegal channels. It is an independent body that assists and monitors Governments' compliance with the international drug control treaties. Its 13 members, elected by ECOSOC, serve in their individual capacities. The Board sends investigative missions and technical visits to drug-affected countries, and sets limits on the amount of drugs needed by countries for medical and scientific purposes. It also reviews trends in the supply of opiate raw materials and the demand for opiates, to ensure their availability for legitimate purposes.

At a **special session of the General Assembly on the world drug problem**, held in June 1998, the world's Governments developed a truly global drug control strategy. Governments committed to work together to streamline existing strategies and to outline practical activities to strengthen international cooperation in curtailing both illicit drug production and consumption. These included: campaigns to reduce the demand for drugs; programmes to restrict availability of materials that can be used in the production of illicit drugs; efforts to improve judicial cooperation among countries to better control drug trafficking and punishment of offenders; and stepped-up efforts to eradicate illicit drug crops.

A series of treaties, adopted under United Nations auspices, require that Governments exercise control over production and distribution of narcotic and psychotropic substances, combat drug abuse and illicit trafficking, maintain the necessary administrative machinery, and report to international organs on their actions. These treaties are:

- The *Single Convention on Narcotic Drugs* (1961), which codifies the use of over 116 natural or synthetic narcotics, including cannabis and cocaine;
- The *Convention on Psychotropic Substances* (1971), which covers hallucinogens, amphetamines, barbiturates, non-barbiturate sedatives and tranquillizers;
- The 1972 *Protocol Amending the Single Convention*, which highlights the need for treatment and rehabilitation of drug addicts; and
- The 1988 *United Nations Convention against Illicit Traffic in Narcotic Drugs and Psychotropic Substances*, which is designed to deprive drug traffickers of their ill-gotten financial gains and freedom of movement. The Convention is the main framework for international cooperation against drug trafficking. It provides for the tracing, freezing and confiscation of proceeds and property derived from drug trafficking. Courts are empowered to make available or to seize bank, financial or commercial records. Bank secrecy cannot be invoked in such cases. The Convention bars all havens to drug traffickers, particularly by providing for the extradition of drug traffickers, mutual legal assistance between States on drug-related investigations and the transfer of proceedings for criminal prosecution. Under the Convention, parties commit themselves to eliminate or reduce illicit demand for drugs.

The central objective of these treaties is to limit the supply of and demand for narcotic drugs and psychotropic substances to medical and scientific needs.

The **United Nations International Drug Control Programme (UNDCP)**, established in 1991 by the General Assembly, coordinates all United Nations drug control activities. It provides leadership in international drug control, monitors trends in drug production, consumption and trafficking, and promotes the implementation of drug control treaties.

UNDCP assists Governments in adopting and implementing national drug control laws and regulations; supports the training of law-enforcement personnel, judges, magistrates and prosecutors; assists Governments in preventing the diversion of drugs into the illicit market; provides advisory services, technical assistance and training to police and customs officials so as to augment their capacity to interdict narcotic drugs; and sponsors cross-border cooperation among drug law enforcement agencies in areas where drug trafficking is high. `

Efforts to reduce drug demand are indispensable for combating the drug problem. But many Governments lack the resources to develop programmes of drug abuse prevention, treatment and rehabilitation. UNDCP provides support focusing on mobilizing civil society, particularly NGOs and the business community, the latter through workplace drug prevention programmes.

To break the economic hold that drug traffickers establish in some regions, UNDCP helps opium poppy and coca bush farmers find alternative legal crops, or other employment that can be just as lucrative. Major projects are ongoing in South America and Asia.

To deprive drug traffickers of their illicit power and influence, UNDCP assists Governments in efforts to counter money-laundering and confiscate assets gained from drug trafficking. It is supporting a $4.3 million global programme to improve the capacity of legal and law enforcement systems, which includes the creation of financial intelligence units to reduce the vulnerability of financial systems.

Crime prevention

The intergovernmental **Commission on Crime Prevention and Criminal Justice**, as a functional body of ECOSOC, was established in 1992 to strengthen United Nations activities in the field. Made up of 40 Member States, it meets every year. As recommended by the Commission, a world ministerial **Conference on Transnational Organized Crime** was held in Naples, Italy, in 1994. The United Nations **Centre for International Crime Prevention** carries out the mandates of the Commission.

Specifically, the Centre:

- Dispenses technical assistance and advisory services, particularly to criminal justice systems of developing countries and countries in transition;
- Encourages cooperation between national legal systems in areas such as extradition, mutual assistance and the transfer of criminal proceedings;
- Helps to forge international accords to combat transnational crime and money-laundering;
- Assists in the use and application of internationally recognized standards of conduct for police, the judiciary and penal institutions, as well as for the protection of victims' rights and for humane treatment of offenders;

- Coordinates a network of international and regional criminological institutes, committed to fostering and promoting United Nations criminal policy in the light of and in response to mandates in this area;
- Disseminates up-to-date statistics and information through the Internet and the World Wide Web, via its Crime and Justice Information Network;
- Promotes the exchange of national experiences and highlights new trends and perspectives, especially at global crime conferences and the annual sessions of the Commission.

Examples of the Centre's work in 1997 included assisting West African States in developing and implementing a regional convention on mutual assistance in criminal matters, helping authorities in South Africa to devise a witness-protection programme, and assisting Romania's capacity to prevent and fight corruption and organized crime.

Under the Commission's auspices, several practical actions followed, including the establishment of databases, together with agreements on monitoring and information exchange. The Commission in 1997 began elaborating a convention to combat transnational crime, and took action on problems such as bribery and corruption, the smuggling of illegal migrants and the illicit traffic in children.

As decided by the General Assembly, a **United Nations Congress on the Prevention of Crime and the Treatment of Offenders** is held every five years, to provide a forum to exchange policies and to stimulate progress in the fight against crime. Participants include criminologists, penologists and senior police officers, as well as experts in criminal law, human rights and rehabilitation.

Established in 1968, the **United Nations Interregional Crime and Justice Research Institute (UNICRI)** undertakes and promotes action-oriented research aimed at the prevention of crime and the treatment of offenders (*see Part One, page 49*). UNICRI operates as the interregional research arm of the United Nations Centre for Crime Prevention. It contributes, through research and information dissemination, to the formulation of improved policies in crime prevention and control.

(For United Nations action against terrorism, see Chapter 6, pages 269-270.)

Science, culture and communication

The United Nations sees cultural and scientific exchanges, as well as communication, as instrumental to the advancement of international peace and development. In addition to its central work around education (*see pages 172-174, above*), the **United Nations Educational, Scientific and Cultural Organization (UNESCO)** focuses its activities on three other areas: science in the service of development; cultural development — heritage and creativity; and communication, information and informatics.

Science

The major programme, *Sciences in the service of development*, fosters the advancement, transfer and sharing of knowledge in the natural, physical, social and human sciences. UNESCO's intergovernmental programmes include *Man and the Biosphere*; the programme of the Intergovernmental Oceanographic Commission; the *Project on Environment and Development in Coastal Regions* (*see also pages 203 and 214 below*); the *Management of Social Transformations Programme*; the *International Hydrological Programme*; and the *International Geological Correlation Programme*. In addition, through education and training initiatives, UNESCO helps to correct the imbalance in scientific and technological manpower, 90 per cent of which is concentrated in the industrialized countries (*see also page 155 above, and page 213 below*).

In the wake of advances in cloning living beings, UNESCO member States adopted in 1997 the *Universal Declaration on the Human Genome and Human Rights* — the first international text on the ethics of genetic research. The Declaration sets universal ethical standards on human genetic research and practice that balance the freedom of scientists to pursue their work with the need to safeguard human rights and protect humanity from potential abuses.

In the social and human sciences, UNESCO focuses on teaching human rights and democracy, combating all forms of discrimination, improving the status of women, and encouraging action to solve the problems faced by youth, such as education for the prevention of AIDS.

Cultural development

UNESCO's cultural activities are concentrated on safeguarding cultural heritage. Under the 1972 *Convention on the Protection of the World Cultural and Natural Heritage*, 152 States have pledged international cooperation to protect over 550 outstanding sites in 112 countries: protected towns, monuments and natural environments which have been placed on the *World Heritage List*. Sites threatened by neglect are included in the *List of World Heritage in Danger*.

A 1970 UNESCO convention prohibits the illicit import, export and transfer of cultural property, and a 1995 convention favours the return of stolen or illegally exported cultural objects to their country of origin.

Cultural activities also concentrate on promoting the cultural dimension of development; encouraging creation and creativity; preserving cultural identities and oral traditions; and promoting books and reading.

Communication, information and informatics

UNESCO has asserted itself as a world leader in promoting press freedom and pluralistic and independent media. Its major programme in this area seeks to promote the free flow of information, and to strengthen the communication capacities of developing countries.

UNESCO promotes press freedom and independence and seeks to reinforce media pluralism. It assists member States in adapting their media laws to democratic standards, and in pursuing editorial independence in public and private media.

When violations of press freedom occur, the UNESCO Director-General intervenes through diplomatic channels or public statements. At the initiative of UNESCO, 3 May is observed as **World Press Freedom Day**.

To reinforce communication infrastructures and human resources in developing countries, UNESCO provides training and technical expertise, and helps to develop national and regional media projects, especially through its *International Programme for the Development of Communication*. For instance, the national news agencies of 40 African countries have been strengthened through projects mainly funded by Germany, while UNESCO has supported a private news agency in Bangladesh. Over 1,800 Cambodian media professionals have been trained thanks to funds from Denmark and France.

UNESCO's *Intergovernmental Informatics Programme* helps developing countries set up their own informatics systems and to secure access to global information flows through information highways. The emphasis in the programme is on training, on establishing computer networks linking scientific and cultural institutions, as well as hooking them up to the Internet (*see also pages 151-153, above*).

The new communication technologies, by multiplying the possibilities for producing, disseminating and receiving information on an unprecedented scale, are leading to an extension of the principle of "free flow of ideas". UNESCO seeks to ensure that as many people as possible benefit from the opportunities that these technologies provide. The social and cultural impact of such technologies, and the policy approaches to legal and ethical issues related to cyberspace, are also questions of concern to UNESCO.

Sustainable development

In the first decades of the United Nations, environmental concerns rarely appeared on the international agenda. The related work of the Organization focused on creating an inventory of the global natural resources available for development, and exploring ways to ensure that their exploitation benefited the developing countries in particular. During the 1960s, there were some agreements made regarding marine pollution, especially oil spills (*see page 208, below*). But with increasing evidence of the deterioration of the environment on a global scale, the international community has been responding since the 1970s with escalating concern over the impact of development on the ecology of the planet and human well-being, and the United Nations has been a leading advocate for environmental concerns, and a chief proponent of new concepts such as "sustainable development".

The relationship between economic development and environmental degradation was first placed on the international agenda in 1972, at the **United Nations Conference on the Human Environment**, held in Stockholm. After the Conference, Governments set up the **United Nations Environment Programme (UNEP)**, which today continues to act as the leading global environmental authority and as a global advocate for action to protect and improve the environment (*see pages 201-203, below*).

In 1973, the United Nations set up the **Sudano-Sahelian Office (UNSO)** to spearhead efforts to reverse the spread of desertification and achieve food self-sufficiency in affected countries in West Africa. Action was slow, however, to integrate environmental concerns into national economic planning and decision-making. Overall, the environment continued to deteriorate, and such problems as ozone depletion, global warming and water pollution grew more serious, while the destruction of natural resources accelerated at an alarming rate.

The 1980s witnessed important reviews and negotiations among Member States to reach agreement on several aspects of environmental concern, including treaties protecting the ozone layer and controlling the movement of toxic wastes (*see pages 203-205, below*). In 1983, the United Nations set up the **World Commission on Environment and Development**, whose work brought about a new understanding and sense of urgency to the need for development that was beneficial both for the environment and for the well-being of people everywhere. Increasingly, environmental degradation — which had been seen as a side effect of industrial pollution in the wealthier nations — was understood to be an issue which threatened the developing nations as well. Led by Gro Harlem Brundtland of Norway, the

Commission put forward in its 1987 report to the General Assembly the concept of *sustainable development* as an alternative approach to one simply based on economic growth — one "which meets the needs of the present without compromising the ability of future generations to meet their own needs".

After considering the report, the General Assembly called for the **United Nations Conference on Environment and Development (UNCED)** (Rio de Janeiro, 1992), which became known as the **Earth Summit**. The primary goals of the world conference were to agree on an approach to development that would protect the environment while ensuring economic development, and to lay the foundation for a global partnership between the developing and the more industrialized countries, based on mutual needs and common interests, to ensure a healthy future for the planet.

Today, awareness of the need to support and sustain the environment is reflected in virtually all areas of the work of the United Nations. Thanks to the ground-breaking work since 1972, new mechanisms have been created and dynamic partnerships between the Organization and Governments, NGOs, the scientific community and the private sector are in the process of bringing new knowledge and concrete action to the environmental problems that are shared by all nations. The United Nations now maintains that the need to protect the environment must be integral to all economic development activities. Environmental goals cannot be achieved unless current patterns of economic development are also changed.

Earth Summit and Agenda 21

Governments took an historic step towards ensuring the future of the planet when they adopted at the Earth Summit in Rio *Agenda 21*, a comprehensive plan for global action in all areas of sustainable development. The Conference took steps to reverse environmental deterioration and establish the basis for a sustainable way of life into the twenty-first century.

In addition to Agenda 21, which in seeking to meet the needs of all peoples addresses both environment and development goals, the Summit also adopted the *Rio Declaration on Environment and Development*, which defines the rights and responsibilities of States; and the *Statement of Forest Principles*, guidelines for the sustainable management of forests worldwide. Two conventions, on climate change and on biological diversity, were negotiated leading up to the Summit and were opened for signature in Rio (*see pages 204 and 206, below*).

In Agenda 21, Governments outlined a detailed blueprint for action which, if implemented, could move the world away from its present unsustainable model of economic development towards activities which will protect and renew the crucial environmental resources on which we depend. Areas for action include protecting the atmosphere; combating deforestation, soil loss and desertification; preventing air and water pollution; halting the depletion of fish stocks; and promoting the safe management of toxic wastes. Agenda 21 also addresses patterns of development which cause stress to the environment: poverty and external debt in developing countries, unsustainable patterns of production and consumption, demographic stress and the structure of the international economy.

The programme of action also recommends ways to strengthen the part played by major groups — women, trade unions, farmers, children and young people, indigenous peoples, the scientific community, local authorities, business, industry and NGOs — in achieving sustainable development.

The *Rio Declaration on Environment and Development* supports Agenda 21 by defining the rights and responsibilities of States regarding these issues. Among its principles:

- That human beings are at the centre of concerns for sustainable development. They are entitled to a healthy and productive life in harmony with nature;
- That scientific uncertainty should not delay measures to prevent environmental degradation where there are threats of serious or irreversible damage;
- That States have a sovereign right to exploit their own resources but not to cause damage to the environment of other States;
- That eradicating poverty and reducing disparities in worldwide standards of living are "indispensable" for sustainable development;
- That the full participation of women is essential for achieving sustainable development; and
- That the developed countries acknowledge the responsibility that they bear in the international pursuit of sustainable development in view of the pressures their societies place on the global environment and of the technologies and financial resources they command.

The non–legally binding *Statement of Forest Principles* for the sustainable management of forests was the first global consensus reached on forests. Among its provisions:

- That all countries, notably developed countries, should make an effort to "green the world" through reforestation and forest conservation;
- That States have a right to develop forests according to their socio-economic needs, in keeping with national sustainable development policies; and
- That specific financial resources should be provided to develop programmes that encourage economic and social substitution policies.

In Rio, the United Nations was given a key role in the implementation of Agenda 21. Since then, the Organization has taken steps to integrate the concept of environmentally sound development into all relevant policies and programmes. Income-generating projects increasingly take into account environmental consequences. Development assistance programmes are increasingly directed towards women, given their central roles as producers of goods, services and food and as caretakers of the environment.

Efforts to manage forests in a sustainable manner begin with finding alternatives to meet the needs of people who are overusing them. The moral and social imperatives for alleviating poverty are given additional urgency by the recognition that poor people can cause damage to the environment. For the same reason, the United Nations is working to ensure that decisions about direct foreign investments consider the fact that drawing down the Earth's natural resources for short-term profit is bad for business over the long term.

In adopting Agenda 21, the Earth Summit also called for several major initiatives in other key areas of sustainable development. These included a global conference on small island developing States, a legally binding Convention on Desertification, and talks on preventing the depletion of highly migratory and straddling fish stocks and avoiding conflicts arising from fishing on the high seas (*see below*).

In addition, two bodies were created within the United Nations to ensure full support for implementation of Agenda 21 worldwide:

- The **Commission on Sustainable Development,** which first met in 1993; and
- The **Inter-agency Committee on Sustainable Development,** set up by the Secretary-General in 1992 to ensure system-wide cooperation and coordination in the follow-up to the Summit.

The General Assembly established the United Nations **Commission on Sustainable Development (CSD)** under the Economic and

Social Council as a means of supporting and encouraging action by Governments, business, industry and other non-governmental groups to bring about the social and economic changes needed for environmentally sustainable development. Its mandate is to review implementation of the Earth Summit agreements, to provide policy guidance to Governments and major groups involved in sustainable development and to strengthen Agenda 21 by devising additional strategies where necessary. The Commission is supported by numerous inter-sessional meetings and activities initiated by Governments, international organizations and major groups.

Between 1994 and 1996, the Commission monitored in stages the early implementation of Agenda 21. Each sectoral issue — health, human settlements, fresh water, toxic chemicals and hazardous waste, land, agriculture, desertification, mountains, forests, biodiversity, atmosphere, oceans and seas — was reviewed once, while progress on most cross-sectoral issues was considered each year. These issues, which must be addressed if action in sectoral areas is to be effective, are grouped as follows: critical elements of sustainability (trade and environment, patterns of production and consumption, combating poverty, demographic dynamics); financial resources and mechanisms; education, science, transfer of environmentally sound technologies, technical cooperation and capacity-building; decision-making; and activities of the major groups, such as business and labour.

Earth Summit + 5

In 1997 — five years after the Earth Summit — the General Assembly held a special session on the implementation of Agenda 21. A UNEP report issued in early 1997 warned that "the global environment has continued to deteriorate and environmental problems remain deeply embedded in the socio-economic fabric of nations in all regions". Delegates from some 165 countries agreed with that assessment, but were unable to decide how best to proceed, largely due to differences among countries on how to finance sustainable development globally. Member States, however, emphasized that implementing Agenda 21 was more urgent than ever. They pledged to ensure that the next review of its implementation would show greater progress in achieving sustainable development.

The final document of the special session recommended measures to improve the implementation of Agenda 21, including:

- Consider adopting legally binding targets to reduce emission of greenhouse gases leading to climate change;

- Continue dialogue among countries on protecting forests, towards a possible legally binding convention;
- Move more forcefully towards sustainable patterns of production, distribution and use of energy;
- Intensify efforts to reverse the decline in development assistance;
- Focus on poverty eradication as a prerequisite for sustainable development.

The programme of work adopted at that session for the period 1998-2002 provides for CSD to monitor progress in one or two major areas each year (*see below*).

Reports submitted annually by Governments continue to be the main basis for monitoring progress and identifying problems faced by countries. By mid-1998, some 140 Governments had established national sustainable development councils or other coordinating bodies. Central to the ability of Governments to formulate policies for sustainability and to regulate their impact is the development of a set of internationally recognized criteria and indicators for sustainable development. CSD is spearheading this work, which will enable countries to gather and report the data needed to measure progress on Agenda 21. It is hoped that a menu of indicators — from which Governments will choose those appropriate to local conditions — will be used by countries in their national plans and strategies and, subsequently, when they report to the Commission.

The United Nations **Department of Economic and Social Affairs** provides the Secretariat for CSD and responds to requests for policy recommendations to facilitate the implementation of sustainable development. It provides analytical, technical and information services within the framework of the commitments made at the Earth Summit. A key element in these services is the forging of partnerships between the governmental, non-governmental and international actors.

Forests

By 1995, the international community, which had adopted a statement on forest principles at the Earth Summit, was ready to discuss additional measures necessary to ensure the sustainable development of the world's forests. The **Intergovernmental Panel on Forests,** set up by CSD, concluded its work in 1997 by adopting some 100 action-specific proposals for the conservation and sustainable management and development of forests.

Responding to the continuing need for a central forum on forests, Governments attending the Earth Summit+5 established the **Intergovernmental Forum on Forests**, which monitors implementation of these proposals and considers what additional measures, including a possible international legal agreement, might be needed to ensure the sustainable development of forests.

Financing sustainable development

At Rio, it was agreed that most financing for Agenda 21 would come from within each country's public and private sectors. However, new and additional external funds were considered necessary to support developing countries' efforts to adopt sustainable development practices. Of the estimated $600 billion required annually by developing countries to implement Agenda 21, most — $475 billion — was to be generated by those countries. A further $125 billion would be needed annually in new and additional funds from external sources, some $70 billion more than 1992 levels of official development assistance.

An important mechanism for the transfer of such funds is the **Global Environment Facility (GEF)** set up in 1991. Run jointly by the World Bank, UNDP and UNEP, GEF has become the main source of multilateral grant funding to developing countries for projects aimed at achieving global environmental benefits. It provides funding for activities in four areas: preventing climate change; conserving biodiversity; pollution of international waters; and the depletion of the ozone layer.

Currently, GEF serves as the interim financial mechanism for activities under the *United Nations Framework Convention on Climate Change* and the *Convention on Biological Diversity* (*see pages 204 and 206, below*). In 1994, GEF's mandate was expanded to include land degradation, primarily desertification and deforestation, in so far as funded projects would ameliorate the global environmental problems of the initial mandate.

By mid-1998, GEF had provided some $1.9 billion to more than 500 projects in 119 countries. An additional $5 billion in co-financing had been raised in support of these projects from recipient Governments, international development agencies such as UNDP and the World Bank, as well as private industry. Its projects have included converting sugarcane residues into energy, reducing methane emissions and landfill pollution in China, biodiversity management in Argentina, reducing pollution in the Danube River Basin and phasing out chlorofluorocarbons and other ozone-depleting substances in Eastern Europe.

Changing human behaviour

Achieving sustainable development worldwide depends largely on changing patterns of production and consumption — what we produce, how it is produced and how much we consume. Finding ways to change our patterns of production and consumption was first put on the international agenda at the Earth Summit. Since then, the Commission on Sustainable Development has spearheaded a programme of work, in cooperation with organizations both within and outside the United Nations, aimed at challenging the behaviour of individual consumers, households, industrial concerns, businesses and Governments.

Central to the issue is the fact that using fewer resources and wasting less is simply better business. It saves money and generates higher profits. It also protects the environment by conserving natural resources and creating less pollution. In doing so, we sustain the planet for the enjoyment and well-being of future generations.

CSD's work programme in this area focuses on projected trends in consumption and production; the impact on developing countries, including trade opportunities; assessment of the effectiveness of policy instruments, including new and innovative instruments; progress by countries through their time-bound voluntary commitments; and extension and revision of United Nations guidelines for consumer protection.

The Commission has a work programme on the transfer of environmentally sound technology, cooperation and capacity-building. The programme places an emphasis on three interrelated priority areas: access to and dissemination of information, capacity-building for managing technological change, and financial and partnership arrangements. The Commission is working with the World Trade Organization, UNCTAD and UNEP to ensure that trade, environment and sustainable development issues are mutually reinforcing.

Action for the environment

While the whole United Nations system is increasingly engaged in environmental protection in diverse ways, its lead agency in this area is the **United Nations Environment Programme (UNEP)** (*see also Part One, pages 38-39*). Created to be the environmental conscience of the United Nations system, UNEP assesses the state of the world's environment and identifies issues requiring international cooperation; helps formulate international environmental law; and helps to integrate environmental considerations in the social and economic policies and programmes of the United Nations system.

UNEP helps solve problems that cannot be handled by countries acting alone. It provides a forum to build consensus and to forge international agreements. In doing so, it strives to enhance the participation of business and industry, the scientific and academic community, NGOs, community groups and others in the achievement of sustainable development.

One of the functions of UNEP is the promotion of scientific knowledge and information on the environment. Research and synthesis of environmental information, promoted and coordinated by UNEP, has generated a variety of *State-of-the-Environment* reports, and created worldwide awareness of emerging environmental problems — some of which triggered international negotiations of several environmental conventions.

UNEP's **Global Environment Monitoring System (GEMS)** and **Global Resource Information Database (GRID)** focus on vital areas of environmental concern, including climate and atmosphere, oceans, renewable resources, transboundary pollution and the health consequences of pollution. GEMS involves some 25 major global monitoring networks, while GRID has 12 network focal points, each with an associated database, and has activities in 142 countries. Over 30,000 scientists and technicians have been involved; the institutions in which they work are funded by Governments and international agencies (*also see related programmes of the World Meteorological Organization, page 208, below*).

INFOTERRA is a worldwide network of national focal points in 171 countries which assists organizations and individuals to obtain environmental information. It processes over 50,000 queries a year.

The **International Register of Potentially Toxic Chemicals (IRPTC)** was established in order to make information about chemicals available to those people who need to use them. Some 70,000 chemicals are in use today, and IRPTC provides vital information for chemical safety decisions. Some 120 countries have appointed national correspondents to inform IRPTC of their latest research and laws and to relay information back to interested parties at home.

UNEP's **Industry and Environment Office** is of central importance to United Nations efforts to encourage business and industry to change their patterns of production in order to reduce activities which cause global warming, the deterioration of the ozone layer, and pollution of freshwater and seas. Located in Paris, the Office provides practical information and brings industry and Governments together to promote environmentally sound industrial development through technical cooperation and information transfer.

UNEP acts to protect oceans and seas and promote the environmentally sound use of marine resources under its 13 *Regional Seas Action Programmes,* which are now in effect in over 140 countries. This programme is expected to expand to additional regions during 1998, which has been proclaimed International Year of the Ocean.

In response to a request made by the Earth Summit, UNEP sponsored talks which led in 1995 to the adoption of the *United Nations Global Programme of Action for the Protection of the Marine Environment*, a milestone in efforts by the international community to protect oceans, estuaries and coastal waters from pollution caused by human activities on land, and to promote the welfare of some 3.5 billion people who live in coastal areas (*see also page 192, above*).

Under its *Water Programme*, UNEP supports global and regional assessments of freshwater, coastal and marine resources; development and application of international agreements on the management of internationally shared water systems; and international cooperation for implementing the *Global Programme of Action for the Protection of the Marine Environment from Land-based Activities*.

Coastal and marine areas cover some 70 per cent of the Earth's surface and are vital to the Planet's life-support system. Most pollution comes from industrial wastes, mining, agricultural activities and emissions from motor vehicles, some of which occurs thousands of miles inland. The Global Programme calls for plans to deal with inadequate treatment of waste water and sewage and for an international legal agreement to reduce the use of persistent organic pollutants — highly toxic, cancer-causing substances such as pesticides, solvents and polychlorinated biphenyls (PCBs) used by the chemical industry (*see also related programmes of the International Maritime Organization, page 207, below*).

Over the years, UNEP has been the catalyst for the negotiation of a number of international agreements which today form the cornerstone of the United Nations efforts to halt and reverse damage to the Planet. UNEP also administers a series of environmental agreements. The historic *Montreal Protocol* (1987) and its subsequent *Amendments* seek to preserve the ozone layer in the upper atmosphere. The *Basel Convention on the Control of Hazardous Wastes and Their Disposal* (1989) has reduced the danger of pollution from toxic waste. The *Convention on International Trade in Endangered Species* (1973) is universally recognized for its achievements in controlling the trade in wildlife products. UNEP has also helped to prepare the 1992 Conventions on biological diversity and on climate change.

In collaboration with FAO, UNEP promoted Governments' consensus towards a *Convention on Prior Informed Consent Procedures for Certain Hazardous Chemicals and Pesticides in International Trade,* which was adopted and opened for signature in 1998. The Convention gives importing countries the power to decide which chemicals they want to receive and exclude those they cannot manage safely. UNEP is now working towards a legally binding treaty to reduce and eliminate releases of persistent organic pollutants.

Climate change and global warming

The 1992 *United Nations Framework Convention on Climate Change* was developed jointly by UNEP and the World Meteorological Organization (WMO). It is the centrepiece of world efforts to combat global warming — the gradual rise in global temperatures as a result of human activities. Under the Convention, signed in Rio, developed countries are obliged to reduce emissions of carbon dioxide and other warming gases they release into the atmosphere to 1990 levels by the year 2000. These countries, which together account for 60 per cent of annual carbon dioxide emissions, also agreed to transfer to developing countries technology and information that would help them respond to the challenges of climate change. By April 1998, the Convention had been ratified by 174 countries.

United Nations work on climate change is informed by the work the **Intergovernmental Panel on Climate Change (IPCC)**. The Panel, a worldwide network of 2,500 leading scientists and experts, reviews scientific research on climate change. Set up in 1988, it is coordinated by UNEP and WMO. In 1989, its finding that human activities could possibly cause changes in the global climate system led to negotiations on the Framework Convention. By 1995, with access to new and more powerful computer models, the Panel found that there was "discernible human influence on the global climate."

By 1995, the evidence presented by IPCC scientists was clear: the 1992 target, even if reached on time, would not prevent global warming and its associated problems. Additional reductions would be necessary. In 1997, countries which had ratified the Convention met in Kyoto, Japan and agreed on a legally binding protocol under which developed countries will reduce their collective emissions of six greenhouse gases by 5.2 per cent from 1990 levels between 2008 and 2012.

Ozone depletion

The ozone layer is a thin layer of gas in the upper atmosphere (about 12 to 45 kilometres above the ground) which shields the Earth's surface from the Sun's damaging ultraviolet rays. Exposure to increased ultraviolet radiation at the Earth's surface is known to result in skin cancer, and to cause unpredictable damage to plants, algae, the food chain and the global ecosystem. UNEP helped to negotiate and now administers the historic *Vienna Convention on the Protection of the Ozone Layer* (1985), the *Montreal Protocol* (1987) and its London (1990) and Copenhagen (1992) *Amendments*. Under these agreements, developed countries have banned the production and sale of chlorofluorocarbons, a chemical that depletes the ozone layer. Schedules are in place to phase out other ozone-depleting substances.

In 1998, a UNEP–WMO assessment of ozone depletion, prepared by more than 200 scientists from around the world, confirmed the effectiveness of the Montreal Protocol. A full recovery of the Earth's protective ozone shield could occur by the middle of the next century — provided the Protocol is fully implemented. According to the assessment:

- The combined total abundance of ozone-depleting compounds in the troposphere (the lowest part of the atmosphere) peaked in 1994 and is now slowly declining;
- If measures had not been taken in accordance with the Montreal Protocol and its Amendments and Adjustments, the ozone decline would have been much stronger and would have continued for many more decades;
- Abundance of ozone-depleting substances in the stratosphere is expected to peak by 2000. However, when changing atmospheric conditions are combined with natural ozone variability, detecting the start of the ozone layer recovery may not be possible for perhaps another 20 years.

Even though the Protocol is working well to reduce the use and release of ozone-depleting substances, the life of chemicals already released in the atmosphere means that the depletion will continue for years to come.

Small islands

As requested by the Earth Summit, the United Nations held the **Global Conference on the Sustainable Development of Small Island Developing States** (Barbados, 1994). The Conference adopted a programme of action on problems affecting small islands, including economic isolation, overpopulation, degradation of land and marine environments, and possible sea-level rise caused by climate change.

Desertification

One quarter of the earth's land is threatened by desertification, according to UNEP estimates. In Africa, some 66 per cent of the continent is desert or drylands, and 73 per cent of agricultural drylands are already degraded. The livelihoods of over 1 billion people in more than 100 countries are jeopardized, as farming and grazing land becomes less productive. Drought can trigger desertification, but human activities

— overcultivation, overgrazing, deforestation, poor irrigation — are usually the most significant causes.

A United Nations treaty, negotiated as a result of the Earth Summit, seeks to address this problem: the *United Nations Convention to Combat Desertification in those Countries Experiencing Serious Drought and/or Desertification, Particularly in Africa.*

The Convention, which entered into force in 1996 and to which 125 countries are parties, provides the framework for all activity to combat desertification. It focuses on improving land productivity, rehabilitation of land, conservation and management of land and water resources. It emphasizes popular participation and an "enabling environment" for local people to help themselves reverse land degradation. It integrates the physical and biological dimensions of desertification with social and economic realities. It contains commitments for the preparation by affected countries of national action programmes, and gives an unprecedented role to NGOs in preparing and carrying out action programmes.

A number of United Nations agencies provide assistance to combat desertification. A special IFAD programme has mobilized $400 million, plus another $350 million contributed through co-financing, for projects in African countries threatened by desertification. UNDP funds activities to combat desertification through UNSO and its **United Nations Trust Fund for Sudano-Sahelian Activities.** Similarly, the World Bank organizes and funds programmes aimed at protecting fragile drylands and increasing agricultural productivity in these areas on a sustainable basis, while the FAO promotes sustainable agricultural development through a wide range of practical help to Governments.

Biodiversity, pollution and overfishing

Biodiversity — the variety of plant and animal species — is essential for human survival. The protection and conservation of the diverse range of species of animal and plant life and their habitats is the aim of the *United Nations Convention on Biological Diversity* (1992), to which 172 States are parties. The Convention obligates States to conserve biodiversity, ensure its sustainable development, and provide for the fair and equitable sharing of benefits from the use of genetic resources. Since 1992, States have been working on a protocol to ensure the safe use of genetically engineered organisms (*see also page 192, above*).

Protection of endangered species is also enforced under the 1973 *Convention on International Trade in Endangered Species*, administered by UNEP. States parties meet periodically to update the list of which plant and animal species or products, such as ivory, should be protected by quotas or outright bans.

Acid rain. Caused by emissions of sulphur dioxide from industrial manufacturing processes, "acid rain" has been significantly reduced in much of Europe and North America thanks to the 1979 *Convention on Long-Range Transboundary Air Pollution.* The Convention, to which 43 States are parties, is administered by the United Nations Economic Commission for Europe.

Hazardous wastes and chemicals. To regulate the 3 million tons of toxic waste that crosses national borders each year, Member States negotiated in 1989 the *Basel Convention on the Control of Transboundary Movements of Hazardous Wastes and their Disposal,* administered by UNEP. The treaty, to which 117 States are parties, was strengthened in 1995 to ban the export of toxic waste to developing countries, which often do not have the technology for safe disposal.

High seas fishing. The overfishing and near exhaustion of many species of commercially valuable fish and the increasing incidence of violence over fishing on the high seas led Governments at the Earth Summit to call for measures to conserve and sustainably manage fish which migrate across broad areas of the ocean or move between more than one country's exclusive economic zone. The 1995 United Nations Agreement on Straddling Fish Stocks and Highly Migratory Fish Stocks, signed by some 60 countries, provides for these species to be subject to quotas designed to ensure the continued survival of fish in the future, as well as steps for peacefully resolving disputes on the high seas.

Protecting the marine environment

The oceans cover two thirds of the Earth's surface, and protecting them has become one of the United Nations' primary concerns. UNEP's work, particularly its diverse efforts to protect the marine environment, has focused world attention on the oceans and seas and provided practical assistance in national and international efforts to address specific problems such as pollution (*see page 202, above*). The International Maritime Organization (IMO) is the United Nations specialized agency responsible for measures to prevent marine pollution from ships and improve the safety of international shipping (*see also Part One, page 60*). In spite of the dramatic expansion of world shipping, oil pollution from ships was cut by around 60 per cent during the 1980s and the number of oil spills during the last two decades has been greatly reduced. This is partly due to the introduction of better methods of controlling the disposal of wastes, and partly to the tightening of controls through conventions.

The pioneer *International Convention for the Prevention of Pollution of the Sea by Oil* was adopted in 1954, and IMO took over responsibility for it in 1959. In the late 1960s, a number of major tanker accidents led to further action. Since then, IMO has developed many measures to prevent accidents at sea and oil spills, to minimize their consequences, and to combat marine pollution — including that caused by the dumping into the seas of wastes generated by land-based activities. The main treaties are:

- *Convention on the Prevention of Marine Pollution by Dumping of Wastes and Other Matters* (1972);
- *International Convention Relating to Intervention on the High Seas in Cases of Oil Pollution Casualties* (1969);
- *International Convention on Oil Pollution Preparedness, Response and Cooperation* (1990).

IMO has also tackled the environmental threats caused by routine operations such as the cleaning of oil cargo tanks and the disposal of engine-room wastes — in tonnage terms a bigger menace than accidents. The most important of these measures is the 1973 *International Convention for the Prevention of Pollution from Ships*, as modified by its 1978 *Protocol (MARPOL 73/78)*. It covers not only accidental and operational oil pollution, but also pollution by chemicals, packaged goods, sewage and garbage. Recent changes to the Convention oblige all new tankers to be fitted with double hulls or a design that provides equivalent cargo protection in the event of a collision or grounding. Since 1995, these changes have also been applied to existing tankers when they reach 25 years of age.

Two IMO treaties establish a system for providing compensation to those who have suffered financially as a result of pollution. The treaties, adopted in 1969 and 1971, enable victims of oil pollution to obtain compensation much more simply and quickly than had been possible before (*for IMO action in transport and communication, see pages 150-151, above*).

Meteorology, climate and water

From weather prediction to climate-change research and tropical-storm forecasting, the **World Meteorological Organization (WMO)** coordinates global scientific efforts to improve accurate weather information, warnings and services for public, private and commercial use, including the airline and shipping industry and agricultural and water resources authorities (*see also Part One, page 59*). WMO's activities contribute to the safety of life and property, economic and social development, and the protection of the environment.

Within the United Nations, WMO provides the authoritative scientific voice on the state and behaviour of the Earth's atmosphere and climate. The agency:

- Facilitates international cooperation in establishing networks of stations for making meteorological, hydrological and other observations;
- Promotes the rapid exchange of meteorological information, the standardization of meteorological observations, and the uniform publication of observations and statistics;
- Furthers the application of meteorology to aviation, shipping, water problems, agriculture and other activities;
- Promotes operational hydrology;
- Encourages research and training.

The backbone of WMO's activities, the *World Weather Watch* programme offers up-to-the-minute worldwide weather information through observation systems and telecommunication links operated by member States, with 9 satellites, 10,000 land observation stations, 3,000 aircraft, 700 weather radars, 7,300 ship stations, and 700 moored and drifting buoys carrying automatic weather stations.

Each day, high-speed links transmit data and weather charts through 3 World, 35 Regional and 185 National Meteorological Centres, which cooperate in preparing weather analyses and forecasts, thus providing an up-to-date global weather watch. Thus ships and airplanes, research scientists, the media and the public are given a constant supply of timely data. It is through WMO that the complex agreements on standards, codes, measurements and communications are established internationally. A *Tropical Cyclone Programme* assists more than 50 countries vulnerable to tropical cyclones to minimize destruction and loss of life by improving forecasting and warning systems and disaster preparedness.

With climate change an issue of growing concern, the *World Climate Programme*, by collecting and preserving climate data, helps Governments to plan in response to the changing situation. The Programme aims at using climate information to improve economic and social planning; to improve understanding of climate processes through research; and to detect and warn Governments of impending climate variations or changes, either natural or man-made. Among its elements are the *World Climate Data and Monitoring Programme*, the *World Climate Applications and Services Programme*, the *World Climate Impact Assessment and Response Strategies Programme*, and the *World Climate Research Programme*. To assess all available information on climate change, WMO and UNEP established in 1988 the Intergovernmental Panel on Climate Change (*see page 204, above*).

The *Atmospheric Research and Environment Programme* coordinates research on the structure and composition of the atmosphere, the physics and chemistry of clouds, weather modification, tropical meteorology, transboundary transport of pollutants and weather forecasting. It helps member States to conduct research projects, to disseminate scientific information, and to incorporate the results of research into forecasting and other techniques. In particular, under the *Global Ozone Observing System*, over 140 ground-based stations, supplemented by satellites, constitute a global network to monitor ozone layer depletion.

Weather-related agricultural losses may approach 20 per cent of annual production in some countries. The *Applications of Meteorology Programme* helps countries to apply meteorology to the protection of life and property and to social and economic development. In agriculture, for instance, prompt meteorological advice can mean a substantial reduction in losses caused by pests and diseases. In drought-prone areas, the use of tailored meteorological bulletins permits increased crop yields. This Programme also supports activities related to public weather services.

The *Hydrology and Water Resources Programme* helps to assess, manage and conserve global water resources (*see also below*). It promotes global cooperation in evaluating water resources and developing hydrological networks and services, including data collection and processing, hydrological forecasting and warning, and the supply of meteorological and hydrological data for design purposes. This programme, for instance, facilitates cooperation within water basins shared between countries, and provides specialized forecasting in flood-prone areas, helping to preserve life and property.

WMO's *Technical Cooperation Programme* helps to build the capacity of developing countries to obtain technical expertise and equipment for improving their national meteorological and hydrological services. It fosters the transfer of technology, as well as of meteorological and hydrological knowledge and information.

The *Education and Training Programme* encourages the exchange of scientific knowledge through courses, seminars and conferences. In the last decade, the Programme awarded more than 3,250 fellowships for the advanced training of specialists from all over the world.

The *Regional Programme*, which cuts across the scientific and technical programmes, contributes to the implementation of global programmes at the regional level through close collaboration with member countries, regional organizations and regional and national offices of the United Nations system.

Natural resources and energy

The United Nations has long been involved in assisting countries in managing their natural resources on a sustainable basis. As early as 1952, the General Assembly declared that developing countries have "the right to determine freely the use of their natural resources" and that they must use such resources towards realizing their economic development plans in accordance with their national interests.

An ECOSOC body, the **Committee on Natural Resources**, develops guidelines on policies and strategies for ECOSOC and Governments; reviews arrangements to coordinate United Nations activities in natural resources development; evaluates trends and issues concerning natural resources exploration and development; and is concerned with the availability and sustainability of resources. Made up of 24 experts, it meets every two years.

Water resources

The United Nations has long been addressing the global crisis caused by growing demands on the world's water resources to meet human, commercial and agricultural needs. The **United Nations Water Conference** (Mar del Plata, Argentina, 1977), the **International Conference on Water and the Environment** (Dublin, 1992), the 1992 Earth Summit and the **International Drinking Water Supply and Sanitation Decade** (1981-1990) all focused on this vital resource. The Decade helped some 1.3 billion people in the developing countries gain access to safe drinking water.

United Nations activities are geared towards the sustainable development of fragile and finite freshwater resources, which are coming under increasing stress from population growth, pollution and increasing demand for agricultural and industrial purposes.

A 1997 United Nations assessment of freshwater resources concluded that overuse and pollution are limiting the amount of fresh water available to safely meet the needs of human society and the ecosystem. With agriculture highly dependent on access to ample freshwater resources, improved irrigation techniques will be necessary if there is to be enough food for the world's growing population. The volume of current consumption can be reduced without necessarily curtailing standards of living or economic growth, and the technologies to make this possible are already available. It is largely a question of adapting human activities to the exigencies of water supply, the assessment concludes. This study, prepared for the Earth

Summit +5 review, found that unless action is taken, by the year 2025 two thirds of the world's population will live in countries facing severe water problems likely to seriously affect human health and the ecosystem and hinder economic development.

In 1998, the Commission on Sustainable Development considered ways to increase access to water through market mechanisms, including pricing, while ensuring that poor people can afford water, mobilize funds for water programmes in developing countries and improve freshwater assessments as a basis for policy-making. The Commission is building on a series of meetings during 1998, both within and outside the United Nations, to forge international agreement on a strategy for freshwater.

Energy

While fossil-fuel use in developed countries is slowly stabilizing, many polluting emissions are on the increase. In many developing countries, rapid growth in fossil-fuel use is leading to severe pollution. Global energy consumption is projected to more than double by 2050. At the same time, over 2 billion people, mostly in rural areas of developing countries, do not have access to commercial energy services.

Many entities of the United Nations system are active in a variety of projects and programmes in the field of energy, often in the form of education and training, generation of awareness and capacity-building. Most of the projects seek to assist specific countries to meet their energy objectives. Other activities reflect the changing energy situation and the environmental impact of the development and use of energy resources.

In this area, the **Committee on New and Renewable Sources of Energy and Energy for Development** acts as an advisory body to ECOSOC. The 24-expert Committee, which meets every two years, seeks to foster environmentally sound and efficient fossil-fuel technologies, the efficient use of energy and materials, the development of renewable energy, and other innovations conducive to sustainable development.

Technical cooperation. The United Nations maintains an active programme of technical cooperation in the field of natural resources and energy. The programme comprises advisory services and capacity-building in formulating policies and strategies; project and programme formulation and implementation in natural resources management; and meetings and workshops.

In water and mineral resources, the United Nations system provides technical cooperation assistance and advisory services, emphasizing environmental protection, investment promotion, legislation and sustainable development.

During the last two decades, hundreds of technical cooperation and pre-investment projects in natural resources and energy involving hundreds of millions of dollars have been implemented by the United Nations and its family of organizations. A roughly equivalent amount was provided by the recipient Governments in the form of national staff, facilities and local operating costs. As a result, each year some 300 field projects assist developing countries in the development of their natural resources. Such projects strengthen national capacities, stimulate further investment and promote sustainable development.

Nuclear safety

Today, some 440 nuclear reactors produce 17 per cent of the world's electricity. In 10 countries, over 40 per cent of energy production comes from nuclear power. In this area, the **International Atomic Energy Agency (IAEA)**, an international organization in the United Nations family, fosters and guides the development of peaceful uses of atomic energy, and establishes standards for nuclear safety and environmental protection (*also see Part One, page 63*).

IAEA serves as the world's central intergovernmental forum for scientific and technical cooperation in the nuclear field. It provides a focal point for the exchange of information and the drawing up of guidelines and norms in the area of nuclear safety, as well as for the submission to Governments, at their request, of ways to improve the safety of reactors and avoid the risk of accidents. It also plays a prominent role in international efforts aimed at ensuring the use of nuclear technology for sustainable development.

On safety, IAEA formulates basic standards for radiation protection and issues regulations and codes of practice on specific types of operations, including the safe transport of radioactive materials. It facilitates emergency assistance to member States in the event of a radiation accident, under the *Convention on Assistance in the Case of a Nuclear Accident or Radiological Emergency* and the *Convention on Early Notification of a Nuclear Accident*. Other international treaties for which IAEA is the depositary include the *Convention on Physical Protection of Nuclear Material*, the *Vienna Convention on Civil Liability for Nuclear Damage*, the *Convention on Nuclear Safety*, and the *Joint Convention on the Safety of Spent Fuel Management and on the Safety of Radioactive Waste Management* — the first legal instrument to address those issues on a global scale.

IAEA aids and advises member countries on atomic-energy programmes, and fosters the exchange of scientific and technical information. Its technical cooperation activities to promote the peaceful uses of atomic energy help countries in the critical areas of water, health, nutrition, medicine and food production. A prime example is the work related to mutation breeding, through which nearly 2,000 new beneficial varieties of crops have been developed using radiation-based technology.

In the current debate on energy options to curb carbon dioxide emissions contributing to global warming, IAEA has stressed the benefits of nuclear power as an energy source economically competitive with coal, but free of greenhouse and other toxic gas emissions.

IAEA collects and disseminates information on virtually every aspect of nuclear science and technology through its *International Nuclear Information System (INIS)* in Vienna. With UNESCO, it operates the **International Centre for Theoretical Physics** in Trieste, Italy, and maintains three laboratories for studies in basic uses. IAEA works with FAO in research on atomic energy in food and agriculture, and with WHO on radiation in medicine and biology. IAEA's **Marine Environment Laboratory** in Monaco carries out worldwide marine pollution studies with UNEP and UNESCO.

(On IAEA's work in nuclear arms proliferation, see Chapter 2, page 113.)

Chapter 4

HUMAN RIGHTS

HUMAN RIGHTS

One of the great achievements of the United Nations is the creation of a comprehensive body of human rights law, which, for the first time in history, provides us with a universal and internationally protected code of human rights, one to which all nations can subscribe and to which all people can aspire. Not only has the Organization painstakingly defined a broad range of internationally accepted rights — including economic, social and cultural, as well as political and civil rights — it has also established mechanisms with which to promote and protect these rights and to assist Governments in carrying out their responsibilities.

Since the adoption of the Universal Declaration of Human Rights in 1948, human rights have received an unprecedented level of global attention and support. Women, children, disabled persons, minorities, indigenous peoples, migrant workers and other vulnerable groups now possess rights that protect them from discriminatory practices that had long been common in many societies. Rights have been extended through groundbreaking General Assembly decisions that have gradually established their universality, indivisibility and inter-relatedness with development and democratization. Education campaigns have tirelessly informed the world's public of their inalienable rights, while numerous national judicial and penal systems have been enhanced with United Nations training programmes and technical advice. The United Nations machinery to monitor compliance with human rights covenants has acquired a remarkable cohesiveness and weight among Member States.

Most recently, the post of the United Nations High Commissioner for Human Rights was created to strengthen and coordinate United Nations work for the protection and promotion of all human rights of all persons around the world. In his reform efforts, Secretary-General Kofi Annan has made human rights the central theme that unifies the Organization's work in the key areas of peace and security, development and humanitarian assistance.

Human rights instruments

At the San Francisco Conference in 1945 at which the United Nations was established, some 40 non-governmental organizations (NGOs) representing women, trade unions, ethnic organizations and religious groups joined forces with delegations, mostly from smaller countries, and pressed for more specific language on human rights than proposed by other States. This determined lobbying resulted in relatively strong provisions on human rights being incorporated into the *Charter of the United Nations*, laying the foundation for the post-1945 era of international law-making.

The Charter Preamble explicitly reaffirms "faith in fundamental human rights, in the dignity and worth of the human person, in the equal rights of men and women and of nations large and small". Article 3 calls for "promoting and encouraging respect for human rights and for fundamental freedoms for all without distinction as to race, sex, language, or religion". Other provisions commit States to take action in cooperation with the United Nations to achieve universal respect for human rights.

International Bill of Human Rights

Three years after the United Nations began work, the General Assembly put into place the first supporting pillar of twentieth-century human rights law: the *Universal Declaration of Human Rights*, which was intended as a "common standard of achievement for all peoples". It was adopted on 10 December 1948, the day which continues to be observed internationally as **Human Rights Day**. Its 30 articles spell out basic civil, cultural, economic, political and social rights that all human beings in every country should enjoy (*see box on facing page*). The fiftieth anniversary of the Universal Declaration is being celebrated during 1998.

Many provisions of the Universal Declaration are generally considered to have the weight of customary international law because they are so widely accepted and used as a yardstick for measuring the conduct of States. Many newly independent countries have cited the Universal Declaration or included its provisions in their basic laws or constitutions.

The Universal Declaration, together with the two International Covenants on Human Rights and their Optional Protocols, comprise the International Bill of Human Rights.

The broadest legally binding human rights agreements negotiated under United Nations auspices are the two International Covenants — one on Economic, Social and Cultural Rights and the other on Civil and Political Rights — the latter with two Optional Protocols which deal with recourse procedures which extend to individuals the right of individual petition, and with the abolition of the death penalty. These agreements, adopted in 1966, take the provisions of the Universal

(*continued on page 220*)

Defining universal rights

The *Universal Declaration of Human Rights*, a cornerstone of the wide-ranging body of human rights law created over the decades, marked its fiftieth anniversary during 1998. Articles 1 and 2 of the Universal Declaration state that "all human beings are born equal in dignity and rights" and are entitled to all the rights and freedoms set forth in the Declaration "without distinction of any kind such as race, colour, sex, language, religion, political or other opinion, national or social origin, property, birth or other status".

Articles 3 to 21 set forth the civil and political rights to which all human beings are entitled, including:

- The right to life, liberty and security;
- Freedom from slavery and servitude;
- Freedom from torture or cruel, inhuman or degrading treatment or punishment;
- The right to recognition as a person before the law; the right to judicial remedy; freedom from arbitrary arrest, detention or exile; the right to a fair trial and public hearing by an independent and impartial tribunal; the right to be presumed innocent until proved guilty;
- Freedom from arbitrary interference with privacy, family, home or correspondence; freedom from attacks upon honour and reputation; the right to protection of the law against such attacks;
- Freedom of movement; the right to seek asylum; the right to a nationality;
- The right to marry and to found a family; the right to own property;
- freedom of thought, conscience and religion; freedom of opinion and expression;
- The right to peaceful assembly and association;
- The right to take part in government and to equal access to public service.

Articles 22 to 27 set forth the economic, social and cultural rights to which all human beings are entitled, including:

- The right to social security;
- The right to work; the right to equal pay for equal work; the right to form and join trade unions;
- The right to rest and leisure;
- The right to a standard of living adequate for health and well-being;
- The right to education;
- The right to participate in the cultural life of the community.

The concluding Articles, 28 to 30, recognize that everyone is entitled to a social and international order in which the human rights set forth in the Declaration may be fully realized; that these rights may only be limited for the sole purpose of securing recognition and respect of the rights and freedoms of others and of meeting the requirements of morality, public order and the general welfare in a democratic society; and that each person has duties to the community in which she or he lives.

Declaration a step further by translating these rights into legally binding commitments and setting up bodies to monitor the compliance of States parties. A large majority of the world's countries are parties to the Covenants.

Economic, social and cultural rights

The *International Covenant on Economic, Social and Cultural Rights* entered into force in January 1976. By May 1998, it had 137 States parties. The States parties submit periodic reports to the Committee on Economic, Social and Cultural Rights, a body established by the Economic and Social Council (ECOSOC), on how they have been implementing its provisions. The human rights which the Covenant seeks to promote and protect are of three kinds:

- The right to work in just and favourable conditions;
- The right to social protection, to an adequate standard of living and to the highest attainable standards of physical and mental well-being;
- The right to education and the enjoyment of benefits of cultural freedom and scientific progress.

The Covenant provides for the realization of these rights without discrimination of any kind.

The Committee on Economic, Social, and Cultural Rights, an 18-member body of experts, studies these reports and discusses them with representatives of the Governments concerned. Its comments on the Covenant aim to help States parties in their task of implementation, as well as to bring to their attention deficiencies in reports and procedures. The Committee may also make recommendations to ECOSOC based on its consideration of individual reports.

Civil and political rights

The *International Covenant on Civil and Political Rights* and the *First Optional Protocol* to that Covenant both entered into force in March 1976. By May 1998, the Covenant had 140 States parties.

- The Covenant deals with such rights as freedom of movement; equality before the law; the right to a fair trial and presumption of innocence; freedom of thought, conscience and religion; freedom of opinion and expression; peaceful assembly; freedom of association, participation in public affairs and elections; and protection of minority rights.
- It prohibits arbitrary deprivation of life; torture, cruel or degrading treatment or punishment; slavery and forced labour; arbitrary

arrest or detention and arbitrary interference with privacy; war propaganda, and advocacy of racial or religious hatred.

The Covenant established an 18-member **Human Rights Committee**, which considers reports submitted by States parties on measures taken to implement the Covenant's provisions. For States parties to the First Optional Protocol, the Committee also receives and considers communications from individuals who claim that their human rights, being those rights protected by the Covenant, have been violated. The Committee considers communications from individuals in private meetings. Their letters and other documentation about individual cases remain confidential. The findings of the Committee, however, are made public immediately after the session at which they were adopted and are reproduced in the Committee's annual report to the General Assembly.

Other conventions

The Universal Declaration has served as the inspiration for some 80 conventions and declarations that have been concluded within the United Nations on a wide range of issues.

- The *Convention on the Prevention and Punishment of the Crime of Genocide* (1948), a direct response to the atrocities of the Second World War, defines the crime of genocide as the commission of certain acts with intent to destroy a national, ethnic, racial or religious group, and commits States to bringing to justice alleged perpetrators.

- The *Convention Relating to the Status of Refugees* (1951) defines the rights and duties of refugees, especially their right not to be forcibly returned to countries where they are at risk, and makes provisions for various aspects of their everyday lives, including their right to work, education, public assistance and social security, and their right to travel documents (*see also page 255*). The *Protocol relating to the Status of Refugees* (1967) ensured the universal application of the Convention, which was originally designed for refugees from the Second World War.

- The *International Convention on the Elimination of All Forms of Racial Discrimination* (1966) is one of the most widely ratified treaties, with 150 States parties as of May 1998. Beginning with the premise that any policy of racial superiority based on racial differences is unjustifiable, scientifically false and morally and legally condemnable, it defines "racial discrimination" and commits States parties to take measures to abolish such discrimination in both law and practice. The Convention established a monitoring body — the Committee on the Elimination of Racial Discrimination — to consider reports from States parties and, if authorized, petitions from individuals alleging a violation of the Convention.

- The *Convention on the Elimination of All Forms of Discrimination against Women* (1979), with 161 States parties as of May 1998, guarantees women equality with men before the law and specifies measures to eliminate discrimination against women with respect to political and public life, nationality, education, employment, health, marriage and the family. The Convention established the **Committee on the Elimination of Discrimination against Women** as the body to monitor its implementation and consider reports from States parties. Discussions have been under way since 1996 on a protocol to the Convention which would allow individuals to submit complaints on violations of the Convention to the Committee.

- The *Convention Against Torture and Other Inhuman or Degrading Treatment or Punishment* (1984), with 105 States parties as of May 1998, defines torture as an international crime, holds States parties accountable for preventing torture and requires them to punish the perpetrators. No exceptional circumstances may be invoked to justify torture, nor may a torturer offer a defence of having acted under orders. The monitoring body set up by the Convention, the **Committee against Torture**, reviews reports of States parties and can initiate investigations regarding countries where it believes the practice of torture is systematic. The United Nations has taken many other steps to prevent torture and assist victims. A **Special Rapporteur on the question of torture**, appointed by the Commission on Human Rights, reports annually on the practice worldwide, and makes recommendations to Governments aimed at stopping torture.

- The *Convention on the Rights of the Child* (1989) recognizes the particular vulnerability of children and brings together in one comprehensive code benefits and protections for children concerning all categories of human rights. The Convention firmly guarantees non-discrimination and recognizes that the best interests of the child must guide all actions. Special attention is paid to children who are refugees, disabled, or members of minorities. States parties are to provide guarantees for children's survival, development, protection and participation. The Convention is the most broadly ratified treaty, with 191 States parties as of May 1998. The **Committee on the Rights of the Child**, established by the Convention, oversees its implementation and considers reports submitted by States parties.

- The *International Convention on the Protection of the Rights of All Migrant Workers and Members of Their Families* (1990) defines basic rights and principles as well as measures to protect migrant workers, whether legal or illegal, throughout the process of migration. Unfortunately, the Convention is not yet in force, because only nine countries have ratified it to date. When it does enter into force, a monitoring committee will be set up.

The Universal Declaration and other United Nations instruments have also inspired several regional agreements, such as the European Convention on Human Rights, the American Convention on Human Rights and the African Charter of Human and Peoples Rights.

Other standards

In addition to these treaties, the United Nations has adopted many other standards and rules relating to the protection of human rights. These "declarations", "codes of conduct", "principles", etc. are not treaties which States become party to, but they have a big impact, not least because they are usually carefully drafted by States and adopted by consensus. Among the most important of these:

- The *Declaration on the Elimination of All Forms of Intolerance and of Discrimination Based on Religion and Belief* (1981) affirms the right of everyone to freedom of thought, conscience and religion and the right not to be subject to discrimination on the grounds of religion or other beliefs. The Commission appointed a Special Rapporteur (1986) to examine incidents and study measures to prevent intolerance based on religion and belief.

- The *Declaration on the Right to Development* (1986) established that right as "an inalienable human right by virtue of which each person and all peoples are entitled to participate in, contribute to and enjoy economic, social, cultural and political development in which all human rights and fundamental freedoms can be fully realized". It adds that "equality of opportunity for development is a prerogative both of nations and of individuals". The right to development was strongly reaffirmed in the Vienna Declaration and Programme of Action adopted by the World Conference on Human Rights in 1993 *(see page 230, below)*.

- The *Declaration on the Rights of Persons Belonging to National or Ethnic, Religious and Linguistic Minorities* (1992) proclaims the right of minorities to enjoy their own culture; to profess and practise their own religion; to use their own language; to establish and maintain contacts with other members of their group; and to leave any country, including their own, and to return to their country. The Declaration calls for action by States to promote and protect these rights.

Other important non-treaty standards include the *Standard Minimum Rules for the Treatment of Prisoners* (1957), the *Basic Principles on the Independence of the Judiciary* (1985), the *Body of Principles for the Protection of All Persons under Any Form of Detention or Imprisonment* (1988) and the *Declaration on the Protection of All Persons from Enforced Disappearance* (1992).

Human rights machinery

The United Nations Commission on Human Rights

The major United Nations body working to promote and protect human rights is the **United Nations Commission on Human Rights**, which was established in 1946 by ECOSOC. The Commission provides overall policy guidance, studies human rights problems, develops and codifies new international norms and monitors the observance of human rights around the world. As the principal intergovernmental policy-making body for human rights at the United Nations, the Commission is authorized to discuss human rights situations anywhere in the world and to examine information from States, NGOs and other sources.

The Commission provides a forum for States, intergovernmental organizations and NGOs to voice their concerns about human rights issues. Made up of 53 Member States elected for three-year terms, the Commission meets for six weeks each year in Geneva. While not entitled to vote, many other States participate in the Commission's work. States as well as NGOs present information on situations of concern to them; the Governments involved often submit replies. In light of the examination of such situations, fact-finding groups or experts may be designated, on-the-spot visits may be organized, discussions with Governments pursued, assistance provided and violations condemned.

If a particular situation is deemed sufficiently serious, the Commission may order an investigation by either a group of independent experts (Working Group) or an individual (Special Rapporteur). Based on information received from these experts, the Commission then calls upon the Government concerned to bring about needed changes.

In 1947, the Commission on Human Rights established the **Subcommission on Prevention of Discrimination and Protection of Minorities**, which meets annually and consists of 26 members who serve as experts in their personal capacity, not as State representatives. Originally dedicated to the issues of discrimination and minority protection, over the years the Subcommission has greatly expanded its scope of concern to cover a broad range of human rights issues. It has initiated many studies of human rights issues, particularly on the development of legal rules, and makes recommendations to the Commission on Human Rights. NGOs take part in the work of the Subcommission.

The High Commissioner for Human Rights

The post of High Commissioner for Human Rights was created in 1993 to strengthen the coordination and impact of United Nations human rights activities. Appointed for a four-year term, the High Commissioner is charged with many tasks, including: promoting and protecting the effective enjoyment by all of all human rights; promoting international cooperation for human rights; stimulating and coordinating action on human rights in the United Nations system; and assisting in developing new human rights standards and promoting ratification of human rights treaties. The High Commissioner is also mandated to respond to serious violations of human rights and to undertake action to prevent violations. The High Commissioner undertakes human rights field activities, and provides advisory service and technical assistance to Governments.

The **Office of the High Commissioner for Human Rights (OHCHR)** is the focal point for United Nations human rights activities and serves as the secretariat for the Commission on Human Rights, the treaty bodies (expert committees monitoring treaty compliance) and other United Nations human rights organs. In addition to the regular budget, some of its activities are financed through voluntary or trust funds.

The first High Commissioner began work in 1994 and was succeeded in 1997 by Mary Robinson, a former President of Ireland. Under the direction and authority of the Secretary-General, the High Commissioner reports on her activities to the Commission on Human Rights and through ECOSOC to the General Assembly. In her work to prevent human rights violations, the High Commissioner seeks to establish a dialogue on human rights issues with all Governments. Within the United Nations system, she works to strengthen and streamline the United Nations human rights machinery to make it more efficient and effective.

In recent years, the High Commissioner has taken concrete steps to institutionalize cooperation and coordination with the United Nations Children's Fund (UNICEF), the United Nations Educational, Scientific and Cultural Organization (UNESCO), the United Nations Development Programme (UNDP), the Office of the United Nations High Commissioner for Refugees (UNHCR), and the United Nations Volunteers. Similarly, the Office works in close cooperation with the Departments of the United Nations Secretariat on efforts to provide early warning of potential crises in order to take action before they escalate.

Technical cooperation programme

One of the most rapidly expanding areas of the United Nations human rights work is its programme of providing, at the request of States, assistance in the promotion and protection of human rights. Technical cooperation projects are undertaken in specific countries, as well as at the regional and international levels. Such programmes often include training courses for members of the armed forces, law enforcement officials, members of the judiciary, lawyers and others involved in the administration of justice, as well as advice on incorporating international human rights standards into national law. Advice and assistance is provided on drawing up national plans of action for the protection of human rights, and on human rights aspects of electoral laws and the carrying out of elections. The programme also provides fellowships and scholarships to persons responsible for promoting and protecting human rights in their countries.

A key function of the technical cooperation programme concerns support to the establishment and strengthening of national institutions for the promotion and protection of human rights. OHCHR encourages States to set up such institutions, offers advice on how to ensure that such institutions are effective, and promotes cooperation between different national institutions.

The technical cooperation programme is carrying out activities in more than 20 countries and on some 10 different regional and international themes.

Field presence

A relatively new feature of the United Nations human rights programme is the establishment of OHCHR field offices and operations. United Nations human rights staff in the field engage in a variety of functions: they provide on-the-spot advice, training or assistance to Governments on such matters as legal reform and strengthening national structures for human rights protection. They may also be given a mandate to monitor respect for human rights or to work with local

NGOs. As of 1998, the OHCHR had field offices in Burundi, Cambodia, Colombia, the Democratic Republic of the Congo, the former Yugoslavia, Gaza (Palestinian Authority), Georgia (Abkhazia), Malawi, Mongolia and Rwanda.

Information

Human rights education and information material is produced by OHCHR and the United Nations Department of Public Information. A key source of information is the OHCHR Web site (www.unhchr.ch). The **United Nations Decade for Human Rights Education** was launched in 1995.

Promoting and protecting human rights

The role and scope of United Nations action in promoting and protecting human rights continue to expand, but the central mandate remains: to ensure that the human dignity of the ultimate constituents, the "peoples" of the United Nations, in whose name the Charter was written, is fully respected. Through the international machinery, the United Nations is at work on several fronts:

- **As global conscience** — The United Nations has set a pace in establishing minimum standards of acceptable behaviour by nations, and keeping the attention of the international community focused on human rights practices that threaten to undermine those standards. Human rights declarations and conventions are adopted by the General Assembly, underscoring their universality.

- **As lawmaker** — An unprecedented codification of international law has taken place. Those human rights pertaining to women, children, prisoners and detainees, and mentally disabled persons, as well as violations such as genocide, racial discrimination and torture, to name just a few, are now a major part of international law which at one time focused almost exclusively on relations between States.

- **As monitor** — The United Nations has played a central role in ensuring that human rights are not just defined in the abstract, but also put into practice. The International Covenants on Civil and Political Rights and on Economic, Social and Cultural Rights (1966) are among the earliest examples of treaties that empower international bodies to monitor how States live up to their commitments. Treaty bodies, Special Rapporteurs and Working Groups of the Commission on Human Rights each have procedures and mechanisms to monitor compliance with international standards and investigate allegations of human rights abuses. Their resolutions on specific cases carry a moral weight that few Governments are willing to defy.

- **As nerve-centre** — OHCHR receives communications from groups and individuals claiming violations of their human rights. On the average, about 100,000 complaints are received per year. OHCHR refers these communications to the appropriate United Nations organs and mechanisms, taking into account the implementation procedures established by conventions and resolutions. OHCHR maintains a 24-hour fax hotline in Geneva (41-22-917-0092) to receive emergency complaints about violations of human rights.

- **As researcher** — The data compiled by the United Nations on human rights issues is indispensable to the development and application of human rights law. For example, some 80 country studies provided the basis of an instrument being drafted to protect the rights of indigenous peoples. OHCHR prepares studies and reports requested by United Nations bodies on human rights issues, pointing the way towards policies, practices and new institutions which can enhance respect for human rights.

- **As forum of appeal** — Under the First Optional Protocol to the International Covenant on Civil and Political Rights, the International Convention on the Elimination of All Forms of Racial Discrimination and the Convention Against Torture, individual complaints may be brought against States that have accepted the relevant international legal procedures, once all domestic remedies have been exhausted. Also, under procedures established by the Commission on Human Rights, the Commission, its Sub-Commission on Prevention of Discrimination and Protection of Minorities and their Working Groups hear numerous complaints annually submitted by NGOs or individuals.

- **As fact-finder** — The Commission on Human Rights has established mechanisms to monitor and report on the incidence of certain kinds of abuses, and on violations in a specific country. The mechanisms entrusted with this politically sensitive, humanitarian and sometimes dangerous task are **Special Rapporteurs/ Representatives** or **Working Groups**. They gather facts, keep contact with local groups and government authorities, conduct on-site visits when Governments permit, and make recommendations on how respect for human rights might be strengthened.

  There are thematic Special Rapporteurs/Representatives and Working Groups that report on enforced or involuntary disappearances, torture, religious intolerance, summary executions, arbitrary detention, freedom of expression, the sale of children, mercenaries, racial discrimination, independence of the judiciary, internally displaced persons, violence against women and the effects of toxic and dangerous products on the enjoyment of human rights.

Country-specific Special Rapporteurs/Representatives are currently reporting on Afghanistan, Cuba, Democratic Republic of the Congo, Equatorial Guinea, Iran, Iraq, Occupied Arab Territories (including Palestine), Myanmar, Sudan, former Yugoslavia, Rwanda, and Burundi. In addition, mandates have been entrusted to the Secretary-General to prepare reports on Bougainville (part of Papua New Guinea), Cyprus, East Timor, Southern Lebanon and West Bekaa, Togo, Occupied Palestine, Occupied Arab Territories, Occupied Syria and Golan, and Chechnya.

- **As discreet diplomat** — The Commission on Human Rights may ask the Secretary-General to intervene or send an expert to examine a human rights situation with a view to preventing flagrant violations. Such efforts of quiet diplomacy are also undertaken by the Secretary-General in the exercise of his "good offices" and may establish the United Nations' legitimate concern and curb abuses. The Secretary-General, or his special representatives, and the High Commissioner for Human Rights, confidentially raise human rights concerns with Member States on items such as the release of prisoners, commutation of death sentences and other issues.

Major conferences

The twentieth anniversary of the adoption of the Universal Declaration of Human Rights was commemorated in 1968 as the **International Year for Human Rights**. The major event of the Year, the **International Conference on Human Rights**, held in Tehran, Iran, was the first worldwide governmental conference devoted exclusively to the subject.

The **World Conference on Human Rights** (Vienna, 1993), the first global review of human rights since the Tehran Conference, was seen as a major reaffirmation of the universality and the central role of human rights at a time when their promotion and protection were under attack in many parts of the world. The Conference, which was marked by an unprecedented degree of participation by government delegates and the non-governmental human rights community, assessed progress made since the adoption of the Universal Declaration of Human Rights in 1948 and identified obstacles and ways in which they might be overcome.

The Conference demonstrated a growing determination among Member States and human rights NGOs and other actors that the existing body of human rights law needed to be implemented by vigorous operational activities undertaken by the United Nations. Human rights — in the words of the **Vienna Declaration** adopted at the World Conference — had become the "legitimate concern of the international community". The Vienna Declaration further proclaimed that "democracy, development and respect for human rights and fundamental freedoms are interdependent and mutually reinforcing".

The Declaration underscores the universal nature of human rights: "All human rights are universal, indivisible, interdependent and interrelated. The international community must treat human rights globally in a fair and equal manner, on the same footing, and with the same emphasis. While the significance of national and regional particularities and various historical, cultural and religious backgrounds must be borne in mind, it is the duty of States, regardless of their political, economic and cultural systems, to promote and protect all human rights and fundamental freedoms."

The Vienna Conference also confirmed the need to make clear that the areas of protection had become increasingly specific: preventing genocide, abolishing slavery, combating torture and eliminating all forms of discrimination based on race, sex, religion or belief. In the same way, the beneficiaries of human rights had become better defined: women's rights, rights of indigenous peoples, protection of refugees, stateless persons, children, physically and mentally disabled persons, protection of detainees and victims of enforced disappearance, and protection of the rights of migrant workers and their families were all specifically highlighted.

The Conference revealed tensions around many difficult issues — such as national sovereignty, universality, the role of NGOs and questions as to the feasibility, viability and impartiality of new or strengthened human rights instruments. The **Vienna Declaration and Programme of Action**, adopted by consensus at the Conference by 171 States, marked historic new steps to promote and protect human rights by:

- Declaring that all human rights are universal, indivisible, interdependent and interrelated;
- Reaffirming the right to development and the inextricable relationship between human rights and development (*see below*);
- Urging the universal ratification of human rights treaties, including setting target dates of 1995 and 2000 for ratification of the

Convention on the Rights of the Child and the Convention on the Elimination of All Forms of Discrimination against Women, respectively;

- Supporting the establishment of a Special Rapporteur on Violence against Women;
- Calling for more resources to be provided to United Nations human rights activities;
- Recommending that the General Assembly proclaim an international decade of the world's indigenous people and a decade for human rights education, which it did in the following months.

The Conference also recommended that the General Assembly consider as a matter of priority the establishment of the position of the High Commissioner for Human Rights; the Assembly established this post later that year.

Right to development

The recognition that grinding poverty and underdevelopment affect the enjoyment of human rights has long been part of the approach of the United Nations to human rights, reflected first in the Universal Declaration itself. The *Declaration on the Right to Development*, adopted by the General Assembly in 1986, marked a major turning point in efforts to turn this recognition into a reality, and which has had practical implications for the way in which national and international development policies related to development are pursued. In the Vienna Declaration, States attached a high priority to the right to development, and this is explicitly reflected in the mandate of the High Commissioner. A **Working Group on the Right to Development** and, most recently, an **Intergovernmental Group of Experts** have been mandated by the Commission on Human Rights to develop strategies for the implementation of the right to development.

The rights of labour

Defining and protecting the rights of labour is another major area of concern for the United Nations. The tripartite **International Labour Conference**, one of the principal bodies of the **International Labour Organization (ILO)**, and which is made up of government, employer and worker representatives, has set international standards through a series of conventions and recommendations (*see also Part One, page 51*). After ratification by member States, conventions create binding obligations to put their provisions into effect. Recommendations provide guidance on policy, legislation and practice.

Over the years, the Governments of member States and their employers' and workers' organizations have built up a system of international standards in all work-related matters. Altogether, some 181 Conventions and 188 Recommendations have been adopted. While many are concerned with matters such as labour administration, industrial relations, employment policy, working conditions, social security, occupational safety and health, others relate to ensuring basic human rights in the work place, and to issues such as the employment of women, children and special categories of workers, such as the disabled.

ILO's supervisory procedure to ensure the application of its conventions in law and practice is the most advanced of all such international procedures. It is based on the objective evaluation by independent experts of the manner in which obligations are complied with, and on the examination of cases by the ILO's tripartite bodies. There is a special procedure to investigate complaints of infringements of freedom of association.

The ILO has brought about many landmark conventions:

* *On Forced Labour* (1930): requires the suppression of forced or compulsory labour in all its forms;

* *On Freedom of Association and Protection of the Right to Organize* (1948): establishes the right of workers and employers to form and join organizations without prior authorization; lays down guarantees for the free functioning of such organizations;

* *On Right to Organize and Collective Bargaining* (1949): provides for protection against anti-union discrimination, for protection of workers' and employers' organizations and for measures to promote collective bargaining;

* *On Equal Remuneration* (1951): calls for equal pay and benefits for work of equal value;

* *On Discrimination* (1958): calls for national policies to promote equality of opportunity and treatment, and to eliminate discrimination in the workplace on grounds of race, colour, sex, religion, political opinion, extraction or social origin;

* *On Minimum Age* (1973): aiming at the abolition of child labour, it stipulates that the minimum age for employment shall not be less than the age of completion of compulsory schooling.

In addition, the General Assembly has taken a number of measures to protect the rights of migrant workers (*see page 242, below*).

The struggle against discrimination

Apartheid

One of the great successes that demonstrated the ways in which the United Nations can bring an end to major injustices in the world is its role in the overthrow of South Africa's apartheid rule. Practically from its inception, the United Nations was involved in the struggle against apartheid, a system of institutionalized racial segregation and discrimination imposed by the South African Government.

When, in 1994, the newly elected President of South Africa, Nelson Mandela, addressed the United Nations General Assembly, he observed that it was the first time in its 49 years that the Assembly had been addressed by a South African head of State drawn from among the African majority. Welcoming the vanquishing of apartheid, President Mandela said: "That historic change has come about not least because of the great efforts in which the United Nations engaged to ensure the suppression of the apartheid crime against humanity."

Condemned by the United Nations in 1966 as a "crime against humanity" incompatible with the Charter and the Universal Declaration of Human Rights, the issue of apartheid was on the agenda of the General Assembly from 1948 until the end of apartheid in 1994. During the 1950s, the General Assembly repeatedly appealed to the South African Government to abandon apartheid in the light of the principles of the Charter.

- The **United Nations Special Committee against Apartheid**, established in 1962 by the General Assembly to keep the racial policies of South Africa under review, became the focal point in the efforts of the international community to promote a comprehensive programme of action against apartheid and to encourage support and assistance to the people of South Africa and to their liberation movements.
- The General Assembly adopted the *International Convention on the Suppression and Punishment of the Crime of Apartheid* in 1973.
- The Security Council instituted a voluntary arms embargo against South Africa in 1963, and made it mandatory in 1977 after determining that the country's aggressions against its neighbours and its potential nuclear capability constituted a threat to international peace and security — the first time the Council had taken such action against a Member State.
- The General Assembly called for a sports boycott of South Africa in 1971, a move which had an ongoing impact on public opinion in South Africa and abroad, and adopted the *International Declaration*

against Apartheid in Sports (1977) and the *International Convention Against Apartheid in Sports* (1985).

- Among its many censures of South Africa, the General Assembly did not accept its credentials to the Assembly's regular sessions from 1970 through 1974, thereby refusing to allow the delegation of South Africa to participate in its work. South Africa did not participate in the proceedings of the Assembly until the overthrow of apartheid in 1994.

- In 1985, when the South African Government proclaimed a state of emergency and escalated repression, the international community again reacted strongly. The Security Council, for the first time, called on Governments to take significant economic measures against South Africa under Chapter VII of the Charter.

- The transition from the apartheid Government to a non-racial democracy, facilitated by a National Peace Accord between the Government and major political parties in 1990, was fully supported by the United Nations. Two Security Council resolutions in 1992 emphasized the involvement by the international community in facilitating the transition. In September, the Security Council deployed the **United Nations Observer Mission in South Africa (UNOMSA)** to strengthen the structures of the peace accord. UNOMSA observed the 1994 elections that led to the establishment of a non-racial and democratic government. With the installation of the new Government and the adoption of the first non-racial, democratic constitution, the apartheid system came to an end.

Racism

In 1963, the General Assembly adopted the *United Nations Declaration on the Elimination of All Forms of Racial Discrimination.* The Declaration affirms the fundamental equality of all persons and confirms that discrimination between human beings on the grounds of race, colour or ethnic origin is a violation of the human rights proclaimed in the Universal Declaration and an obstacle to friendly and peaceful relations among nations and peoples.

Two years later, the General Assembly adopted the *International Convention on the Elimination of All Forms of Racial Discrimination*, which among other provisions allowed the Committee on the Elimination of Racial Discrimination, where the State had accepted its competence, to consider complaints from individuals and obliged States parties to adopt legislative, judicial, administrative and other measures to prevent and punish racial discrimination.

The General Assembly in 1993 proclaimed the **Third Decade to Combat Racism and Racial Discrimination (1993-2003)** and called on all States to take measures to combat new forms of racism, especially through laws, administrative measures, education and information. The Assembly declared that all forms of racism and racial discrimination, including those resulting from official doctrines of racial superiority, such as ethnic cleansing, are among the most serious violations of human rights in the contemporary world and must be combatted by all available means. The first Decade had been proclaimed in 1973, and the second in 1983.

Also, in 1993 the Commission on Human Rights appointed a **Special Rapporteur on Contemporary Forms of Racism, Racial Discrimination, Xenophobia and Related Intolerance**, whose mandate is to examine incidents worldwide of contemporary forms of racism; racial discrimination; any form of discrimination against blacks, Arabs and Muslims; xenophobia; anti-semitism; and related intolerance, as well as governmental measures to overcome them. Two **World Conferences to Combat Racism and Racial Discrimination** were held in Geneva in 1978 and 1983. The General Assembly has decided to hold a third conference by 2001.

The rights of women

Equality for women has been a focus of the work of the United Nations since its founding 50 years ago and the establishment of the Commission on the Status of Women in 1946 as a special body to deal with women's issues. The United Nations has been a staunch ally in the struggle to attain women's rights universally and the efforts to ensure that women have equal access to public life and to opportunities in all aspects of economic and social development (*see also Chapter 3, pages 178-180*).

In recent years, the United Nations family of organizations have all undertaken reviews of their work to ensure that women are better integrated into decision-making bodies and considered a central component of their policies and programmes in the field. In addition, steps have been taken to ensure the advancement of women in the work of the Organization itself.

Commission on the Status of Women

The **Commission on the Status of Women**, made up of 45 Member States, examines women's progress towards equality throughout the world, prepares recommendations on promoting women's rights in political, economic, social and educational fields, and addresses problems requiring immediate attention in the field of women's rights. It also drafts treaties and other instruments aimed at improving the status of women in law and in practice.

The Beijing Platform for Action

The action plan adopted by the Fourth World Conference on Women identified 12 critical areas of concern:

- The persistent and increasing burden of poverty on women;
- Unequal access to and inadequate educational opportunities;
- Inequalities in health status, and unequal access to and inadequate health-care services;
- Violence against women;
- Effects of armed or other kinds of conflict on women;
- Inequality in women's access to and participation in the definition of economic structures and policies and the production process itself;
- Inequality between men and women in the sharing of power and decision-making at all levels;
- Insufficient mechanisms at all levels to promote the advancement of women;
- Lack of awareness of, and commitment to, internationally and nationally recognized women's human rights;
- Insufficient mobilization of mass media to promote women's positive contribution to society;
- Lack of adequate recognition and support for women's contribution to managing natural resources and safeguarding the environment;
- The girl child.

The activities of the Commission have evolved from defining rights to exploring factors that have prevented women from enjoying them. Thus, emphasis has shifted to the underlying social and cultural causes of gender discrimination. In 1993, for example, a *Declaration on the Elimination of Violence against Women*, elaborated by the Commission, was adopted by the General Assembly. The Declaration includes a clear definition of violence as being physical, sexual and psychological violence occurring in the family or the community and perpetrated or condoned by the State.

The United Nations has facilitated international guidelines and law for the advancement of women, most notably the **Convention on the Elimination of Discrimination against Women (CEDAW)** in 1979. The Commission is drafting a protocol to the Convention which would allow individuals to submit complaints to the **Committee on the Elimination of Discrimination against Women**, the body overseeing the implementation of the Convention.

World conferences

Three world conferences during the United Nations–sponsored **International Women's Decade (1976-1985)** — Mexico City, 1975; Copenhagen, 1980; and Nairobi, 1985 — greatly enhanced international awareness of the concerns of women and provided the groundwork for invaluable links between national women's movements and the international community. The *Nairobi Forward-looking Strategies for the Advancement of Women to the Year 2000*, produced by the Third World Conference on Women in 1985, continues, along with the Convention, to be a benchmark in advancing and monitoring the global progress of women.

Despite clear signs of progress in education, health and access to employment, the Commission on the Status of Women has continued to press its concerns that implementation of the Nairobi Forward-looking Strategies has been inadequate in many areas. In calling for the **Fourth World Conference on Women** in Beijing (1995), the Commission warned that the failure of societies to achieve true gender equality would result in slow economic and diminished social and political development, misuse of human resources and reduced progress for society as a whole.

Together with the World Food Summit and Habitat II in 1996, the Beijing Conference marked the culmination of the cycle of major United Nations conferences which, combined with the energy of national women's movements, have galvanized understanding, interest and action concerning the advancement of women around the world. These United Nations conferences and summits on education, children, the environment, human rights, population and social development as well as that on women have reflected a common concern regarding the pivotal role of women in development and society.

The World Conference on Human Rights, in particular, achieved a major breakthrough by responding to the worldwide campaign that "women's rights are human rights". The Conference called for the integration of women's human rights in the work of United Nations human rights bodies. It considered issues of violence against women in public and private life as human rights issues. In a unique international statement, the Conference called for the eradication of any conflicts which may arise between the rights of women and the harmful effects of certain traditional or customary practices, cultural prejudices and religious extremism.

Through its operational bodies, the United Nations is able to further the empowerment of women, particularly in regard to overall development efforts (*see Chapter 3, page 178*). In addition to the work done by the United Nations Secretariat, in particular the Division for the Advancement of Women, and the specialized agencies, funds and programmes, there are two other entities dedicated exclusively to women: the **United Nations Development Fund for Women**

(UNIFEM) and the **International Research and Training Institute for the Advancement of Women (INSTRAW)**. Both were created to support programmes and projects that improve the quality of life for women (*see Chapter 3, pages 179-180*).

The rights of children

Millions of children die every year from malnutrition and disease. Countless others become victims of armed conflict and extreme forms of exploitation and abuse such as sexual exploitation. The **United Nations Children's Fund (UNICEF)**, the lead advocate for children in the United Nations system, has described the world's children as the "forgotten quarter" of the Earth's people (*see also Chapter 3, pages 181-183*). Guided by the Convention on the Rights of the Child, UNICEF strives to establish child rights as enduring ethical principles and international standards of behaviour towards children.

The *Declaration of the Rights of the Child*, adopted by the General Assembly in 1959, affirms the right of children to special protection, opportunities and facilities for healthy, normal development. These and other rights were transformed into binding legal obligations through the adoption by the Assembly in 1989 of the *Convention on the Rights of the Child*, now almost universally ratified, except for two countries. The **Committee on the Rights of the Child**, established under the Convention, meets regularly to monitor the progress made by States parties in fulfilling their obligations. The Committee can make suggestions and recommendations to Governments and to the General Assembly on ways in which the objectives of the Convention may be met.

The Convention on the Rights of the Child provides a standard against which the behaviour of nations can be measured and improved. Working groups of the Commission on Human Rights are currently drafting two protocols to the Convention, one that would prevent the recruitment of children under 18 into armed forces or their participation in hostilities, another that would strengthen international prohibitions concerning the sale of children, child prostitution and child pornography.

Regarding the problem of child labour, the goals of the United Nations are to protect working children from exploitation and hazardous conditions that endanger their physical and mental development, to ensure children's access to at least minimum levels of education, nutrition and health care, and, over the long term, to achieve the progressive elimination of child labour.

- In 1990, the **International Labour Organization (ILO)** launched a major global offensive by establishing the International Programme on the Elimination of Child Labour. Upon the request of individuals, the programme provides technical advisory services focusing on the worst abuses: hazardous work, forced labour, street children, girls and the employment of children who are less than 13 years old.
- In 1992, the General Assembly urged Governments and the Commission on Human Rights to take action on the problem of street children, who are increasingly involved in and affected by serious crime, drug abuse, violence and prostitution.
- The **Subcommission on Prevention of Discrimination and Protection of Minorities** has called for steps to halt the recruitment or conscription of children into armed forces. On the basis of a wide-ranging report prepared by Ms. Graça Machel, the former Minister of Education of Mozambique, in 1996, the Secretary-General in 1997 appointed a **Special Representative for Children in Conflict**, Mr. Olara Otunnu.
- The Commission on Human Rights has appointed a **Special Rapporteur on the Sale of Children, Child Prostitution and Child Pornography and the Use of Adoption for Commercial Purposes**.

The rights of minorities

The United Nations has from its inception sought to place minority rights high on its human rights agenda. The protection of the human rights of members of minority ethnic, religious or linguistic groups is guaranteed specifically in the International Covenant on Civil and Political Rights, and more generally in the principle of non-discrimination which is basic to all United Nations human rights law. The adoption by the General Assembly of the *Declaration on the Rights of Persons Belonging to National or Ethnic, Religious and Linguistic Minorities* in 1992 gave a new impetus to the United Nations, and in 1995 the Commission on Human Rights approved the establishment by its Subcommission of a **Working Group on Minorities**. The Working Group recommends practical measures for the better promotion and protection of the rights of persons belonging to minorities.

Indigenous people

The United Nations has increasingly taken up the cause of indigenous people, who are considered, among the world's minorities, one of the most disadvantaged groups. Indigenous people are also called "first peoples", tribal peoples, aboriginals and autochthons. There are at least

5,000 indigenous groups, made up of 300 million people, living in over 70 countries on five continents. Excluded from decision-making processes, many have been marginalized, exploited, forcefully assimilated and subjected to repression, torture and murder when they speak out in defence of their rights. Fearing persecution, they often become refugees and sometimes must hide their identity, abandoning their languages and traditional customs and clothing.

In 1982, the Subcommission of the Commission on Human Rights established a **Working Group on Indigenous Populations**, which prepared a draft *Declaration on the Rights of Indigenous Peoples* for eventual adoption by the General Assembly. The draft was approved by the Subcommission in 1994 and is being considered by the Commission. A voluntary fund provides financial assistance to representatives of indigenous groups who wish to travel to participate in official meetings where the draft declaration is being discussed.

The 1992 Earth Summit heard the collective voice of indigenous peoples as they expressed their concerns about the deteriorating state of their lands and the environment. UNDP, UNICEF, the International Fund for Agricultural Development (IFAD), UNESCO, the World Bank and the World Health Organization (WHO) all have programmes directed at specific indigenous groups working to improve health and literacy and combat environmental degradation of their native lands.

At the conclusion of the **International Year of the World's Indigenous People (1993)**, the Assembly proclaimed the **International Decade of the World's Indigenous People (1994-2004)**.

Persons with disabilities

More than 500 million persons — 10 per cent of the world's population, an estimated 80 per cent of them living in the developing world — suffer from some type of physical, mental or sensory impairment.

- Disabled persons are often denied basic educational opportunities as children and, as adults, are often given menial or poorly paid jobs.
- Physical restrictions often bar them from public buildings and transport.
- Social attitudes exclude them from cultural life and normal social relationships.
- Prejudice and ignorance lead to unnecessary institutionalization.
- Society also suffers, since the loss of their enormous potential as human beings impoverishes humankind.

The rights of disabled persons do not appear in any single formal listing but are scattered throughout court rulings, ILO recommendations and a number of legal instruments. Thus, they find themselves at a legal disadvantage in relation to other vulnerable groups such as refugees and migrant workers.

The **International Year of Disabled Persons (1981)** saw the adoption of a **World Programme of Action Concerning Disabled Persons**, the primary statement of principles for disabled persons, and led to the **United Nations Decade of Disabled Persons (1983-1992)**. Two monitoring exercises during the Decade, in 1987 and in 1992, acknowledged that despite many efforts, disabled persons continued to be denied equal opportunities and in many societies remained isolated.

It has been the United Nations call for global "equalization of opportunity" for persons with disabilities that has prompted cities and towns throughout the world to provide such seemingly simple, basic and obvious services as access ramps and sidewalk indentations for the convenience of disabled people.

Eleven years in the making, a new set of standards for the protection of people with mental illness — the *Principles for the protection of persons with mental illness and the improvement of health care* — was adopted by the General Assembly in 1991. The standards cover a wide range of issues and rights, and state, among other things, that:

- Determination of mental illness should never be made on the basis of political, economic or social status; membership of a cultural, racial or religious group; or any other reason not directly relevant to mental health status;

- Physical restraint or involuntary seclusion should not be used, except as the only means available to prevent immediate harm to the patient or others;

- Sterilization should never be a treatment for mental illness;

- Psychosurgery and other intrusive and irreversible treatments should not be carried out involuntarily;

- Every effort should be made to avoid involuntary hospitalization.

In 1994, the General Assembly endorsed a long-term strategy to further the implementation of the World Programme of Action Concerning Disabled Persons. The strategy set as its ultimate goal "a society for all", encompassing human diversity and the development of the human potential of each person.

Migrant workers

With increasing movement of people across international frontiers in search of work, a new human rights convention was approved to curb discrimination against migrant workers. In 1990, following 10 years of negotiations, the *International Convention on the Protection of the Rights of All Migrant Workers and Members of Their Families* was adopted by the General Assembly.

- The Convention makes it illegal to expel migrant workers on a collective basis or to destroy their identity documents, work permits or passports.
- It also states, among other things, that migrant workers are entitled to receive the same remuneration, social benefits and medical care as nationals; to join or take part in meetings of trade unions; and, upon ending their employment, to transfer earnings, savings and personal belongings.
- Children of migrant workers have the right to registration of birth and nationality and of access to education.

As of May 1998, the Convention had not yet acquired the necessary number of ratifications (20) to enter into force.

Administration of justice

The United Nations has taken many steps to strengthen the protection of human rights in the judicial process. When individuals are under investigation by State authorities, when they are arrested, detained, charged, tried or imprisoned, there is always the need to ensure that the application of the law shows due regard for human rights protections. The United Nations has worked to develop standards and codes to serve as models for national legislation, covering matters such as the treatment of prisoners, the protection of detained juveniles, the use of firearms by police, the conduct of law-enforcement officials, the role of lawyers and prosecutors, and the independence of the judiciary. Many of these standards have been developed through the United Nations **Commission on Crime Prevention and Criminal Justice** and the Centre for International Crime Prevention (*see Chapter Three, pages 190-191*). The OHCHR has a programme of technical assistance providing advice to many countries on human rights in the administration of justice.

Future priorities

Despite the United Nations work in the area of human rights, there continue to be massive and widespread violations of human rights. In

1998, as the fiftieth anniversary of the Universal Declaration of Human Rights was celebrated, violations across the broad spectrum of human rights continued to dominate news from around the world. At least part of this can be attributed to the heightened awareness of human rights and the stepped-up monitoring of problem areas, particularly child abuse, violence against women, and abuses that until only recently have been considered acceptable behaviour by traditional standards.

Indeed, measures to promote and protect human rights are stronger than ever and increasingly linked to the fight for social justice, economic development and democracy. In his reform programme for the United Nations, Secretary-General Kofi Annan declared that human rights would be the cross-cutting theme in the multifaceted work of the Organization, thus highlighting the central role their promotion and protection would play in all its policy and programme decisions. His appointment of a new High Commissioner for Human Rights and other steps taken to enhance institutional cooperation and coordination with partners like UNICEF, UNESCO, UNDP, the United Nations Volunteers and UNHCR are an expression of the concrete efforts being taken to strengthen the Organization's ability to fight for human rights.

PART TWO

Chapter 5

HUMANITARIAN ASSISTANCE

HUMANITARIAN ASSISTANCE

Since it first coordinated humanitarian relief operations in Europe following the devastation and massive displacement of people in the Second World War, the United Nations has been relied on by the international community to respond to natural and man-made disasters that are beyond the capacity of national authorities alone. Today, the Organization is a major provider of emergency relief and longer-term assistance, including food, shelter, medical supplies and logistical support, primarily through its operational agencies, and a catalyst for action by Governments and other relief agencies (*see Coordinating emergency relief, page 249*).

During the 1990s, civil conflicts have become a central cause of emergency situations. By 1997, an estimated 50 million people had been forced to flee their homes — 1 out of every 120 people on earth. In 1997 alone, the United Nations launched 10 new consolidated inter-agency appeals which raised more than $800 million to assist 15 million people in some 15 countries. In recent years, the **Office of the United Nations High Commissioner for Refugees** has provided international protection and assistance to over 20 million people annually — refugees as well as a growing number of displaced people. The **World Food Programme** has regularly delivered two thirds of the world's emergency food assistance, saving millions of lives.

Providing immediate assistance to victims of an emergency is the first, essential step. But humanitarian action by the United Nations system goes beyond relief, to involve long-term rehabilitation and development. In 1997, natural disasters such as storms, floods, landslides and earthquakes killed some 13,000 people and caused $30 billion in economic losses. Some 90 per cent of this total occurred in developing countries, a striking indicator of the degree to which poverty, population pressures and environmental degradation magnify the scale of suffering and destruction.

A central component of United Nations policy is to ensure that emergency relief contributes to recovery and longer-term development in the affected area. Economic and social development remains the best protection against disaster — whether natural or, as is increasingly the case, man-made.

The United Nations also assists countries in incorporating disaster prevention and preparedness into their overall development plans. In an effort to raise awareness of the need for prevention and preparedness, the General Assembly declared the 1990s as the **International Decade for Natural Disaster Reduction**. The Decade's objective is to reduce loss of life, economic damage and social disruption caused by natural disasters. Major themes include assessing the risk of and vulnerability to such hazard, vulnerability and risk assessment; early warning; disasters and sustainable development; political commitments; and shared knowledge and technology transfer.

The **World Conference on Disaster Reduction** (Yokohama, Japan, 1994) helped to develop new strategies to reduce the effects of disasters. At the Decade's end in 1999, the international community will evaluate its achievements and map a comprehensive strategy for the next century.

Emergency relief coordination

Since the end of the cold war, the growing number of civil conflicts and emergencies — in countries such as Afghanistan, the former Yugoslavia, Iraq, Liberia and in the Great Lakes region of Africa — has strained the capacity of the international system to provide humanitarian assistance. But as the number of emergency situations has risen, the United Nations has upgraded its capacity to respond quickly and effectively.

In 1991, the General Assembly established the **Inter-Agency Standing Committee** to coordinate the international response to humanitarian emergencies. The **United Nations Emergency Relief Coordinator** is the Organization's focal point for this endeavour, acting as the system's principal policy adviser, coordinator and advocate on issues pertaining to humanitarian emergencies. The **Office for the Coordination of Humanitarian Affairs (OCHA)**, working closely with United Nations agencies, Governments, intergovernmental humanitarian organizations and non-governmental organizations (NGOs), facilitates the complex planning, coordination, logistics, diplomatic efforts and resource mobilization that are integral to virtually every international emergency response (*see Part One, pages 27-28*).

The Office coordinates field missions by United Nations agencies to assess needs; issues consolidated inter-agency appeals for funding humanitarian assistance; organizes donor meetings and follow-up arrangements; monitors the status of contributions in response to the appeals; and issues reports to keep donors and others apprised of developments. Since 1992, the Office has launched some 80 inter-agency appeals, which have raised over $11 billion for emergencies.

Coordinating emergency relief

The Inter-Agency Standing Committee, chaired by the United Nations Emergency Relief Coordinator, oversees the international response to humanitarian emergencies. Its participants are:

* The *United Nations Children's Fund,* which provides assistance to women and children, particularly health care, safe water and sanitation and nutrition (humanitarian assistance amounted to $151 million in 1997);
* The *United Nations Development Programme,* which provides funds for assistance and coordinates humanitarian aid in countries in crisis through its Resident Coordinator in the country (humanitarian assistance and disaster management budget, excluding co-sharing: $63.4 million in 1997);
* The *United Nations High Commissioner for Refugees*, which provides humanitarian assistance to refugees and displaced persons (special programmes/budget: $737.4 million in 1997);
* The *World Food Programme*, which provides food aid to victims of emergencies and disaster (expenditures in relief activities: $828 million in 1997).
* The *World Health Organization*, which provides assistance in the area of health (humanitarian assistance budget: $59.6 million in 1996-1997);
* The *Food and Agriculture Organization of the United Nations*, which provides assistance for re-establishing agricultural production in affected areas (relief operations budget: $62.4 million in 1997);
* The *Office of the High Commissioner for Human Rights,* which promotes, through legal expertise and field presence, the protection of human rights;
* *Major intergovernmental humanitarian organizations* — the International Organization for Migration, the International Committee of the Red Cross, the International Federation of Red Cross and Red Crescent Societies;
* *Major non-governmental organizations* — e.g. InterAction, the International Council of Voluntary Agencies, the Steering Committee for Humanitarian Response.

The Secretary-General's Representative for Internally Displaced People is a standing invitee. Other agencies may be invited on an ad hoc basis.

A $50 million **Central Emergency Revolving Fund** facilitates rapid humanitarian action in emergency situations until funds are made available by the donor community. By 1998, humanitarian agencies had borrowed from the Fund on 50 occasions, drawing some $126 million since it became operational in 1992 and paying back some $116 million.

Responding to emergencies

The Office for the Coordination of Humanitarian Affairs operates a 24-hour duty system for immediate response and dissemination of information. To permit rapid response to emergencies, particularly natural disasters, it has established, with the participation of donor Governments, United Nations Disaster Assessment and Coordination Teams which can be immediately deployed to affected countries to help the authorities determine relief requirements and coordinate the response. The Office may also call upon civil and military emergency teams and expertise. A warehouse in Pisa, Italy, stocks relief items ready for airlift.

United Nations Disaster Management Teams, consisting of country-level heads of the United Nations agencies under the leadership of the Resident Coordinator (usually from UNDP), have been established in many disaster-prone developing countries. Such teams make arrangements to coordinate relief activities in anticipation of an emergency.

In collaboration with international bodies and NGOs, the United Nations has helped launch programmes aimed at improving disaster preparedness in more than 70 countries. An early-warning system seeks to identify potential humanitarian crises. A Disaster Management Training Programme has provided training to some 5,000 people from 65 countries. A Central Register of Disaster Management Capacities keeps track of emergency stockpiles run by humanitarian organizations, of disaster management expertise and of military and civil defence assets available for relief assistance.

Delivering assistance

Four United Nations entities — UNDP, UNHCR, UNICEF and WFP — have primary roles in the delivery of relief assistance.

During the past decade, war and civil strife have left an estimated 1 million children orphaned or separated from their parents. A further 12 million children have been made homeless and 10 million have been severely traumatized. The **United Nations Children's Fund (UNICEF)** has sought to meet their needs by supplying food, safe water, medicine and shelter. UNICEF also aims to assist development by supporting activities such as immunization and education (through "school-in-a-box" kits) in refugee camps. Special programmes assist traumatized children and help unaccompanied children to reunite with parents or extended families. In 1997, UNICEF provided emergency assistance to 26 countries affected by conflict.

To deliver humanitarian relief to children during armed conflict, UNICEF has pioneered the concept of "children as zones of peace" and created "days of tranquillity" and "corridors of peace" in Africa, Asia, Europe and Central America (*see also Chapter 3, page 181*).

UNICEF has drawn world attention to the plight of children in war. Since 1987, some 2 million children have been killed, 6 million have been seriously injured or disabled, and thousands have fought in armed conflicts. The Secretary-General appointed in 1997 a **Special Representative for Children in Armed Conflict**, Mr. Olara Otunnu, to strengthen the protection of children in conflict situations.

There are millions of landmines buried in 70 countries around the world, waiting to maim and kill 8,000 to 10,000 children every year. UNICEF supports the campaign for a total ban on the use, production, stockpiling and transfer of anti-personnel landmines. In 1997, the Ottawa Conference was held, at which the Convention on anti-personnel mines was signed by 123 countries (*see Chapter 2, page 111*). UNICEF and other members of the United Nations system are promoting ratification of the Convention and supporting mine-awareness programmes.

The **United Nations Development Programme (UNDP)** is the agency responsible for operational activities for natural disaster mitigation, prevention and preparedness. When emergencies and natural disasters occur, UNDP Resident Representatives coordinate relief and rehabilitation efforts at the national level. On many occasions, Governments call on UNDP to help design rehabilitation programmes and to direct donor aid.

UNDP helps to ensure that recovery activities are integrated with relief operations. Humanitarian aid and development support are thus linked, bringing the earliest possible resumption of sustainable development to a troubled area. UNDP rehabilitation projects aim to alleviate poverty, often the root cause of civil strife. To ensure that the resources provided will have the greatest possible impact, each project is carried out in consultation with local and national government officials. This community-based approach has helped provide urgent but lasting relief for hundreds of thousands of victims of war or civil upheaval. Today, many conflict-scarred communities have improved their living standards thanks to training programmes, credit schemes and infrastructure projects (*see also Chapter 3, pages 131-135 and 160*).

On the **Office of the United Nations High Commissioner for Refugees (UNHCR)**, see *Assistance to Refugees*, below.

The **World Food Programme (WFP)** provides relief to millions of people who are the victims of disasters. It is responsible for mobilizing food and funds for transport for all large-scale refugee-feeding operations managed by UNHCR.

Getting food to where it is needed

The World Food Programme prides itself on its unique capacity to coordinate food aid operations worldwide. Ocean transport is the backbone of WFP's food shipments. Forty WFP-chartered ships loaded with food aid are at sea at any given time, and can be re-routed quickly when emergencies arise. Transporting the food is usually even more complex once it has arrived in the country concerned. But when the job requires it, WFP's transport and logistics experts can ship diesel locomotives from Russia to Georgia to move food inland, or ferry tons of food by barge hundreds of miles up the White Nile in Sudan. WFP crews have packed supplies on the backs of donkeys and elephants, paddled them up rivers in canoes or parachuted them into remote areas.

Every day, WFP emergency response teams rush supplies to millions of the victims of war, ethnic conflict and political strife or flood, drought and crop failure. Such crises, especially man-made disasters, consume most of WFP's resources. A decade ago, two out of three tons of the food aid provided by WFP was used to help people become self-reliant. Today, the picture is reversed, with 70 per cent of WFP resources going to victims of conflict. In 1997, WFP assisted 14.9 million internally displaced, 4.2 million refugees and 10 million victims of earthquakes, floods and droughts (*see also Chapter 3, pages 163-164*).

The **Food and Agriculture Organization of the United Nations (FAO)** is often called on to help farmers re-establish production following floods, outbreaks of livestock disease and similar emergencies. FAO's disaster relief assistance is coordinated by its Special Relief Operations Service.

The FAO **Global Information and Early Warning System** issues monthly reports on the world food situation. Special alerts identify, for Governments and relief organizations, countries threatened by food shortages (*see also Chapter 3, page 144*).

Within the United Nations system, the **World Health Organization (WHO)** Division of Emergency and Humanitarian Action (EHA) coordinates the international response to emergencies in the area of health. WHO provides expert advice on epidemiological surveillance, control of communicable diseases, public-health information and health-emergency training.

EHA's emergency relief activities include the provision of emergency drugs and supplies, fielding of emergency-assessment missions and technical support. In emergency preparedness, EHA's main objective is to strengthen the capacity of Member States to reduce the adverse health consequences of emergencies. In 1997, WHO provided emergency and humanitarian relief in 31 countries (*see also Chapter 3, pages 164-168*).

International protection and assistance to refugees

Throughout 1997, the **Office of the United Nations High Commissioner for Refugees (UNHCR)** provided international protection and assistance to more than 22 million people who had fled war or persecution, of whom some 12 million were refugees and some 4.4 million were internally displaced persons (*see also Part One, page 44*). Recently, internal conflicts have been the main cause of refugee crises. As of end-1997, UNHCR assisted 2.6 million refugees from Afghanistan, 631,000 from Iraq, 525,000 from Somalia, 517,000 from Burundi and 487,000 from Liberia.

Although UNHCR's mandate is to protect and assist refugees, it has been called upon more and more to come to the aid of a wider range of people living in refugee-like situations. In recent years, the distinction between refugees and displaced persons (those who have not crossed international borders) has become increasingly blurred, with the number of people displaced within their own country — the "internally displaced" — overtaking the number of refugees.

During the conflict in the former Yugoslavia — which produced the largest refugee flows in Europe since the Second World War — UNHCR was the lead humanitarian agency, helping refugees, the internally displaced and residents of some beseiged communities, such as Sarajevo (*see Chapter 2, page 105*). UNHCR has also been assisting refugees, displaced people and returnees in the Great Lakes region of central Africa, including Rwanda. Of the 4.4 million internally displaced people assisted by UNHCR in 1997, the largest groups were in Bosnia and Herzegovina (816,000), Sierra Leone (655,000), Burundi (586,100) and Azerbaijan (551,100). However, the total number of people internally displaced by conflicts was far higher (*see table on page 254*).

The 1990s have been marked not only by major emergencies but by positive developments in the solution of refugee problems. By end-1997, nearly 4 million Afghan refugees had returned home, some 2 million people had returned to Rwanda after the tragedies of 1994 and 1996 (*see Chapter 2, page 85*) and 1.5 million people had returned to Iraq.

However, the sudden return of large numbers of people can quickly overwhelm fragile economic and social infrastructures. To ensure that

People in flight

By 1997, over 50 million people had to flee their homes because of conflict or disaster.

Number of people of concern to UNHCR*

Total	22.3 million
By region:	
Africa	7.2 million (Somalia, Burundi, Liberia)
Asia	7.4 million (Afghanistan)
Europe	6.2 million (Bosnia and Herzegovina, Croatia)
Latin America & Caribbean	0.1 million
North America	1.3 million
Oceania	0.08 million

In addition, UNRWA provides essential services to some 3.2 million Palestinian refugees on an ongoing basis.

---

*Includes refugees, asylum seekers, returnees, displaced people and others of concern as of end-1997.
Source: UNHCR

---

refugees and internally displaced persons can rebuild their lives after they return home, UNHCR works with a range of organizations to facilitate reintegration. This requires emergency assistance for those in need, development programmes for the areas that have been devastated and job-creation schemes. To this end, UNHCR implements "quick-impact projects" and works with development agencies.

In 1997, UNHCR offered such assistance to some 3.5 million returnees. One of the most successful repatriation operations has been the return of nearly 1.7 million refugees to Mozambique following a peaceful settlement of its internal conflict in 1993 (*see Chapter 2, page 82*). In 1997, the largest repatriation movements assisted by UNHCR were to Rwanda (220,000), Bosnia and Herzegovina (105,000), Burundi (89,000) and Afghanistan (87,000).

To provide international protection to refugees, UNHCR promotes the adoption and application of international standards for the treatment of refugees, notably protection of refugees' rights in countries of asylum, and protection against forced return to the country of origin. In seeking durable solutions to refugees' problems, the Office attempts to facilitate the voluntary repatriation of refugees and reintegration into their country of origin or, where this is not feasible, their integration in the country of asylum or their resettlement in a third country.

The legal status of refugees is defined in two international treaties, the 1951 *Convention relating to the Status of Refugees* and its 1967 **Protocol**, which define their rights and duties. As of mid-1998, 136 States were parties to one or both treaties. A key element of the refugees' international legal status is the widely accepted principle of "non-refoulement", which prohibits the expulsion or forcible return of persons to a country where they may have reason to fear persecution.

The links between peace, stability, security, respect for human rights and sustainable development are increasingly seen as crucial in the search for durable solutions to the refugee problem.

Palestine refugees

The **United Nations Relief and Works Agency for Palestine Refugees in the Near East (UNRWA)** has been providing education, health, relief and social services to Palestine refugees since 1950 (*see Part One, page 40*). UNRWA initially provided emergency relief to some 750,000 Palestine refugees who had lost their homes and livelihoods as a result of the 1948 Arab-Israeli conflict (*see Chapter 2, page 95*). By 1997, UNRWA was providing essential services to more than 3.2 million registered Palestine refugees in Jordan, Lebanon, the Syrian Arab Republic, and the West Bank and Gaza Strip.

UNRWA's humanitarian role has been reinforced by recurrent conflicts in the Middle East, such as the civil war in Lebanon, the Palestinian uprising (*intifada*) and the Persian Gulf War, which led to the displacement of over 300,000 Palestinians into the UNRWA area of operations (*see Chapter 2, page 101*).

UNRWA's operations are supervised and supported by its Headquarters in Gaza and in Amman, Jordan. The Commissioner-General, who reports to the General Assembly, heads all UNRWA operations, assisted by an Advisory Commission comprised of Belgium, Egypt, France, Japan, Jordan, Lebanon, Syria, Turkey, the United Kingdom and the United States. In addition to its international staff, UNRWA employs 22,000 local staff, mainly Palestine refugees.

The Agency's 648 elementary and preparatory schools accommodated more than 447,000 pupils during the 1997/98 school year, while the 8 UNRWA vocational training centres had over 6,200 students. The Agency's network of 122 health centres handled 7.2 million patient visits in 1997. Environmental health services were provided to the 1.1 million refugees living in 59 refugee camps.

Some 192,000 people received special hardship assistance, which sought to ensure minimum standards of nutrition and shelter and to promote self-reliance through poverty-alleviation programmes. The income-generation programme has provided more than 10,500 loans totalling $22.1 million to Palestinian-owned enterprises.

After the 1993 accords between Israel and the Palestine Liberation Organization and the establishment of the Palestinian Authority in the West Bank and Gaza Strip, UNRWA entered a new era in its relationship with the Palestinian people (*see Chapter 2, page 98*). In support of the peace process, the Agency started its **Peace Implementation Programme** to upgrade infrastructure, create employment and improve living conditions in refugee communities throughout its area of operations. By 1997, the Programme had received nearly $220 million in contributions and pledges. UNRWA has cooperated closely with the Palestinian Authority.

The international community considers UNRWA a stabilizing factor in the Middle East. The refugees themselves look upon UNRWA's programmes as a symbol of the international community's commitment to a solution of the Palestine refugee issue.

Chapter 6

INTERNATIONAL LAW

Among the United Nations most pervasive achievements has been the development of a body of international law — conventions, treaties and standards — that play a central role in promoting economic and social development, as well as international peace and security. Many of the treaties brought about by the United Nations form the basis of the law governing relations among nations. While the United Nations work in this area does not always receive attention, it has a daily impact on the lives of people everywhere in the world.

The United Nations Charter specifically calls on the United Nations to help in the settlement of international disputes by peaceful means, including arbitration and judicial settlement (Art. 33), and to encourage "the progressive development of international law and its codification" (Art. 13). Over the years, the United Nations has sponsored over 480 multilateral agreements, which address a broad range of common concerns among States and are legally binding for the States that ratify them.

The United Nations legal work has been in the forefront of tackling problems as they take on an international dimension — providing the legal framework for protecting the environment, ensuring the peaceful use of outer space, regulating migrant labour, and combating drug trafficking and terrorism, to mention a few. (*For conventions on outer space, and on human rights and workers' rights, see Chapter 2 and Chapter 4.*)

Judicial settlement of disputes

The primary organ of the United Nations for the settlement of disputes is the **International Court of Justice** (*see also Part One, pages 14-15*). Since its founding in 1946, States have submitted 75 cases to it, and 22 advisory opinions have been requested by international organizations. Most cases have been dealt with by the full Court, but since 1981 cases may be referred to special chambers at the request of the parties.

The World Court, as it is popularly known, has made scores of judgements on international disputes involving economic rights, rights of passage, the non-use of force, non-interference in the internal affairs of States, diplomatic relations, hostage-taking, the right of asylum and nationality. Such disputes are brought before the Court by countries in search of an impartial solution to their differences. By achieving a peaceful settlement of disputes on questions such as land frontiers, maritime boundaries and territorial sovereignty, the Court has often helped to prevent the escalation of disputes.

In a typical case of territorial rights, a Chamber of the Court in 1986 resolved a dispute over the delineation of a section of the border between Burkina Faso and Mali. In 1994, after Nigerian forces clashed with Cameroonian police, Cameroon instituted proceedings against Nigeria in a sovereignty dispute over the oil-rich Bakassi peninsula, and then over the whole land and sea border. The case is now before the Court. Another border dispute was jointly referred to the Court by the Libyan Arab Jamahiriya and Chad. The Court ruled in 1994 that the border was defined by a 1955 treaty between Libya and France; Libya then withdrew its forces from an area along its southern border with Chad, known as the Aouzou Strip.

Various cases have been referred to the Court against the background of political upheaval or regional conflict. In 1980, the United States brought a case arising from the seizure of its Embassy in Tehran and the detention of its staff. The Court held that Iran must release the hostages, hand back the Embassy and make reparation. However, before the Court could fix the amount of reparation, the case was withdrawn following an agreement between the two countries. In 1989, Iran asked the Court to condemn the shooting down of an Iranian airliner by the United States warship *Vincennes*, and to find the United States responsible to pay Iran compensation. The case was closed in 1996 following a compensation settlement.

In 1992, Libya brought the two "Lockerbie" cases — one against the United Kingdom and one against the United States — concerning the interpretation or application of the *Convention for the Suppression of Unlawful Acts against the Safety of Civil Aviation*, arising out of the crash, in 1988, of Pan American flight 103 at Lockerbie, Scotland. The cases are before the Court.

In 1993, Bosnia and Herzegovina brought a case against the Federal Republic of Yugoslavia concerning the application of the *Convention on the Prevention and Punishment of the Crime of Genocide*. The Court in 1993 called upon the parties to prevent further commission of the crime of genocide and further aggravation of the dispute. In 1996, the Court rejected the objections to its jurisdiction raised by Yugoslavia; the case is now before the Court.

The Court in 1996 rejected objections by the United States to its jurisdiction in a case concerning the destruction of Iranian oil platforms by United States warships, and found that it had jurisdiction to consider some of Iran's claims.

States have also submitted questions of economic rights. For instance, a Chamber of the Court in 1989 rejected a claim for compensation put forward by the United States against Italy for the requisition of an Italian company owned by United States corporations. In 1995, in the context of a dispute over fisheries jurisdiction between Canada and the European Union, Spain instituted a case against Canada, concerning the Canadian Coastal Fisheries Protection Act and its application, after the seizing on the high seas by Canada of a Spanish fishing trawler.

A recent case involving claims of environmental protection, concerning a dispute over a project for a barrage system on the Danube river, was brought by Hungary and the Slovak Republic. In 1997, the Court found both States in breach of their legal obligations, and called on them to carry out a 1977 treaty they had concluded on the building of the system.

The Court's advisory opinions have dealt with, among other things, admission to United Nations membership, reparation for injuries suffered in the service of the United Nations, the territorial status of Western Sahara, and the expenses of certain peacekeeping operations, such as that in the Congo (1960-1964). Two opinions, rendered in 1996 on the request of the General Assembly and the World Health Organization, concerned the legality of the threat or use of nuclear weapons.

In a 1971 advisory opinion requested by the Security Council, the Court stated that the continued presence of South Africa in Namibia was illegal and that South Africa was under obligation to withdraw its administration and end its occupation of the Territory, clearing the way for the eventual independence of Namibia (*see Chapter 7, page 280*).

Progressive development and codification of international law

The **International Law Commission** was established by the General Assembly in 1947 to promote the progressive development of international law and its codification. The Commission, which meets annually, is composed of 34 members elected by the General Assembly for five-year terms. Collectively, they represent the principal legal systems of the world, and serve as experts in their individual capacity, not as representatives of their Governments. The work of the Commission covers a wide range of topics of public international law regulating relations among States.

Most of the Commission's work involves the preparation of drafts on topics of international law. Some topics are chosen by the

Commission, others are referred to it by the General Assembly or the Economic and Social Council. When the Commission completes work on a topic, the General Assembly usually convenes an international conference of plenipotentiaries to incorporate the draft into a convention, which is then "opened to States to become parties", meaning that countries formally agree to be bound by its provisions.

Some of these conventions form the very foundation of the law governing relations among States. For example:

- The *Convention on the Non-navigational Uses of International Watercourses*, adopted by the General Assembly in 1997, which regulates the equitable and reasonable utilization of watercourses shared by two or more countries;

- The *Convention on the Law of Treaties between States and International Organizations or between International Organizations*, adopted at a conference in Vienna in 1986;

- The *Convention on the Succession of States in Respect of State Property, Archives and Debts* (1983), adopted at a conference in Vienna;

- The *Convention on the Prevention and Punishment of Crimes against Internationally Protected Persons, including Diplomatic Agents*, adopted by the General Assembly in 1973;

- The *Convention on the Law of Treaties* (1969), adopted at a conference in Vienna;

- The *Conventions on Diplomatic Relations* (1961) and *on Consular Relations* (1963), adopted at conferences held in Vienna;

- The four *Conventions on the Law of the Sea* (*see pages 265-267, below*) adopted at a United Nations conference in 1958.

The Commission in 1996 adopted a set of draft articles on the law of State responsibility for international wrongful acts, and completed the draft of the Code of Crimes against the Peace and Security of Mankind. The Commission's draft statute for an international criminal court is under consideration by the General Assembly (*see page 268, below*).

The Commission is currently addressing such issues as the international liability for injurious consequences arising out of acts not prohibited by international law; nationality of individuals in cases of State succession; State responsibility; the right to diplomatic protection; and reservations to treaties.

International trade law

The **United Nations Commission on International Trade Law (UNCITRAL)** facilitates world trade by developing conventions, model laws, rules and legal guides designed to harmonize international trade law. Established by the General Assembly in 1966, the 36-nation body brings together representatives of the world's geographic regions and principal economic and legal systems.

UNCITRAL has become the core legal body of the United Nations system in the field of international trade law. The International Trade Law Branch of the United Nations Office of Legal Affairs serves as the secretariat of UNCITRAL. Over its 30-year history, the Commission has developed widely accepted texts that are viewed as landmarks in various fields of law. These include the 1980 *United Nations Convention on Contracts for the International Sale of Goods*, the 1985 *UNCITRAL Model Law on International Commercial Arbitration*, the 1976 *UNCITRAL Arbitration Rules*, the 1980 *UNCITRAL Conciliation Rules*, the 1994 *UNCITRAL Model Law on Procurement of Goods, Construction and Services*, the 1996 *UNCITRAL Notes on Organizing Arbitral Proceedings* and the 1996 *Model Law on Electronic Commerce*.

Other notable texts developed by UNCITRAL include: the 1974 *Convention on the Limitation Period in the International Sale of Goods*; the 1978 *United Nations Convention on the Carriage of Goods by Sea ("Hamburg Rules")*; the 1988 *United Nations Convention on International Bills of Exchange and International Promissory Notes*; the 1988 *UNCITRAL Legal Guide on Drawing Up International Contracts for the Construction of Industrial Works*; the 1991 *United Nations Convention on the Liability of Operators of Transport Terminals in International Trade*; the 1992 *UNCITRAL Legal Guide on International Countertrade Transactions*; and the 1995 *United Nations Convention on Independent Guarantees and Standby Letters of Credit*.

In 1997, the Commission adopted the *UNCITRAL Model Law on Cross-Border Insolvency*, intended to assist States to improve their national insolvency legislation, so as to cope with the growing number of bankruptcies involving enterprises operating in more than one country.

Current work includes the preparation of a legislative guide on privately financed infrastructure projects, which would provide guidance to States preparing or modernizing legislation relevant to those projects; the preparation of rules on certain aspects of digital signatures and certification authorities; compilation and publication of Case Law on UNCITRAL Texts (CLOUT); and a draft convention on Assignment in Receivables Financing, which will facilitate the availability of credit at lower cost.

Environmental law

The United Nations has pioneered the development of international environmental law, brokering major treaties that have advanced environmental protection everywhere. The United Nations Environment Programme administers many of these treaties (*see also Chapter 3, pages 201-203*).

* The *International Convention to Combat Desertification in Those Countries Experiencing Serious Drought and/or Desertification, Particularly in Africa* (1994) seeks to promote international cooperation in taking action to combat desertification and mitigate the effects of drought in the countries affected;

* The *Convention on Biological Diversity* (1992) seeks to conserve biological diversity, promote the sustainable use of its components, and encourage equitable sharing of the benefits arising from the utilization of genetic resources;

* The *Framework Convention on Climate Change* (1992) obligates States parties to reduce emissions of greenhouse gases causing global warming and related atmospheric problems;

* The *Basel Convention on the Control of Transboundary Movement of Hazardous Wastes and their Disposal* (1989) obligates States parties to reduce shipping and dumping of dangerous wastes across borders, to minimize the amount and toxicity generated by hazardous waste, and to ensure their environmentally sound management as close as possible to the source of generation;

* The *Vienna Convention on the Ozone Layer* (1985), the *Montreal Protocol* (1987) and its *Amendments* seek to reduce damage to the ozone layer in the earth's atmosphere, which shields life from the sun's harmful ultraviolet radiations;

The 1979 *Convention on Long-range Transboundary Air Pollution* ("Acid Rain Convention") and its four *Protocols*, negotiated under the auspices of the United Nations Economic Commission for Europe (ECE), provide for the control and reduction of air pollution in Europe and North America.

The 1971 *Convention on Wetlands of International Importance Especially as Waterfowl Habitat* obligates contracting parties to use wisely all wetlands under their jurisdiction. The 1972 *Convention Concerning the Protection of the World Cultural and Natural Heritage* obligates States parties to protect unique natural and cultural areas. Both were promoted by the United Nations Educational, Scientific and Cultural Organization (UNESCO).

The Conventions promoted by the International Maritime Organization (IMO) have helped to reduce marine pollution (*see also page 00*). Among them are *International Conventions on Oil Pollution Preparedness, Response and Cooperation* (1990), *on the Prevention of Marine Pollution from Ships* (1973/1978), *on the Prevention of Marine Pollution by Dumping of Wastes* (1972), *on the Intervention on the High Seas in Cases of Oil Pollution Casualties* (1969), and *on the Prevention of Pollution of the Sea by Oil* (1954).

Law of the sea

The *United Nations Convention on the Law of the Sea* is considered one of the most comprehensive instruments of international law. This landmark Convention provides the basic framework for all aspects of ocean sovereignty, jurisdiction, use, and State rights, as well as obligations. Its aim is to establish a uniform rule in the uses of the ocean, avoiding conflict and contributing to international peace and security.

The Convention covers all aspects of ocean space and its uses — navigation and overflight, resource exploration and exploitation, conservation and pollution, fishing and shipping. Its 320 articles and 9 annexes constitute a guide for behaviour by States in the world's oceans, defining maritime zones, laying down rules for delineating sea boundaries, assigning legal rights, duties and responsibilities, and providing machinery for the settlement of disputes.

The Convention was the outcome of complex negotiations initiated at the Third Conference on the Law of the Sea in 1973. It was opened for signature in 1982 at Montego Bay, Jamaica, and it entered into force in 1994, one year after it received its sixtieth ratification or accession. By 1997, it had more than 120 States parties.

Impact of the Convention

States have consistently, through national and international legislation and through related decision-making, asserted the authority of the Convention as the pre-eminent international legal instrument in the field. Thus far, its major impact has been on the almost universal acceptance of 12 nautical miles as the limit of the territorial sea, as well

Law of the Sea Convention, key features

- Coastal States exercise sovereignty over their territorial sea up to 12 nautical miles, while all States enjoy the freedom of navigation through the territorial sea of a coastal State;

- Ships and aircraft of all countries are allowed "transit passage" through straits used for international navigation; States alongside the straits can regulate navigation and other aspects of passage;

- Coastal States have sovereign rights in a 200-nautical-mile "exclusive economic zone" (EEZ) on natural resources and certain economic activities, and also exercise jurisdiction over marine science research and environmental protection; all other States have freedom of navigation and overflight in the zone, as well as freedom to lay submarine cables and pipelines;

- "Archipelagic States" — States made up of closely related islands — have sovereignty over a sea area enclosed by straight lines drawn between the outermost points of the islands;

- Coastal States have jurisdiction over the resources of their continental shelf (the under-sea extension of a State's land territory); a Commission on the Limits of the Continental Shelf (*see facing page*) is to make recommendations to coastal States that claim that their continental shelf extends beyond 200 miles;

- All States are obliged to adopt measures to manage and conserve living resources; States are bound to prevent and control marine pollution and are liable for damage caused by violation of their international obligations to combat pollution;

- States are obliged to settle by peaceful means their disputes concerning the interpretation or application of the Convention; disputes can be submitted to the International Tribunal for the Law of the Sea (*see facing page*) established under the Convention, to the International Court of Justice, to arbitration or to conciliation. The Tribunal has exclusive jurisdiction over deep seabed mining disputes.

---

as coastal States' jurisdiction over the resources of an exclusive economic zone up to the limit of 200 nautical miles.

The Convention has been recognized for its impact on the rights of international navigation, as well as on other aspects affecting coastal State control over marine scientific research, prevention of pollution and access by landlocked States to and from the sea. Moreover, it is now recognized as the framework and foundation for any future instruments that seek to further define rights and obligations in the oceans — a fact that has been, for instance, reflected in the adoption of the 1995 *Agreement on Straddling Fish Stocks and Highly Migratory Fish Stocks* (*see Chapter 3, pages 206-207*).

Deep seabed mining

For years following the adoption of the Convention, the provisions of Part XI, dealing with deep seabed mining, were viewed as an obstacle, particularly by industrialized countries, to the universal acceptance of the Convention. Objections dealt mainly with the detailed procedures for authorizing production from the deep seabed; cumbersome financial rules of contracts; decision-making in the Council of the Seabed Authority; and mandatory transfer of technology.

To overcome these objections, the General Assembly in 1994 adopted the *Agreement Relating to the Implementation of Part XI of the Convention*. The Agreement removes the obstacles to universal acceptance by substituting general provisions for the detailed procedures contained in the Convention, and by leaving it to the Authority to determine the exact nature of the rules on the authorization of deep seabed mining operations. The Agreement also removes the obligation for mandatory transfer of technology and ensures the representation of certain countries, or groups of countries, in the Council while giving those countries certain rights over decision-making.

Bodies established under the Convention

The **International Seabed Authority**, located in Kingston, Jamaica, established in 1994, is the organization through which States parties to the Convention organize and control activities relating to the deep seabed's mineral resources in the international seabed area, beyond the limits of national jurisdiction.

The **International Tribunal for the Law of the Sea**, operational since 1996, is a forum for settling disputes arising out of the interpretation or application of the Convention. Made up of 21 judges elected by the States parties, it is located in the German seaport of Hamburg.

The **Commission on the Limits of the Continental Shelf** makes recommendations to States that claim that their continental shelf extends beyond 200 miles from their coast. It is based at United Nations Headquarters; its 21 members, elected by the States parties, serve in their personal capacity. The Commission held its first two sessions in 1997.

International humanitarian law

The United Nations has traditionally played a limited role in the development of international humanitarian law — the principles and rules regulating the means and methods of warfare as well as the humanitarian protection of the civilian population, of sick and wounded combatants and of prisoners of war.

While the 1949 Geneva Conventions and the two 1977 Additional Protocols were concluded under the auspices of the International Committee of the Red Cross, the General Assembly, as a political forum of the United Nations, contributed to the elaboration of a number of international conventions, such as the 1948 *Convention on the Prevention and Punishment of the Crime of Genocide*, the 1968 *Convention on the Non-Applicability of Statutory Limitations to War Crimes and Crimes Against Humanity*, the 1980 *Convention on Prohibition and Restrictions on the Use of Certain Conventional Weapons which may be deemed to be Excessively Injurious or to have Indiscriminate Effects* and its four *Protocols*, and the *Principles of International Cooperation in the Detection, Arrest, Extradition and Punishment of Persons Guilty of War Crimes and Crimes Against Humanity*, which the Assembly adopted in 1973.

Moreover, the Security Council has established the two International Criminal Tribunals for the Former Yugoslavia and for Rwanda (*see below*).

International Criminal Court (ICC)

The idea of a permanent international court to prosecute genocide, crimes against humanity, war crimes and aggression was first considered at the United Nations in the context of the adoption of the Genocide Convention of 1948. Further development was forestalled through differences of opinion for many years. In 1992, the General Assembly directed the International Law Commission to prepare a draft Statute for the Court.

A plenipotentiary conference, held in Rome in June/July 1998, adopted the Statute, which calls for the establishment of a permanent International Criminal Court with power to investigate and bring to justice individuals who commit the most serious crimes of international concern, including genocide, crimes against humanity and war crimes. The Court will also have jurisdiction over "the crime of aggression" once a provision is adopted defining the crime and setting out the conditions under which the Court shall exercise jurisdiction. It also gives precedence to national courts. The **Rome Statute of the International Criminal Court**, as the formal document is called, was adopted by a vote of 120 in favour to 7 against, with 21 abstentions, and was then opened for signature. The treaty needs to be ratified by at least 60 States Parties before taking effect.

The organs of the Court are the Presidency; an Appeals Division, a Trial Division and a Pre-Trial Division; the Office of the Prosecutor; and the Registry. The Court will have 18 judges, elected by the Assembly of States Parties for a term limited to nine years. No two judges may be nationals of the same State. The judges will elect the President, while the Court's Prosecutor will be elected by secret ballot by the Assembly of States Parties. The precise nature of the relationship between the Court and the United Nations is to be defined through an agreement to be approved by the Assembly of States Parties to the Statute. The seat of the Court will be located at The Hague in the Netherlands, but it may convene elsewhere.

International tribunals

Mass violations of international humanitarian law in the former Yugoslavia and in Rwanda (*see also Chapter 2, pages 105 and 85*) led the Security Council to establish two international tribunals to prosecute persons responsible for such violation. Both tribunals were established under Chapter VII of the Charter, which deals with enforcement measures, and are subsidiary organs of the Security Council.

- The **International Criminal Tribunal for the Former Yugoslavia**, established in 1993, is composed of three chambers (two Trial Chambers and an Appeals Chamber), a Prosecutor and the Registry. The seat of the Tribunal is located in The Hague, the Netherlands.
- The **International Tribunal for Rwanda**, established in 1994, is composed of three Trial Chambers, a Prosecutor and the Registry. The seat of the Tribunal is in Arusha, Tanzania; the Office of the Prosecutor is in Kigali, Rwanda.

The Tribunals have a common Appeals Chamber and a common Prosecutor, and are engaged in a number of trial proceedings.

International terrorism

The United Nations has consistently addressed the problem of terrorism, taking both legal and political steps.

In the legal sphere, the United Nations and its specialized agencies — such as the International Civil Aviation Organization (ICAO), the International Maritime Organization (IMO) and the International Atomic Energy Agency (IAEA) — have developed a network of international agreements that constitute the basic legal instruments against terrorism. These are:

- The *Convention on Offences and Certain Other Acts Committed on Board Aircraft* (adopted in Tokyo in 1963);
- The *Convention for the Suppression of Unlawful Seizure of Aircraft* (The Hague, 1970);
- The *Convention for the Suppression of Unlawful Acts against the Safety of Civil Aviation* (Montreal, 1971);
- The *Convention on the Prevention and Punishment of Crimes against Internationally Protected Persons, including Diplomatic Agents* (New York, 1973);
- The *Convention on the Physical Protection of Nuclear Material* (Vienna, 1980);
- The *Protocol for the Suppression of Unlawful Acts of Violence at Airports Serving International Civil Aviation* (Montreal, 1988);
- The *Convention for the Suppression of Unlawful Acts against the Safety of Maritime Navigation* (Rome, 1988);
- The *Protocol for the Suppression of Unlawful Acts against the Safety of Fixed Platforms located on the Continental Shelf* (Rome, 1988); and
- The *Convention on the Marking of Plastic Explosives for the Purpose of Detection* (Montreal, 1991).

The General Assembly has brought about three conventions:
- The *Convention against the Taking of Hostages* (1979), in which States parties agree to make the taking of hostages punishable by appropriate penalties. They also agree to prohibit certain activities within their territories, to exchange information, and to enable any criminal or extradition proceedings to take place. If a State party does not extradite an alleged offender, it must submit the case to its own authorities for prosecution. As of mid-1998, the Convention had 83 States parties.
- The *Convention on the Safety of United Nations and Associated Personnel*, requested by the Assembly in 1993 following many instances of attacks against United Nations staff which resulted in injury and death. Adopted by the Assembly in 1994, the Convention will enter into force when ratified by 22 Member States; 19 had ratified it as of 1998.
- The *International Convention for the Suppression of Terrorist Bombings*, adopted by the Assembly in 1997. It is aimed at denying "safe havens" to persons wanted for terrorist bombings by obligating each State party to prosecute such persons if it does

not extradite them to another State which has issued an extradition request.

An ad hoc committee established by the Assembly in 1996 is elaborating an international convention for the suppression of acts of nuclear terrorism.

In the political sphere, the General Assembly adopted in 1994 the *Declaration on Measures to Eliminate International Terrorism*, which condemned "all acts and practices of terrorism as criminal and unjustifiable, wherever and by whomever they were committed". The Assembly urged States to take measures at the national and international level to eliminate international terrorism.

Other legal questions

The General Assembly has adopted conventions and legal instruments on various other questions. Among them are the *International Convention against the Recruitment, Use, Financing and Training of Mercenaries* (1989), the *Body of Principles for the Protection of All Persons under Any Form of Detention or Imprisonment* (1988) and the *Declaration on the Enhancement of the Effectiveness of the Principle of Refraining from the Threat or Use of Force in International Relations* (1987).

The Assembly has adopted numerous international instruments on the recommendation of the 47-member **Special Committee on the Charter of the United Nations and on the Strengthening of the Role of the Organization**, established by the Assembly in 1974. These include the 1995 *United Nations Model Rules for the Conciliation of Disputes between States*, the 1994 *Declaration on the Enhancement of Cooperation between the United Nations and Regional Arrangements or Agencies in the Maintenance of International Peace and Security*, the 1991 *Declaration on Fact-finding by the United Nations in the field of the Maintenance of International Peace and Security*, the 1988 *Declaration on the Prevention and Removal of Disputes and Situations which May Threaten International Peace and Security and on the Role of the United Nations in this Field*, the 1982 *Declaration on the Peaceful Settlement of International Disputes*, and the 1990 draft on the rationalization of United Nations procedures.

Under the Charter (article 102), Member States should register with the United Nations the international agreements they enter into. The United Nations **Office of Legal Affairs** (*see Part One, pages 25-26*) is responsible for the registration, deposit and publication of treaties and conventions. It publishes the *United Nations Treaty Series*, which contains the text of over 30,000 treaties and related action. It also issues the volume *Multilateral Treaties Deposited with the Secretary-General*, which includes some 486 major treaties deposited by Member States (*available on Internet at www.un.org/Depts/Treaty*).

(*On amendments to the United Nations Charter, see Part One page 4.*)

Chapter 7

DECOLONIZATION

DECOLONIZATION

More than 80 nations whose peoples were formerly under colonial rule have joined the United Nations as sovereign independent States since the world Organization was founded in 1945. Additionally, many other Territories have achieved self-determination through political association with other independent States or through integration with other States. The United Nations has played a crucial role in that historic change by encouraging the aspirations of dependent peoples and by setting goals and standards to accelerate their attainment of independence. United Nations missions supervised elections leading to independence — in Togoland (1956 and 1968), Western Samoa (1961) and most recently in Namibia (*see page 280, below*).

The decolonization efforts of the United Nations derive from the Charter principle of "equal rights and self-determination of peoples", as well as from three specific chapters in the Charter — XI, XII and XIII — devoted to the interests of dependent peoples. Since 1960, the United Nations has also been guided by the General Assembly's *Declaration on the Granting of Independence to Colonial Countries and Peoples* (*see page 277, below*), also known as the Declaration on decolonization, by which Member States proclaimed the necessity of bringing colonialism to a speedy end. The United Nations has also been guided by General Assembly resolution 1541(XV) of 15 December 1960, which defined the three options offering full self-government for Non-Self-Governing Territories (*see page 277, below*).

Despite the great progress made against colonialism, some 1.3 million people still live under colonial rule, and the United Nations continues its efforts to help achieve self-determination or independence in the remaining Non-Self-Governing Territories.

International Trusteeship System

Under Chapter XII of the Charter, the United Nations established the International Trusteeship System for the supervision of Trust Territories placed under it by individual agreements with the States administering them.

The System applied to: (i) Territories held under Mandates established by the League of Nations after the First World War; (ii) Territories detached from "enemy States" as a result of the Second World War; and (iii) Territories voluntarily placed under the System by States responsible for their administration. The basic objective of the System was to promote the political, economic and social advancement of the Territories and their development towards self-government and self-determination.

The **Trusteeship Council** (*see Part One, pages 13-14*) was established under Chapter XIII of the Charter to supervise the administration of Trust Territories and to ensure that Governments responsible for their administration took adequate steps to prepare them for the achievement of the Charter goals.

In the early years of the United Nations, 11 Territories were placed under the Trusteeship System (*see Part Three, pages 298-299*). Today, all 11 Territories have either become independent States or have voluntarily associated themselves with a State.

The Security Council in 1994 terminated the United Nations Trusteeship Agreement for the last Territory — the Trust Territory of the Pacific Islands (Palau), administered by the United States — after it chose self-government in a 1993 popular plebiscite. Palau became independent in 1994, joining the United Nations as its 185th Member State.

With no territories left on its agenda, the Trusteeship System had completed its historic task.

Non-Self-Governing Territories

The United Nations Charter also addresses the issue of other Non-Self-Governing Territories not brought into the Trusteeship System.

Chapter XI of the Charter — the Declaration regarding Non-Self-Governing Territories — provides that Member States administering Territories which have not attained self-government recognize "that the interests of the inhabitants of these Territories is paramount" and accept as a "sacred trust" the obligation to promote their well-being.

To this end, administering Powers, in addition to ensuring the political, economic, social and educational advancement of the peoples, undertake to assist them in developing self-government and democratic political institutions. Administering Powers have an obligation to transmit regularly to the Secretary-General information on the economic, social and educational conditions in the Territories under their administration.

In 1946, eight Member States — Australia, Belgium, Denmark, France, the Netherlands, New Zealand, the United Kingdom and the United States — enumerated the Territories under their administration which they considered to be non-self-governing. In all, 72 Territories were enumerated, of which eight became independent before 1959.

Transmission of information by the administering Power was discontinued for 21 others for various reasons. In some cases, such as Puerto Rico, Greenland, Alaska and Hawaii, the General Assembly accepted the cessation of information; in others, the decision was taken unilaterally by the administering Power.

In 1963, the Assembly approved a revised list of 64 Territories to which the 1960 Declaration on decolonization applied. The list included the two remaining Trust Territories at that time (Nauru and the Trust Territory of the Pacific Islands); the Non-Self-Governing Territories for which information was transmitted under Chapter XI of the Charter (article 73e), including four administered by Spain; Namibia (then referred to as South West Africa); and those Non-Self-Governing Territories about which no information had been transmitted, but which the Assembly had deemed to be Non-Self-Governing — namely the Territories under Portuguese administration and Southern Rhodesia (now Zimbabwe). The list was further expanded in 1965 to include French Somaliland (now Djibouti) and Oman. The Comoro Islands were included in 1972 and New Caledonia in 1986.

From 1960 to 1990, 53 Territories attained self-government. As of 1997, there were 17 Non-Self-Governing Territories (*see table on the following page*).

Declaration on the Granting of Independence to Colonial Countries and Peoples

The demands of the peoples of the Territories to achieve self-determination, and the international community's perception that Charter principles were being too slowly applied, led to the General Assembly's proclamation on 14 December 1960 of the *Declaration on the Granting of Independence to Colonial Countries and Peoples* (resolution 1514(XV)).

The Declaration states that the subjection of peoples to alien subjugation, domination and exploitation constitutes a denial of fundamental human rights, is contrary to the Charter, and is an impediment to the promotion of world peace and cooperation, and that "immediate steps shall be taken, in Trust and Non-Self-Governing Territories or all other Territories which have not yet attained independence, to transfer all powers to the peoples of those Territories, without any conditions or reservations, in accordance with their freely expressed will and desire, without any distinction as to race, creed or colour in order to enable them to enjoy complete independence and freedom".

Also in 1960, the Assembly approved resolution 1541(XV), defining free association with an independent State, integration into an

Territories to which the Declaration on the Granting of Independence to Colonial Countries and Peoples continues to apply (as of 1998)

TERRITORY	ADMINISTERING AUTHORITY
Africa:	
Western Sahara	Spain[1]
Asia and the Pacific:	
American Samoa	United States
East Timor	Portugal[2]
Guam	United States
New Caledonia[3]	France
Pitcairn	United Kingdom
Tokelau	New Zealand
Atlantic Ocean, Caribbean and Mediterranean:	
Anguilla	United Kingdom
Bermuda	United Kingdom
British Virgin Islands	United Kingdom
Cayman Islands	United Kingdom
Falkland Islands (Malvinas)	United Kingdom
Gibraltar	United Kingdom
Montserrat	United Kingdom
St. Helena	United Kingdom
Turks and Caicos Islands	United Kingdom
United States Virgin Islands	United States

---

[1] On 26 February 1976, Spain informed the Secretary-General that as of that date it had terminated its presence in the Territory of the Sahara and deemed it necessary to place on record that Spain considered itself thenceforth exempt from any responsibility of an international nature in connection with the administration of the Territory, in view of the cessation of its participation in the temporary administration established for the Territory. In 1990, the General Assembly reaffirmed that the question of Western Sahara was a question of decolonization which remained to be completed by the people of Western Sahara.

[2] Since 1977, Portugal, in its capacity as administering Power of the Non-Self-Governing Territory of East Timor, has been annually informing the Secretary-General that it continues to be prevented de facto from exercising its responsibilities for the administration of the Territory due to the latter's illegal occupation by a third country.

[3] On 2 December 1986, the General Assembly determined that New Caledonia was a Non-Self-Governing Territory.

---

independent State or independence as the three legitimate political status options offering full self-government. (*For the list of dependent*

Territories that have become integrated or associated with independent States since the adoption of the Declaration on decolonization, see Part Three, page 297.)

The Assembly, in 1961, established a 17-member Special Committee — enlarged to 24 members in 1962 — to examine the application of the Declaration, and to make recommendations on its implementation. Commonly referred to as the **Special Committee of 24 on Decolonization**, its full title is the **Special Committee on the Situation with Regard to the Implementation of the Declaration on the Granting of Independence to Colonial Countries and Peoples**.

The Committee meets annually, hears appointed and elected representatives of the Territories and petitioners, dispatches visiting missions to the Territories, and organizes seminars on the political, social, economic and educational situations in the Territories. In recent years, three administering Powers have not participated in the work of the Committee. The United States has maintained that it remains conscious of its role as an administering Power and will continue to meet its responsibilities under the Charter. The United Kingdom has stated that while most of the Territories under its administration chose independence, a small number have preferred to remain associated with it. France has not extended cooperation to the Special Committee *vis-à-vis* New Caledonia.

In the years following the adoption of the Declaration, some 60 former colonial Territories, inhabited by more than 80 million people, attained self-determination through independence and joined the United Nations as sovereign Members (*see Part Three, pages 295-296*).

In considering the Non-Self-Governing Territories, the General Assembly has each year reaffirmed that the continuation of colonialism in any form and manifestation is incompatible with the Charter, the Universal Declaration of Human Rights and the Declaration on decolonization.

The Assembly has called upon the administering Powers to take all necessary steps to enable the peoples of the Non-Self-Governing Territories to exercise fully as soon as possible their right to self-determination and independence. It has called upon the administering Powers to complete the withdrawal of the remaining military bases from the Territories, and to ensure that no activity of foreign economic and other interests hinders the implementation of the Declaration.

To mark the thirtieth anniversary of the Declaration in 1990, the Assembly in 1988 declared 1990-2000 as the **International Decade**

for the Eradication of Colonialism. In 1991, the Assembly adopted the action plan for the Decade.

In respect to certain territories, such as East Timor and Western Sahara, the Assembly has entrusted the Secretary-General with specific tasks to facilitate the process of decolonization, in accordance with the United Nations Charter and the objectives of the Declaration (*see pages 282-284, below*).

Namibia

In one of its recent and successful efforts, the United Nations helped bring about in 1990 the independence of Namibia — a case history that reveals the complexity of the efforts required to ensure a peaceful transition.

Formerly known as South West Africa, Namibia was an African Territory once held under the League of Nations Mandate System. The General Assembly in 1946 asked South Africa to administer the Territory under the Trusteeship System. South Africa refused, and in 1949 informed the United Nations that it would no longer transmit information on the Territory, maintaining that the Mandate had ended with the demise of the League.

The International Court of Justice held in 1950 that South Africa continued to have international obligations towards the Territory and that the United Nations should supervise its administration — an opinion South Africa rejected.

The General Assembly in 1966, stating that South Africa had not fulfilled its obligations, terminated that Mandate and placed the Territory under the responsibility of the United Nations — the only case of a Territory for which the United Nations, not a Member State, assumed responsibility.

To administer the Territory until independence, the Assembly in 1967 established the United Nations Council for South West Africa. It was renamed the Council for Namibia in 1968, when the Assembly proclaimed that the Territory would be known as Namibia, in accordance with the wishes of its people. The Council in 1974 established, in Lusaka, Zambia, the Institute for Namibia, to educate and train Namibians for administering a free Namibia.

The Security Council in 1969 termed the presence of South Africa illegal and called for its withdrawal. The International Court of Justice stated in 1971 that South Africa was obligated to withdraw. But South Africa remained, imposing apartheid laws and continuing to exploit Namibia's resources.

In 1976, the Security Council demanded that South Africa accept elections for the Territory under United Nations supervision. The General Assembly stated that independence talks must involve the South West Africa People's Organization (SWAPO) — the sole representative of the Namibian people.

In 1978, Canada, France, the Federal Republic of Germany, the United Kingdom and the United States submitted to the Security Council a settlement proposal. This provided for elections for a Constituent Assembly, under United Nations auspices. The Council, by *resolution 435*, endorsed the Secretary-General's recommendations for implementing the proposal, asked him to appoint a Special Representative for Namibia, and established the **United Nations Transition Assistance Group (UNTAG)**.

South Africa in 1980 accepted the proposal, but did not agree on a ceasefire with SWAPO and linked progress on Namibia's independence to the withdrawal of Cuban troops from Angola. Years of negotiations by the Secretary-General and his Special Representative removed all the obstacles, except the one related to troop withdrawal.

Negotiations mediated by the United States led to agreements, signed at United Nations Headquarters in 1988, to achieve peace in southern Africa. South Africa undertook to cooperate with the Secretary-General to ensure Namibia's independence through elections. Angola and Cuba signed an agreement on the withdrawal of Cuban troops from Angola, which the United Nations oversaw (*see Chapter 2, pages 81-82*).

The operation that led to Namibia's independence started in April 1989. UNTAG's international civilian staff observed the entire electoral process, conducted by the Namibian authorities. UNTAG's 4,300 military staff monitored the ceasefire between SWAPO and South Africa and the demobilization of all military forces. Its 1,500 police officers ensured a smooth electoral process and monitored the local police.

Over 700,000 voters registered at centres all over the country. The elections, monitored by UNTAG, were held in November; 97 per cent of registered voters went to the polls to choose the 72 members of the Constituent Assembly. SWAPO obtained 41 seats, the Democratic Turnhalle Alliance 21 and five small parties 10. The Secretary-General's Special Representative, Martti Ahtisaari, declared the elections "free and fair".

South Africa withdrew its remaining troops. The Constituent Assembly drafted a new Constitution, which was approved on 9 February 1990. On 16 February, the Assembly elected SWAPO leader Sam Nujoma as President for a five-year term. On 21 March, Namibia became independent, with the Secretary-General administering the oath of office to Namibia's first President. In April, Namibia became the 160th Member of the United Nations.

Western Sahara

The United Nations has been dealing since 1963 with an ongoing dispute on Western Sahara — a Territory on the north-west coast of Africa bordering with Morocco, Mauritania and Algeria.

In 1963, Western Sahara was administered by Spain, but both Morocco and Mauritania laid claim to it. The International Court of Justice, in a 1975 opinion requested by the General Assembly, rejected the claims of territorial sovereignty by Morocco or Mauritania.

The United Nations has been seeking a settlement in Western Sahara since the withdrawal of Spain in 1976 (*see footnote on page 278*) and the ensuing fighting between Morocco, which had "reintegrated" the Territory, and the Popular Front for the Liberation of Saguia el-Hamra and Río de Oro (Frente POLISARIO), supported by Algeria.

The Organization of African Unity (OAU) called in 1979 for a referendum allowing the people of the Territory to exercise their right to self-determination. Morocco agreed in 1981 to a ceasefire and to an internationally supervised referendum, while making it clear that it would not negotiate directly with POLISARIO. By 1982, 26 OAU member States had recognized the "Saharawi Arab Democratic Republic (SADR)" proclaimed by POLISARIO in 1976. When POLISARIO was seated at the 1984 OAU summit, Morocco withdrew from the OAU.

The General Assembly reaffirmed in 1983 and 1984 that the people of the Territory had yet to exercise their right to self-determination and independence, and that the parties should negotiate a ceasefire allowing for a referendum.

A joint good offices mission by the Secretary-General and the OAU Chairman led to their 1988 settlement proposal providing for a ceasefire and a referendum to choose between independence and integration with Morocco — a proposal both parties accepted.

The Security Council in 1990 approved the Secretary-General's proposal that, during a transitional period, a Special Representative of the Secretary-General would be responsible for all matters relating to the referendum, assisted by the **United Nations Mission for the Referendum in Western Sahara (MINURSO)**. All Western Saharans aged 18 and over counted in the 1974 Spanish census would have the right to vote, whether living in the Territory or outside. An Identification Commission would update the census and identify voters. Refugees living outside the Territory would be identified with the assistance of the Office of the United Nations High Commissioner for Refugees.

The Security Council established MINURSO in 1991. The Secretary-General called for a formal ceasefire to come into effect on 6 September and, in view of continued sporadic fighting, the Security Council dispatched 228 MINURSO military observers to verify the end of hostilities.

While both parties reiterated their confidence in the United Nations and their commitment to the plan, they continued to have different views, in particular on the criteria for voter eligibility.

The Secretary-General had set out such criteria in a 1991 report to the Security Council. Morocco accepted them, while considering them unduly restrictive. POLISARIO stated that it had been originally agreed that the sole basis of the electorate would be the list of Saharans counted in the 1974 census, and that the criteria would unduly expand the electorate beyond the persons included in the census, with the possible inclusion of persons who were not Saharans from the Territory.

In 1994, the Security Council asked the Identification Commission to start the identification and registration of voters, on the basis of a compromise proposed by the Secretary-General and accepted by both parties. Morocco intended to present for identification 100,000 applicants residing outside the Territory, but POLISARIO objected.

In spite of the mediation of the Secretary-General and his Special Representative, disagreements over voter eligibility continued, bringing the identification process to a halt in late 1995. The Security Council suspended the process until the parties showed commitment to completing it. Out of the some 77,000 persons convoked, 60,000 had been identified.

Talks mediated by the Secretary-General's new Personal Envoy, former United States Secretary of State James A. Baker III, led in 1997 to agreements on the resumption of the identification process and on a code of conduct for the referendum. It was estimated that the referendum would involve some 80,000 voters.

East Timor

Another ongoing dispute that continues to receive attention is the question of East Timor. The island of Timor lies to the north of Australia, in the south-central part of the chain of islands forming the Republic of Indonesia. The western part of the island was a Dutch colony and became part of Indonesia when the country attained independence. East Timor was a Portuguese colony.

The General Assembly in 1960 placed East Timor on the list of Non-Self-Governing Territories. In 1974, recognizing the right to self-determination and independence of its colonies, Portugal sought to establish a provisional government and a popular assembly which would determine the status of East Timor.

But civil war broke out in 1975 between those advocating independence and those advocating integration with Indonesia. Portugal withdrew, stating that it was unable to control the situation (*see footnote on page 278*). One East Timorese side declared independence as a separate country, while another proclaimed independence and integration with Indonesia. In December, Indonesian troops landed in East Timor, and a "provisional government" was formed. Portugal broke off relations with Indonesia and brought the matter before the Security Council.

The Council and the General Assembly called on Indonesia to withdraw its forces and called on all States to respect East Timor's territorial integrity, as well as the inalienable rights of its people to self-determination in accordance with the Declaration on decolonization.

In 1976, the "provisional Government" held elections for an assembly, which called for integration with Indonesia. Indonesia issued a law for the integration of the Territory, and the pro-independence movement started armed resistance and an international campaign of opposition.

Portugal has maintained that the people of East Timor have not exerted their right to self-determination. Indonesia has maintained that the process of decolonization in East Timor is complete and that its people chose independence through integration with Indonesia.

Since 1982, at the request of the General Assembly, the Secretary-General has been holding talks with Indonesia and Portugal to promote a just and comprehensive settlement. To give new impetus to his good offices on the question, the Secretary-General appointed, in 1997, a Personal Representative for East Timor, and has continued to consult with East Timorese personalities of various political persuasions facilitating meetings of the All-inclusive Intra-Timorese dialogue. Both Governments have expressed their desire to find a peaceful negotiated settlement to the problem.

PART THREE

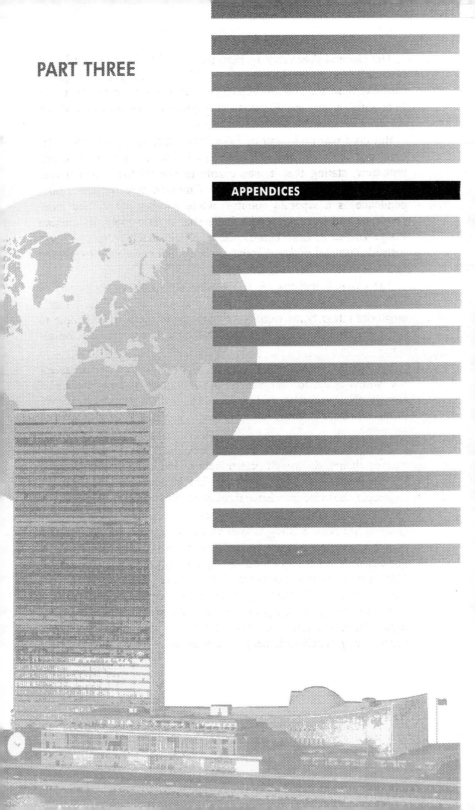

APPENDICES

UNITED NATIONS MEMBER STATES

(as of June 1998)

Member State	Date of Admission	Scale of Assessments for 1998 (per cent)	Population (est.)
Afghanistan	19 November 1946	0.004	20,883,000
Albania	14 December 1955	0.003	3,650,000
Algeria	8 October 1962	0.116	29,168,000
Andorra	28 July 1993	0.004	71,000
Angola	1 December 1976	0.010	11,185,000
Antigua and Barbuda	11 November 1981	0.002	67,000
Argentina	24 October 1945	0.768	35,220,000
Armenia	2 March 1992	0.027	3,764,000
Australia	1 November 1945	1.471	18,289,000
Austria	14 December 1955	0.935	8,106,000
Azerbaijan	2 March 1992	0.060	7,554,000
Bahamas	18 September 1973	0.015	284,000
Bahrain	21 September 1971	0.018	599,000
Bangladesh	17 September 1974	0.010	120,073,000
Barbados	9 December 1966	0.008	265,000
Belarus[a]	24 October 1945	0.164	10,247,000
Belgium	27 December 1945	1.096	10,159,000
Belize	25 September 1981	0.001	222,000
Benin	20 September 1960	0.002	5,514,000
Bhutan	21 September 1971	0.001	1,812,000
Bolivia	14 November 1945	0.008	7,588,000
Bosnia and Herzegovina	22 May 1992	0.005	4,510,000
Botswana	17 October 1966	0.010	1,490,000
Brazil	24 October 1945	1.514	157,872,000
Brunei Darussalam	21 September 1984	0.020	300,000
Bulgaria	14 December 1955	0.045	8,356,000
Burkina Faso	20 September 1960	0.002	10,870,000
Burundi	18 September 1962	0.001	6,088,000
Cambodia	14 December 1955	0.001	10,702,000
Cameroon	20 September 1960	0.014	13,560,000
Canada	9 November 1945	2.825	29,964,000
Cape Verde	16 September 1975	0.001	396,000
Central African Republic	20 September 1960	0.002	3,334,000
Chad	20 September 1960	0.001	6,515,000
Chile	24 October 1945	0.113	14,419,000
China	24 October 1945	0.901	1,232,083,000
Colombia	5 November 1945	0.108	36,626,000
Comoros	12 November 1975	0.001	632,000
Congo	20 September 1960	0.003	2,668,000
Costa Rica	2 November 1945	0.017	3,398,000
Côte d'Ivoire	20 September 1960	0.012	14,781,000

Member State	Date of Admission	Scale of Assessments for 1998 (per cent)	Population (est.)
Croatia	22 May 1992	0.056	4,501,000
Cuba	24 October 1945	0.039	11,019,000
Cyprus	20 September 1960	0.034	756,000
Czech Republic	19 January 1993	0.169	10,315,000
Democratic People's Republic of Korea	17 September 1991	0.031	22,466,000
Democratic Republic of the Congo[b]	20 September 1960	0.008	46,812,000
Denmark	24 October 1945	0.687	5,262,000
Djibouti	20 September 1977	0.001	617,000
Dominica	18 December 1978	0.001	74,000
Dominican Republic	24 October 1945	0.016	8,052,000
Ecuador	21 December 1945	0.022	11,698,000
Egypt[c]	24 October 1945	0.069	60,603,000
El Salvador	24 October 1945	0.012	5,796,000
Equatorial Guinea	12 November 1968	0.001	410,000
Eritrea	28 May 1993	0.001	3,280,000
Estonia	17 September 1991	0.023	1,470,000
Ethiopia	13 November 1945	0.007	58,506,000
Federated States of Micronesia	17 September 1991	0.001	109,000
Fiji	13 October 1970	0.004	797,000
Finland	14 December 1955	0.538	5,125,000
France	24 October 1945	6.494	58,375,000
Gabon	20 September 1960	0.018	1,106,000
Gambia	21 September 1965	0.001	1,141,000
Georgia	31 July 1992	0.058	5,411,000
Germany	18 September 1973	9.630	81,912,000
Ghana	8 March 1957	0.007	17,832,000
Greece	25 October 1945	0.368	10,475,000
Grenada	17 September 1974	0.001	99,000
Guatemala	21 November 1945	0.019	10,928,000
Guinea	12 December 1958	0.003	7,518,000
Guinea-Bissau	17 September 1974	0.001	1,091,000
Guyana	20 September 1966	0.001	838,000
Haiti	24 October 1945	0.002	7,336,000
Honduras	17 December 1945	0.004	6,140,000
Hungary	14 December 1955	0.119	10,193,000
Iceland	19 November 1946	0.032	271,000
India	30 October 1945	0.305	939,409,000
Indonesia[d]	28 September 1950	0.173	196,813,000
Iran (Islamic Republic of)	24 October 1945	0.303	61,128,000
Iraq	21 December 1945	0.087	20,607,000
Ireland	14 December 1955	0.223	3,521,000
Israel	11 May 1949	0.329	5,696,000
Italy	14 December 1955	5.394	57,399,000
Jamaica	18 September 1962	0.006	2,491,000

Member State	Date of Admission	Scale of Assessments for 1998 (per cent)	Population (est.)
Japan	18 December 1956	17.981	125,761,000
Jordan	14 December 1955	0.008	5,581,000
Kazakhstan	2 March 1992	0.124	16,526,000
Kenya	16 December 1963	0.007	31,806,000
Kuwait	14 May 1963	0.154	1,687,000
Kyrgyzstan	2 March 1992	0.015	4,575,000
Lao People's Democratic Republic	14 December 1955	0.001	5,035,000
Latvia	17 September 1991	0.046	2,491,000
Lebanon	24 October 1945	0.016	3,084,000
Lesotho	17 October 1966	0.002	2,078,000
Liberia	2 November 1945	0.002	2,820,000
Libyan Arab Jamahiriya	14 December 1955	0.160	5,593,000
Liechtenstein	18 September 1990	0.005	32,000
Lithuania	17 September 1991	0.045	3,710,000
Luxembourg	24 October 1945	0.066	416,000
Madagascar	20 September 1960	0.003	15,353,000
Malawi	1 December 1964	0.002	10,114,000
Malaysia[e]	17 September 1957	0.168	20,565,000
Maldives	21 September 1965	0.001	263,000
Mali	28 September 1960	0.003	11,134,000
Malta	1 December 1964	0.014	373,000
Marshall Islands	17 September 1991	0.001	57,000
Mauritania	27 October 1961	0.001	2,351,000
Mauritius	24 April 1968	0.009	1,134,000
Mexico	7 November 1945	0.941	96,578,000
Monaco	28 May 1993	0.003	32,000
Mongolia	27 October 1961	0.002	2,354,000
Morocco	12 November 1956	0.041	27,623,000
Mozambique	16 September 1975	0.002	17,796,000
Myanmar	19 April 1948	0.009	45,922,000
Namibia	23 April 1990	0.007	1,575,000
Nepal	14 December 1955	0.004	21,127,000
Netherlands	10 December 1945	1.619	15,517,000
New Zealand	24 October 1945	0.221	3,570,000
Nicaragua	24 October 1945	0.002	4,238,000
Niger	20 September 1960	0.002	9,465,000
Nigeria	7 October 1960	0.070	115,020,000
Norway	27 November 1945	0.605	4,381,000
Oman	7 October 1971	0.050	2,302,000
Pakistan	30 September 1947	0.060	134,146,000
Palau	15 December 1994	0.001	17,000
Panama	13 November 1945	0.016	2,674,000
Papua New Guinea	10 October 1975	0.007	4,400,000
Paraguay	24 October 1945	0.014	4,955,000
Peru	31 October 1945	0.085	23,947,000
Philippines	24 October 1945	0.077	71,899,000

Member State	Date of Admission	Scale of Assessments for 1998 (per cent)	Population (est.)
Poland	24 October 1945	0.251	38,618,000
Portugal	14 December 1955	0.368	9,808,000
Qatar	21 September 1971	0.033	558,000
Republic of Korea	17 September 1991	0.955	45,545,000
Republic of Moldova	2 March 1992	0.043	4,237,000
Romania	14 December 1955	0.102	22,608,000
Russian Federation[f]	24 October 1945	2.873	147,739,000
Rwanda	18 September 1962	0.002	5,397,000
Saint Kitts and Nevis	23 September 1983	0.001	41,000
Saint Lucia	18 September 1979	0.001	144,000
Saint Vincent and the Grenadines	16 September 1980	0.001	113,000
Samoa	15 December 1976	0.001	166,000
San Marino	2 March 1992	0.002	26,000
Sao Tome and Principe	16 September 1975	0.001	135,000
Saudi Arabia	24 October 1945	0.594	18,836,000
Senegal	28 September 1960	0.006	8,572,000
Seychelles	21 September 1976	0.002	76,000
Sierra Leone	27 September 1961	0.001	4,297,000
Singapore	21 September 1965	0.167	3,044,000
Slovakia	19 January 1993	0.053	5,374,000
Slovenia	22 May 1992	0.060	1,991,000
Solomon Islands	19 September 1978	0.001	391,000
Somalia	20 September 1960	0.001	9,822,000
South Africa	7 November 1945	0.365	42,393,000
Spain	14 December 1955	2.571	39,270,000
Sri Lanka	14 December 1955	0.013	18,300,000
Sudan	12 November 1956	0.009	27,291,000
Suriname	4 December 1975	0.004	432,000
Swaziland	24 September 1968	0.002	936,000
Sweden	19 November 1946	1.099	8,843,000
Syrian Arab Republic[g]	24 October 1945	0.062	14,619,000
Tajikistan	2 March 1992	0.008	5,919,000
Thailand	16 December 1946	0.158	60,003,000
The former Yugoslav Republic of Macedonia [h]	8 April 1993	0.005	2,163,000
Togo	20 September 1960	0.002	4,201,000
Trinidad and Tobago	18 September 1962	0.018	1,297,000
Tunisia	12 November 1956	0.028	9,092,000
Turkey	24 October 1945	0.440	62,697,000
Turkmenistan	2 March 1992	0.015	4,569,000
Uganda	25 October 1962	0.004	19,848,000
Ukraine	24 October 1945	1.678	51,094,000
United Arab Emirates	9 December 1971	0.177	2,260,000
United Kingdom	24 October 1945	5.076	58,784,000
United Republic of Tanzania[i]	14 December 1961	0.004	30,799,000

Member State	Date of Admission	Scale of Assessments for 1998 (per cent)	Population (est.)
United States of America	24 October 1945	25.000	266,557,000
Uruguay	18 December 1945	0.049	3,203,000
Uzbekistan	2 March 1992	0.077	22,912,000
Vanuatu	15 September 1981	0.001	169,000
Venezuela	15 November 1945	0.235	22,311,000
Viet Nam	20 September 1977	0.010	75,181,000
Yemen	30 September 1947	0.010	15,919,000
Yugoslavia	24 October 1945	0.060	10,574,000
Zambia	1 December 1964	0.003	8,275,000
Zimbabwe	25 August 1980	0.009	11,908,000

States which are not Members of the United Nations but which participate in certain of its activities, shall be called upon to contribute towards the expneses of the Organization on the basis of the following percentage rates:

Holy See	0.001
Nauru	0.001
Switzerland	1.215
Tonga	0.001

---

[a] On 19 September 1991, Byelorussia informed the United Nations that it had changed its name to Belarus.

[b] The Republic of Zaire informed the United Nations that, effective 17 May 1997, it had changed its name to Democratic Republic of the Congo.

[c] Egypt and Syria were original Members of the United Nations from 24 October 1945. Following a plebiscite on 21 February 1958, the United Arab Republic was established by a union of Egypt and Syria and continued as a single Member. On 13 October 1961, Syria, having resumed its status as an independent State, resumed its separate membership in the United Nations. On 2 September 1971, the United Arab Republic changed its name to the Arab Republic of Egypt.

[d] By letter of 20 January 1965, Indonesia announced its decision to withdraw from the United Nations "at this stage and under the present circumstances". By telegram of 19 September 1966, it announced its decision "to resume full cooperation with the United Nations and to resume participation in its activities". On 28 September 1966, the General Assembly took note of this decision and the President invited representatives of Indonesia to take seats in the Assembly.

[e] The Federation of Malaya joined the United Nations on 17 September 1957. On 16 September 1963, its name was changed to Malaysia, following the admission to the new federation of Singapore, Sabah (North Borneo) and Sarawak. Singapore became an independent State on 9 August 1965 and a United Nations Member on 21 September 1965.

[f] The Union of Soviet Socialist Republics was an original Member of the United Nations from 24 October 1945. In a letter dated 24 December 1991, Boris Yeltsin, the President of the Russian Federation, informed the Secretary-General that the membership of the Soviet Union in the Security Council and all other

United Nations organs was being continued by the Russian Federation with the support of the 11 member countries of the Commonwealth of Independent States.
[g] Egypt and Syria were original Members of the United Nations from 24 October 1945. Following a plebiscite on 21 January 1958, the United Arab Republic was established by a union of Egypt and Syria and continued as a single Member. On 13 October 1961, Syria, having resumed its status as an independent State, resumed its separate membership in the United Nations.
[h] The General Assembly decided on 8 April 1993 to admit to United Nations membership the States being provisionally referred to for all purposes within the United Nations as "the former Yugoslavia Republic of Macedonia" pending settlement of the difference that had arisen over its name.
[i] Tanganyika was a United Nations Member from 14 December 1961 and Zanzibar was a Member from 16 December 1963. Following the ratification on 26 April 1964 of Articles of Union between Tanganyika and Zanzibar, the United Republic of Tanganyika and Zanzibar continued as a single Member, changing its name to the United Republic of Tanzania on 1 November 1964.

GROWTH IN UNITED NATIONS
MEMBERSHIP, 1945-1998

Year	Number	Member States
1945	Original 51	Argentina, Australia, Belgium, Bolivia. Brazil, Belarus, Canada, Chile, China, Colombia, Costa Rica, Cuba, Czechoslovakia, Denmark, Dominican Republic, Ecuador, Egypt, El Salvador, Ethiopia, France, Greece, Guatemala, Haiti, Honduras, India, Iran, Iraq, Lebanon, Liberia, Luxembourg, Mexico, Netherlands, New Zealand, Nicaragua, Norway, Panama, Paraguay, Peru, Philippines, Poland, Russian Federation, Saudi Arabia, South Africa, Syrian Arab Republic, Turkey, Ukraine, United Kingdom of Great Britain and Northern Ireland, United States of America, Uruguay, Venezuela, Yugoslavia
1946	55	Afghanistan, Iceland, Sweden, Thailand
1947	57	Pakistan, Yemen[1]
1948	58	Myanmar
1949	59	Israel
1950	60	Indonesia
1955	76	Albania, Austria, Bulgaria, Cambodia, Finland, Hungary, Ireland, Italy, Jordan, Lao People's Democratic Republic, Libyan Arab Jamahiriya, Nepal, Portugal, Romania, Spain, Sri Lanka
1956	80	Japan, Morocco, Sudan, Tunisia
1957	82	Ghana, Malaysia
1958	82[2]	Guinea
1960	99	Benin, Burkina Faso, Cameroon, Central African Republic, Chad, Congo, Côte d'Ivoire, Cyprus, Gabon, Madagascar, Mali, Niger, Nigeria, Senegal, Somalia, Togo, Democratic Republic of the Congo
1961	104[3]	Mauritania, Mongolia, Sierra Leone, United Republic of Tanzania
1962	110	Algeria, Burundi, Jamaica, Rwanda, Trinidad and Tobago, Uganda
1963	112	Kenya, Kuwait
1964	115	Malawi, Malta, Zambia
1965	117[4]	Gambia, Maldives, Singapore
1966	1225	Barbados, Botswana, Guyana, Lesotho
1967	123	Democratic Yemen[1]
1968	126	Equatorial Guinea, Mauritius, Swaziland
1970	127	Fiji
1971	132	Bahrain, Bhutan, Oman, Qatar, United Arab Emirates
1973	135	Bahamas, German Democratic Republic, Germany, Federal Republic of[6]
1974	138	Bangladesh, Grenada, Guinea-Bissau

Year	Number	Member States
1975	144	Cape Verde, Comoros, Mozambique, Papua New Guinea, Sao Tome and Principe, Suriname
1976	147	Angola, Samoa, Seychelles
1977	149	Djibouti, Viet Nam
1978	151	Dominica, Solomon Islands
1979	152	Saint Lucia
1980	154	Saint Vincent and the Grenadines, Zimbabwe
1981	157	Antigua and Barbuda, Belize, Vanuatu
1983	158	Saint Kitts and Nevis
1984	159	Brunei Darussalam
1990	159[1,6]	Liechtenstein, Namibia
1991	166	Democratic People's Republic of Korea, Estonia, Federated States of Micronesia, Latvia, Lithuania, Marshall Islands, Republic of Korea
1992	179	Armenia, Azerbaijan, Bosnia and Herzegovina, Croatia, Georgia, Kazakhstan, Kyrgyzstan, Moldova, San Marino, Slovenia, Tajikistan, Turkmenistan, Uzbekistan
1993	184[7]	Andorra, Czech Republic, Eritrea, Monaco, Slovak Republic, The former Yugoslav Republic of Macedonia
1994	185	Palau

---

[1] Yemen was admitted to membership in the United Nations on 30 September 1947 and Democratic Yemen on 14 December 1967. On 22 May 1990, the two countries merged and have since been represented as one Member with the name "Yemen".

[2] The total remains the same because from 21 January 1958 Syria and Egypt continued as a single member (United Arab Republic)

[3] Syria resumed its status as an independent State.

[4] Indonesia withdrew as of 20 January 1965.

[5] Indonesia resumed its membership as of 28 September 1966.

[6] The Federal Republic of Germany and the German Democratic Republic were admitted to membership in the United Nations on 18 September 1973. Through the accession of the German Democratic Republic to the Federal Republic of Germany, effective from 3 October 1990, the two German States have united to form one sovereign State.

[7] Czechoslovakia was an original Member of the United Nations from 24 October 1945. In a letter dated 10 December 1992, its Permanent Representative informed the Secretary-General that the Czech and Slovak Federal Republic would cease to exist on 31 December 1992 and that the Czech Republic and the Slovak Republic, as successor States, would apply for membership in the United Nations. Following the receipt of such applications, the Security Council, on 8 January 1993, recommended to the General Assembly that the Czech Republic and the Slovak Republic be admitted to United Nations membership. They were thus admitted on 19 January 1993 as Member States.

DECOLONIZATION

Trust and Non-Self-Governing Territories that have achieved
independence since the adoption of the 1960 Declaration*

State or entity   **Date of admission to the United Nations**

Africa

State or entity	Date of admission to the United Nations
Algeria	8 October 1962
Angola	1 December 1976
Botswana	17 October 1966
Burundi	18 September 1962
Cape Verde	16 September 1975
Comoros	12 November 1975
Djibouti	20 September 1977
Equatorial Guinea	12 November 1968
Gambia	21 September 1965
Guinea-Bissau	17 September 1974
Kenya	16 December 1963
Lesotho	17 October 1966
Malawi	1 December 1964
Mauritius	24 April 1968
Mozambique	16 September 1975
Namibia	23 April 1990
Rwanda	18 September 1962
Sao Tome and Principe	26 September 1975
Seychelles	21 September 1976
Sierra Leone	27 September 1961
Swaziland	24 September 1968
Uganda	25 October 1962
United Republic of Tanzania[1]	14 December 1961
Zambia	1 December 1964
Zimbabwe	18 April 1980

Asia

State or entity	Date of admission to the United Nations
Brunei Darussalam	21 September 1984
Democratic Yemen	14 December 1967
Oman	7 October 1971
Singapore	21 September 1965

Declaration on the Granting of Independence to Colonial Countries and Peoples, adopted by the General Assembly on 14 December 1960.

State or entity	Date of admission to the United Nations

Caribbean

Antigua and Barbuda	11 November 1981
Bahamas	18 September 1973
Barbados	9 December 1966
Belize	25 September 1981
Dominica	18 December 1978
Grenada	17 December 1974
Guyana	20 September 1966
Jamaica	18 September 1962
Saint Christopher and Nevis	23 September 1983
Saint Lucia	18 September 1979
Saint Vincent and the Grenadines	16 September 1980
Suriname[2]	4 December 1975
Trinidad and Tobago	18 September 1962

Europe

Malta	1 December 1964

Pacific

Federated States of Micronesia	17 September 1991
Fiji	13 October 1970
Kiribati[3]	—
Marshall Islands	17 September 1991
Nauru[3]	—
Papua New Guinea	10 October 1975
Palau	15 December 1994
Samoa	15 December 1976
Solomon Islands	19 September 1978
Tuvalu[3]	—
Vanuatu	15 September 1981

---

[1] The former Trust Territory of Tanganyika, which became independent in December 1961, and the former Protectorate of Zanzibar, which achieved independence in December 1963, united into a single State in April 1964.

[2] By resolution 945(X), the General Assembly accepted the cessation of the transmission of information regarding Suriname following constitutional changes in the relationship between the Netherlands, Suriname and the Netherlands Antilles.

[3] Kiribati, Nauru and Tuvalu, which became independent on 12 July 1979, 31 January 1968 and 1 October 1978, respectively, have not applied for United Nations membership.

DECOLONIZATION

Dependent Territories that have become integrated
or associated with independent States since
the adoption of the 1960 Declaration*

Territory	Remarks
Cameroons under British administration	The northern part of the Trust Territory joined the Federation of Nigeria on 1 June 1961 and the southern part joined the Republic of Cameroon on 1 October 1961
Cook Islands	Fully self-governing in free association with New Zealand since August 1965
Ifni	Returned to Morocco in June 1969
Niue	Fully self-governing in free association with New Zealand since August 1974
North Borneo	North Borneo and Sarawak joined the Federation of Malaya in 1963 to form the Federation of Malaysia
São Joao Batista de Ajuda	Nationally united with Dahomey (now Benin) in August 1961
Sarawak	Sarawak and North Borneo joined the Federation of Malaya in 1963 to form the Federation of Malaysia
West New Guinea (West Irian)	United with Indonesia in 1963
Cocos (Keeling) Islands	Integrated with Australia in 1984

Declaration on the Granting of Independence to Colonial Countries and Peoples, adopted by the General Assembly on 14 December 1960.

DECOLONIZATION

Territories to which the Declaration on Decolonization continues to apply (as of 1998)*

Territory	Administering Authority
Africa	
Western Sahara	Spain[1]
Asia and the Pacific	
American Samoa	United States
East Timor	Portugal[2]
Guam	United States
New Caledonia[3]	France
Pitcairn	United Kingdom
Tokelau	New Zealand
Atlantic Ocean, Caribbean and Mediterranean	
Anguilla	United Kingdom
Bermuda	United Kingdom
British Virgin Islands	United Kingdom
Cayman Islands	United Kingdom
Falkland Islands (Malvinas)	United Kingdom
Gibraltar	United Kingdom
Montserrat	United Kingdom
St. Helena	United Kingdom
Turks and Caicos Islands	United Kingdom
United States Virgin Islands	United States

---

*Declaration on the Granting of Independence to Colonial Countries and Peoples, adopted by the General Assembly on 14 December 1960.

[1] On 26 February 1976, Spain informed the Secretary-General that as of that date it had terminated its presence in the Territory of the Sahara and deemed it necessary to place on record that Spain considered itself thenceforth exempt from any responsibility of an international nature in connection with the administration of the Territory, in view of the cessation of its participation in the temporary administration established for the Territory. In 1990, the General Assembly reaffirmed that the question of Western Sahara was a question of decolonization which remained to be completed by the people of Western Sahara.

[2] Since 1977, Portugal, in its capacity as administering Power of the Non-Self-Governing Territory of East Timor, has annually been informing the Secretary-General that it continues to be prevented de facto from exercising its responsibilities for the administration of the Territory due to the latter's illegal occupation by a third country.

[3] On 2 December 1986, the General Assembly determined that New Caledonia was a Non-Self-Governing Territory.

DECOLONIZATION

Trust Territories that have achieved self-determination

Togoland (under British administration)
>United with the Gold Coast (Colony and Protectorate), a Non-Self-Governing Territory administered by the United Kingdom, in 1957 to form Ghana

Somaliland (under Italian administration)
>United with British Somaliland Protectorate in 1960 to form Somalia

Togoland (under French administration)
>Became independent as Togo in 1960

Cameroons (under French administration)
>Became independent as Cameroon in 1960

Cameroons (under British administration)
>The northern part of the Trust Territory joined the Federation of Nigeria on 1 June 1961 and the southern part joined the Republic of Cameroon on 1 October 1961

Tanganyika (under British administration)
>Became independent in 1961 (in 1964, Tanganyika and the former Protectorate of Zanzibar, which had become independent in 1963, united as a single State under the name of the United Republic of Tanzania)

Ruanda-Urundi (under Belgian administration)
>Voted to divide into the two sovereign States of Rwanda and Burundi in 1962

Western Samoa (under New Zealand administration)
>Became independent as Samoa in 1962

Nauru (administered by Australia on behalf of Australia, New Zealand and the United Kingdom)
>Became independent in 1968

New Guinea (administered by Australia)
>United with the Non-Self-Governing Territory of Papua, also administered by Australia, to become the independent State of Papua New Guinea in 1975

Trust Territory of the Pacific Islands:
  (a) **Federated States of Micronesia**
          Became fully self-governing in free Association with the United States in 1990
  (b) **Republic of the Marshall Islands**
          Became fully self-governing in free Association with the United States in 1990
  (c) **Commonwealth of the Northern Mariana Islands**
          Became fully self-governing as a Commonwealth of the United States in 1990
  (d) **Palau**
          Became fully self-governing in free Association with the United States in 1994

PEACEKEEPING OPERATIONS: PAST AND PRESENT

(As of June 1998)

*UNTSO
United Nations Truce Supervision Organization (Jerusalem)
June 1948–

*UNMOGIP
United Nations Military Observer Group in India and Pakistan
January 1949–

UNEF I
First United Nations Emergency Force (Gaza)
November 1956–June 1967

UNOGIL
United Nations Observation Group in Lebanon
June–December 1958

ONUC
United Nations Operation in the Congo
July 1960–June 1964

UNSF
United Nations Security Force in West New Guinea (West Irian)
October 1962–April 1963

UNYOM
United Nations Yemen Observation Mission
July 1963–September 1964

*UNFICYP
United Nations Peacekeeping Force in Cyprus
March 1964–

DOMREP
Mission of the Representative of the Secretary-General in the Dominican Republic
May 1965–October 1966

UNIPOM
United Nations India-Pakistan Observation Mission
September 1965–March 1966

UNEF II
Second United Nations Emergency Force (Suez Canal and later Sinai peninsula)
October 1973–July 1979

*UNDOF
United Nations Disengagement Observer Force (Syrian Golan Heights)
June 1974–

*UNIFIL
United Nations Interim Force in Lebanon
March 1978–

UNGOMAP
United Nations Good Offices Mission in Afghanistan and Pakistan
May 1988–March 1990

UNIIMOG
United Nations Iran-Iraq Military Observer Group
August 1988–February 1991

UNAVEM I
United Nations Angola Verification Mission I
January 1989–June 1991

UNTAG
United Nations Transition Assistance Group (Namibia and Angola)
April 1989–March 1990

ONUCA
United Nations Observer Group in Central America
November 1989–January 1992

*UNIKOM
United Nations Iraq-Kuwait Observation Mission
April 1991–

UNAVEM II
United Nations Angola Verification Mission II
June 1991–February 1995

ONUSAL
United Nations Observer Mission in El Salvador
July 1991–April 1995

*MINURSO
United Nations Mission for the Referendum in Western Sahara
April 1991–

UNAMIC
United Nations Advance Mission in Cambodia
October 1991–March 1992

UNPROFOR
United Nations Protection Force (former Yugoslavia)
March 1992–December 1995

UNTAC
United Nations Transitional Authority in Cambodia
March 1992–September 1993

UNOSOM I
United Nations Operation in Somalia I
April 1992–March 1993

ONUMOZ
United Nations Operation in Mozambique
December 1992–December 1994

UNOSOM II
United Nations Operation in Somalia II
March 1993–March 1995

UNOMUR
United Nations Observer Mission Uganda-Rwanda
June 1993–September 1994

*UNOMIG
United Nations Observer Mission in Georgia
August 1993–

UNOMIL
United Nations Observer Mission in Liberia
September 1993–September 1997

UNMIH
United Nations Mission in Haiti
September 1993–June 1996

UNAMIR
United Nations Assistance Mission for Rwanda
October 1993–March 1996

UNASOG
United Nations Aouzou Strip Observer Group (Republic of Chad)
May–June 1994

*UNMOT
United Nations Mission of Observers in Tajikistan
December 1994–

UNAVEM III
United Nations Angola Verification Mission III
February 1995–June 1997

UNCRO
United Nations Confidence Restoration Operation in Croatia
March 1995–January 1996

*UNPREDEP
United Nations Preventive Deployment Force (former Yugoslav Republic of Macedonia)
March 1995–

*UNMIBH
United Nations Mission in Bosnia and Herzegovina
December 1995–

UNTAES
United Nations Transitional Administration for Eastern Slavо. ʾя, Baranja and Western Sirmium (Croatia)
January 1996–January 1998

*UNMOP
United Nations Mission of Observers in Prevlaka (Croatia)
January 1996–

UNSMIH
United Nations Support Mission in Haiti
July 1996–July 1997

MINUGUA
United Nations Verification Mission in Guatemala
January–May 1997

*MONUA
United Nations Observer Mission in Angola
July 1997–

UNTMIH
United Nations Transition Mission in Haiti
August-November 1997

*MIPONUH
United Nations Civilian Police Mission in Haiti
December 1997–

*United Nations Civilian Police Support Group (Croatia)
January 1998–

*MINURCA
United Nations Mission in the Central African Republic
March 1998–

*UNOMSIL
United Nations Observer Mission in Sierra Leone
July 1998–

---

*Current, as of July 1998 operation.

BUDGET OF THE UNITED NATIONS

For the 1998-1999 biennium, the appropriation for the regular budget of the United Nations (i.e. excluding the bulk of Offices and Programmes, as well as the Specialized Agencies and other associated bodies), as initially approved in 1997, totalled $2,532,331,200, divided into 13 main categories of expenditures, as follows (in United States dollars):

1.	Overall policy-making, direction and coordination	478,283,700
2.	Political affairs	206,100,100
3.	International justice and law	53,514,700
4.	International cooperation for development	272,593,900
5.	Regional cooperation for development	370,368,900
6.	Human rights and humanitarian affairs	127,362,900
7.	Public information	138,040,400
8.	Common support services	446,190,700
9.	Internal oversight	8,359,600
10.	Jointly financed activities and special expenses	58,464,400
11.	Capital expenditures	34,550,300
12.	Staff assessment*	315,436,700
13.	Development account	13,065,000

*To equalize the net pay of all United Nations staff members, whatever their national tax obligations, the Organization deducts from their salaries a sum of money designated as "staff assessment". The rate of withholding is roughly equivalent to the amount paid by United States citizens for federal, state and local taxes calculated at the standard rate. The money collected by the United Nations from the staff assessment is then credited towards the United Nations membership "dues" of the staff member's home country.

Most Governments excuse nationals who are United Nations employees from further taxation. The United States is the main exception; its citizens who work for the Secretariat must pay the same income taxes as all other United States citizens. To enable them to pay their taxes, the United Nations refunds to United States employees that part of their staff assessment which is equal to what the national revenue authorities require for taxes. The citizen then pays that amount to those authorities. In this way, United States nationals are not required to pay taxes twice.

The regular programme budget to which these assessments apply covers expenses relating to substantive programmes, programme support and administrative activities of the Organization both at Headquarters and around the globe.

The main source of funds for the regular budget is the contributions of Member States, who are assessed on a scale specified by the Assembly on the recommendation of the 18-member Committee on Contributions. The fundamental criterion on which the scale of assessments is based is the real capacity of Member States to pay. The Assembly has fixed a maximum of 25 per cent of the budget for any one contributor and, beginning in 1998, a minimum of 0.001 per cent. (*For scale of assessments of Member States, see pages 287-291.*)

Initial income estimates for the biennium 1998-1999, other than assessments on Member States, totalled $363,840,300.

1.	Income from staff assessment*	325,486,700
2.	General income	33,743,600
3.	Services to the public	4,610,000

---

* See footnote on page 305.

UNITED NATIONS SPECIAL OBSERVANCES

INTERNATIONAL DECADES AND YEARS

1990-1999	Third Disarmament Decade
1990-1999	International Decade for Natural Disaster Reduction
1990-2000	International Decade for the Eradication of Colonialism
1990-1999	United Nations Decade of International Law
1991-2000	Fourth United Nations Development Decade
1991-2000	Second Transport and Communications Decade in Africa
1991-2000	United Nations Decade against Drug Abuse
1993-2002	Second Industrial Development Decade for Africa
1993-2002	Asian and Pacific Decade of Disabled Persons
1993-2003	Third Decade to Combat Racism and Racial Discrimination
1994-2004	International Decade of the World's Indigenous People
1995-2004	United Nations Decade for Human Rights Education
1997-2006	United Nations Decade for the Eradication of Poverty
1998	International Year of the Ocean
1999	International Year of Older Persons
2000	International Year for the Culture of Peace
2000	International Year of Thanksgivings
2001	International Year of Volunteers

ANNUAL DAYS AND WEEKS

8 March	United Nations Day for Women's Rights and International Peace
21 March	International Day for the Elimination of Racial Discrimination
Beginning 21 March	Week of Solidarity with the Peoples Struggling against Racism and Racial Discrimination
22 March	World Day for Water
3 May	World Press Freedom Day
15 May	International Day of Families
Beginning 21 May	Week of Solidarity with the Peoples of All Colonial Territories
4 June	International Day of Innocent Children Victims of Aggression
5 June	World Environment Day
17 June	World Day to Combat Desertification and Drought
26 June	International Day against Drug Abuse and Illicit Trafficking
26 June	International Day in Support of Victims of Torture
First Saturday of July	International Day of Cooperatives
11 July	World Population Day

9 August	International Day of the World's Indigenous People
16 September	International Day for the Preservation of the Ozone Layer
September	International Day of Peace
(Opening day of the regular annual session of the General Assembly)	
1 October	International Day of Older Persons
First Monday of October	World Habitat Day
Second Wednesday of October	International Day for Natural Disaster Reduction
16 October	World Food Day
17 October	International Day for the Eradication of Poverty
24 October	United Nations Day
24-30 October	Disarmament Week
16 November	International Day for Tolerance
20 November	Africa Industrialization Day
29 November	International Day of Solidarity with the Palestinian People
2 December	International Day for the Abolition of Slavery
3 December	International Day of Disabled Persons
10 December	Human Rights Day
29 December	International Day for Biological Diversity

OTHER INTERNATIONAL DAYS

Other international days observed throughout the United Nations system include:

23 March	World Meteorological Day
7 April	World Health Day
23 April	World Book and Copyright Day
17 May	World Telecommunication Day
31 May	World No-Tobacco Day
8 September	International Literacy Day
Last week in September	World Maritime Day
9 October	World Post Day
24 October	World Development Information Day
20 November, varies	Universal Children's Day
21 November	World Television Day
1 December	World AIDS Day
5 December	International Volunteer Day for Economic and Social Development
7 December	International Civil Aviation Day

UNITED NATIONS INFORMATION CENTRES, SERVICES AND OFFICES

AFRICA

Accra

United Nations Information Centre, Gamel Abdul Nassar/Liberia Roads
(P.O. Box 2339), Accra, Ghana
Telephone: (233-21) 665-511/666-851-5
Fax: (233-21) 665-578/668-427(FAO)
E-mail: unicar@ncs.com.gh
Services to: Ghana, Sierra Leone

Addis Ababa

United Nations Information Service, Africa Hall, Economic Commission for
Africa (P.O. Box 3001), Addis Ababa, Ethiopia
Telephone: (251-1) 510-172, (251-1) 517-200 ext. 108
Fax: (251-1) 51-4416 (ECA) or (251-1) 51-6027
Services to: Ethiopia, Economic Commission for Africa

Algiers

United Nations Information Centre, 9A, rue Emile Payen, Hydra (Boite postale
823), Algiers, Algeria
Telephone: (213-2) 69 12 12
Fax: (213-2) 69 23 55
Services to: Algeria

Antananarivo

United Nations Information Centre, 22 rue Rainitovo, Antananarivo, Madagascar
Telephone: (261-2) 24 115
Fax: (261-2) 33 315
E-mail: cinu.tana@undp.dts.mg
Services to: Madagascar

Brazzaville

United Nations Information Centre, Avenue Foch, Case Ortf 15 (P.O. ⌐ox 13210
or 1018), Brazzaville, Congo
Telephone: (242) 83-50-90/83-58-48
Fax: (242) 83-61-40
Services to: Congo

Bujumbura

United Nations Information Centre, 117, Avenue de la Révolution (P.O. Box
2160), Bujumbura, Burundi
Telephone: (257) 225-018; 228-569
Fax: (257) 225-850 (UNDP)
E-mail:un.inf.centre.burundi@undp.org
Services to: Burundi

Cairo

United Nations Information Centre, 1, Osoris St. Garden City (P.O. Box 262), Cairo, Egypt
Telephone: (20-2) 3545153
Fax: (20-2) 3553705
E-mail: unic@foegy.undp.org.eg
Services to: Egypt, Saudi Arabia

Dakar

United Nations Information Centre, 12, Avenue Roume, Immeuble UNESCO, (P.O. Box 154) Dakar, Senegal
Telephone: (221) 823 30 70, 823 40 66
Fax: (221) 822 26 79
E-mail: loum@sonatel.senet.net
Services to: Senegal, Cape Verde, Gambia, Guinea-Bissau, Côte d'Ivoire, Mauritania, Guinea

Dar es Salaam

United Nations Information Centre, Marogoro Road/Sokoine Drive, Old Boma Building, Ground Floor (P.O. Box 9224), Dar es Salaam
Telephone: (255-51) 112923, 119510
Fax: (255-51)-113272 (UNDP)
E-mail: fo.urt@undp.org
Services to: United Republic of Tanzania

Harare

United Nations Information Centre, Zimre Centre, 3rd Floor, L. Takawira Street/Union Avenue
(P.O. Box 4408), Harare, Zimbabwe
Telephone: (263-4) 79-15-21/70-46-79, 79-20-87
Fax: (263-4) 750 476
Services to: Zimbabwe

Khartoum

United Nations Information Centre, United Nations Compound, Gamma'a Ave (P.O. Box 913), Khartoum, Republic of the Sudan
Telephone: (249-11) 777816
Fax: (249-11) 773772, 773128, 783764
E-mail: fo.sdn@un.org
Services to: Sudan, Somalia

Kinshasa

United Nations Information Centre, Bâtiment Deuxième République, Boulevard du 30 Juin (P.O. Box 7248), Kinshasa, Democratic Republic of the Congo
Telephone: (243-12) 33431, 33424, 33425 ext. 213/203
Fax: (871) 150-3261
Services to: Democratic Republic of the Congo

Lagos

United Nations Information Centre, 17 Kingsway Road, Ikoyi (P.O. Box 1068), Lagos, Nigeria
Telephone: (234-1) 269 4886
Fax: (234-1) 269-1934
E-mail: nir0uni%remote.undp-nir@nylan.undp.org
Services to: Nigeria

Lomé

United Nations Information Centre, 107 Boulevard du 13 Janvier (P.O. Box 911) Lomé, Togo
Telephone: (228) 212-306
Fax: (228) 212-306 (same as telephone no.)
E-mail: fo.tog@undp.org
Services to: Togo

Lusaka

United Nations Information Centre, P.O. Box 32905, Lusaka 10101, Republic of Zambia
Telephone: (260-1) 228-487, 228-488,
Fax: (260-1) 222-958
E-mail: unic@zamnet.zm
Services to: Zambia, Botswana, Malawi, Swaziland

Maseru

United Nations Information Centre, Letsie Road, Food Aid Compound (P.O. Box 301), Maseru 100, Lesotho
Telephone: (266) 312 496
Fax: (266) 310 042 (UNDP)
E-mail: fo.les@undp.org
Services to: Lesotho

Nairobi

United Nations Information Centre, United Nations Office, Gigiri (P.O. Box 30552), Nairobi, Kenya
Telephone: (254-2) 623292/3, 623677, 623798
Fax: (254-2) 624349
E-mail: irene.mwakes@unep.org
Services to: Kenya, Seychelles, Uganda

Ouagadougou

United Nations Information Centre, Avenue Georges Konseiga, Secteur No. 4 (P.O. Box 135), Ouagadougou 01, Burkina Faso
Telephone: (226) 30-60-76/33-65-03
Fax: (226) 31-13-22
E-mail: cinu.oui@fasonet.bf
Services to: Burkina Faso, Chad, Mali, Niger

Pretoria

United Nations Information Centre, Metro Park Building, 351 Schoeman Street
(P.O. Box 12677), Tramshed 0126, Pretoria, South Africa
Telephone: (27-12) 338-5077, 338-5078
Fax: (27-12) 320-1122
E-mail: fo.saf@undp.org
Services to: South Africa

Rabat

United Nations Information Centre, Angle Charia Ibnouzaid, Et Zankat Roundanat, No. 6, (P.O. Box 601), Rabat, Morocco
Telephone: (212-77) 686-33/632-04
Fax: (212-77) 683-77
E-mail: rabat@ccmail.unicc.org
Services to: Morocco

Tripoli

United Nations Information Centre, Muzzafar Al Aftas St., Hay El-Andalous (2)
(P.O. Box 286), Tripoli, Libyan Arab Jamahiriya
Telephone: (218-21) 477-0251; 477-7885
Fax: (218-21) 477-7343
Services to: Libyan Arab Jamahiriya

Tunis

United Nations Information Centre, 61 Boulevard Bab-Benat (P.O. Box 863),
Tunis, Tunisia
Telephone: (216-1) 560-203
Fax: (216-1) 568-811
E-mail: cinfo.tunis@un.intl.tn
Services to: Tunisia

Windhoek

United Nations Information Centre, 372 Paratus Building, Independence Avenue
(Private Bag 13351), Windhoek, Namibia
Telephone: (264)-61-233034/5
Fax: (264) 61 233036
E-mail: unic@un.na
Services to: Namibia

Yaoundé

United Nations Information Centre, Immeuble Kamdem, rue Joseph Clère (P.O.
Box 836), Yaoundé, Republic of Cameroon
Telephone: (237) 22-50-43/22-08-26
Fax: (237) 23-51-73
Services to: Cameroon, Gabon, Central African Republic

The Americas

Asunción

United Nations Information Centre, Estrella 345, Edificio City – 3er. Piso
Asunción, Paraguay
Telephone: (595-21) 493025/493026/493027
Fax:(595-21) 449611
E-mail: unic@undp.org.py
Services to: Paraguay

Buenos Aires

United Nations Information Centre, Junín 1940, 1er piso, 1113 Buenos Aires,
Argentina
Telephone: (54-1) 803-7671, 7672, 803-0738
Fax: (54-1) 804-7545, 801-6092
E-mail: buenosaires@ccmail.unicc.org
Services to: Argentina, Uruguay

La Paz

United Nations Information Centre, Av. Mariscal Santa Cruz No. 1350
(P.O. Box 9072), La Paz, Bolivia
Telephone: (591-2) 358-590/358-591 thru 595
Fax: (591-2) 391-368 (UNDP)
E-mail: unicbol@eos.pnud.bo
Services to: Bolivia

Lima

United Nations Information Centre, Lord Cochrane 130, San Isidro (L-27)
(P.O. Box 14-0199), Lima, Perú
Telephone: (511) 441-8745, 422-4149, 422-0879
Fax: (511) 441-8735
E-mail: uniclima@chiva.rcp.net.pe
Services to: Peru

Managua

United Nations Information Centre, Del Portón del Hospital Militar, 1 c. al lago
y 1 c. abajo
(P.O. Box 3260), Managua, Nicaragua
Telephone: (505-2) 66-42-53,
Fax: (505-2) 666 909 (UNDP)
Services to: Nicaragua

Mexico City

United Nations Information Centre, Presidente Masaryk 29-6°. piso, 11570
México, D.F.
Telephone: (52-5) 250-1364, 250-1555, 203-9406
Fax: (52-5) 203-8638
E-mail: dpi-mexico@un.org
Services to: Mexico, Cuba, Dominican Republic

Panama City

United Nations Information Centre, Calle Gerardo Ortega y Ave. Samuel Lewis, Banco Central Hispano Building, 1st floor (P.O. Box 6-9083 El Dorado), Panamá, Republic of Panama
Telephone: (507) 223-0557/269-6280
Fax: (507) 223 2198
E-mail: cinup@sinfo.net
Services to: Panama

Port of Spain

United Nations Information Centre, Bretton Hall, 2nd Floor, 16 Victoria Avenue (P.O. Box 130), Port of Spain, Trinidad, West Indies
Telephone: (1-868) 623-4813, 623-8438
Fax: (1-868) 623-4332
E-mail: dpi-prospa@un.org
Services to: Trinidad and Tobago, Antigua and Barbuda, Bahamas, Barbados, Belize, Dominica, Saint Kitts and Nevis, Grenada, Guyana, Jamaica, Saint Lucia, Netherlands Antilles, Saint Vincent and the Grenadines, Suriname

Rio de Janeiro

United Nations Information Centre, Palácio Itamaraty, Av. Marechal Floriano 196, 20080-002 Rio de Janeiro, RJ Brazil
Telephone: (55-21) 253-2211
Fax: (55-21) 233-5753
E-mail: nacoes.unidas@openlink.com.br
Services to: Brazil

San Salvador

United Nations Information Centre (temporarily inactive)
Edificio Escalón, 2o. Piso, Paseo General Escalón y 87 Avenida Norte, Colonia Escalón (P.O. Box 2157), San Salvador, El Salvador
Telephone: (503) 279-1925 (UNDP)
Fax: (503) 279 1929 (UNDP)
Services to: El Salvador

Santa Fé de Bogotá

United Nations Information Centre, Calle 100 No. 8A-55, Of. 815 (P.O. Box 058964), Santa Fé de Bogotá 2, Colombia
Telephone: (57-1) 257-6044/7576/7916/6065
Fax: (57-1) 257-6244
E-mail: santafe@ccmail.unicc.org
Services to: Colombia, Ecuador, Venezuela

Santiago

United Nations Information Service, Edificio Naciones Unidas, Comisión Económica para América Latina y el Caribe, Avenida Dag Hammarskjöld, Casilla 179-D, Santiago, Chile
Telephone: (56-2) 210-2000, 210-2371, 210-2202
Fax: (56-2) 208-1947/208-0252 (ECLAC)
E-mail: dpisantiago@eclac.cl
Services to: Chile, Economic Commission for Latin America and the Caribbean

Washington, D.C.

United Nations Information Centre, 1775 K Street, N.W., Suite 400, Washington, D.C. 20006, United States
Telephone: (202) 331 8670
Fax: (202) 331 9191, 331 9155
E-mail: dpi-washington@un.org
Services to: United States of America

Asia and the Pacific

Bangkok

United Nations Information Service, United Nations Economic and Social Commission for Asia and the Pacific (ESCAP), United Nations Building, Rajdamnern Avenue Bangkok 10200, Thailand
Telephone: (66-2) 288-1866, 288-2127
Fax: (66-2) 288-1052
E-mail: unisbkk.unescap@un.org
Services to: Thailand, Cambodia, Lao People's Democratic Republic, Malaysia, Singapore, Socialist Republic of Viet Nam, Hong Kong, ESCAP

Beirut

United Nations Information Service, Riad El Solh Square (P.O. Box No.11-8575) Beirut, Lebanon
Telephone: (961-1) 981-301/311/401
Fax: (961-1) 740-340
Services to: Lebanon, Kuwait, Syrian Arab Republic, Economic and Social Commission for Western Asia

Colombo

United Nations Information Centre, 202-204 Bauddhaloka Mawatha (P.O. Box 1505), Colombo 7, Sri Lanka
Telephone: (94-1) 580-691
Fax: (94-1) 581-116 (UNDP)
E-mail: unic.sri@undp.org
Services to: Sri Lanka

Dhaka

United Nations Information Centre, House 60, Road 11A, Dhanmondi (P.O. Box 3658), Dhaka 1000,
Bangladesh
Telephone: (880-2) 818-600; (880-2) 817-868
Fax: (880-2) 812-343
E-mail: loum@sonatel.senet.net
Services to: Bangladesh

Islamabad

United Nations Information Centre, House No. 26, 88th Street, G-6/3 (P.O. Box 1107), Islamabad, Pakistan
Telephone: (92-51) 270-610/812-012/213-553, (92-51) 823-976
Fax: (92-51) 271-856
E-mail: unic@paknet2.ptc.pk
Services to: Pakistan

Jakarta

United Nations Information Centre, Gedung Dewan Pers, 5th Floor, 32-34 Jalan Kebon Sirih, Jakarta, Indonesia
Telephone: (62-21) 380-0292/385-4550
Fax: (62-21) 380-0274
E-mail: unicjak@rad.net.id
Services to: Indonesia

Kabul

United Nations Information Centre (temporarily inactive)
Shah Mahmoud Ghazi Watt (P.O. Box 5), Kabul, Afghanistan
Services to: Afghanistan

Kathmandu

United Nations Information Centre, (P.O. Box 107) Pulchowk, Patan, Kathmandu, Nepal
Telephone: (977-1) 524366
Fax: (977-1) 523-991/986 (UNDP)
E-mail:fo.nep@undp.org
Services to: Nepal

Manama

United Nations Information Centre, Villa 131, Road 2803, Segaya (P.O. Box 26004), Manama 328, Bahrain
Telephone: (973) 231-046
Fax: (973) 270-749
E-mail: undpbah@batelco.com.bh
Services to: Bahrain, Qatar, United Arab Emirates

Manila

United Nations Information Centre, NEDA Building, 106 Amorsolo Street, Legaspi Village, Makati City (P.O. Box 7285 ADC (DAPO) Pasay City), Metro Manila, Philippines
Telephone: (63-2) 892-0611 thru 25, Exts. 255-258, 893-3882; 892-4445/4483
Fax: (63-2) 816-3011, 817-8539
E-mail: unic-mla@philonline.com.ph
Services to: Philippines, Papua New Guinea, Solomon Islands

New Delhi

United Nations Information Centre, 55 Lodi Estate, New Delhi-110003, India
Telephone: (91-11) 462 34 39 and 462 88 77
Fax: (91-11) 462-0293
E-mail: feodor@giasdl01.vsnl.net.in
Services to: India, Bhutan

Sana'a

United Nations Information Centre, Handhal Street, 4, Al-Boniya Area (P.O. Box 237), Sana'a, Republic of Yemen
Telephone: (967-1) 274-000
Fax: (967-1) 274-043
E-mail: unicyem@y.net.ye
Services to: Yemen

Sydney

United Nations Information Centre, 46-48 York Street, 5th Floor (GPO Box 4045), Sydney, NSW, 2001 Australia
Telephone: (61-2) 9262-5111
Fax: (61-2) 9262-5886
E-mail: sydney@ccmail.unicc.org
Services to: Australia, Fiji, Kiribati, Nauru, New Zealand, Tonga, Tuvalu, Vanuatu, Western Samoa

Tehran

United Nations Information Centre, 185 Ghaem Magham Farahani Ave, Tehran – 15868 Iran (P.O. Box 15875-4557), Tehran, Islamic Republic of Iran
Telephone: (98-21) 873-1534
Fax: (98-21) 204-4523
E-mail: iftikhar%ira01.undp-ira@nylan.undp.org
Services to: Iran

Tokyo

United Nations Information Centre, UNU Building, 8th Floor, 53-70, Jingumae 5-chome, Shibuya-ku, Tokyo 150, Japan
Telephone: (81-3) 5467-4451/4454
Fax: (81-3) 5467 4455
E-mail: unictok@orange.ifnet.or.jp
Services to: Japan

Yangon

United Nations Information Centre, 6 Natmauk Road (P.O. Box 230), Yangon, Myanmar
Telephone: (95-1) 292619, 292622
Fax: (95-1) 292739
E-mail: unic.myanmar@undp.org
Services to: Myanmar

EUROPE

Ankara

United Nations Information Centre, 197 Atatürk Bulvari, Ankara, Turkey
Telephone: (90-312) 426-8113
Fax: (90-312) 468-9719
E-mail: unic@undp.un.org.tr
Services to: Turkey

Athens

United Nations Information Centre, 36 Amalias Avenue GR-10558 Athens, Greece
Telephone: (30-1) 523-0640
Fax:(30-1) 523-3639
E-mail: athens@ccmail.unicc.org
Services to: Greece, Cyprus, Israel

Bonn

United Nations Information Centre, Haus Carstanjen, Martin-Luther-King-Strasse, 8D-53175 Bonn, Germany
Telephone: (49 228) 815 2770
Fax: (49 228) 815 2777
E-mail: unic@uno.de
Services to: Germany

Brussels

United Nations Information Centre and Liaison Office with the European Community, Avenue de Broqueville 40, 1200 Brussels, Belgium
Telephone: (32-2) 775-8280/8288
Fax: (32-2) 770-7759
E-mail: unicbel@mbox.unicc.org
Services to: Belgium, Luxembourg, the Netherlands

Bucharest

United Nations Information Centre, 16 Aurel Vlaicu (P.O.Box 1-701), Bucharest, Romania
Telephone: (40-1) 211-32-42, 211-88-28, 211-35-06
Fax: (40-1) 211-35-06
E-mail: fo.rom@undp.org
Services to: Romania

Copenhagen

United Nations Information Centre, Centre Midtermolen 3, DK-2100 Copenhagen, Denmark
Telephone: (45) 35 46 73 00
Fax: (45) 35 46 73 01
E-mail: unic@un.dk
Services to: Denmark, Finland, Iceland, Norway, Sweden

Geneva

United Nations Information Service, UN Office at Geneva, Palais des Nations, 1211 Geneva 10, Switzerland
Telephone: (41-22) 917-2300; 917-2302; 917-2325
Fax: (41-22) 917 0030, 917 0073
E-mail: dpi_geneva@un.org
Services to: Switzerland, Bulgaria

Lisbon

United Nations Information Centre, Rua Latino Coelho, 1, Edificio Aviz, Bloco A-1, 10º, 1000 Lisboa, Portugal
Telephone: (351-1) 319 0790
Fax: (351-1) 352-0559
E-mail: lisbon@ccmail.unicc.org
Services to: Portugal

London

United Nations Information Centre, Millbank Tower (21st floor), 21-24 Millbank, London SW1P 4QH, United Kingdom
Telephone: (44-171) 630-1981
Fax: (44-171) 976-6478
E-mail: info@uniclondon.org
Services to: United Kingdom, Ireland

Madrid

United Nations Information Centre, Avenida General Perón, 32-1 (P.O. Box 3400), 28020 Madrid, Spain
Telephone: (34-91) 555-8087/555-8142
Fax: (34-91) 597-1231
E-mail: unicspa@mbox.unicc.org
Services to: Spain

Moscow

United Nations Information Centre, 4/16 Glazovsky Per, Moscow 121002, Russian Federation
Telephone: (7-095) 241-2894, (7-095) 241-2537
Fax: (7-095) 230-2138
E-mail: dpi_moscow@un.org
Services to: Russian Federation

Paris

United Nations Information Centre, 1 rue Miollis, 75732, Paris Cedex 15, France
Telephone: (33-1) 45-68-10-00
Fax: (33-1) 43-06-46-78
E-mail: unic.paris@unesco.org
Services to: France

Prague

United Nations Information Centre, Panska 5, 11000 Prague 1, Czech Republic
Telephone: (420-2) 24-21-10-49
Fax: (420-2) 24 22 54 25
E-mail: unicprg@terminal.cz
Services to: Czech Republic

Rome

United Nations Information Centre, Palazzetto Venezia, Piazza San Marco 50, 00186 Rome, Italy
Telephone: (39-6) 678-9907
Fax: (39-6) 679-3337
E-mail: dpi-roma-cc@un.org
Services to: Italy, Holy See, Malta, San Marino

Vienna

United Nations Information Service, Vienna International Centre, Wagramer Strasse 5, A-1220 Vienna (UN Office at Vienna, P.O. Box 500, A-1400 Vienna), Austria
Telephone: (43-1) 21345-4666, 21345-5139
Fax: (43-1) 21345-5899
E-mail: agius@un.org
Services to: Austria, Hungary, Slovakia

Warsaw

United Nations Information Centre, Al. Niepodleglosci 186, 00-608 Warszawa (UN Centre, P.O. Box 1, 02-514 Warsaw 12), Poland
Telephone: (48-22) 25-57-84
Fax: (48-22) 25-49-58
E-mail: fo.pol@undp.org
Services to: Poland

OFFICES IN THE COMMONWEALTH OF INDEPENDENT STATES AND ERITREA

Almaty

United Nations Office, c/o KIMEP, 4 Abai Avenue, 480100 Almaty, Kazakhstan
Telephone: (7-3272) 642-618/480/271
Fax: (7-3272) 642-608
Services to: Kazakhstan

Asmara

United Nations Office, Andinet Street, Zone 4 Admin. 07
Airport Road, (near Expo), Asmara, Eritrea
Telephone: (291-1) 182 018, 182 166
Fax: (291-1) 182-573
Services to: Eritrea

Baku

United Nations Office, 3 Isteglaliyat Street, Baku 1, Baku, Azerbaijan
Telephone: (99412) 98 98 88/98 16 28/98 16 89
Fax: (99412) 98 32 35
Services to: Azerbaijan

Kiev

United Nations Office, 6 Klovsky Uzviz, 1, Kiev 252020, Ukraine
Telephone: (380-44) 293-3412/9363/2248
Fax: (380-44) 293-26-07
Services to: Ukraine

Minsk

United Nations Office, 17 Kirov Street, 6th Floor (G.P.O. Box 103) 220000 Minsk, Belarus
Telephone: (375-172) 27-48-76, 27-81-49, 27-45-27
Fax: (375-172) 26-03-40
Services to: Belarus

Tashkent

United Nations Office, 4 Taras Shevchenko St., Tashkent 700029, Uzbekistan
Telephone: (7-3712) 891 167/330 977/560 606
Fax: (7-3712) 891 291
Services to: Uzbekistan

Tbilisi

United Nations Office, Eristavi St. 9, Tbilisi 380079, Republic of Georgia
Telephone: (995-32) 99 85 58; 25 11 26/28/29/31
Fax: (1-995-32) 2502 71 or 72
Services to: Georgia

Yerevan

United Nations Office, 14 Karl Libknekht Street, 1st floor, 375001 Yerevan, Armenia
Telephone: (374-2) 151-647
Fax: (374-2) 151-647
Services to: Armenia

UNITED NATIONS WEB SITES

United Nations: www.un.org

United Nations system: www.unsyst.org

United Nations Offices and Programmes:

United Nations Development Programme (UNDP): www.undp.org

United Nations Volunteers (UNV): www.unv.org

United Nations Conference on Trade and Development (UNCTAD): www.unicc.org/unctad

United Nations Environment Programme (UNEP): www.unep.org

United Nations Centre for Human Settlements (Habitat): www.unhcs.org

United Nations International Research and Training Institute for the Advancement of Women (INSTRAW): www.un.org/instraw

United Nations Children's Fund (UNICEF): www.unicef.org

World Food Programme (WFP): www.wfp.org

United Nations Population Fund (UNFPA): www.unfpa.org

United Nations International Drug Control Programme (UNDCP): www.undcp.org

United Nations High Commissioner for Human Rights: www.unchr.ch

United Nations High Commissioner for Refugees (UNHCR): www.unhcr.ch

United Nations University (UNU): www.unu.edu

United Nations Institute for Training and Research (UNITAR): www.unitar.org

United Nations Research Institute for Social Development (UNRISD): www.unrisd.org

United Nations Specialized Agencies:

International Labour Organization (ILO): www.ilo.org

Food and Agriculture Organization of the United Nations (FAO): www.fao.org.

United Nations Educational, Scientific and Cultural Organization (UNESCO): www.unesco.org

World Health Organization (WHO): www.who.ch

World Bank: www.worldbank.org

International Monetary Fund (IMF): www.imf.org

International Civil Aviation Organization (ICAO): www.cam.org/icao

Universal Postal Union (UPU): ibis.ib.upu.org

International Telecommunication Union (ITU): www.un.itu.ch

World Meteorological Organization (WMO): www.wmo.ch

International Maritime Organization (IMO): www.imo.org

World Intellectual Property Organization (WIPO): www.wipo.int

International Fund for Agricultural Development (IFAD): www.unicc.org/ifad

United Nations Industrial Development Organization (UNIDO): www.unido.org

International Atomic Energy Agency (IAEA): www.iaea.or.at

This selection of United Nations publications and products can be obtained from the Organization, some at no charge and other as sales items. The letters in parentheses at the end of each entry refer to where the publications can be obtained (*see Where to Order, page 333*).

General

UN Chronicle. UN/DPI. Annual subscription, $20.00. E/F **(a)ii**
Quarterly magazine providing coverage of the wide-ranging activities of the UN system. Information is presented on issues ranging from food and health to peacekeeping and the world economy. Also provides perspectives on highlights of Security Council and General Assembly sessions.

Yearbook of the United Nations, Vol. 49. UN/DPI. 1,615 pages. Sales No. E.96.I.1. ISBN: 90-411-0376-7. $150. E. **(a)iii**
The most comprehensive and authoritative reference book on all aspects of the work of the United Nations and its common system. Published annually in a single volume, the *Yearbook* is designed to provide government offices, libraries and the research community with detailed and factual accounts of United Nations activities during a given calendar year.

Yearbook of the United Nations, 50th Anniversary Edition. UN/DPI. 1995. 440 pages. Sales No. E.95.I.50. ISBN: 0-7923-3112-5. $ 95. E. **(a)iii**
This special edition of the *United Nations Yearbook* provides, through a combination of narrative and key historical documents, a comprehensive picture of the achievements of the United Nations over the past 50 years.

Image and Reality: Questions and Answers about the United Nations. UN/DPI. New York. 1997. 58 pages. DPI/1838/Rev.1. Sales No. E.97I.13. ISBN: 92-1-100627-9. **(a) ii**
Provides simple answers to some of the most frequently asked questions about the UN, including: How are peacekeeping operations organized? What kind of development and humanitarian assistance does the UN provide? How is the UN addressing environmental problems? How is the budget determined? What reforms are being undertaken to improve its work?

Notes for Speakers: The United Nations at 50. UN/DPI. New York. 1995. DPI/1698. 88 pages. E/F/S. **(a)i**
Briefing paper designed for use by UN officials and governmental, academic, media and NGO representatives highlighting the work and accomplishments of the United Nations during its first 50 years.

The Quotable Kofi Annan: Selections from Speeches and Statements by the Secretary-General. UN/DPI. New York. 1998. 52 pages. DPI/1971. Sales No.98.I.10. ISBN: 92-1-100653-8. $5.00. E. **(a)ii**
Presents a selection of quotations from the speeches and statements of UN Secretary-General Kofi Annan, covering the period from his election in December 1996 through March 1998. Topics include: The UN in Transition;

Peace and Security; Development; Human Rights; Democracy and Good Governance; and the UN and its Partners.

Renewal amid Transition, 1997, Annual Report on the Work of the Organization. By UN Secretary-General Kofi Annan. UN/DPI. New York. 75 pages. Sales No. E.97.I.1. ISBN: 92-1-100643-0. $7.50. **(a)ii**

The United Nations in Our Daily Lives. New York. 1998. 116 pages. Sales No. E.98.I.11. ISBN: 92-1-1-100654-6. $5.00. E. **(a)ii**

In a story format designed for a general audience, illustrates the many ways in which the United Nations is a part of everyone's life and how much we rely on its programmes.

Peace and Security

An Agenda for Peace, Second Edition. By UN Secretary-General Boutros Boutros-Ghali. New York. UN/DPI. 1995. 155 pages. DPI/1623/PKO. Sales No. E.95.I.15. ISBN 92-1-100555-8. $7.50. A/C/E/F/R/S. **(a)ii**

Recommends ways of strengthening the capacity of the UN for preventive diplomacy, peacemaking, peacekeeping and post-conflict peace-building.

The Blue Helmets. UN/DPI. 1996. 820 pages. DPI/1800. Sales No. E.96.I.14. ISBN: 92-1-100611-2. E/F. **(a)ii**

A review of United Nations peacekeeping, with a comprehensive account of the United Nations peacekeeping operations from their inception in 1948 up to early 1996.

The United Nations and Cambodia, 1991-1995. UN/DPI. 1995. DPI/1450. Sales No. E.95.I.9. ISBN: 92-1-100548-5. 360 pages. $29.95 **(a)ii**

The United Nations and Nuclear Non-Proliferation. UN/DPI. 1995. DPI/1628. Sales No. E.95.I.17. ISBN: 92-1-100557-4. 200 pages. $29.95 **(a)ii**

The United Nations and El Salvador, 1990-1995. UN/DPI. 1995. DPI/1475. Sales No. E.95.I.12. ISBN 92-1-100552-3. 612 pages. $29.95 **(a)ii**

The United Nations and the Iraq-Kuwait Conflict, 1990-1996. UN/DPI. 1996. DPI/1770. Sales No. E.96.I.3. ISBN 92-1-100596-5. 864 pages. $49.95 **(a)ii**

The United Nations and Mozambique, 1992-1995. UN/DPI. 1995. DPI/1675. Sales No. E.95.I.20. ISBN 92-1-100559-0. 321 pages. $29.95 **(a)ii**

The United Nations and Rwanda, 1993-1996. UN/DPI. 1996. DPI/1678. Sales No. E.96.I.20. ISBN 92-1-100561-2. 740 pages. $49.95 **(a)ii**

The United Nations and Somalia, 1992-1996. UN/DPI. 1996. DPI/1677. Sales No. E.96.I.8. ISBN 92-1-100566-3. 516 pages. $29.95 **(a)ii**

Economic and Social

Africa Recovery. Annual subscription: $20. **a(iv)**

Quarterly magazine covering issues of economic and social reform in Africa and international cooperation for development, in particular by the United Nations.

An Agenda for Development. UN/DPI. New York. 1997. 110 pages. DPI/1935 Sales No. E.98.I.3. ISBN: 92-1-100644-9. $7.50. A/C/E/F/R/S. **(a)ii**

Outlines principles to guide global development. Shows how the development process is linked to peace, economy, environment, society and democracy.

Agenda 21: The UN Programme of Action from Rio. UN/DPI. New York. 1992. 294 pages. DPI/1344. Sales No. E.93.I.11. ISBN: 92-1-100509-4. $25. E/F/S. **(a)ii**

The complete text of the recommendations adopted at the Earth Summit in Rio de Janeiro, 1992 — the UN Conference on Environment and Development — which together set out a comprehensive blueprint for achieving sustainable development.

The following Earth Summit publications are available from the Project Manager for Sustainable Development, Room S-1040, UN Department of Public Information, New York, NY 10017. Tel.: (212) 963-7704. Fax: (212) 963-1186.

Agreement on High Seas Fishing. UN/DPI. 1996. New York. 33 pages. DPI/SD/1746. Free. E/F/S.

Convention on Biological Diversity. UN/DPI. 1996. New York. 25 pages. DPI/SD/1307. Free. E/F/S.

Convention on Climate Change. UN/DPI. 1996. New York. 21 pages. DPI/SD/1300. Free. E/F/S.

Convention on Desertification. UN/DPI. 1996. New York. 44 pages. DPI/SD/1576. Free. E/F/S.

Programme of Action for Small Island States. UN/DPI. 1996. New York. 51 pages. DPI/SD/1609. Free. E/F/S.

Rio Declaration and Forest Principles. UN/DPI. 1996. New York. 10 pages. DPI/SD/1299. Free. E/F/S.

Copenhagen Declaration and Programme of Action. UN/DPI. 1995. New York. 137 pages. DPI/1707. $15. E/F/ S in 1997. **(a)ii**

The complete programme of action adopted at the Social Summit — the World Summit for Social Development (Copenhagen, 1995).

Global Environment Outlook 1997. UNEP/Oxford University Press. New York. 264 pages. $25. ISBN: 0-19-521349-1. **(a)iii**

The United Nations Environment Programme's annual review of the state of the planet's environment, featuring regional reports and policy reviews from institutes around the world. Focuses on five questions: what are the main regional and global environment problems of today and of the future; what causes these problems; what will happen if we do not solve them; what do we want from our future; and what is being done, and what can be done, to prevent the destruction of our environment?

Platform for Action and the Beijing Declaration: Fourth World Conference on Women. UN/DPI. 184 pages. Sales No. DPI/1766. $7.50. E. **(a)ii**

The complete text of the recommendations adopted at the 1995 Fourth World Conference on Women.

Population and Development: Programme of Action adopted at the International Conference on Population and Development, Volume 1. United Nations/UNFPA. 1995. 100 pages. Sales No. E.95.13.7. ISBN: 92-1-151278-6. $10. E/S. **a(ii); (n)**

Programme of Action of the 1994 Conference, which emphasized the imperatives of empowering women and guaranteeing choice with regard to family planning, as well as the statements and reservations expressed on the Programme of Action.

Summary of the Programme of Action of the International Conference on Population and Development. UN/DPI. 1995. New York. 27 pages. DPI/1618/POP. E/F/S/A. **a(i)**

The World Summit for Children. UNICEF. New York. 1990. 44 pages. Sales No. E.90.XX.USA.13. $10. E. **a(ii) and (d)**

The recommendations adopted at the Summit (New York, 1990).

Change: Threat or Opportunity for Human Progress? New York. UNDP. 1991. Sales No. E.91.III.B.10. 5-volume set. $75.00. E. **(b)**

Analysis of worldwide changes and their possible impact on humankind's future. Reflects views and visions of more than 80 world-renowned experts. Vol. 1: Political Change; vol. 2: Economic Change; vol. 3: Globalization of Markets; vol. 4: Changes in the Human Dimension of Development, Ethics and Values; vol. 5: Ecological Change: Environment, Development and Poverty Linkages.

The Cultural Dimension of Development: Towards a Practical Approach. Paris. UNESCO. 1994. 200 pages. ISBN: 92-3-103043-4. $20. E/F/S. **(e)**

Describes the means for integrating cultural factors into development.

Environment, Employment and Development (ed. A. S. Bhalla). Geneva. ILO. 1992. ISBN: 92-2-108250-4. SwF 25.00. E. **(g)**

Examines employment implications of sustainable development, reviews approaches to minimizing environmental degradation and looks at environmentally sound approaches to employment promotion.

Human Development Report 1997: Human Development to Eradicate Poverty. New York. UNDP/Oxford University Press. 229 pages. ISBN: 0-19-511997-1. $19.95 paperback. E/F/S. **(a)iii**

Assesses the state of human development worldwide and suggests practical actions for increasing the national and external aid resources allocated to health, education and employment. This edition focuses on poverty, providing an overview of global poverty trends and an assessment of the scale of poverty problems worldwide; outlines six priorities for tackling poverty at the country level, and a global agenda for supportive action.

International Cooperation for the Eradication of Poverty in Developing Countries. New York. Secretary-General's Report, A/46/454. 1991. E.94.II.D.4. $55.00. E/F/S. **(a)i**

Contains a review of national experience in combating poverty and proposals for international measures for the eradication of poverty.

The Least Developed Countries 1997 Report. 1997. 192 pages. E.97.II.D.6. ISBN: 92-1-112410-7. E/F/S. **(a)ii**
Reviews recent socio-economic developments in the least developed countries and the progress in implementing support measures. Deals with such issues as: socio-economic developments and policy reforms, agricultural performance, the manufacturing sector, transport and communications infrastructure and services, national actions and international support measures.

Monitoring Social Progress in the 1990s: Data Constraints, Concerns and Priorities (by David G. Westendorff and Dharam Ghai). UK/USA. UNRISD. 1993. 348 pages. E. **(f)**
Examines the limitations of social data, especially in developing countries, and identifies strategies for improving data quality in the short and medium term.

Notes for Speakers: Social Development. UN/DPI. 1995. DPI/1625/SOC/CON. 78 pages. E. **(a)i**
Briefing paper designed for use by UN officials and governmental, academic, media and NGO representatives reviewing the issues of social development, with particular focus on the work of the United Nations in the areas of poverty, employment and social integration.

Notes for Speakers: The Advancement of Women. UN/DPI. 1995. DPI/1674/WOM/CON.92 pages. $10. E/F/S. **(a)ii and (a)i**
Briefing paper designed for use by UN officials and governmental, academic, media and NGO representatives reviewing the issues around the advancement of women with particular attention to the role of the United Nations system and the Fourth World Conference on Women (Beijing, 1995.)

The Progress of Nations 1997. New York. UNICEF. 1997. 68 pages. Sales No. E.97.XX.USA.1. ISBN: 92-806-3314-7. $6.95. E/F/S/R/A (and other languages). **(d)**
The nations of the world ranked according to their achievements in health, nutrition, education, family planning and progress for women.

Report on the World Social Situation. New York. United Nations. 1997. Sales No. E.97.IV.1. ISBN: 92-1-130182-3. $35.00. Issued every four years. E/F/S. **(a)ii**
Discusses the balance between economic efficiency and social justice; the interaction between the social functions of the State, market responses to social demands and the imperatives of sustainable development; the equalization of opportunity for all members of society; the more effective delivery of social services for the disadvantaged sectors of society; and the mobilization of resources for social development at the local, national, regional and international levels.

The State of Food and Agriculture 1997. Rome. FAO. 290 pages. ISBN: 92-5-104005-2. $45.00. E/F/S. **(m)**
FAO's annual report on current developments in world agriculture. Presents basic information on the global agricultural situation and a review of the economic environment surrounding agriculture. The 1997 edition focuses on: forests in a global context; raising women's productivity in agriculture; and global climate change abatement policies. Examines trends and issues of importance to agriculture in the various developing country regions, focusing in detail on Angola, Bangladesh, Egypt, Mozambique and Peru.

The State of the World's Children 1998. New York. UNICEF Annual Report. UNICEF/Oxford University Press. 104 pages. ISBN: 0-19-829401-8. $12.95. E/F/S/A and other languages. A free 12-page summary is available. **(d)**

Focuses on the impact of sound nutrition on children's physical and mental development, their health and their potential for productive lives. Provides an overview of the underlying causes and impact of malnutrition, which accounts for more than half of the nearly 12 million under-five deaths in developing countries each year, as well as the strategies required for its concerted eradication.

The State of World Population 1997. The Right to Choose: Reproductive Rights and Reproductive Health. New York. UNFPA Annual Report. 138 pages. Sales No.97.III.H.1. ISBN: 0-89714-409-0. $9.95. E/F/S/A and other languages. **(n)**

Annual report on population issues and their impact on world development. Provides easily accessible tables representing trends and statistics for world population. The 1997 edition deals with sexual and reproductive rights.

The State of the World's Refugees: A Humanitarian Agenda. UNHCR/Oxford University Press. 1997. Biennial Report. 264 pages. ISBN: 0-19-828043-2. $14.00. E/F/S. **(o)**

Outlines UNHCR policies to protect the 22 million refugees and displaced people under its care. Focuses on the increasing determination by rich and poor nations alike not to accept refugees, regarded as political, social or economic threats. Suggests a plan of action to counter forced displacement, including steps to eradicate poverty, promote human rights and democracy, and ensure that those responsible for forcing millions from their homes are brought to account.

The State of World Rural Poverty: An Inquiry into Its Causes and Consequences, IFAD/New York University Press. 1993. 513 pages. ISBN: 08-147375-44. $25. Available through New York University Press (Tel.: 1-800-996-6987 or 212-998-2575). E.

Proposes new approaches to poverty alleviation among rural poor, particularly in developing countries, and counters long-standing misconceptions that have discouraged effective utilization of human resources potential in rural areas.

Statistical Yearbook, 42nd edition. UN Statistical Office. 1995. 946 pages. Sales No. B.97.XVII.1. ISBN: 92-1-061174-8. $120. E. **(a) ii**

A comprehensive compendium of vital internationally comparable data for the analysis of socio-economic development at the world, regional and national levels. Provides data on the world economy, its structure, major trends and current performance, as well as on issues such as world population, employment, inflation, food supply, external debt of developing countries, education, housing, energy production, development of new energy sources, and environmental pollution and management.

Trade and Development Report, 1997: Globalization, Distribution and Growth. Sales No. E.97.II.D.8. ISBN: 92-1-112411-5. 195 pages. $48.00 **(j)**

Sheds light on some of the pressing policy issues facing developing countries and the international community as a whole. Explores the interaction of trends in the international economy with the prospects of developing countries. Compares current economic performance with that of the preceding year and examines future economic prospects at the regional and global levels. Makes compelling reading for those seeking new knowledge and insights into the effects of globalization.

The United Nations and the Advancement of Women, 1945-1996. UN/DPI. 1996. DPI/1679. Sales No. E.96.I.9. ISBN: 92-1-100603-1. 846 pages. $49.95 **(a)ii**

UN Briefing Papers: The World Conferences — Developing Priorities for the 21st Century. UN/DPI. 112 pages. Sales No. E.97.I.5. ISBN: 92-1-100631-7. $12.00 **(a)ii**

The first in a new series of UN Briefing Papers, provides a broad perspective on the recommendations and actions flowing from the conferences on Children, Human Rights, Social Development, Crime, Environment, Women, Population, Food, Human Settlements, Small Islands, Trade and Natural Disasters. The efforts now under way at the international and national levels to realize the goals they have set for the international community are clearly and concisely explained.

UN Development Update. Bi-monthly 8-page newsletter. UN/DPI. Free. **a (i)**

Gives updated information on all activities of the UN system spanning a two-month period.

World Development Report 1997: The State in a Changing World. World Bank/Oxford University Press. 1997. 354 pages. Paperback: ISBN: 0-19-521114-6. $25.95. E/F/S. **(k)**

Focuses on the role and effectiveness of the State, what is should do; how it should do it; and how it can do better in a rapidly changing world. Previous reports focused on: Transition from plan to a market orientation (1996); Workers in an integrating world (1995); Infrastructure for development (1994); Investing in health (1993); Development and the environment (1992); The challenge of development (1991); Poverty (1990).

World Economic and Social Survey 1997: Trends and Policies in the World Economy. United Nations. New York. 1997. 293 pages. Sales No. E.97.II.C.1. ISBN: 92-1-109133-90. $55.00. E/F/S. **(a)ii**

Provides a detailed assessment of the state of the world economic and social situation. Contains forecasts for the upcoming year and descriptions of national and international economic policies, as well as emerging issues and trends. The 1997 edition focuses on the strengthening of the world economy, the positive turnaround of the transition economies since 1989 and the escalated growth of electronic product exports for developing countries.

The World Health Report 1998: Life in the 21st Century — A Vision for All. Geneva. WHO. 1998. 230 pages. ISBN: 92-4-156189-0. $15.30. E/F. **(i)**

Takes an expert look at health trends over the past five decades; assesses the global situation and predicts how health conditions, diseases, and the tools for managing them will evolve up to the year 2025.

World Investment Report 1997: Transnational Corporations and Competitiveness. UNCTAD. 368 pages. Sales No. E.96.II.A.14. ISBN: 92-1-104468-5. $45.00. E. **(a)ii**

Provides a better understanding of the role of foreign direct investment, the world economy and the current discussion on the evolution of international arrangements for foreign direct investment. Highlights global and regional trends, the linkages between trade and foreign direct investment and the current international arrangements governing foreign direct investment.

World Labour Report 1997-98. Geneva. ILO. 1997. 83 pages. ISBN: 92-2-110331-5. $40. E/F/S. **(g)**
Examines the relevance and limits of the social forces that are bringing about the disruption and marginalization of industrial relations. Draws attention to a range of mechanisms that govern relations between employers and the organized workforce. Provides a reflection of the effort that has been made to adapt the structures, venues, and strategies to the new economic reality and to its international dimension.

The World's Women 1970-1995: Trends and Statistics. New York. 202 pages. UN Statistical Office. 1994. Sales No. E.95.XVII.2. ISBN: 92-1-161372-8. $15.95. E. **(a)ii**
Updated and expanded, this book remains the most complete description to-date of women's conditions worldwide. Shows women's contributions to economic, political and family life.

Human Rights

Human Rights: A Compilation of International Instruments. 950 pages. Sales No. 94.XIV.1. ISBN: 92-1-154099-2. $55. **(a)ii**
This two-volume set constitutes a comprehensive catalogue of the existing human rights instruments adopted at both universal and regional levels. Contributes to a wider knowledge and increased awareness of international human rights standards. A valuable source for all those interested and engaged in the promotion and protection of human rights and fundamental freedoms.

Integrating Human Rights with Sustainable Human Development. 1998. 44 pages. Sales No. 98.III.B.10. ISBN: 92-1-126087-6. $7.50. E. **(a)ii**
Marking the fiftieth anniversary of the Universal Declaration of Human Rights, promotes awareness of the links between human rights and development. Discusses human rights and their implications for sustainable human development; underscores the UN Development Programme's support for human rights and its implementing strategy.

International Criminal Tribunal for the Former Yugoslavia: Basic Documents. 1995. 524 pages. Sales No. B.95III.P.1. ISBN: 92-1-056701. $48. **(a)ii**
Contains all the texts regulating the functioning of the Tribunal. Will capture the attention of observers of the Tribunal's proceedings and all those interested in the possibility of administering international criminal justice.

The United Nations and Apartheid, 1948-1994. UN/DPI. 1995. DPI/1568. Sales No. E.95.I.7. ISBN: 92-1-100546-9. 565 pages. $29.95 **(a)ii**

The United Nations and Human Rights, 1945-1995. UN/DPI. 1996. DPI/1676. Sales No. E.95.I.21. ISBN: 92-1-100560-4. 536 pages. $29.95 **(a)ii**

World Conference on Human Rights: The Vienna Declaration and Programme of Action. DPI. New York. 71 pages. DPI/1394/Rev.1/HR. Reprint: April 1995. E/F/S. **a(i)**
Text of the Programme of Action adopted at the World Conference on Human Rights, Vienna, 1993.

WHERE TO ORDER

(a)i   United Nations. Public Inquiries Unit. Room GA-057. New York. NY 10017. USA.

Tel.: (212) 963-4475. Fax: (212) 963-0071.

If sales item:

(a)ii   United Nations Publications. Room DC2-0853. New York, NY 10017. USA.

Tel.: (212) 963-8302, (800) 253-9646. Fax: (212) 963-3489.

E-mail: publications@un.org. Internet: www.un.org/Pubs/Sales.

For Europe, Africa and the Middle East: UN Publications, Palais des Nations, CH-1211 Geneva 10, Switzerland Tel.: (41 22) 917-2614. Fax: (41 22) 917-0027. E-mail: unpubli@unog.ch.

(a)iii United Nations Bookshop. Tel: (212) 963-7680. Fax: (212) 963-3489.

(b)   UNDP (United Nations Development Programme):

Division of Public Affairs. 1 UN Plaza, Room DC1-1922. New York, NY 10017. USA.

Tel.: (212) 906-5301. Fax: (212) 906-5364.

(c)   United Nations ECE (Economic Commission for Europe):

ECE Information Office. Palais des Nations. CH 1211 Geneva 10. Switzerland.

Tel. (41-22) 917-2893. Fax: (41-22) 917-0036.

(d)   UNICEF (United Nations Children's Fund):

UNICEF. 3 UN Plaza. New York, NY 10017. USA.

Fax: (212) 326-7768.

(e)   UNESCO (United Nations Educational, Scientific and Cultural Organization):

UNESCO Press. 7, Place de Fontenoy. 75700 Paris, France.

Tel. (45) 681000. Fax: (45) 671690.

In the USA: UNIPUB. Tel: (800) 274-4888.

(f)   UNRISD (United Nations Research Institute for Social Development):

Reference Centre. UNRISD. Palais des Nations. 1211 Geneva 10. Switzerland.

Tel.: (41-22) 798-8400. Fax: (41-22) 740-0791.

(g)   ILO (International Labour Office):

ILO Publications. CH-1211 Geneva 22. Switzerland.

Tel.: (41-22) 799-7301. Fax: (41-22) 798-6358.

E-mail: publivente@ilo.org.

(h)   UNCHS (United Nations Centre for Human Settlements — Habitat):

Information, Audio-visual and Documentation Division.

P.O. Box 30030. Nairobi. Kenya.

Tel.: (254-2) 623043. Fax: (254-2) 624266/7.

(i)   WHO (World Health Organization):
Distribution and Sales. 20. Avenue Appia. CH 1211 Geneva 27.
   Switzerland.
Tel.:(41-22) 791-2476. Fax: (41-22) 791-4857. 788-0401.
E-mail: publications@who.ch.
In the USA: WHO Publications, Albany New York. Tel: (518) 436-9686.

(j)   UNCTAD (United Nations Conference on Trade and Development):
Palais des Nations. CH 1211 Geneva 10. Switzerland.
Tel.: (41-22) 907-5712. Fax: (41-22) 907-0043.

(k)   World Bank:
P.O. Box 960, Herndon, VA 20172-0960. Tel.: (703) 661-1580.
Fax: (703) 661-1501. E-mail: books@worldbank.org.
Box 7247-7956. Philadelphia. PA 19170-7956. USA.
Tel.: (202) 473-1155. Fax: (202) 676-0581.

(l)   INSTRAW (International Research and Training Institute for
   the Advancement of Women):
P.O. Box 21747. Santo Domingo. Dominican Republic.
Tel.: (809) 685-2111. Fax: (809) 685-2117.

(m)   FAO (Food and Agriculture Organization of the United Nations):
Distribution and Sales Section. FAO. Viale delle Terme di Caracalla.
   00100 Rome. Italy.
Tel.: (39-6) 5225-4608. Fax: (39-6) 5225-3152.

(n)   UNFPA (United Nations Population Fund):
Information and External Relations Division. 220 East 42nd Street.
   New York, NY 10017. USA.
Tel.: (212) 297-5029. Fax: (212) 557-6416.

(o)   UNHCR (Office of the United Nations High Commissioner
   for Refugees):
Public Information. Case Postale 2500. 1211 Geneva 2 Depot.
   Switzerland.
Tel.: (41-22) 739-8111. Fax: (41-22) 739-7314/5.

INDEX

Global Environment Facility (GEF), 38, 132, 136, 200
Global Environment Monitoring System (GEMS), 202
Global Environment Outlook, 38
Global Information and Early Warning System, 144, 163, 252
Global Maritime Distress and Safety System, 151
Global Resource Information Database, 202
Global Trade Point Programme, 140, 142
Global warming, 204–205, 212–213
Governance, 126, 132
Greenhouse gases, 198, 200, 203–204
1997 Kyoto agreement, 204
Guatemala
peacekeeping operations, 92–93
Guinea worm disease, 168, 181

H

Habitat. *See* United Nations Centre for Human Settlements
Haiti
peacekeeping operations, 93–95
Hazardous wastes, 194, 196, 203, 264
1989 Convention, 203, 207
Health, 53–54, 131, 164–168. *See also* child health; disease prevention; mental illness; reproductive health
HIV/AIDS. *See* AIDS
Housing. *See* human settlements
Human Development Report, 36
Human rights, 42–43, 217–243
administration of justice, 242
conventions, instruments and standards, 218–224
Day, 218
Decade for Human Rights Education, 227
disabled persons, 240–241
field offices, 226–227
indigenous people, 239–240
machinery, 224–229
migrant workers, 242
minorities, 225, 239
special rapporteurs/representatives, 222–223, 228–229, 231, 233, 238–239, 251

technical cooperation, 226, 242
Universal Declaration, 217–220, 229
Vienna Declaration and Programme of Action, 230–231
World Conference, 157, 229–231, 237
Human Rights Committee, 221
Human settlements, 43–44, 169–172
UN Conference, 157, 170
Humanitarian assistance, 27–28, 40–42, 44, 131–132, 247–256
Hunger, 41–42, 52, 61–62, 129, 131, 159, 162–164. *See also* food

I

IAEA. *See* International Atomic Energy Agency
ICAO. *See* International Civil Aviation Organization
ICJ. *See* International Court of Justice
IFAD. *See* International Fund for Agricultural Development
Illicit drugs. *See* drug control
Illiteracy, 172
ILO. *See* International Labour Organization
IMF. *See* International Monetary Fund
Immunization, 165, 182
IMO. *See* International Maritime Organization
Implementation Force (IFOR), 108
Indigenous people
human rights, 239–240
International Decade, 240
International Year, 240
Industrial development, 62, 145–146
Infant mortality, 167, 181–182
Informatics, 193
Information centres, 30, 309–321
INFOTERRA, 202
Inhumane Weapons Convention (1980), 78, 115
INSTRAW. *See* International Research and Training Institute for the Advancement of Women
Intellectual property, 60–61, 154–155
conventions, 155
Inter-Agency Committee on Sustainable Development, 197

International Telecommunication Union (ITU), 58–59, 151–153
International Trade Centre UNCTAD/WTO, 50, 142–143
International trade law
conventions, model laws, rules, 141, 263–265
International Tribunal for Rwanda, 87, 269
International Tribunal for the Law of the Sea, 266
International Trusteeship System, 275–277
Internet, 152–153, 191, 193. *See also* web sites
Intifada, 98, 255
Iraq, 16, 101–104, 253–254
Iraq-Kuwait Boundary Demarcation Commission, 102–103
ITC. *See* International Trade Centre UNCTAD/WTO

J

Jammu and Kashmir, 99–100
Joint UN Programme on HIV/AIDS (UNAIDS), 133, 166

K

Kashmir. *See* Jammu and Kashmir
Korean peninsula, 95
Kuwait
Iraq invasion, 101–102

L

Labour, 51, 146–148, 239
conventions, 232
rights, 231–232
Landmines, 27, 78, 251
1997 Ottawa Convention, 111, 115, 117
clearance, 78
Latin America and the Caribbean
peacekeeping operations, 90–95
Law of the sea, 265–267
Least Developed Countries, 129–130
Programme of Action, 130
UN Conference, 157
Lebanon
peacekeeping operations, 97–98
Legal Committee (6th Committee), 8, 25
Legal Counsel, 25–26

Liberia
emergency relief, 253–254
peacekeeping operations, 90
Lifelong education, 173
Loans
for development, 54-56, 135–137

M

Marine Environment Laboratory, 214
Marine pollution, 193, 203, 207–208, 214
conventions, 208, 265
Maritime safety
conventions, 150–151
Maternal health, 168
Mental illness, 241
Meteorology, 59, 208–210
Middle East
1991 Peace Conference, 98
peacekeeping operations, 71, 95–99
Migrant workers
1990 Convention, 242
Minorities
human rights, 223–225, 239
Montreal Protocol, 204–205, 264
Mozambique
peacekeeping operations, 82–83
Multilateral Investment Guarantee Agency (MIGA), 56, 136, 138

N

Namibia, 79, 81, 261, 280–282
Natural resources, 211–213
technical cooperation, 212
Nobel Peace Prize, 34, 44, 51, 71
Non-governmental organizations (NGOs), 13, 18, 28, 50, 135, 170, 173, 177, 183–184, 190, 195-196, 205, 217, 225, 230, 249-250
Non-self-governing territories, 275–280, 295–300
North Atlantic Treaty Organization (NATO), 107–108
Nuclear disarmament, 111–114
Nuclear energy, 63, 213–214
Nuclear safety, 213–214
conventions, 213
Nuclear weapons
1996 Comprehensive Test-Ban Treaty, 110–111, 117

The former Yugoslav Republic of Macedonia, 71, 106
The former Yugoslavia, 71, 75, 105–108
Georgia, 105
Guatemala, 92
Haiti, 93–95
Iraq-Kuwait, 101–104
Jammu and Kashmir, 99–100
Korean peninsula, 95
Latin America and the Caribbean, 90–95
Lebanon, 97–98
Liberia, 90
Middle East, 71, 95–99
Mozambique, 82
Namibia, 79
ongoing, 80
Republic of the Congo, 84
Rwanda, 85–87
Somalia, 88–90
South Africa, 232
Southern Africa, 80
strengthening, 74–75
Tajikistan, 104–105
Uganda-Rwanda, 85–86
Western Sahara, 282–283
Peacemaking and peace-building, 27, 67, 69–71, 75, 77–79
Pollution. *See* marine pollution
Population, 39–40, 157, 176–178, 338–339
of Member States, 287–291
Postal services, 57–58, 153–154
Poverty eradication, 35, 55, 132–136, 145, 159–162, 198
International Decade, 160
Press freedom
World Day, 193
Preventive diplomacy, 69–71. *See also* peacemaking and peace-building
Private sector, 130, 136, 138–142
Progress of Nations, 34
Public information, 29–30, 227

R

Racism and racial discrimination, 221–222, 234–235
Convention, 221, 234
decades, 234-235

World Conference, 235
Rapid deployment, 74
Referendum
Eritrea, 87
Refugees, 40, 44–45, 247–256
1951 Convention, 255
assistance and protection, 247, 253–255
Reform of the United Nations, 18–19
Regional Commissions, 12–13, 31–33, 128
Register of Conventional arms, 110, 116
Reproductive health, 39–40, 177–178
Republic of the Congo
Peacekeeping operations, 84
Rights of the child, 34, 238–239
1989 Convention, 34, 222-223, 238
Rio Declaration on Environment and Development, 195–196
River blindness, 165
Rural development, 52, 61–62, 142–145, 162–163
Rwanda
emergency relief, 253–254
International Tribunal, 87, 268–269
peacekeeping operations, 85–87

S

Safe drinking water, 129, 168
Safe motherhood, 168
Sanctions and embargoes, 76
Science and technology, 35, 41, 51, 155–156, 173–176, 192
Seabed mining, 267
1971 Sea-bed Treaty, 116
Secretariat, 15–16, 21, 24–31, 226
Secretary-General, 10, 15–18
Deputy, 18, 128
Office of, 21
as peacemaker, 69–71, 283–284
Security Council, 9–11, 17, 19, 67–68
Africa, 79
enforcement, 76–77
functions and powers, 9–10
members, 4, 9
voting, 9
Security Council resolutions
242 (1967), 96–98
338 (1973), 97–98
425 (1978), 97
435 (1978), 281

Urban development, 169–172
Uruguay Round, 63

V

Veto, 9
Vienna Declaration and Programme of
    Action, 230–231
Volunteers, 36–37
    International Year, 37
Vulnerable groups
    social integration, 183–187

W

Water resources, 210–212
    Conferences, 211
    Decade, 211
Web sites, 181, 227, 271, 322–323
Western Sahara, 278, 282–283, 298
WFP. *See* World Food Programme
WHO. *See* World Health Organization
WIPO. *See* World Intellectual Prop-
    erty Organization
WMO. *See* World Meterological Or-
    ganization
Women. *See also* girls
    advancement of, 45–47, 177–181,
        235–238
    conferences, 46, 157, 178–179, 236–
        237
    1979 Convention, 179, 222, 236
    discrimination, 179, 222, 236
    empowerment of, 45, 179–181,
        237–238
    International Decade, 236
    rights of, 231, 235– 238
    Special Adviser on Gender Issues
        and Advancement of Women,
        180
Working Capital Fund, 20
World Assembly on Ageing, 186
World Bank, 54–56, 130–132, 135–
    136, 161, 165–166, 172–173,
    200, 206, 240
World Commission on Environment
    and Development, 194
World Conference on Education for
    All (1990:Jomtien, Thailand),
    157, 173

World Conference on Human Rights
    (1993:Vienna), 157, 229–231,
    237
World Conference on Natural Disaster
    Reduction (1994:Yokohama),
    157, 248
World Conference on Women (4th:
    1995:Beijing), 46, 157, 179,
    236–237
World Court. *See* International Court
    of Justice
World Development Report, 54
World Economic Outlook, 57
World Food Programme (WFP),
    41–42, 133, 163–164, 180, 247, 249–
    252
World Food Summit (1996:Rome),
    157, 162
World Health Organization (WHO),
    53–54, 165–168, 181, 214, 240,
    249, 252–253
World Intellectual Property Organiza-
    tion (WIPO), 60–61, 154–155
World Investment Report, 138–139
World Maritime University, 60, 151
World Meteorological Organization
    (WMO), 59, 156, 204–205, 208–
    211
World Summit for Children (1990:
    New York), 34, 157, 181
World Summit for Social Develop-
    ment (1995:Copenhagen), 156–
    158
World Trade Organization (WTO), 50,
    63–64, 142, 201
World Weather Watch, 209
World Youth Forum, 185
WTO. *See* World Trade Organization

Y

Youth, 184–185
    International Year, 185
    UN Fund, 185
    World Forum, 185
    World Programme of Action to the
        Year 2000, 185